BREAKING BARRIERS!

ADVANCEMENTS OF WOMEN'S RIGHTS in MODERN SOCIETY

SUZANNE A. KENNEDY

About The Author

Suzanne A. Kennedy

Suzanne A. Kennedy was born with a passion for words and music in the historic city of Boston. Raised by educated parents - a college professor father and high school teacher mother - Suzanne inherited an insatiable curiosity about the world from a young age.

Her quest for knowledge and drive for social justice truly blossomed in her twenties when she discovered the vibrant women's rights movement while attending college. With an open mind and a fierce determination, Suzanne became a voice for the voiceless, her writing fueled by personal witnesses to the plight of women across the globe.

A citizen of the world, Suzanne has traveled extensively, living in cultural capitals like Washington D.C., New York, and New Jersey. From these vantage points, she has borne witness to the harsh realities and systematic oppression faced by women in every corner of the planet. Her works shine a light on these injustices, while offering empowering perspectives and calls to action.

When not tirelessly advocating through her writing, Suzanne finds solace in the loving company of her rescued chihuahua and two cats. These furry companions remind her of the fundamental desires all living beings share - to live in peace, freedom, and with dignity. It is this universal truth that Suzanne channels into her work, inspiring generations of women to persevere in their fight for equality.

With an unwavering moral compass and a gift for prose, Suzanne A. Kennedy has emerged as a true literary force. Her writings blaze like a beacon, guiding humanity towards a more just and equitable future for all women around the world.

Table of Contents

About The Author..iv

Chapter 1 Introduction...1

Section A: Definition and significance of women's rights 1

Section B: Overview of the historical context of women's rights movement..22

Section C: Introduction to the advancements and challenges faced by women in modern society 40

Chapter 2 Historical Context of Women's Rights Movements. 63

Section A. Overview of early women's rights movements, such as suffrage and first-wave feminism 63

Section B. Key Milestones and Achievements in the Fight for Gender Equality Throughout History 72

Section C. Impact of Past Movements on Shaping the Current Landscape of Women's Rights...92

Chapter 3 Legal and Political Advances.................................105

Section A: Overview of legislative and policy advancements promoting women's rights...105

Section B: Analysis of landmark legal cases and rulings pertaining to gender equality..118

Section C: Examination of women's representation in political leadership roles and government institutions.......................135

Chapter 4 Economic Empowerment and Workplace Equality
....157

Section A: Discussion of advancements in women's economic rights and opportunities...157

Section B: Analysis of gender wage gap trends and efforts to achieve pay equity..174

Section C: Exploration of workplace policies and initiatives promoting gender diversity and inclusion..........................201

Chapter 5 Education and Access to Opportunities **235**

Section A: Overview of advancements in women's access to education and academic opportunities 235

Section B: Analysis of efforts to address gender disparities in STEM fields and higher education 261

Section C: Examination of initiatives promoting girls' education and empowerment globally...277

Chapter 6 Social and Cultural Transformations **295**

Section A: Exploration of changing societal attitudes towards gender roles and stereotypes in women 295

Section B: Analysis of media representations of women and their impact on social perceptions...308

Section C: Examination of cultural movements and grassroots activism driving social change...315

Chapter 7 Intersectionality and Inclusivity...............................**330**

Section A: Discussion of the intersectional nature of women's rights and the importance of inclusivity 330

Section B: Analysis of challenges faced by marginalized communities within the women's rights movement..................344

Section C: Examination of efforts to prioritize diversity, equity, and inclusion in feminist activism 352

Chapter 8 Global Perspectives on Women's Rights **367**

Section A: Overview of women's rights movements and challenges worldwide 367

Section B: Analysis of cultural and legal barriers to gender equality in different regions...375

Section C: Examination of international collaborations and initiatives advancing women's rights globally........................383

Chapter 9 Remaining Challenges and Future Directions **401**

Section A: Identification of Persistent Barriers to Gender Equality and Women's Rights 401

Section B: Analysis of Emerging Issues and Challenges Facing Women in the Modern Era.. 416

Section C: Discussion of Future Directions and Strategies for Achieving Full Gender Equality 428

Chapter 10 Conclusion 448

Section A: Summary of Key Advancements and Milestones in Women's Rights 448

Section B: Reflections on the Ongoing Journey Towards Gender Equality 459

Section C: Call to Action for Continued Advocacy and Activism in Support of Women's Rights and Empowerment.................. 470

Chapter 1
Introduction

Section A: Definition and significance of women's rights

In the intricate mosaic of human rights, women's rights emerge as a vital thread, weaving together the principles of equality, non-discrimination, autonomy, and dignity. At its core, the concept of women's rights seeks to craft a world where women are accorded equal treatment and opportunities, whether in the workplace, educational institutions, or the corridors of political power. This encompasses the notion of equal pay for equal work, unfettered access to education and healthcare, and the unimpeded right to partake in decision-making processes, irrespective of gender.

The pursuit of gender equality faces deep-rooted systemic barriers that have persisted across generations. According to the World Economic Forum's Global Gender Gap Report 2022, it may take another 132 years to close the global gender gap at the current rate of progress. This staggering statistic underscores the urgency and magnitude of the challenge before us, highlighting the need for more concerted and accelerated efforts to dismantle the structural impediments to women's rights and equality.

The pursuit of women's rights is intrinsically linked to the broader struggle for human rights and social justice. Gender equality is not only a moral and legal imperative but also a fundamental prerequisite for the achievement of sustainable development, peace, and security. When women are empowered and their rights are upheld, societies as a whole thrive, benefiting from the full potential and contributions of half their population. Conversely, the denial of women's rights perpetuates a cycle of marginalization, poverty, and conflict, hindering progress for all.

Women's rights are not merely a women's issue but a human issue that affects us all. According to a study by the McKinsey Global Institute, advancing women's equality could add $12 trillion to global GDP by 2025. This economic imperative, coupled with the moral and social justice arguments, underscores the need for a holistic and intersectional approach to promoting women's rights, one that recognizes the interconnected nature of gender equality with other pressing global challenges such as poverty, climate change, and conflict resolution.

Non-discrimination, akin to a gentle rainfall nourishing the earth, ensures that women are shielded from the bitter winds of prejudice and bias. It strives to dismantle the barriers erected by gender identity, sexual orientation, race, ethnicity, religion, and disability, allowing women to stand tall and proud in their uniqueness without fear of discrimination or marginalization.

Despite legal frameworks and policies aimed at promoting non-discrimination, implicit biases and deep-rooted cultural norms often perpetuate discriminatory practices. According to a report by the United Nations Development Programme, up to 90% of people hold biases against women, stemming from societal conditioning and gender stereotypes. Addressing these unconscious biases and challenging harmful cultural narratives is crucial to creating an enabling environment where women can thrive without facing discrimination in their daily lives.

Discrimination against women takes many insidious forms, from overt acts of violence and harassment to more subtle forms of marginalization and exclusion. The United Nations has identified several areas where discrimination persists, including unequal access to education, healthcare, and economic opportunities, as well as disparities in legal status and political representation. Addressing these multifaceted manifestations of discrimination is crucial to achieving substantive equality and realizing the full potential of women's rights.

Autonomy, much like a butterfly dancing freely among the blossoms, embodies the right of women to chart their own destinies.

It encompasses the freedom to make choices about their bodies, lives, and futures, including decisions about reproductive rights, marriage, career, and lifestyle, free from the shadows of coercion or interference. Reproductive rights, in particular, stand as a cornerstone of women's autonomy, affirming their agency over their own bodies and the right to make informed choices about their sexual and reproductive health.

However, even in countries with progressive laws protecting reproductive rights, access to comprehensive sexual and reproductive healthcare remains a significant challenge. According to the Guttmacher Institute, an estimated 218 million women in developing regions have an unmet need for modern contraception. Addressing these access barriers, through investments in healthcare infrastructure, training of healthcare providers, and comprehensive sexuality education, is essential to ensuring women's autonomy and bodily integrity.

Reproductive rights are a critical battleground in the fight for women's autonomy and bodily integrity. Access to comprehensive reproductive healthcare, including contraception, safe abortion services, and maternal care, is essential for women to exercise control over their bodies and life choices. However, in many parts of the world, restrictive laws, social stigma, and lack of access to services continue to undermine women's reproductive rights, perpetuating cycles of disempowerment and gender inequality

According to the World Health Organization, around 25 million unsafe abortions are estimated to take place worldwide each year, putting women's lives and health at risk. This staggering statistic highlights the urgent need to decriminalize abortion, remove legal barriers, and provide safe, accessible, and affordable abortion services as part of a comprehensive reproductive healthcare package for women..

Dignity, as delicate as a dew-kissed rose at dawn, encapsulates the inherent worth and value of every individual. Women's rights seek to safeguard this dignity by challenging gender-based violence, exploitation, objectification, and dehumanization, ensuring that every woman's voice is heard and her agency respected.

The fight for women's dignity extends beyond physical violence to encompass psychological and economic forms of abuse. According to UN Women, an estimated 736 million women worldwide have been subjected to intimate partner violence, coercive control, or non-partner sexual violence at least once in their lifetime. Addressing the root causes of gender-based violence, including harmful gender norms, unequal power dynamics, and systemic inequalities, is crucial to upholding women's dignity and creating a world free from fear and oppression.

Gender-based violence, in its many forms – physical, sexual, psychological, and economic – represents one of the most egregious violations of women's dignity and human rights. According to the World Health Organization, one in three women worldwide experience physical or sexual violence in their lifetime, primarily perpetrated by an intimate partner. This pandemic of violence not only causes immense suffering and trauma but also reinforces gender inequalities, undermining women's autonomy, participation, and overall well-being.

The costs of gender-based violence extend far beyond the individual, imposing a significant economic burden on societies. According to a report by the Copenhagen Consensus Center, the global cost of violence against women is estimated to be around $4.4 trillion, or 5.5% of the global GDP. Investing in prevention, protection, and support services for survivors is not only a moral imperative but also an economic necessity to mitigate the far-reaching impacts of this pervasive human rights violation.

Gender-based violence has ripple effects that extend across generations, impacting not only the survivors but also their families and communities. Children who witness or experience violence in the home are more likely to experience cognitive and emotional difficulties, perpetuating cycles of trauma and adversity. According to UNICEF, exposure to violence in childhood can lead to a 63% increase in the risk of perpetrating or experiencing violence later in life. Addressing gender-based violence through comprehensive prevention programs, trauma-informed support services, and community-level interventions is crucial for breaking these intergenerational cycles and fostering more resilient, peaceful societies.

The significance of women's rights reverberates like a melody that harmonizes with the very essence of humanity. At its core, it is the cornerstone of gender equality, a fundamental human right that underpins sustainable development and social progress. By dismantling systemic barriers and biases, women's rights pave the way for a world where every individual can flourish, unencumbered by the shackles of inequality.

The pursuit of women's rights is intrinsically linked to the broader quest for human dignity and social justice. As Dr. Martin Luther King Jr. famously stated, "Injustice anywhere is a threat to justice everywhere." The denial of women's rights not only perpetuates gender inequality but also undermines the fundamental principles of human rights and the inherent worth of every individual. Conversely, by upholding women's rights, we reaffirm our shared humanity and commitment to creating a more just and equitable world for all.

The impact of women's rights extends far beyond the individual, shaping the trajectory of entire societies and nations. Countries that prioritize gender equality and women's empowerment tend to have lower rates of poverty, better health outcomes, and higher levels of economic growth. Conversely, gender inequality acts as a brake on development, perpetuating cycles of poverty, poor health, and economic stagnation. This underscores the importance of women's rights as a catalyst for sustainable and inclusive development globally.

A study by the International Monetary Fund found that closing the gender gap in labor force participation could boost economic growth by up to 35% in some countries. Furthermore, according to the World Bank, if women had the same access to productive resources as men, they could increase yields on their farms by 20-30%, potentially reducing the number of hungry people in the world by 100-150 million. These staggering figures demonstrate the profound economic and developmental impacts of empowering women and upholding their rights, underscoring the urgency of addressing gender inequalities as a critical pathway to sustainable development.

Moreover, women's rights are enshrined in international human rights instruments, such as the Universal Declaration of Human Rights and the Convention on the Elimination of All Forms of Discrimination Against Women (CEDAW), weaving a protective cocoon around the well-being and equality of women. These frameworks serve as guiding lights, reinforcing the duty of governments and societies to champion the cause of women, ensuring their equality, dignity, and well-being.

Despite the existence of these international legal frameworks, significant gaps remain in their implementation and enforcement. Many countries have yet to ratify CEDAW or have done so with reservations that undermine the convention's spirit and intent. Even where national laws align with international standards, discriminatory social norms, lack of political will, and inadequate resource allocation often impede the full realization of women's rights on the ground. Strengthening accountability mechanisms and fostering greater political commitment are essential to translating legal protections into tangible progress.

The role of civil society organizations and grassroots movements is crucial in holding governments accountable and advocating for the effective implementation of international commitments on women's rights. These organizations often serve as a vital link between policymakers and the communities they serve, amplifying the voices and experiences of women and girls while also monitoring progress and identifying gaps in implementation. Fostering an enabling environment for civil society engagement, including adequate funding and protection for human rights defenders, is essential for driving sustainable progress in advancing women's rights.

Despite the existence of these international legal frameworks, significant gaps remain in their implementation and enforcement. Many countries have yet to ratify CEDAW or have done so with reservations that undermine the convention's spirit and intent. Even where national laws align with international standards, discriminatory social norms, lack of political will, and inadequate resource allocation often impede the full realization of women's rights on the ground. Strengthening accountability mechanisms and fostering greater political commitment are essential to translating legal protections into tangible progress.

Indigenous women's rights represent a critical yet often overlooked dimension of the global women's rights agenda. Indigenous communities worldwide face systemic discrimination, land dispossession, and threats to their cultural survival – burdens that disproportionately impact indigenous women and girls. Upholding their collective rights to self-determination, traditional knowledge, and natural resource management is inextricably linked to advancing indigenous women's individual rights to education, healthcare, and freedom from violence and exploitation.

Indigenous women play a vital role in preserving and transmitting traditional knowledge systems, which often hold invaluable insights into sustainable resource management, biodiversity conservation, and climate resilience. However, their contributions and expertise are frequently marginalized or overlooked in decision-making processes. Ensuring the meaningful participation and leadership of indigenous women in environmental governance and sustainable development initiatives is crucial for building more equitable and sustainable societies that respect and value diverse knowledge systems and ways of life.

Empowerment is a radiant jewel in the crown of women's rights, bestowing upon women and girls the courage to challenge societal norms, pursue education and career opportunities, and assert their rights and autonomy. As they stand tall and empowered, they become beacons of change, guiding their communities towards a brighter, more inclusive future.

Women's empowerment is not merely an individual journey but a collective endeavor that requires transformative shifts in social, cultural, and economic structures. It necessitates addressing the root causes of gender inequality, such as patriarchal power dynamics, unequal distribution of resources, and discriminatory institutional practices. By fostering an enabling environment that challenges gender stereotypes, promotes equal opportunities, and provides support systems for women and girls, we can catalyze a ripple effect of empowerment that transcends generations and communities.

The importance of women's rights extends its caring embrace to encompass health and well-being, fostering a world where women have access to quality healthcare services, leading to lower maternal mortality rates and improved overall public health. Education, too, is not a distant dream but a beacon of hope that illuminates the path to intergenerational benefits for families and societies. By investing in girls' education and promoting gender equality in learning opportunities, we sow the seeds of empowerment, agency, and transformative change.

Education is a powerful catalyst for women's empowerment, with far-reaching impacts on health, economic opportunities, and civic engagement. According to UNESCO, each additional year of schooling for girls can increase their future earnings by up to 20%. Furthermore, educated mothers are more likely to invest in the health and education of their children, creating a virtuous cycle of intergenerational progress. By prioritizing girls' education and ensuring access to quality learning opportunities, we not only uplift individual women but also catalyze broader societal transformations towards greater gender equality and sustainable development.

Moreover, women's participation in peacebuilding and conflict resolution efforts is crucial for fostering sustainable peace and security. By addressing the root causes of conflict and advocating for reconciliation, women's rights play a pivotal role in building inclusive societies that honor the rights and dignity of all individuals.

Research has consistently shown that women's participation in peace processes leads to more sustainable and durable peace agreements. According to a study by the International Peace Institute, peace agreements are 35% more likely to last at least 15 years when women are included as witnesses, signatories, mediators, and negotiators. Women's unique perspectives and experiences often broaden the scope of peace negotiations to address issues such as gender-based violence, human rights, and the specific needs of marginalized communities, leading to more comprehensive and inclusive peace-building efforts.

Economic development, too, is profoundly influenced by women's rights, as closing gender gaps in employment and entrepreneurship leads to enhanced economic productivity and sustainable development. By investing in women's rights and gender equality, societies sow the seeds of poverty reduction, economic growth, and social cohesion.

According to the World Bank, closing the gender gap in labor force participation could boost global GDP by $7.7 trillion by 2025. Furthermore, investing in women's entrepreneurship has a multiplier effect, as women tend to reinvest a higher proportion of their earnings into their families and communities, leading to improved health, education, and overall well-being. By removing barriers to women's economic participation and supporting their entrepreneurial endeavors, societies can unlock a vast reservoir of untapped potential and drive inclusive economic growth.

The gender pay gap and occupational segregation remain persistent barriers to women's economic empowerment globally. On average, women earn only 77 cents for every dollar earned by men for work of equal value, according to UN Women. This disparity not only undermines women's financial independence but also deprives economies of much-needed productivity and innovation. Closing these gaps requires a multi-pronged approach – from strengthening pay equity laws and promoting women's leadership in male-dominated fields to addressing unconscious biases and providing affordable childcare.

The gender pay gap is not only a moral issue but also an economic one. According to a study by the International Labour Organization (ILO), the global gender pay gap represents a loss of $1.6 trillion in income each year. This lost income translates into reduced economic growth, lower tax revenues, and decreased consumption, hindering overall economic development. Addressing the pay gap through comprehensive policy interventions, such as pay transparency measures, gender-neutral job evaluations, and workplace diversity initiatives, is essential for unlocking the full economic potential of women and driving sustainable growth.

In the field of climate change and environmental justice, women's rights are inextricably linked to the health of the planet. Women, particularly in developing countries, are disproportionately impacted by environmental degradation, natural disasters, and resource scarcity due to their roles in agriculture, water collection, and household management. Ensuring women's participation in environmental decision-making, promoting sustainable livelihoods, and integrating gender perspectives into climate policies are vital for building resilient communities and a habitable future for all.

Women's traditional knowledge and sustainable practices often hold invaluable insights for addressing climate change and preserving biodiversity. For instance, many indigenous communities have developed sophisticated systems for managing natural resources, such as rotational farming, seed preservation, and water harvesting techniques. By recognizing and integrating these knowledge systems into climate adaptation and mitigation strategies, we can leverage women's unique perspectives and experiences to build more sustainable and resilient communities.

Women's rights intersect with broader struggles for social justice, encompassing racial justice, economic justice, environmental justice, and LGBTQ+ rights. Recognizing the interconnectedness of these issues is pivotal in addressing systemic inequalities and building more inclusive and equitable societies for all.

The intersections of gender, race, and class reveal the compounded forms of discrimination and marginalization faced by many women of color. For instance, Black women in the United States earn only 63 cents for every dollar earned by white men, according to the National Women's Law Center. This stark disparity highlights the need for an intersectional approach that addresses the unique challenges faced by women at the intersection of multiple identities and systems of oppression. By centering the voices and experiences of these women, we can develop more holistic and effective strategies for achieving gender equality and social justice.

The principle of intersectionality is central to understanding the complexities and nuances of women's rights. Women's experiences are shaped not only by their gender but also by intersecting identities and systems of oppression based on race, class, sexual orientation, disability, and other factors. An intersectional approach to women's rights recognizes these compounded forms of discrimination and advocates for holistic solutions that address the unique needs and challenges faced by diverse groups of women.

The experiences of LGBTQ+ women highlight the compounded discrimination and marginalization faced by those with intersecting identities. LGBTQ+ women often face heightened risks of violence, discrimination in employment and housing, and barriers to accessing healthcare services. According to a report by the United Nations Office of the High Commissioner for Human Rights, transgender women are particularly vulnerable, facing high rates of violence, criminalisation, and human rights violations. An intersectional approach to women's rights must prioritize the needs and safety of LGBTQ+ women, challenging societal norms and advocating for inclusive policies and legal protections.

Feminist theory and activism have evolved to encompass a wide range of perspectives and approaches, reflecting the diversity of women's experiences and the intersectional nature of oppression. From liberal feminism's focus on equal rights and opportunities to radical feminism's challenge of patriarchal power structures, and from Black feminism's centering of race and intersectionality to ecofeminism's exploration of gender and environmental justice, these varied lenses enrich and propel the global women's rights movement forward.

The emergence of transnational feminism has broadened the scope of feminist theory and activism, recognizing the interconnected nature of women's struggles across borders and cultures. Transnational feminism acknowledges the diversity of women's experiences, while also highlighting the shared challenges faced by women worldwide, such as gender-based violence, economic inequality, and restricted access to reproductive rights. By fostering solidarity and collective action among women's movements globally, transnational feminism offers a powerful framework for advancing women's rights and challenging systems of oppression that transcend national boundaries.

The United Nations Sustainable Development Goals (SDGs), particularly SDG 5 on gender equality, stand as a clarion call for the global community to prioritize women's rights and empowerment. By working towards these goals, we weave a narrative of progress, where the threads of equality, justice, and dignity are interwoven into the fabric of our shared future.

Despite the ambitious targets set by the SDGs, progress towards gender equality has been uneven and slow. According to UN Women's 2022 report, at the current rate of progress, it may take nearly three centuries to close the gender gap in economic participation and opportunities. This highlights the need for accelerated action, increased investment, and robust accountability mechanisms to ensure that the SDGs are not just aspirational goals but tangible achievements. By prioritizing gender-responsive budgeting, promoting institutional reforms, and fostering multi-stakeholder partnerships, we can drive transformative change and realize the promise of the SDGs for women's empowerment.

While the SDGs represent an ambitious and comprehensive global agenda, their implementation has been uneven, with significant gaps persisting in achieving gender equality targets. According to UN Women's 2022 monitoring report, no country has yet achieved full gender equality, and the COVID-19 pandemic has exacerbated existing inequalities, rolling back hard-won gains in areas such as women's employment, education, and freedom from violence. Redoubling efforts and mobilizing sufficient resources to implement the SDGs is critical to realizing their transformative potential for women's rights.

The COVID-19 pandemic has had a disproportionate impact on women, exacerbating existing gender inequalities and exposing the vulnerabilities inherent in our systems. According to a report by UN

Women, the pandemic has led to a dramatic increase in domestic violence cases, with lockdowns and economic insecurity amplifying the risk factors for gender-based violence. Additionally, women have borne the brunt of job losses and economic hardship, particularly in the informal and service sectors. Addressing the gendered impacts of the pandemic through targeted policies and investments is crucial for ensuring a gender-responsive recovery and building more resilient societies.

The digital revolution has emerged as both an opportunity and a challenge for women's rights. On one hand, digital technologies have enabled greater access to information, education, and economic opportunities for women, while also providing platforms for advocacy and solidarity-building. However, the online sphere has also exposed women to new forms of gender-based violence, such as cyber harassment, non-consensual image sharing, and online stalking. Ensuring women's digital security and safety while harnessing the empowering potential of technology is a critical frontier in the fight for women's rights.

The digital gender divide remains a significant barrier, with women in many parts of the world still lacking equal access to the internet and digital technologies. According to the International Telecommunication Union, the global internet user gender gap stood at 62.5% for men and 57.1% for women in 2022. This digital exclusion not only limits women's economic and educational opportunities but also hinders their ability to access information, express themselves, and participate in online advocacy and movements. Bridging this gap through investments in digital infrastructure, skills training, and gender-responsive policies is crucial for ensuring that the digital revolution is inclusive and empowering for all women.

In summary, women's rights are a mosaic of interconnected principles, each thread telling a story of resilience, empowerment, and progress. Upholding and advancing women's rights is not just an aspiration; it is an imperative for achieving gender equality, promoting human rights, empowering women and girls, improving health and well-being, fostering peace and stability, driving economic development, and advancing social justice globally.

The pursuit of women's rights is not a linear path but a multi-generational struggle that has witnessed both triumphs and setbacks throughout history. From the women's suffrage movement to the ongoing battles for reproductive rights, pay equity, and freedom from violence, each victory has been hard-won, fueled by the resilience and determination of countless women's rights activists and advocates. As we continue this journey, it is essential to honor the sacrifices and contributions of those who came before us, while also recognizing the ongoing challenges and the intersectional nature of the struggles that lie ahead.

As we navigate the landscape of women's rights, we encounter challenges and barriers, like thorns in a garden of roses, that demand our attention and resolve.

Legal and policy gaps, like tangled vines obstructing the path, hinder the full realization of women's rights in many countries. Discriminatory laws and policies continue to restrict women's mobility, inheritance rights, access to divorce, and participation in public life. Addressing these gaps is imperative for dismantling the barriers that impede women's progress.

One of the most pernicious legal barriers to women's rights is the persistence of discriminatory family laws in many countries. These laws often restrict women's rights to inheritance, divorce, child custody, and reproductive autonomy, perpetuating gender inequalities within the family unit. According to a report by the World Bank, over 90 countries still have legal barriers that prevent women from working in certain jobs, owning and managing assets, or making decisions about their reproductive health. Reforming these discriminatory laws and ensuring gender-equal legal frameworks is a fundamental step in advancing women's rights and gender equality.

In some countries, women remain legally barred from owning property, obtaining passports, or making decisions about their children without the consent of a male guardian. These discriminatory legal frameworks not only violate women's autonomy but also perpetuate cycles of economic disempowerment, social marginalization, and vulnerability to exploitation. Reforming such laws and ensuring gender-neutral legal frameworks is a critical step in advancing women's rights.

The persistence of male guardianship laws in several countries represents a severe infringement on women's autonomy and legal personhood. Under these laws, women are treated as legal minors, requiring the approval of a male guardian (typically a husband, father, or brother) for decisions related to travel, employment, healthcare, and even basic daily activities. These laws not only perpetuate gender discrimination but also facilitate various forms of abuse and exploitation, including economic deprivation and restricted freedom of movement. Abolishing male guardianship laws and ensuring that women have equal legal capacity and agency is a crucial step in advancing women's rights and empowerment.

Women's political participation and representation remain severely limited in many parts of the world, hindering their ability to shape the policies and decisions that affect their lives. As of 2022, only 26.1% of national parliamentary seats globally were held by women, according to the Inter-Parliamentary Union. This democratic deficit not only undermines women's rights but also deprives societies of the diverse perspectives and experiences that women bring to decision-making processes. Overcoming structural barriers, challenging gender stereotypes, and promoting women's leadership at all levels of governance are essential for achieving substantive gender equality.

Beyond numerical representation, it is crucial to ensure that women's voices and priorities are substantively reflected in policymaking and legislative processes. According to a study by the Inter-Parliamentary Union, even when women are present in parliament, their ability to influence decision-making can be limited by factors such as gender biases, lack of access to leadership positions, and the marginalization of women's issues. Addressing these systemic barriers through measures such as gender-sensitive parliamentary practices, capacity-building programs, and the prioritization of women's concerns in policy agendas is essential for translating numerical representation into substantive and transformative change.

Gender-based violence, a dark cloud looming over the horizon, remains a pervasive human rights violation worldwide. Efforts to combat such violence and support survivors are crucial in upholding women's rights and fostering a world free from fear and oppression.

The COVID-19 pandemic has exacerbated the global crisis of gender-based violence, with lockdowns and economic insecurity amplifying the risk factors for domestic abuse and intimate partner violence. According to UN Women, there has been an alarming increase in reported cases of violence against women during the pandemic, with some countries experiencing a surge of up to 30% in emergency calls related to domestic violence. Addressing this "shadow pandemic" requires a comprehensive approach that includes strengthening support services for survivors, implementing preventive measures through education and community engagement, and addressing the underlying gender norms and power imbalances that perpetuate violence against women.

Deeply ingrained gender norms and cultural practices, like ancient roots anchoring the tree of inequality, often perpetuate discrimination against women. Challenging and changing these norms is essential for creating an environment where every woman can flourish unencumbered by limitations imposed by tradition.

Gender norms and stereotypes are often reinforced and perpetuated through various socialization agents, such as family, education systems, media, and religious institutions. From an early age, girls and boys are exposed to messages and expectations that reinforce traditional gender roles, limiting their aspirations and choices. Challenging these deeply entrenched norms requires a multi-pronged approach that involves transforming curricula, media representations, and community-level interventions. By engaging men and boys as allies and champions of gender equality, we can foster a shift in societal attitudes and create an enabling environment for the full realization of women's rights.

Gender socialization from an early age plays a significant role in perpetuating harmful norms and stereotypes that restrict women's rights and opportunities. Girls are often socialized to prioritize domestic roles, defer to male authority, and suppress their ambitions and leadership potential. Comprehensive efforts to challenge these norms through gender-sensitive education, media campaigns, and community engagement are crucial for fostering an enabling environment for women's empowerment.

Educational institutions play a pivotal role in shaping gender norms and attitudes from a young age. According to a UNESCO report, textbooks and learning materials in many countries still perpetuate gender stereotypes, reinforcing traditional roles and limiting girls' aspirations. Integrating gender-sensitive curricula, promoting positive role models, and training educators on gender-responsive pedagogy are crucial steps in disrupting harmful gender socialization processes. By empowering girls and boys with knowledge, skills, and confidence to challenge gender norms, we can foster a more equitable and inclusive society that values the contributions and potential of all individuals, regardless of gender.

Religious and cultural traditions can sometimes be invoked to justify discriminatory practices against women, such as child marriage, female genital mutilation, or restrictions on women's mobility and decision-making autonomy. However, it is essential to recognize that no culture or religion is monolithic, and there are often progressive interpretations and reform movements within these traditions that champion women's rights and gender equality. Engaging with these progressive voices and supporting their efforts to reinterpret and reshape cultural narratives can be a powerful force for positive change.

Child marriage, in particular, represents a severe violation of human rights and a significant barrier to achieving gender equality. According to UNICEF, an estimated 650 million girls and women alive today were married before their 18th birthday, with the highest rates occurring in sub-Saharan Africa, South Asia, and parts of the Middle East. Child marriage perpetuates cycles of poverty, poor health outcomes, and gender-based violence, while also limiting girls' access to education and economic opportunities. Addressing this harmful practice requires a comprehensive approach that involves legal reforms, community engagement, and investments in girls' empowerment and education.

Economic disparities, much like a turbulent current threatening to sweep away the foundation of progress, continue to affect women worldwide. Bridging the wage gaps, ensuring equal access to credit and resources, and promoting women's entrepreneurship are pivotal steps in achieving economic gender equality.

Despite progress in recent decades, the global gender gap in labor force participation remains stubbornly wide. According to the International Labour Organization (ILO), the labor force participation rate for women aged 25-54 was 63% in 2022, compared to 94% for men in the same age group. This gap not only perpetuates economic inequalities but also hinders economic growth and productivity, as it represents a vast pool of untapped talent and potential. Closing this gap requires comprehensive efforts to address the root causes, such as discriminatory social norms, lack of access to quality childcare and family-friendly policies, and occupational segregation.

Women's unpaid care work, such as household chores, childcare, and caring for the elderly, represents a significant and often invisible economic burden that perpetuates gender inequalities. According to UN Women, women perform 76.2% of total hours of unpaid care work globally, limiting their ability to participate in the formal labor market and accumulate economic assets. Recognizing and redistributing this care work through policies like paid family leave, affordable childcare, and engaging men and boys in caregiving roles is essential for advancing women's economic empowerment.

The disproportionate burden of unpaid care work on women is not only a gender equality issue but also a macroeconomic concern. According to the International Labour Organization (ILO), the value of unpaid care work globally is estimated to be as high as $10.8 trillion annually, or 9% of global GDP. By failing to recognize and redistribute this work, economies are effectively overlooking a substantial contribution to societal well-being and economic productivity. Implementing policies that support the equal sharing of care responsibilities and investing in care infrastructure can unlock substantial economic benefits while promoting gender equality and women's empowerment.

Access to financial services and resources remains a significant barrier for many women worldwide, particularly in developing countries and rural areas. According to the World Bank, women are still 20% less likely than men to have a formal bank account, limiting their ability to save, borrow, and invest in income-generating activities. Promoting financial inclusion through gender-responsive financial products, digital financial services, and financial literacy programs is crucial for unlocking women's economic potential and fostering inclusive economic growth.

The gender gap in financial inclusion is particularly pronounced in rural areas and among marginalized communities. For instance, in sub-Saharan Africa, only 37% of women have access to formal financial services, compared to 48% of men, according to the World Bank. This lack of access to financial resources not only perpetuates poverty and economic insecurity but also limits women's ability to invest in their businesses, accumulate assets, and build resilience against economic shocks. Addressing this gap requires a multi-pronged approach that involves improving financial literacy, tailoring financial products to women's needs, and leveraging digital technologies to expand access to remote and underserved communities.

The concept of intersectionality, akin to a kaleidoscope of diverse identities blending seamlessly, recognizes that women's experiences of oppression and discrimination are shaped by intersecting factors such as race, ethnicity, class, sexuality, disability, and migration status. Embracing intersectional approaches to women's rights enables us to champion inclusive policies and interventions that address the unique needs and challenges faced by diverse groups of women.

The experiences of indigenous women highlight the compounded forms of discrimination and marginalization faced by those with intersecting identities. Indigenous women often face higher rates of poverty, limited access to healthcare and education, and increased vulnerability to violence and exploitation. According to the United Nations Permanent Forum on Indigenous Issues, indigenous women are disproportionately affected by environmental degradation, land dispossession, and the loss of traditional livelihoods, further exacerbating their economic and social marginalization. Addressing the specific needs and priorities of indigenous women is crucial for advancing their rights and ensuring their participation in decision-making processes that impact their lives and communities.

Immigrant and refugee women often face compounded challenges in asserting their rights due to language barriers, lack of legal status, and social isolation. They may be particularly vulnerable to exploitation, human trafficking, and gender-based violence, while also facing barriers in accessing essential services and support systems. Addressing the specific needs of migrant and refugee women, including ensuring their access to healthcare, education, and legal protections, is crucial for upholding their fundamental rights and dignity.

The experiences of refugee women highlight the intersections of gender, displacement, and conflict. According to the United Nations High Commissioner for Refugees (UNHCR), women and girls account for approximately half of the world's refugee population, and they often face heightened risks of sexual and gender-based violence, limited access to reproductive healthcare, and obstacles to economic empowerment. Addressing the specific needs of refugee women, including providing safe spaces, access to education and livelihoods, and trauma-informed support services, is essential for ensuring their protection, dignity, and empowerment in the face of displacement and adversity.

Women with disabilities encounter multiple forms of discrimination and marginalization, both due to their gender and their disability status. They face higher rates of poverty, lack of access to education and employment opportunities, and an increased risk of gender-based violence, including sexual abuse and forced sterilization. Promoting the rights of women with disabilities, including their participation in decision-making processes, access to assistive technologies, and freedom from discrimination and violence, is essential for achieving inclusive and equitable societies.

The intersections of gender and disability often create compounded barriers and vulnerabilities for women with disabilities. According to the United Nations Department of Economic and Social Affairs, women with disabilities are three times more likely to experience gender-based violence than women without disabilities, and they often face increased social isolation, limited access to sexual and reproductive health services, and heightened discrimination in employment and education. Addressing these intersectional challenges requires a multi-faceted approach that involves promoting inclusive policies, challenging societal attitudes and stereotypes, and ensuring accessible services and support systems that cater to the specific needs of women with disabilities.

The drumbeat of change resonates through the efforts of women's rights activists and movements, as they tirelessly advocate for policy changes, raise awareness, and mobilize communities to advance women's rights. Global campaigns, such as #MeToo, #TimesUp, and the Women's March, have galvanized attention to issues such as sexual violence, workplace harassment, and reproductive rights, sparking dialogue and propelling social change.

The power of social media and digital activism has amplified the reach and impact of women's rights movements, enabling the rapid dissemination of information, the mobilization of collective action, and the formation of transnational solidarities. Platforms like Twitter, Facebook, and Instagram have become virtual spaces for advocacy, storytelling, and consciousness-raising, empowering women and girls to share their experiences, challenge societal norms, and demand accountability from institutions and decision-makers. However, the digital sphere has also exposed women's rights activists to new forms of harassment, surveillance, and online violence, underscoring the need for digital security and safety measures to protect these critical voices for change.

International organizations, such as the United Nations and its agencies, play a pivotal role in promoting and protecting women's rights through treaties, conventions, and initiatives. Instruments such as CEDAW, the Beijing Declaration and Platform for Action, and the Sustainable Development Goals (SDGs) serve as guiding lights in the global effort to advance women's rights and gender equality.

Education and awareness-raising efforts are the gentle winds that carry the seeds of change, fostering positive attitudes and behaviors while combatting gender-based discrimination and violence. Comprehensive sexuality education, media literacy programs, and gender-sensitive curricula are vital tools in promoting gender equality and empowering women and girls.

In conclusion, advancing women's rights demands a collective effort to surmount persistent challenges, embrace intersectional approaches, mobilize global advocacy and movements, strengthen international frameworks and mechanisms, and invest in education and awareness-raising efforts. As we start at the crossroads of history, let us embark on this journey with open hearts and unwavering determination, for in championing women's rights, we nurture a world that flourishes in the light of equality and inclusion.

Section B: Overview of the historical context of women's rights movement

In the grand scheme of human history, the narrative of women's rights unfolds as a vibrant and compelling saga, its threads weaving through the fabric of time and society. To truly understand the present and envision the future, one must embark on a journey through the annals of history, where the aspirations for equality and dignity have blossomed into movements that have reshaped the very essence of modern society.

Throughout history, the struggle for women's rights has been inextricably linked to broader social, political, and economic movements. The abolitionist movement, for instance, shared common ground with the early women's rights advocates, as they recognized the interconnected nature of oppression based on gender and race. Figures like Sojourner Truth, a former slave and renowned abolitionist, delivered powerful speeches that highlighted the intersections of racial and gender-based injustice, such as her famous "Ain't I a Woman?" address at the 1851 Women's Rights Convention in Akron, Ohio. Truth's words resonated with both the anti-slavery and women's rights movements, underscoring the importance of intersectional solidarity in the pursuit of equality.

The roots of the quest for women's rights can be traced back to ancient civilizations, where exceptional women challenged patriarchal norms through their actions and words. In ancient Egypt, women like Hatshepsut and Nefertiti wielded significant power and influence, defying gender constraints. Meanwhile, in ancient Greece, the playwright Aristophanes satirized gender roles in his works, hinting at undercurrents of dissent against the status quo.

Recent archaeological discoveries have shed light on the influential roles played by women in ancient civilizations. For instance, the discovery of the tomb of Puabi, a powerful priestess who ruled over the ancient Sumerian city-state of Ur around 2500 BCE, revealed her wealth and status, challenging the notion that women were relegated to subordinate roles in those times. Similarly, the unearthing of the remains of the legendary Amazons, a society of female warriors, in regions of modern-day Russia and Ukraine, has provided tangible evidence of the existence of matriarchal societies that defied traditional gender norms.

Throughout history, various religious and philosophical traditions have grappled with the concept of gender equality. Within the Islamic tradition, scholars like Ibn Arabi and Al-Ghazali advocated for women's rights to education and inheritance, while figures like Rabi'a al-Adawiyya and Fatima al-Fihri challenged conventional gender roles through their spiritual leadership and intellectual pursuits. In Buddhism, the establishment of the Bhikkhuni order by the Buddha allowed women to pursue a religious vocation, albeit with limitations.

In the Christian tradition, early figures such as St. Thecla and St. Perpetua challenged patriarchal norms and served as role models for women's empowerment. During the Middle Ages, influential mystics and scholars like Hildegard of Bingen and Julian of Norwich made significant contributions to theology and philosophy, defying the gender constraints of their time. These examples illustrate how various faith traditions have grappled with the concept of gender equality, with some voices advocating for greater rights and recognition for women, even as patriarchal structures persisted.

The quest for women's rights has its roots in the ancient world, where pioneering thinkers and philosophers challenged the prevailing patriarchal norms of their times. In ancient Greece, Plato advocated for gender equality in education, while the mathematician Hypatia of Alexandria became a symbol of intellectual prowess and defiance against the constraints imposed on women. These early voices, though often marginalized, planted the seeds of a movement that would eventually flourish across continents and civilizations.

In this milieu of burgeoning ideas, Mary Wollstonecraft emerged as a luminary, her words etching indelible marks upon the canvas of feminist philosophy. In her seminal work, "A Vindication of the Rights of Woman" (1792), she fervently championed the cause of women's education and social equality, igniting a flame that would endure through the ages. Through her eloquence, she beckoned society to embrace the notion that women were not merely passive bystanders but agents of change, deserving of equal rights and opportunities.

Wollstonecraft's ideas were not only influential in her time but also laid the foundation for subsequent feminist thought and activism. Her emphasis on the importance of education for women was a revolutionary concept, challenging the prevailing notion that women's primary role was confined to the domestic sphere. Wollstonecraft's arguments were grounded in the Enlightenment ideals of reason, rationality, and natural rights, paving the way for future generations of feminists to build upon her philosophical framework.

Let us set the stage amidst the fervent winds of change that swept through the Enlightenment period, a time when the seeds of individual rights and equality were sown. It was during this era that the intellectual landscape began to shift, ushering in the dawning of a new understanding of human rights. From the fertile grounds of philosophical discourse emerged the nascent whispers of equality, which would later echo through the corridors of feminist movements.

The Enlightenment philosophers, while championing ideas of liberty, equality, and natural rights, often failed to extend these principles to women. Figures like Jean-Jacques Rousseau and Immanuel Kant propagated beliefs about the inherent inferiority of women, reinforcing patriarchal notions that would later be challenged by feminist thinkers and activists.

In this milieu of burgeoning ideas, Mary Wollstonecraft emerged as a luminary, her words etching indelible marks upon the canvas of feminist philosophy. In her seminal work, "A Vindication of the Rights of Woman" (1792), she fervently championed the cause of women's education and social equality, igniting a flame that would endure through the ages. Through her eloquence, she beckoned society to embrace the notion that women were not merely passive bystanders but agents of change, deserving of equal rights and opportunities.

Wollstonecraft's legacy inspired a wave of feminist activism across Europe and North America, as women took up the mantle of advocating for their rights in various spheres of life. Figures like Lucretia Mott, Elizabeth Cady Stanton, and Sojourner Truth emerged as influential voices, challenging the intertwined oppressions of gender, race, and class in their pursuit of equality and justice.

The Seneca Falls Convention of 1848 stands as a milestone in the chronicles of women's suffrage, a pivotal moment that heralded the birth of an enduring movement. It was here that the clarion call for women's right to vote resounded, encapsulated in the resolute words of the Declaration of Sentiments. This historic gathering reverberated with the collective determination of women to cast off the shackles of inequality and claim their rightful place in the annals of governance.

The Convention was organized by notable figures like Elizabeth Cady Stanton and Lucretia Mott, who drew inspiration from the abolitionist movement and the fight for racial equality. The Declaration of Sentiments, modeled after the Declaration of Independence, asserted that "all men and women are created equal" and called for women's suffrage, access to education, and equal rights in the workplace and society.

The Seneca Falls Convention marked the beginning of a protracted and arduous struggle for women's suffrage, spanning decades and spanning across multiple nations. Pioneers like Susan B. Anthony, Ida B. Wells, and Emmeline Pankhurst dedicated their lives to this cause, employing a range of tactics, from peaceful protests to civil disobedience, to raise awareness and challenge the entrenched patriarchal systems that denied women their fundamental right to participate in the democratic process.

As the suffragists fervently championed their cause, their methods of advocacy evolved into a multifaceted landscape of activism. From lobbying and civil disobedience to public demonstrations, their resolve remained unwavering, their voices echoing across the terrain of societal change. Their tireless efforts, woven with courage and resilience, bore witness to the unwavering spirit of women who refused to be relegated to the sidelines of history.

Iconic figures like Susan B. Anthony, Ida B. Wells, and Millicent Fawcett became emblems of the suffrage movement, employing diverse tactics to further their cause. Anthony was arrested and fined for illegally voting in the 1872 presidential election, while Wells fearlessly confronted the intersections of racism and sexism through her activism. Fawcett, a leading figure in the British suffrage movement, orchestrated large-scale demonstrations and lobbied parliament relentlessly for women's enfranchisement.

As the suffragists fervently championed their cause, their methods of advocacy evolved into a multifaceted landscape of activism. From lobbying and civil disobedience to public demonstrations, their resolve remained unwavering, their voices echoing across the terrain of societal change. Their tireless efforts, woven with courage and resilience, bore witness to the unwavering spirit of women who refused to be relegated to the sidelines of history.

One particularly notable example of the suffragists' innovative tactics was the "Silent Sentinels" protest, organized by the National Woman's Party in 1917. Led by figures like Inez Milholland and Lucy

Burns, this peaceful protest saw women standing silently outside the White House, holding banners advocating for women's suffrage. Their unwavering presence and refusal to back down in the face of arrests and abuse from authorities drew national attention to their cause and served as a powerful symbol of nonviolent resistance in the pursuit of women's rights.

Notable events such as the Women's Suffrage Parade in Washington, D.C., in 1913, and the Night of Terror in 1917, when suffragists were brutally assaulted by authorities, exemplified the sacrifices made by these activists in the face of fierce opposition. Their perseverance ultimately paid off, with the ratification of the 19th Amendment to the U.S. Constitution in 1920, granting American women the right to vote.

The tumultuous tides of history, marked by the crucible of wars and conflicts, served as catalysts for transformative change in the societal perceptions of women's roles. Women's profound contributions to the war efforts challenged traditional gender norms, shattering the confines of domesticity and heralding a new era of increased participation in the workforce and public life. Through their toil and resilience, they etched their names onto the pages of history, weaving a narrative of empowerment and resilience.

During World War II, for instance, women played crucial roles in manufacturing, transportation, and various industries, filling the void left by men who had gone off to war. The iconic image of "Rosie the Riveter" became a symbol of women's newfound economic empowerment and their ability to contribute to the war effort while challenging traditional gender roles. These experiences laid the groundwork for the second wave of feminism that would emerge in the post-war era.

The experiences of women during World War II had a profound impact on societal attitudes and expectations. As women demonstrated their capabilities in traditionally male-dominated fields, it became increasingly difficult to justify their exclusion from various spheres of public life. Furthermore, the economic contributions of women during the war effort highlighted the importance of their participation in the workforce, paving the way for greater recognition of women's economic rights and opportunities in the post-war period.

The fervent winds of change that swept through the 1960s, characterized by the Civil Rights Movement and anti-war protests, provided fertile ground for the burgeoning waves of feminist activism. The voices of women, interwoven with the chorus of social change, echoed with an unyielding determination to carve out a space for gender equality within the collective conscience of society.

The publication of Betty Friedan's "The Feminine Mystique" in 1963 ignited a firestorm of debate and activism, challenging the prevailing notions of domesticity and encouraging women to seek fulfillment beyond the confines of the household. Organizations like the National Organization for Women (NOW) emerged as powerful advocates for women's rights, lobbying for legislative changes and raising awareness about issues such as workplace discrimination, reproductive rights, and equal pay.

The Sexual Revolution and the introduction of birth control marked a pivotal shift in women's bodily autonomy and reproductive rights. The ability to control their fertility and make informed choices about their sexual health empowered women to challenge societal norms and assert their agency over their own bodies. This revolution in reproductive freedom paved the way for greater gender equality and the pursuit of personal and professional aspirations.

The concept of intersectionality emerged as a beacon of understanding, illuminating the interconnected nature of gender with race, class, sexuality, and other identities. This profound insight, championed by scholars like Kimberlé Crenshaw, underscored the multifaceted dimensions of oppression and served as a clarion call for inclusive and holistic approaches to feminist advocacy and policy-making.

The recognition of intersectionality has been instrumental in shaping more nuanced and inclusive feminist movements. For example, the emergence of Black feminism, led by figures like bell hooks, Patricia Hill Collins, and Audre Lorde, highlighted the unique experiences and challenges faced by Black women, who often encountered multiple forms of discrimination based on their race, gender, and class. Similarly, the LGBTQ+ feminist movement has advocated for the rights and representation of queer women, challenging the heteronormative assumptions that have historically dominated mainstream feminist discourse.

The development of oral contraceptives and the landmark Roe v. Wade decision by the U.S. Supreme Court in 1973, which legalized abortion nationwide, were significant milestones in the fight for reproductive rights. However, these gains have been met with fierce opposition and ongoing efforts to restrict access to abortion and contraception, highlighting the ongoing nature of the struggle for bodily autonomy and reproductive justice.

The concept of intersectionality emerged as a beacon of understanding, illuminating the interconnected nature of gender with race, class, sexuality, and other identities. This profound insight, championed by scholars like Kimberlé Crenshaw, underscored the multifaceted dimensions of oppression and served as a clarion call for inclusive and holistic approaches to feminist advocacy and policy-making.

Intersectionality recognized that the experiences of women of color, LGBTQ+ individuals, and those from marginalized communities were shaped by multiple, overlapping forms of discrimination and oppression. This understanding gave rise to more nuanced and inclusive feminist movements, such as Black feminism and LGBTQ+ feminism, which sought to address the unique challenges faced by these communities while advocating for intersectional approaches to achieving true equality.<

Across the globe, women's voices rose in unison, each thread contributing to the rich voice of the global feminist movement. From the revolutionary women in Russia who fought for political and social equality to the anti-colonial feminists in Africa and Asia who challenged the intersections of gender, race, and imperialism, these diverse perspectives enriched the discourse and highlighted the importance of intersectional solidarity.

Prominent figures like Olympe Audouard in France, Rokeya Sakhawat Hossain in Bengal, and Fatima Ahmed Ibrahim in Egypt were instrumental in shaping feminist thought and activism within their respective regions. Their contributions underscored the global nature of the women's rights movement and the need for cross-cultural dialogue and cooperation in the pursuit of gender equality.

Olympe Audouard, a French feminist and activist during the French Revolution, was a vocal advocate for women's political rights and their inclusion in the principles of liberty and equality espoused by the revolution. Her writings, such as the "Declaration of the Rights of Woman and the Female Citizen," challenged the exclusion of women from the revolutionary ideals and inspired future generations of French feminists. In Bengal, Rokeya Sakhawat Hossain's works, like "Sultana's Dream," envisioned a utopian world where gender roles were reversed, challenging the patriarchal norms of her time and advocating for women's education and empowerment. Fatima Ahmed Ibrahim, often referred to as the "Doria Shafik of Egypt," was a pioneering feminist who fought for women's suffrage, political representation, and legal reforms to protect women's rights in Egypt.

International conferences, such as the World Conferences on Women, served as pivotal platforms for shaping global feminist agendas and policies. The Beijing Declaration and Platform for Action, adopted at the Fourth World Conference on Women in 1995, stands as a landmark document, setting forth a comprehensive framework for advancing women's rights and gender equality worldwide.

The Beijing Platform for Action covered a wide range of critical areas, including women's economic empowerment, education, health, violence against women, and political participation. It also recognized the importance of addressing intersecting forms of discrimination and called for the mainstreaming of gender perspectives across all areas of policy and programming. This document provided a blueprint for governments, civil society organizations, and international bodies to work towards the realization of women's rights and gender equality.

In the contemporary landscape, the advent of social media platforms has heralded a new chapter in feminist discourse and activism. Spaces like Twitter and Instagram have become virtual arenas for mobilization, community-building, and the dissemination of feminist ideals. The digital realm has emerged as a vibrant canvas, where voices once silenced find resonance and solidarity, where the echoes of advocacy reverberate across the digital expanse.

Online campaigns and hashtags like #BringBackOurGirls, #YesAllWomen, and #MujeresEnLaDelantera have galvanized global attention and solidarity around issues such as gender-based violence, workplace harassment, and the representation of women in various fields. These digital movements have amplified marginalized voices, facilitated cross-border collaboration, and demonstrated the power of collective action in the digital age.

One notable example is the #BringBackOurGirls campaign, which emerged in response to the abduction of over 200 schoolgirls by the Boko Haram terrorist group in Nigeria in 2014. The hashtag quickly went viral, drawing international attention to the issue and putting pressure on governments and organizations to take action. The campaign not only raised awareness about the plight of the abducted girls but also highlighted the broader issues of gender-based violence, access to education for girls, and the importance of women's empowerment in conflict-affected regions.

The #MeToo movement, a seismic wave that surged through the late 2010s, unveiled the harrowing prevalence of sexual harassment and assault, sparking conversations about power dynamics and accountability. It served as a poignant testament to the enduring spirit of women who dared to raise their voices, demanding recognition and justice in the face of systemic oppression.

The development of oral contraceptives and the landmark Roe v. Wade decision by the U.S. Supreme Court in 1973, which legalized abortion nationwide, were significant milestones in the fight for reproductive rights. However, these gains have been met with fierce opposition and ongoing efforts to restrict access to abortion and contraception, highlighting the ongoing nature of the struggle for bodily autonomy and reproductive justice.

An intricate global mosaic of efforts to promote gender equality is enshrined within frameworks like the United Nations Sustainable Development Goals (SDGs), where targets related to women's empowerment and gender equality stand as beacons of hope and progress. These global endeavors, woven with compassion and determination, serve as testaments to the collective resolve to forge a world where women's rights are not just aspirations but tangible realities.

The SDGs, which were adopted by the United Nations in 2015, represent a comprehensive blueprint for addressing the most pressing global challenges, including gender inequality. Goal 5, titled "Achieve Gender Equality and Empower All Women and Girls," encompasses a range of targets aimed at eliminating discrimination, violence, and harmful practices against women and girls, ensuring equal opportunities in leadership and decision-making, and recognizing and valuing unpaid care and domestic work. By integrating gender equality as a cross-cutting issue, the SDGs acknowledge the interconnected nature of sustainable development and the pivotal role of women's empowerment in achieving economic, social, and environmental progress.

Specific targets under Goal 5 of the SDGs include ending all forms of discrimination against women and girls, eliminating all forms of violence against women and girls, ensuring women's full and effective participation in leadership and decision-making processes, and recognizing and valuing unpaid care and domestic work. Progress towards these targets is monitored through indicators such as the proportion of women in managerial positions, the prevalence of gender-based violence, and the existence of legal frameworks to promote gender equality. By setting measurable goals and tracking progress, the SDGs provide a framework for accountability and sustained action towards achieving gender equality on a global scale.

One of the key targets under Goal 5 is to eliminate all forms of violence against women and girls, including trafficking, sexual exploitation, and other types of abuse. According to the United Nations, an estimated one in three women worldwide has experienced physical or sexual violence in their lifetime, with grave consequences for their physical, mental, and emotional well-being. Addressing this pervasive issue requires a multifaceted approach, encompassing legal reforms, improved access to support services for survivors, and widespread awareness-raising campaigns to challenge harmful societal norms and attitudes that perpetuate gender-based violence.

Initiated by activist Tarana Burke and amplified by the allegations against powerful figures like Harvey Weinstein, the #MeToo movement encouraged survivors to share their stories and hold perpetrators accountable. It sparked a global reckoning with the pervasive nature of sexual misconduct and prompted a re-evaluation of workplace cultures, reporting mechanisms, and legal frameworks surrounding these issues. While progress has been made, the movement continues to push for systemic change and a safer, more equitable environment for all.

The #MeToo movement has had a profound impact on raising awareness about sexual harassment and assault, and has sparked important conversations about power dynamics, consent, and accountability in various sectors, including entertainment, media, and politics. However, despite the progress made, significant challenges remain in addressing the deep-rooted cultural attitudes and institutional barriers that enable sexual misconduct to persist. Sustained efforts are needed to implement comprehensive policies and practices that prioritize prevention, support for survivors, and fostering safe and inclusive environments across all spheres of society.

An intricate global mosaic of efforts to promote gender equality is enshrined within frameworks like the United Nations Sustainable Development Goals (SDGs), where targets related to women's empowerment and gender equality stand as beacons of hope and progress. These global endeavors, woven with compassion and determination, serve as testaments to the collective resolve to forge a world where women's rights are not just aspirations but tangible realities.

In addition to the SDGs, various international conventions and treaties have been established to promote and protect women's rights on a global scale. The Convention on the Elimination of All Forms of Discrimination Against Women (CEDAW), adopted by the United Nations in 1979, is often referred to as an international bill of rights for women. It defines discrimination against women and establishes an agenda for national action to end such discrimination, covering areas such as political and public life, education, employment, health care, and family life. As of 2023, 189 countries have ratified CEDAW, demonstrating a widespread commitment to upholding women's rights and gender equality.

The SDGs, adopted by the United Nations in 2015, recognized gender equality as a cross-cutting issue essential for sustainable development. Goal 5, dedicated to achieving gender equality and empowering all women and girls, encompasses targets related to ending all forms of discrimination, violence, and harmful practices, ensuring equal opportunities in leadership and decision-making, and recognizing and valuing unpaid care and domestic work. By integrating gender equality into the global development agenda, the SDGs have provided a framework for coordinated action and accountability towards these critical objectives.

Despite the global commitments and frameworks in place, progress towards gender equality has been uneven across regions and countries. According to the United Nations, no country has yet achieved full gender equality, and significant gaps persist in areas such as economic participation, access to education, and political representation. In some regions, deeply entrenched cultural norms, discriminatory laws, and inadequate resources continue to hinder progress. Addressing these challenges requires sustained political will, increased investment in gender-responsive policies and programs, and the active engagement of all stakeholders, including civil society organizations, the private sector, and local communities.

As we journey through the annals of history, the threads of women's rights movements emerge as a vibrant mosaic, woven with the indomitable spirit of resilience, the enduring call for equality, and the unwavering pursuit of dignity. Each chapter, etched with the ink of perseverance and courage, bears witness to the collective journey of humanity towards a more equitable and just future.

Throughout history, women's rights movements have faced formidable opposition and backlash from those who sought to maintain the status quo and preserve patriarchal power structures. From the violent suppression of suffragettes to the ongoing efforts to restrict reproductive rights and roll back gender equality policies, these reactionary forces have posed significant challenges to the advancement of women's rights. However, the resilience and determination of activists, advocates, and allies have ensured that the movement continues to forge ahead, adapting to new challenges and finding innovative ways to amplify the call for gender justice.

While significant progress has been made, the fight for women's rights is an ongoing battle, with new challenges emerging alongside societal shifts and changing global dynamics. Issues such as the persistent gender pay gap, underrepresentation in leadership and decision-making roles, and the disproportionate impact of crises and conflicts on women and girls remain pressing concerns. Additionally, the rise of anti-feminist and reactionary movements threatens to roll back hard-won gains, necessitating continued vigilance and activism.

The gender pay gap, where women earn less than men for the same work, remains a pervasive issue globally. According to the International Labour Organization (ILO), the global gender pay gap stands at around 20%, with significant variations across regions and sectors. Closing this gap is not only a matter of fairness and equal opportunity but also has significant economic implications. Studies have shown that promoting gender equality and women's economic empowerment can lead to increased productivity, economic growth, and poverty reduction. Addressing the gender pay gap requires a multifaceted approach, including strengthening laws and policies, promoting pay transparency, and challenging gender stereotypes and discrimination in the workplace.

The historical context of the women's rights movement is a testament to the power of collective action, the strength of unity, and the transformative potential of unwavering dedication to a righteous cause. From the early suffragettes who fought for the right to vote to the contemporary activists who challenge systemic inequalities, these trailblazers have left an indelible mark on the fabric of society, paving the way for future generations to continue the fight for gender equality.

One of the key lessons from the historical context of the women's rights movement is the importance of intersectional solidarity. While the early waves of feminism were often led by white, middle-class women, subsequent movements have recognized the need to amplify the voices and experiences of women from diverse backgrounds, including women of color, Indigenous women, LGBTQ+ women, and women with disabilities. By embracing intersectionality and recognizing the multiple and intertwined forms of oppression faced by different groups of women, the movement has become more inclusive, more representative, and better equipped to address the complex and nuanced challenges faced by women across various social locations.

As we reflect on this rich history, we are reminded that the struggle for women's rights is an ongoing journey, a continuous unfolding of progress and setbacks, triumphs and challenges. Each generation builds upon the foundations laid by those who came before, adding their own unique threads to the voices of change.

One of the most significant challenges facing the contemporary women's rights movement is the rise of anti-feminist and reactionary movements that seek to roll back hard-won gains and perpetuate patriarchal structures. These movements often employ tactics such as disinformation campaigns, online harassment, and legislative efforts to restrict reproductive rights, curtail gender equality policies, and promote regressive gender norms. Countering these movements requires a multifaceted approach that combines grassroots activism, educational initiatives, and strategic litigation to protect and advance women's rights at the local, national, and global levels.

In the face of adversity, women have shown remarkable resilience, adapting their strategies and methods to suit the ever-changing landscape of social, political, and technological realities. From the streets to the ballot box, from the written word to the digital platform, women have harnessed the power of their voices and the strength of their convictions to challenge the status quo and demand change.

The rise of digital technologies and social media platforms has presented both opportunities and challenges for the women's rights movement. On one hand, these platforms have facilitated the rapid dissemination of information, mobilization of activists, and amplification of marginalized voices. Campaigns like #MeToo and #BringBackOurGirls have demonstrated the power of digital activism in raising awareness and catalyzing social change. On the other hand, online spaces have also been breeding grounds for misogyny, harassment, and the spread of disinformation, posing new challenges for the movement to navigate. Harnessing the potential of digital tools while mitigating their risks will be crucial for the future of feminist advocacy and activism.

The historical context of the women's rights movement also underscores the importance of intersectionality and the recognition that women's experiences are shaped by a complex interplay of identities and social locations. By embracing the diversity of women's voices and experiences, the movement has become more inclusive, more representative, and more effective in advocating for the rights and dignity of all women.

The concept of intersectionality has also highlighted the unique challenges faced by women in conflict and crisis situations. Women and girls are disproportionately affected by armed conflicts, displacement, and humanitarian emergencies, facing heightened risks of gender-based violence, limited access to essential services, and disruptions to their education and economic opportunities. Addressing the specific needs and vulnerabilities of women and girls in these contexts is crucial for ensuring their protection, empowerment, and participation in peacebuilding and recovery efforts. Organizations like the United Nations Entity for Gender Equality and the Empowerment of Women (UN Women) and the Women's Refugee Commission have been at the forefront of advocating for gender-responsive humanitarian action and promoting the leadership and resilience of women in crisis settings.

As we move forward, we carry with us the lessons of history, the wisdom of our foremothers, and the hope for a brighter future. We stand on the shoulders of giants, those brave women who dared to dream of a world where gender equality is not just an aspiration but a reality. Their legacy inspires us to continue the fight, to challenge the barriers that still stand in the way of women's full participation and empowerment.

One of the most important lessons we can draw from the historical context of the women's rights movement is the power of collective action and solidarity. Throughout history, women have come together, transcending boundaries of race, class, and nationality, to unite their voices and amplify their calls for equality. From the international suffrage movement to the global campaigns for reproductive rights, the strength of women's solidarity has been a driving force for change. As we move forward, cultivating and nurturing this spirit of collective action and intersectional solidarity will be crucial in addressing the complex and interconnected challenges facing women worldwide.

The historical context of the women's rights movement is not just a chronicle of the past; it is a living, breathing testament to the power of women's agency, resilience, and determination. It is a reminder that change is possible, that progress is achievable, and that the fight for gender equality is a collective responsibility that requires the commitment and dedication of all members of society.

The historical context also reminds us of the importance of intergenerational dialogue and knowledge transfer. Each generation of women's rights activists has built upon the foundations laid by their predecessors, adapting strategies and tactics to meet the evolving challenges of their time. By fostering intergenerational connections and ensuring that the stories, experiences, and wisdom of previous generations are passed down, we can ensure continuity in the movement while also embracing new perspectives and approaches. Initiatives like mentorship programs, oral history projects, and collaborative platforms can help bridge the generational divide and strengthen the movement's collective memory and resilience.

As we navigate the challenges and opportunities of the present and look towards the future, let us draw strength and inspiration from the rich history of the women's rights movement. Let us honor the sacrifices and celebrate the victories of those who came before us, while also recognizing the work that still lies ahead.

One of the key challenges we face in the present is the persistent gender gap in access to education and educational attainment. According to UNESCO, despite significant progress, women and girls still face multiple barriers to accessing quality education, including poverty, cultural norms, and gender-based violence. Ensuring equal access to education is not only a fundamental human right but also a critical enabler for women's economic empowerment, political participation, and overall well-being. Addressing this challenge requires a multifaceted approach that tackles the root causes of educational inequality, including investing in infrastructure, providing safe and inclusive learning environments, and challenging gender stereotypes and biases in educational materials and curricula.

Together, let us weave a new chapter in the ongoing story of women's rights, one that is characterized by equality, justice, and dignity for all. Let us create a world where every woman can live free from discrimination, violence, and oppression, where every girl can reach her full potential and dream without limits.

The historical context of the women's rights movement is a powerful reminder that change is possible, that progress is inevitable, and that the fight for gender equality is a noble and necessary struggle. As we carry this legacy forward, let us do so with courage, conviction, and an unwavering commitment to creating a better world for all.

As we look to the future, it is essential to recognize that the fight for gender equality is not a linear journey, but rather a continuous process of overcoming obstacles, adapting to new challenges, and seizing opportunities for transformative change. The women's rights movement must remain vigilant and responsive, anticipating and addressing emerging issues and barriers that threaten to undermine progress. This may include addressing the impact of technology on gender equality, combating the rise of extremist ideologies that seek to roll back women's rights, or addressing the disproportionate impact of climate change and environmental degradation on women and girls. By remaining proactive and adaptable, the movement can continue to shape a more just and equitable future for all.

Section C: Introduction to the advancements and challenges faced by women in modern society

In the ever-evolving landscape of women's rights, the contemporary terrain of modern society presents a panorama marked by both advancements and challenges. As we delve into this chapter, we find ourselves at the nexus of progress and perseverance, where the indomitable spirit of women continues to shape the fabric of our societal ethos.

The advancements in women's rights and gender equality are the result of decades of arduous struggles, advocacy, and collective action. From the suffragette movements of the late 19th and early 20th centuries to the second wave of feminism in the 1960s and 1970s, women have fought tirelessly to dismantle systemic barriers and challenge patriarchal structures that have historically marginalized and oppressed them.

Amidst the kaleidoscope of societal change, one of the most resplendent hues is the remarkable surge in the enrollment of girls in education. Efforts to promote girls' education have unfurled like delicate petals in the springtime, ushering in a new era of inclusivity and opportunity. Scholarships, infrastructure improvements, and awareness campaigns have coalesced to create an environment where the pursuit of knowledge knows no gender bounds. Across continents, the corridors of learning resonate with the laughter and dreams of girls and young women, their aspirations unfurling like the pages of an unwritten symphony.

According to UNESCO, the global enrollment rate for girls in primary education has increased from 79% in 1970 to 89% in 2018. However, significant disparities persist, particularly in sub-Saharan Africa and parts of South Asia, where cultural norms, poverty, and conflict continue to impede girls' access to education. Organizations like Malala Fund and CAMFED have been at the forefront of advocating for girls' education and providing resources to overcome these challenges.

In classrooms and lecture halls, a new generation of trailblazers is emerging, their minds kindled with the fire of possibility and promise. The once-distant horizon of tertiary education now beckons with an ethereal allure, inviting girls to carve their indelible marks upon the annals of academia. With each pen stroke and keystroke, they inscribe their narratives of resilience and ambition, heralding a future where knowledge is a beacon that illuminates the path to equality.

The impact of higher education on women's empowerment is profound. According to a study by the World Bank, each additional year of schooling for girls can increase their future earnings by 10-20%. Furthermore, educated women are more likely to participate in decision-making processes within their households and communities, contributing to the overall development and progress of society.

The impact of education on women's empowerment and agency cannot be overstated. It serves as a catalyst for personal growth, social mobility, and economic independence. By equipping girls and women with the tools of critical thinking, problem-solving, and self-expression, education becomes a transformative force that challenges gender norms, breaks down barriers, and opens up new possibilities for women to shape their own destinies.

However, the journey towards gender parity in education is not without its challenges. In many parts of the world, girls face barriers such as child marriage, gender-based violence, and cultural biases that prioritize the education of boys over girls. Addressing these deep-rooted issues requires a comprehensive approach that involves legislative reforms, community engagement, and the dismantling of harmful sociocultural norms and practices.

Moreover, the ripple effects of girls' education extend far beyond the individual, benefiting families, communities, and entire nations. Educated women are more likely to participate in the workforce, contribute to economic growth, and make informed decisions about their health and well-being. They become agents of change, advocating for their rights and the rights of others, and inspiring future generations to follow in their footsteps.

The benefits of girls' education are not limited to economic and social empowerment; they also have far-reaching implications for global development. According to a report by the United Nations Population Fund (UNFPA), investing in girls' education can contribute to reducing poverty, improving maternal and child health, and promoting sustainable development practices. When women are educated and empowered, they can play a pivotal role in addressing complex global challenges such as climate change, food security, and conflict resolution.

The panorama of career paths has undergone a metamorphosis, with women boldly traversing uncharted territories and shattering the glass ceilings that once confined their aspirations. From the sprawling vistas of engineering to the intricate latticework of finance, women have ventured into traditionally male-dominated fields, infusing them with the iridescent hues of diversity and innovation. Their footsteps echo through the corridors of progress, harmonizing with the cadence of change and heralding an era where professional landscapes are aglow with the mosaic of gender inclusivity.

Despite the progress made, women continue to face significant barriers and biases in the workplace. According to a report by the International Labour Organization (ILO), women are overrepresented in lower-paying occupations and underrepresented in managerial and leadership positions. This occupational segregation is often rooted in deep-seated gender stereotypes, discrimination, and the lack of supportive policies and structures that enable women to balance work and family responsibilities.

In boardrooms and laboratories, women stand as architects of transformation, their intellect and acumen sculpting a future where gender stereotypes are but relics of a bygone era. Their presence in leadership roles reverberates as a testament to the enduring spirit of resilience and fortitude, illuminating a path for future generations to traverse with unwavering confidence and determination.

Notably, countries and organizations that have actively promoted gender diversity in leadership and decision-making roles have reaped significant benefits. A study by McKinsey & Company found that companies in the top quartile for gender diversity on their executive teams were 25% more likely to achieve above-average profitability. Furthermore, research has shown that diverse teams foster innovation, creativity, and better problem-solving abilities, ultimately contributing to organizational success.

The diversification of women's occupational choices is not just a matter of personal fulfillment; it is a crucial step towards achieving gender equality in the workplace. When women are represented across a wide spectrum of industries and roles, it challenges the notion that certain fields are inherently "masculine" or "feminine." It dismantles the barriers that have historically limited women's opportunities and perpetuated gender-based discrimination.

However, breaking down occupational segregation requires a multifaceted approach that addresses the root causes of gender imbalances. This includes providing equal access to education and training opportunities, challenging societal stereotypes and biases, and implementing policies that support work-life balance and promote family-friendly workplaces. Additionally, mentorship programs and role models can play a crucial role in inspiring and empowering young women to pursue non-traditional career paths.

Moreover, women's occupational diversity brings a wealth of perspectives, experiences, and skills to the table, enriching the fabric of the workforce and driving innovation and progress. When women's voices are heard and their contributions are valued, it creates a more inclusive and equitable work environment that benefits everyone.

The benefits of gender diversity in the workplace extend beyond the individual and organizational levels; it also has broader societal implications. When women are financially empowered and engaged in diverse sectors of the economy, it can contribute to reducing poverty, promoting economic growth, and fostering sustainable development. Furthermore, having women in leadership roles can positively influence policies and decision-making processes, ensuring that issues related to gender equality, healthcare, and social welfare are given due consideration.

A symphony of voices, resonant with the chords of advocacy and empowerment, has risen to prominence within the hallowed halls of political institutions. The landscape of governance bears witness to the increasing representation of women, their influential roles shaping policies that reverberate with the harmonies of gender equality, social welfare, healthcare, and education. Through their stewardship, they weave a narrative of governance that is attuned to the needs and aspirations of diverse communities, infusing the fabric of legislation with the delicate threads of empathy and understanding.

According to data from the Inter-Parliamentary Union, as of January 2023, the global average of women's representation in national parliaments stands at 26.1%. While this figure represents progress, it also highlights the persistent underrepresentation of women in decision-making processes worldwide. Factors such as gender stereotypes, lack of support systems, and structural barriers continue to impede women's political participation and leadership.

One of the most significant barriers to women's political participation is the prevalence of gender-based violence, harassment, and intimidation. According to a report by the Inter-Parliamentary Union and the United Nations Development Programme (UNDP), women in politics are frequently subjected to various forms of violence, including physical assault, sexual harassment, online abuse, and psychological intimidation. These acts not only pose a threat to individual women but also undermine the principles of democratic representation and equal participation. Addressing this challenge requires a multifaceted approach that involves legal and policy reforms, capacity-building initiatives, and a cultural shift that rejects and condemns all forms of violence against women in politics.

As the echelons of power echo with the resonance of women's voices, the collective conscience of society bears witness to a paradigm shift, where governance mirrors the kaleidoscopic richness of diverse perspectives. Each policy and proclamation emerges as a brushstroke that paints a portrait of a more equitable and just society, where the rights of women are enshrined within the very fabric of governance.

The impact of women's political representation goes beyond the realm of policymaking and governance. When women occupy positions of leadership and influence, they serve as powerful role models, challenging traditional gender stereotypes and inspiring future generations of girls and young women to pursue their ambitions without limitations. Furthermore, the presence of women in leadership roles can help shape societal narratives and public discourse, amplifying the voices and perspectives of women and promoting a more inclusive and equitable cultural landscape.

The increased representation of women in political leadership has yielded tangible benefits for society. Research has shown that countries with higher levels of women's political participation tend to have stronger policies addressing issues such as gender-based violence, reproductive rights, and childcare support. Furthermore, women in leadership positions often prioritize social welfare programs, education, and environmental protection, reflecting the diverse needs and priorities of their constituents.

The benefits of women's political representation extend beyond the realm of policymaking and governance. When women occupy positions of leadership and influence in various sectors, they serve as powerful role models, challenging traditional gender stereotypes and inspiring future generations of girls and young women to pursue their ambitions without limitations. Furthermore, the presence of women in leadership roles can help shape societal narratives and public discourse, amplifying the voices and perspectives of women and promoting a more inclusive and equitable cultural landscape.

Women's political participation is a cornerstone of democratic governance and a fundamental human right. When women have a seat at the decision-making table, they bring their unique experiences, perspectives, and priorities to the forefront, ensuring that policies and legislation reflect the diverse needs and aspirations of all members of society.

However, the path to achieving meaningful political representation for women is fraught with challenges. In many parts of the world, women face systemic barriers such as violence, intimidation, and lack of access to resources and networks that are essential for successful political campaigns. Additionally, deeply entrenched sociocultural norms and gender stereotypes often discourage women from seeking leadership roles, perpetuating the cycle of underrepresentation.

One promising approach to increasing women's political representation is the implementation of gender quotas or reserved seats in legislative bodies. While controversial in some contexts, gender quotas have been shown to be an effective temporary measure for increasing the number of women in decision-making roles and challenging the systemic barriers that have historically excluded women from political participation. However, it is important to note that quotas should be complemented by broader efforts to address the underlying societal and cultural factors that perpetuate gender inequality in politics, such as promoting women's leadership development, challenging discriminatory attitudes, and ensuring equal access to resources and support networks.

Moreover, women's political representation serves as a powerful symbol of progress and equality, challenging traditional gender roles and inspiring future generations of women to pursue leadership positions. It sends a clear message that women's voices matter, that their contributions are valued, and that their leadership is essential for building a more just and equitable world.

Addressing the underrepresentation of women in political spheres requires a multifaceted approach that involves legal reforms, awareness campaigns, capacity-building initiatives, and the dismantling of structural barriers. Additionally, promoting gender-sensitive policies and creating a supportive environment for women in politics can help foster a more inclusive and representative political landscape.

The path towards achieving gender parity in political representation is a long and arduous one, but it is a journey that must be undertaken with unwavering resolve and collective action. By addressing the systemic barriers, challenging discriminatory attitudes, and fostering an environment that empowers and supports women's political leadership, we can create a more equitable and representative political landscape that reflects the diversity and richness of our societies. Ultimately, the full realization of women's political representation is not only a matter of fairness and justice but also a prerequisite for the development of truly democratic and inclusive societies that uphold the fundamental principles of human rights and equal opportunities for all.

Amidst the labyrinthine corridors of the professional world, the persistent specter of the gender pay gap looms as a challenge that demands unyielding resolve and comprehensive strategies. The arduous journey towards pay equity unfolds as a narrative woven with the threads of steadfast advocacy, encompassing measures such as pay transparency, equal pay laws, workplace diversity initiatives, and support for work-life balance. Each endeavor, however small, contributes to the gradual unravelling of the gender pay gap, heralding a future where remuneration reflects the intrinsic worth of every individual, irrespective of gender.

The persistence of the gender pay gap is a multidimensional issue that requires a holistic approach to address its underlying causes. Beyond the implementation of pay transparency measures and equal pay legislation, it is crucial to challenge the deeply entrenched societal norms and unconscious biases that perpetuate the undervaluation of women's work and the occupational segregation that concentrates women in lower-paying sectors. This may involve initiatives aimed at promoting gender-neutral job evaluations, encouraging women's participation in traditionally male-dominated and higher-paying fields, and providing equal access to training and professional development opportunities.

According to the International Labour Organization (ILO), the global gender pay gap stands at approximately 20%, meaning that women earn around 80% of what men earn for work of equal value. This disparity persists across various sectors and occupations, reflecting deep-rooted biases, discrimination, and structural barriers that women face in the labor market.

The gender pay gap is not only a matter of individual fairness and economic justice but also has broader societal implications. When women earn less than their male counterparts for work of equal value, it perpetuates the cycle of poverty, limits their ability to invest in their children's education and well-being, and hinders their overall economic empowerment. This, in turn, can have ripple effects on entire communities and economies, hindering economic growth, exacerbating income inequality, and undermining efforts towards sustainable development.

Within this landscape, the collective efforts of organizations and advocacy groups resonate as a sonnet of determination, each stanza a testament to the unwavering pursuit of economic parity. As the tendrils of change unfurl, the professional world bears witness to a transformation where the fruits of labor are adorned not with the tarnished vestiges of inequality, but with the radiant laurels of equity and fairness.

The fight for pay equity is not only a matter of legislative reforms and policy changes but also a cultural battle against deeply ingrained stereotypes and biases. It requires a concerted effort to challenge the societal narratives that devalue women's work, undermine their achievements, and perpetuate the notion that certain occupations or industries are inherently "masculine" or "feminine." This can involve public awareness campaigns, educational initiatives, and the amplification of diverse voices and role models that challenge traditional gender norms and celebrate the contributions of women across all sectors and occupations.

Addressing the gender pay gap requires a multidimensional approach that involves legislative reforms, pay transparency measures, and the elimination of discriminatory practices in recruitment, promotion, and performance evaluation processes. Additionally, promoting gender-neutral job evaluations, encouraging women's participation in higher-paying fields, and providing equal access to training and professional development opportunities can help narrow the pay gap.

The gender pay gap is not just a matter of individual fairness; it is a systemic issue that perpetuates economic inequality and undermines women's financial security and independence. By addressing the root causes of the pay gap, such as occupational segregation, discrimination, and the undervaluing of women's work, we can create a more equitable and just society where everyone is fairly compensated for their contributions.

The fight for pay equity is not only an economic and social justice issue but also a matter of recognizing the inherent dignity and worth of all individuals, regardless of gender. When women are fairly compensated for their work, it sends a powerful message about their value and contributions to society, challenging the deeply entrenched patriarchal narratives that have historically devalued and marginalized women's labor. Ultimately, achieving pay equity is not just about closing a numerical gap; it is about creating a more equitable and just society that upholds the fundamental principles of human rights, equality, and respect for all.

The consequences of the gender pay gap extend beyond the individual level, impacting families, communities, and entire economies. When women earn less than their male counterparts, it perpetuates the cycle of poverty, limits their ability to invest in their children's education and well-being, and hinders their economic empowerment. Closing the pay gap is not only a matter of fairness but also a crucial step towards achieving sustainable development and promoting inclusive economic growth.

Moreover, closing the gender pay gap has far-reaching economic benefits, as it boosts women's purchasing power, reduces poverty rates, and stimulates economic growth. When women have equal access to economic opportunities and fair compensation, it creates a ripple effect that benefits families, communities, and entire nations.

The economic benefits of closing the gender pay gap extend beyond the individual and household levels. According to a report by the International Monetary Fund (IMF), reducing the gender gap in labor force participation and earnings could increase economic growth by up to 35% in some countries. Furthermore, promoting pay equity and women's economic empowerment can contribute to the achievement of several Sustainable Development Goals, including those related to poverty reduction, economic growth, and gender equality.

Despite the challenges, there are pockets of progress in addressing the gender pay gap. Countries like Iceland, Norway, and Sweden have implemented robust equal pay legislation, pay transparency measures, and policies that support work-life balance, contributing to narrowing the pay gap. Additionally, some companies have proactively conducted pay audits and implemented pay equity initiatives, recognizing the benefits of fostering a diverse and equitable workforce.

While legislative and policy measures are crucial, addressing the gender pay gap also requires a cultural shift and a collective effort to challenge the deeply ingrained biases and stereotypes that perpetuate unequal pay for equal work. This can involve public awareness campaigns, educational initiatives, and the amplification of diverse voices and role models that celebrate the contributions of women across all sectors and occupations. By fostering a culture of respect, inclusion, and equal opportunities, we can create a more equitable and just society where everyone is fairly compensated for their work, regardless of gender.

The symphony of career aspirations harmonizes with the delicate cadence of family responsibilities, weaving a melodic narrative of challenges that resonate within the hearts of women across the globe. The pursuit of work-life balance unfolds as a sonnet of resilience, each verse a testament to the enduring fortitude of women who navigate the labyrinthine paths of professional aspirations and familial obligations. Policies such as paid parental leave, flexible work arrangements, and support for eldercare emerge as gentle zephyrs that brush against the fabric of societal norms, heralding an era where the dichotomy between career and family is but a vestige of the past.

The challenges of work-life balance are not unique to women, but they are often exacerbated by the persistent gender norms and expectations that place a disproportionate burden of unpaid domestic and caregiving responsibilities on women. This "second shift" of household labor, combined with the demands of professional careers, can lead to burnout, stress, and limited opportunities for advancement. Addressing this issue requires a comprehensive approach that not only promotes family-friendly policies and flexible work arrangements but also challenges the societal narratives and gender roles that perpetuate the unequal distribution of domestic and caregiving responsibilities.

According to a report by the International Labour Organization (ILO), women perform approximately three times as much unpaid care work as men, including childcare, household chores, and caring for elderly or sick family members. This disproportionate burden often forces women to make difficult choices between their careers and family responsibilities, hindering their professional advancement and economic empowerment.

The COVID-19 pandemic has further exacerbated the challenges of work-life balance for women, as they have taken on a disproportionate share of additional caregiving and domestic responsibilities during lockdowns and school closures. According to a report by the United Nations Entity for Gender Equality and the Empowerment of Women (UN Women), the pandemic has set back progress towards gender equality, with women being more likely to experience job losses, increased unpaid care work, and greater risks of domestic violence. Addressing the long-term impacts of the pandemic on women's work-life balance will require targeted policies and support systems, such as accessible and affordable childcare, flexible work arrangements, and initiatives to promote an equitable distribution of domestic and caregiving responsibilities within households.

In this landscape, the collective yearning for balance and fulfillment emerges as an ethereal melody, echoing through the corridors of societal change. Each policy and initiative, crafted with empathy and understanding, becomes a gentle embrace that cradles the aspirations of women, nurturing their ambitions and fortifying their resilience.

The pursuit of work-life balance is not just a matter of personal well-being but also has broader societal implications. When women are able to balance their professional and personal responsibilities, they are better positioned to contribute to the workforce, advance in their careers, and achieve economic empowerment. This, in turn, can have positive ripple effects on families, communities, and the overall economic growth and development of nations. Furthermore, promoting work-life balance can contribute to the achievement of gender equality and the empowerment of women, which are crucial for sustainable development and the realization of human rights.

Progressive policies that support work-life balance, such as paid parental leave, flexible work arrangements, and affordable childcare, have been shown to have positive impacts on women's labor force participation, career advancement, and overall well-being. Countries like Sweden, Denmark, and Canada have implemented comprehensive family-friendly policies, which have contributed to higher rates of female employment and a more equitable distribution of unpaid care work.

The implementation of progressive work-life balance policies has not only benefited women but also contributed to broader societal and economic gains. According to a report by the Organization for Economic Cooperation and Development (OECD), countries with more generous parental leave policies and affordable childcare options tend to have higher rates of labor force participation for women, which in turn contributes to economic growth and productivity. Furthermore, studies have shown that when both parents are able to balance work and family responsibilities, it can lead to better child outcomes, including improved cognitive development and overall well-being.

While policy interventions are crucial, achieving a sustainable work-life balance for women also requires a cultural shift that promotes shared responsibility within households and society. This can involve initiatives aimed at challenging traditional gender roles and stereotypes, encouraging men and boys to take on a more active role in domestic and caregiving responsibilities, and fostering a more equitable distribution of unpaid labor. Additionally, promoting positive role models and amplifying the voices of individuals and couples who have successfully navigated the challenges of work-life balance can inspire and empower others to pursue a more balanced and fulfilling life.

One example of a successful initiative aimed at promoting shared responsibility and challenging gender stereotypes is the "HeForShe" campaign launched by the United Nations Entity for Gender Equality and the Empowerment of Women (UN Women). This global initiative engages men and boys as advocates for gender equality, encouraging them to recognize the benefits of a more equitable distribution of domestic and caregiving responsibilities. By involving men and boys in the conversation, the campaign aims to create a cultural shift that challenges traditional gender roles and promotes a more balanced and fulfilling life for both women and men.

The challenges of work-life balance are not unique to women, but they are often disproportionately borne by women due to persistent gender roles and expectations. Women continue to shoulder the majority of unpaid care work, such as childrearing and eldercare, while also navigating the demands of their professional lives. This double burden can lead to stress, burnout, and limited opportunities for career advancement.

The impact of work-life balance challenges on women's mental health and well-being is significant. According to a study by the American Psychological Association, women who struggle to balance work and family responsibilities are more likely to experience stress, anxiety, and depression. Furthermore, the constant juggling of multiple roles can lead to burnout, which can have negative consequences for both personal and professional life. Addressing these mental health implications is crucial, as women's well-being is not only a matter of individual concern but also has broader societal and economic implications, given the vital roles women play in the workforce and in their communities.

In addition to policy interventions, addressing the challenges of work-life balance requires a cultural shift that challenges traditional gender norms and promotes shared responsibility within households and society. Engaging men and boys in discussions about gender equality and encouraging them to take on a more active role in caregiving and domestic work can help alleviate the disproportionate burden on women and foster more equitable and supportive family dynamics.

The role of educational institutions and media in shaping societal attitudes and norms around work-life balance and gender roles cannot be overstated. From an early age, children are exposed to gender stereotypes and traditional role models through various channels, including textbooks, advertising, and popular culture. Incorporating gender-sensitive curricula, promoting diverse representations of family structures and caregiving roles, and challenging harmful stereotypes through media campaigns can play a crucial role in shaping the next generation's attitudes and behaviors towards work-life balance and shared responsibility.

Addressing the challenges of work-life balance requires a multifaceted approach that includes policy changes, workplace culture shifts, and a redistribution of unpaid care work. By providing comprehensive parental leave policies, flexible work arrangements, and affordable childcare options, we can create a more supportive environment that allows women to thrive both personally and professionally.

The role of technology in enabling work-life balance should not be overlooked. The rise of remote work, virtual communication tools, and digital platforms has opened up new opportunities for flexible work arrangements that can help employees better manage their professional and personal responsibilities. However, it is also important to recognize the potential downsides of technology, such as the blurring of boundaries between work and personal life, and the need to establish healthy digital habits and boundaries. Employers and policymakers should explore ways to leverage technology while also promoting a healthy work-life balance and protecting employee well-being.

Employers also play a crucial role in promoting work-life balance by implementing family-friendly policies, offering flexible work arrangements, and fostering a corporate culture that values and supports employees' personal and family commitments. By creating an environment that enables employees to strike a healthy balance between their professional and personal responsibilities, organizations can benefit from increased productivity, employee satisfaction, and talent retention.

In addition to implementing family-friendly policies, employers can promote work-life balance by providing resources and support services for employees, such as on-site childcare facilities, counseling services, and employee assistance programs. Furthermore, fostering a culture of open communication and transparency can help employees feel comfortable discussing their work-life challenges and exploring potential solutions without fear of stigma or repercussions. By prioritizing employee well-being and creating a supportive work environment, organizations can not only retain top talent but also foster a more engaged, productive, and loyal workforce.

Moreover, promoting a culture of shared responsibility and gender equality within households can help alleviate the disproportionate burden of care work on women. When men are encouraged and supported to take on more active roles in parenting and domestic responsibilities, it creates a more balanced and equitable distribution of labor, enabling women to pursue their career aspirations without sacrificing their personal and family lives.

The role of community organizations and civil society groups in promoting shared responsibility and challenging gender stereotypes should not be underestimated. These organizations can provide valuable resources, support networks, and advocacy efforts that encourage men and boys to take on more active roles in caregiving and domestic responsibilities. By fostering a sense of community and collective responsibility, these groups can help create a cultural shift that normalizes and celebrates men's involvement in traditionally "feminine" domains, ultimately contributing to a more equitable distribution of unpaid labor and promoting work-life balance for all.

Amidst the varied landscape of women's experiences, the narrative of intersectionality emerges as a nuanced and profound depiction of depth and complexity. Women from marginalized groups, bearing the weight of intersecting forms of discrimination and oppression, traverse a landscape where their identities intersect with the myriad facets of societal prejudice. Their narratives unfurl with a poignancy that resonates across the fabric of humanity, illuminating the path towards inclusive approaches to addressing gender inequality.

The intersectional challenges faced by women from marginalized groups are often compounded by economic factors and limited access to resources. For example, women of color and women from low-income backgrounds may face additional barriers in accessing quality education, healthcare, and employment opportunities, which can further exacerbate existing inequalities and limit their ability to achieve economic empowerment and independence. Addressing these intersectional challenges requires a holistic approach that not only tackles gender-based discrimination but also addresses the systemic barriers and structural inequalities that perpetuate poverty, racial discrimination, and economic marginalization.

As we navigate the labyrinth of intersectional challenges, the call for inclusivity and understanding reverberates as a symphony that embraces the diversity of women's experiences. Each chord, woven with empathy and solidarity, becomes a testament to the enduring pursuit of a world where the barriers of discrimination are dismantled, and the landscape of equality is enriched with the vibrant hues of diversity.

One powerful example of an intersectional approach to addressing gender inequality is the work of the FRIDA | The Young Feminist Fund, an organization that supports and amplifies the voices of young feminist activists and organizations worldwide. By centering the experiences and perspectives of women and gender-diverse individuals from diverse backgrounds, including indigenous communities, rural areas, and marginalized groups, FRIDA aims to create a more inclusive and intersectional feminist movement that addresses the multifaceted challenges faced by women across different contexts and identities.

Intersectionality recognizes that women's experiences are shaped by the complex interplay of multiple identities, such as race, ethnicity, class, sexuality, disability, and migration status. Women who face multiple forms of marginalization often encounter unique challenges and barriers that are not adequately addressed by mainstream feminist movements.

For example, women of color may face the compounded effects of racism and sexism, leading to higher rates of poverty, health disparities, and limited access to education and employment opportunities. LGBTQ+ women may confront discrimination based on both their gender and sexual orientation, while women with disabilities may encounter ableism and inaccessibility in addition to gender-based discrimination.

The experiences of indigenous women and women from refugee or migrant backgrounds also highlight the importance of an intersectional approach to gender equality. These groups often face unique cultural, linguistic, and legal barriers, as well as discrimination and marginalization within their own communities and broader society. Addressing the intersectional challenges faced by these groups requires a deep understanding of their specific contexts, as well as partnerships and collaborations with community leaders and organizations that can provide culturally relevant support and advocacy.

Addressing intersectional challenges requires a holistic and inclusive approach that centers the voices and experiences of marginalized women. It demands that we listen to and amplify the perspectives of those who have been historically excluded from feminist discourse and policymaking. By embracing intersectionality, we can create a more nuanced and effective framework for advancing women's rights and gender equality.

One example of an intersectional approach to policymaking is the Equality Act introduced in the United States Congress, which aims to provide comprehensive non-discrimination protections for individuals based on sexual orientation and gender identity. This legislation recognizes that LGBTQ+ individuals, particularly those who belong to other marginalized groups, face compounded forms of discrimination and barriers in areas such as employment, housing, education, and access to public services. By addressing these intersectional challenges through comprehensive legal protections, the Equality Act aims to create a more equitable and inclusive society for all individuals, regardless of their gender identity, sexual orientation, or other intersecting identities.

Moreover, intersectionality highlights the importance of building coalitions and solidarity across different social justice movements. By recognizing the interconnectedness of various forms of oppression, we can work towards dismantling the systemic barriers that perpetuate inequality and discrimination. This requires a commitment to inclusive feminism that is anti-racist, anti-classist, anti-ableist, and anti-oppressive in all its forms.

Building coalitions and fostering solidarity across social justice movements requires a willingness to listen, learn, and collaborate with individuals and organizations that represent diverse experiences and perspectives. It also involves acknowledging and addressing the power imbalances and privilege that may exist within movements, and actively working to create inclusive spaces where all voices are valued and heard. By embracing intersectionality and building coalitions, we can create a more powerful and unified movement for social change that addresses the interconnected systems of oppression and marginalization that affect women and other marginalized groups.

As we gaze upon the resplendent landscape of advancements and challenges, we find ourselves at the nexus of a harmonic convergence, where the symphony of progress harmonizes with the cadence of perseverance. The threads of this narrative, woven with the delicate fibers of hope and resilience, bear witness to a future where the barriers that confine the aspirations of women are but vestiges of a bygone era.

In the next chapter, we shall delve deeper into the evocative narratives that unfurl within the fabric of women's rights, each thread a testament to the enduring spirit of humanity's collective journey towards a more equitable and just future. As we embark on this odyssey, let us heed the call of history and envision a future where the grand mosaic of women's rights is not just a saga of aspirations, but a living testament to the indelible resilience and fortitude of women in modern society.

As we look towards the future, it is essential to recognize that the journey towards gender equality is not a linear path, but rather a continuous process of reflection, adaptation, and collective action. The challenges we face today may differ from those of the past, but the underlying principles of justice, equality, and human rights remain constant. By embracing a spirit of resilience, innovation, and intersectionality, we can create a more inclusive and equitable future for all women, regardless of their backgrounds or identities.

The advancements and challenges faced by women in modern society are a reflection of the ongoing struggle for gender equality and the complex interplay of social, economic, and political factors that shape women's lives. While significant progress has been made in areas such as education, occupational diversity, and political participation, there is still much work to be done to address persistent challenges such as the gender pay gap, work-life balance, and intersectional forms of discrimination.

Despite the challenges that lie ahead, there is reason for hope and optimism. The growing global movement for gender equality, fueled by the voices and activism of women from diverse backgrounds, has gained unprecedented momentum. From grassroots organizations to international advocacy groups, a vibrant network of individuals and organizations is working tirelessly to dismantle systemic barriers, challenge discriminatory norms, and create a more equitable world for all women. By harnessing the power of collective action, amplifying marginalized voices, and embracing a spirit of intersectionality, we can continue to push the boundaries of progress and create lasting, transformative change.

As we move forward, it is crucial that we approach these issues with a spirit of inclusivity, empathy, and solidarity. We must listen to and amplify the voices of marginalized women, recognizing that their experiences and perspectives are essential for creating a more just and equitable world.

Moreover, we must continue to advocate for policy changes, cultural shifts, and systemic reforms that address the root causes of gender inequality. This requires a sustained commitment from individuals, communities, organizations, and governments to challenge the status quo and work towards a future where every woman can thrive and reach her full potential.

The path towards gender equality is not an easy one, but it is a journey that must be undertaken with unwavering resolve and a deep commitment to justice and human rights. It requires a holistic approach that addresses the multifaceted nature of gender discrimination, including economic, social, political, and cultural factors. By fostering intersectional collaborations, championing inclusive policies and practices, and empowering women from diverse backgrounds, we can create a more equitable and just world for all.

The path ahead may be challenging, but it is also filled with hope and possibility. By building on the progress of the past, learning from the wisdom of our foremothers, and embracing the power of collective action, we can create a world where women's rights are not just an aspiration, but a lived reality for all.

So let us move forward with courage, determination, and an unwavering commitment to justice. Let us weave a new chapter in the ongoing story of women's rights, one that is characterized by equality, dignity, and opportunity for all. Together, we can create a future where every woman can rise, shine, and take her rightful place as an equal partner in the great human endeavor.

62

Chapter 2
Historical Context of Women's Rights Movements

Section A. Overview of early women's rights movements, such as suffrage and first-wave feminism

In the annals of history, the genesis of the women's rights movement unfurled as a pivotal moment of societal evolution. These early murmurs of change, propelled by courage and steadfast conviction, initiated a transformative journey that reverberates through the corridors of time.

The roots of the women's rights movement can be traced back even further, to the philosophical and religious traditions that challenged patriarchal norms and advocated for gender equality. In ancient Greece, the philosopher Plato argued for the equal education of women, stating that "if women are expected to have the same duties as men, they must have the same nurture and education." Similarly, in the Islamic tradition, the Prophet Muhammad's teachings emphasized the spiritual equality of men and women and advocated for women's rights in areas such as inheritance and education.

The origins of the women's rights movement can be traced back to the late 18th century, when the ideals of the Enlightenment and the American and French revolutions inspired a growing consciousness about the principles of equality and natural rights. Women like Mary Wollstonecraft, considered one of the pioneers of feminist philosophy, began to challenge the prevailing notions of gender roles and inequality through their writings and activism. Wollstonecraft's seminal work, "A Vindication of the Rights of Woman," published in

1792, laid the groundwork for the later women's rights movements by advocating for equal educational opportunities and challenging the entrenched beliefs about female inferiority.

Wollstonecraft's work was groundbreaking not only in its critique of the societal and legal subjugation of women but also in its assertion that women's perceived inferiority was a result of their lack of access to education and societal restrictions, rather than an innate condition. Her call for equal educational opportunities for women challenged the prevailing belief that women were intellectually inferior and incapable of higher learning. Wollstonecraft's ideas laid the foundation for the later feminist movement's demands for access to education and intellectual pursuits.

The foundation of the women's rights movement is infused with the elements of enduring perseverance, resilience, and steadfast determination. In the annals of history, the suffragettes stand as luminous beacons of resilience, adorned in sashes of vibrant hues and armed with placards emblazoned with calls for justice. With unwavering determination, they took to the streets, their footsteps echoing the cadence of change, as they rallied for the fundamental right to cast their ballots, to have their voices reverberate through the hallowed halls of democracy. Their crusade was not without sacrifice; it bore witness to the resilience of the human spirit in the face of adversity.

The suffrage movement was not limited to the United States and Britain; it was a global phenomenon, with women in various countries and regions organizing and advocating for their right to vote. In New Zealand, Kate Sheppard led the suffrage movement, resulting in the country becoming the first self-governing nation to grant women the right to vote in 1893. In Australia, the suffragette Vida Goldstein campaigned tirelessly for women's suffrage, eventually achieving success with the passage of the Commonwealth Franchise Act in 1902, which granted women the right to vote in federal elections.

The suffrage movement gained significant momentum in the late 19th and early 20th centuries, with various organizations and leaders spearheading the fight for women's voting rights. In the United States, organizations like the National American Woman Suffrage Association (NAWSA), led by figures such as Susan B. Anthony and Carrie Chapman Catt, employed a combination of lobbying, public speeches, and grassroots organizing to push for the 19th Amendment, which was finally ratified in 1920, granting American women the right to vote.

The tactics employed by the suffrage movement in the United States were diverse and innovative. In addition to lobbying and public demonstrations, suffragists utilized various forms of media to spread their message and garner support. Publications like "The Revolution," edited by Susan B. Anthony and Elizabeth Cady Stanton, served as platforms for disseminating information, sharing ideas, and mobilizing supporters. Furthermore, suffragists organized massive parades and public spectacles, such as the 1913 Woman Suffrage Procession in Washington, D.C., which drew tens of thousands of participants and spectators, showcasing the movement's growing momentum and widespread appeal.

Many brave women faced violent opposition from those who sought to preserve the status quo, enduring physical assaults, arrests, and imprisonment for their activism. The suffragettes encountered legal barriers that denied them the right to vote, as well as social barriers that discouraged their participation in the public sphere. Despite these formidable challenges, they persisted, employing a range of tactics that included peaceful protests, civil disobedience, and even hunger strikes to draw attention to their cause.

The violence and brutality faced by the suffragettes was a stark reminder of the entrenched opposition they confronted. In Britain, suffragettes like Emily Wilding Davison were subjected to forcible feeding while imprisoned for their activism, a traumatic and inhumane practice that drew widespread condemnation and further fueled public support for the movement. Davison's ultimate sacrifice – her death after being trampled by a horse at the 1913 Epsom Derby while attempting to raise awareness for the cause – became a powerful symbol of the lengths to which women were willing to go to secure their democratic rights.

In Britain, the Women's Social and Political Union (WSPU), led by Emmeline Pankhurst and her daughters Christabel and Sylvia, adopted more militant tactics, such as chaining themselves to railings, setting fire to mailboxes, and smashing windows. These actions, though controversial, drew significant attention to their cause and contributed to the eventual passage of the Representation of the People Act in 1918, which granted some women over the age of 30 the right to vote. The suffrage movement in Britain also faced backlash and opposition, with many activists being imprisoned and facing brutal treatment, including force-feeding during hunger strikes.

The use of militant tactics by the WSPU was a strategic decision born out of frustration with the slow pace of progress and the perceived ineffectiveness of more moderate approaches. Emmeline Pankhurst famously declared, "We are not here to make a revolution – we are here to make things so unbearable for the government that they will give women the vote to keep things peaceful." While controversial, these tactics garnered significant media attention and public discourse, forcing the suffrage issue to the forefront of the national conversation and challenging the complacency of the status quo.

Icons like Susan B. Anthony, Elizabeth Cady Stanton, and the indomitable Emmeline Pankhurst, along with her daughters Christabel and Sylvia, emerged as torchbearers, their spirits indomitable in the face of adversity. Their unwavering commitment to the cause of suffrage became a clarion call that reverberated through generations, inspiring women from all walks of life to stand in solidarity and amplify their collective voices.

The iconic status of these suffrage leaders was not merely a result of their activism but also a testament to their oratorical skills and ability to inspire and mobilize others. Susan B. Anthony's impassioned speeches, such as her iconic "Ain't I a Woman?" address, challenged societal norms and stereotypes, asserting the inherent equality and dignity of women. Similarly, Emmeline Pankhurst's fiery rhetoric and unwavering determination galvanized supporters and captured the public's imagination, transforming the suffrage movement into a powerful force that could not be ignored.

The suffragettes' struggle was not an isolated effort but a chorus of voices harmonizing across continents, transcending geographical boundaries. Figures like Ida B. Wells-Barnett, a pioneering journalist and activist, advocated tirelessly for women's rights while also confronting the scourge of racial discrimination and violence against African Americans. Sojourner Truth, a former slave turned abolitionist and women's rights advocate, delivered her famous "Ain't I a Woman?" speech in 1851, highlighting the intersectionality of women's rights and racial equality, and challenging the notion that women of color were excluded from the movement's vision of emancipation.

The intersectionality of the women's rights movement with other social justice movements was not merely a matter of shared ideals but also a recognition of the interconnected nature of oppression. Activists like Ida B. Wells-Barnett and Sojourner Truth understood that the fight for women's rights could not be separated from the struggle against racism and racial violence. Their advocacy highlighted the need for an intersectional approach that addressed the unique challenges faced by women of color, who often faced compounded forms of discrimination based on both their gender and race.

The suffrage movement also faced internal divisions and debates over strategies, priorities, and inclusivity. Some advocates, like the National Association of Colored Women (NACW), led by figures such as Mary Church Terrell and Ida B. Wells-Barnett, argued for a more inclusive approach that addressed the intersectional challenges faced by women of color. Others, like the National Woman's Party, embraced more radical tactics and focused primarily on securing the vote for white women, leading to criticism for their exclusionary practices and failure to fully embrace intersectionality.

The Women's Christian Temperance Union (WCTU), founded in 1873, played a pivotal role in championing women's suffrage, with its members believing that giving women the right to vote would help curb societal ills like alcoholism and domestic violence. However, debates and divisions within the broader women's rights movement arose regarding strategies and priorities, with some advocating for a more gradualist approach focused on incremental reforms, while others embraced a more militant stance, determined to catalyze change through unyielding resistance and direct action.

Insert after this paragraph: The suffrage movement also faced opposition from anti-suffrage groups, who argued that women's place was in the home and that granting them the right to vote would disrupt the natural order of society. These groups, often led by wealthy and influential women, employed tactics such as lobbying, public campaigns, and legal challenges to obstruct the suffrage movement's progress. Despite these obstacles, the determination and resilience of the suffragettes ultimately prevailed, securing a landmark victory for women's rights.

The abolitionist movements and the fight against slavery also profoundly influenced and intersected with the women's rights cause, as many prominent figures, such as Lucretia Mott and Elizabeth Cady Stanton, were actively involved in both struggles. The experiences of these activists highlighted the inextricable link between the oppression of women and other marginalized groups, fueling a broader recognition of the need for an intersectional approach to address the multifaceted barriers they faced.

The intersection of the women's rights movement with other social justice movements, such as the abolitionist movement and the labor movement, underscored the interconnectedness of various forms of oppression and discrimination. This recognition paved the way for a more intersectional approach to addressing the multifaceted challenges faced by women from diverse backgrounds and identities, challenging the notion of a monolithic women's experience and highlighting the importance of acknowledging and addressing the unique struggles faced by marginalized groups within the broader movement.

The Seneca Falls Convention of 1848, organized by Stanton and Mott, among others, marked a pivotal moment in the history of the women's rights movement. The Convention's Declaration of Sentiments, modeled after the Declaration of Independence, became a catalyst for the global spread of the suffrage movement, inspiring women worldwide to rally for their inalienable rights and igniting a flame that would illuminate the path for generations to come.

The Seneca Falls Convention and its Declaration of Sentiments laid the foundation for the broader women's rights movement, extending beyond the specific issue of suffrage. The document called for equal rights in various spheres, including education, employment, and property ownership, and challenged the prevailing societal norms and legal frameworks that restricted women's autonomy and agency. The Convention's legacy resonated far beyond its immediate impact, inspiring subsequent generations of women's rights advocates to build upon its principles and push for further advancements.

The first-wave feminism, rooted in the suffrage movement, burgeoned into a broader campaign encompassing a wide range of issues that impacted women's lives. It became a clarion call that resonated far beyond the confines of the ballot box, encompassing demands for property rights, reforms to parental and marriage laws, and equal access to employment and educational opportunities. The pioneers of first-wave feminism, with their pens as mighty swords, inscribed the annals of history with narratives that championed the inalienable rights of women, carving out spaces of empowerment and autonomy amidst the rigid contours of societal norms.

The first-wave feminism also saw the emergence of influential theorists and writers, such as Virginia Woolf, whose seminal work "A Room of One's Own" (1929) challenged the patriarchal literary establishment and advocated for women's intellectual and creative freedom. Woolf's concept of a "room of one's own" became a metaphor for the need for women to have both literal and figurative spaces to pursue their ambitions and develop their talents, free from the constraints and limitations imposed by societal expectations.

However, the experiences of women of color, working-class women, and other marginalized groups within the early women's rights movements highlighted the need for an intersectional approach to address the multifaceted barriers they faced. While the suffrage movement achieved a significant milestone in securing voting rights for a segment of women, the voices and perspectives of these marginalized groups were often overlooked or sidelined, exposing the limitations of a movement that failed to fully embrace the diversity of women's experiences and struggles.

Despite the remarkable achievements of the early women's rights movements, their limitations and shortcomings served as a catalyst for subsequent waves of feminism that sought to address the intersectional challenges faced by women of color, LGBTQ+ individuals, and other marginalized groups. The second wave of feminism, which emerged in the 1960s and 1970s, built upon the foundations laid by the first wave while broadening the scope of the movement to encompass issues such as reproductive rights, workplace discrimination, and sexuality, among others.

The early women's rights movements were not isolated phenomena but intertwined with other social and political reforms of the time, such as the abolition of slavery, the growth of labor movements, and the push for educational reforms. Literature, art, and cultural expressions also played a crucial role in raising awareness and inspiring the movement, through the works of pioneering authors like Mary Wollstonecraft, whose 1792 treatise "A Vindication of the Rights of Woman" challenged the prevailing notions of female inferiority and advocated for equal educational opportunities for women.

The influence of literature and art on the women's rights movement extended beyond the written word. Visual artists like Mary Cassatt and Berthe Morisot, members of the Impressionist movement, depicted the everyday experiences of women in their paintings, challenging the traditional artistic conventions and gender norms of the time. Their works not only celebrated the domestic sphere but also elevated the representation of women's lives and experiences, contributing to a broader cultural shift in perceptions and attitudes.

Virginia Woolf's seminal essay "A Room of One's Own," published in 1929, explored the obstacles that women writers faced in a male-dominated literary landscape, and became a rallying cry for the need for women to have both literal and figurative spaces to cultivate their creativity and intellectual pursuits. The works of these authors and artists not only reflected the zeitgeist of their times but also helped shape public discourse and galvanize support for the women's rights movement.

The suffrage movement witnessed the convergence of diverse philosophies and approaches, with some advocates favoring a more gradualist strategy, believing in the power of gradual change to permeate the fabric of society, while others, emboldened by a fierce urgency, adopted a more militant stance, determined to catalyze change through unyielding resistance and acts of civil disobedience. Figures like Alice Paul and the members of the National Woman's Party embraced militant tactics, staging protests, picketing the White House, and even engaging in hunger strikes when imprisoned, drawing widespread attention to their cause and pressuring the government to act.

The debates over strategies and tactics within the suffrage movement were not only a reflection of differing philosophies but also a product of the diverse backgrounds and experiences of the advocates involved. For some, the gradualist approach was seen as a more pragmatic and inclusive way to build broad-based support, while others viewed militant tactics as a necessary means of exerting pressure and disrupting the status quo. These debates highlighted the complexity and multifaceted nature of the movement, as well as the diversity of perspectives and priorities among its leaders and supporters.

The victory of suffrage, achieved after decades of struggle and sacrifice, sparked a resounding ripple effect, galvanizing women across the globe and signaling a new chapter in the fight for gender equality. It became a testament to the transformative power of collective action, a beacon that illuminated the path for future generations to tread with purpose and determination, emboldened by the knowledge that even the most formidable barriers could be overcome through perseverance and unity.

The suffrage victory, while a monumental achievement, was not the end of the struggle for women's rights. In many countries, the fight for universal suffrage continued, as the initial voting rights granted often excluded women of color, indigenous women, or women from certain social or economic backgrounds. Additionally, the movement's focus shifted to addressing other areas of inequality, such as discrimination in employment, education, and legal rights, paving the way for the subsequent waves of feminism and the ongoing pursuit of gender equality.

As we navigate the panorama of history, we are beckoned to listen to the whispers of the past, to imbibe the wisdom of those who paved the way for the emancipation of women worldwide. Their stories, etched in the annals of time, serve as a reminder of the resilience of the human spirit and the enduring legacy of those who dared to challenge the status quo. In the chapters that follow, we will continue to unravel the constellation of women's advancements, exploring the myriad ways in which women have broken barriers, reshaped narratives, and championed their rights in the ever-evolving fabric of modern society. Let us collectively embark on a journey that honors the triumphs, confronts the barriers, and collectively shapes a future where women's rights are not mere aspirations, but tangible realities intricately integrated into the framework of a more just and equitable world.

Section B. Key Milestones and Achievements in the Fight for Gender Equality Throughout History

Imagine a timeline, steeped in the struggles and triumphs of countless women who have fought for gender equality over the centuries. This timeline is not just a chronicle of events; it's a testament to the indomitable spirit of those who dared to challenge the status quo and push the boundaries of what society deemed possible for women. What were the pivotal moments that have shaped the ongoing journey toward gender parity?

The origins of the fight for gender equality can be traced back to ancient civilizations, where women's roles and rights were often heavily circumscribed by societal norms and cultural traditions. In ancient Greece, for example, women were largely confined to the domestic sphere and excluded from political participation and decision-making. However, even in these early societies, there were voices that challenged the prevailing gender norms and advocated for greater equality and respect for women's rights.

According to the World Economic Forum's Global Gender Gap Report 2022, no country has yet achieved full gender parity, with the global gender gap standing at 68.1%. This underscores the persistent challenges and inequalities that women continue to face across various domains, including economic participation, political empowerment, education, and health. While progress has been made, the data highlights the pressing need for sustained efforts to close the remaining gaps and ensure equal opportunities and rights for all genders.

The Global Gender Gap Report, published annually by the World Economic Forum, provides a comprehensive assessment of gender disparities across four key dimensions: economic participation and opportunity, educational attainment, health and survival, and political empowerment. By analyzing data from over 150 countries, the report serves as a valuable tool for tracking progress, identifying areas of concern, and informing policy decisions aimed at promoting gender equality.

The early victories in the suffrage movement were certainly monumental, marking a seismic shift in the recognition of women's fundamental rights. The ratification of the 19th Amendment to the United States Constitution in 1920, guaranteeing women the right to vote, was a hard-won triumph after decades of relentless campaigning by suffragists like Susan B. Anthony, Elizabeth Cady Stanton, and Ida B. Wells-Barnett. This achievement not only empowered women to have a voice in the democratic process but also shattered the notion that they were unfit for political participation.

The suffrage movement's victory in the United States was not an isolated event but part of a global wave of women's enfranchisement. In the years following the ratification of the 19th Amendment, other nations, including Canada (1918), Germany (1919), and the United Kingdom (1928), granted women the right to vote, reflecting the growing momentum and international influence of the suffrage movement.

The suffrage movement's success was not limited to the United States. In countries like New Zealand (1893), Australia (1902), and Finland (1906), women were granted the right to vote and participate in elections, challenging the prevailing patriarchal norms and paving the way for greater political representation. However, the journey toward universal suffrage was a gradual process, with many countries granting voting rights to women decades after the initial victories, and some regions still grappling with barriers to women's full political participation.

The path to universal suffrage was not always a linear progression, with setbacks and resistance encountered in various regions and contexts. In some cases, voting rights were initially granted to a limited segment of women, often based on age, property ownership, or other qualifications, before being expanded to all adult women. Additionally, cultural and societal norms often posed significant obstacles to the full exercise of women's political rights, even after legal barriers were removed.

However, the journey didn't end with women securing the right to vote. The mid-20th century saw a resurgence of feminist activism, often referred to as the second wave of feminism. This era was marked by a more nuanced understanding of equality, addressing issues such as sexuality, reproductive rights, and workplace discrimination. The 1963 publication of Betty Friedan's groundbreaking book "The Feminine Mystique" resonated profoundly with the frustrations of many women who felt confined by societal expectations and the cult of domesticity. Friedan's words ignited a spark that would grow into a roaring flame of advocacy for women's liberation, challenging the narrow gender roles imposed on women and demanding equal opportunities in all spheres of life.

The impact of "The Feminine Mystique" cannot be overstated. Friedan's critique of the societal pressures on women to conform to traditional gender roles and find fulfillment solely through marriage and motherhood struck a chord with countless women who felt trapped and unfulfilled by the narrow confines of domesticity. The book became a rallying cry for a generation of women seeking greater autonomy, personal growth, and equal opportunities in the workplace and beyond.

The second wave of feminism was characterized by diverse approaches and ideologies, ranging from liberal feminism, which sought equality within existing societal structures, to radical feminism, which called for a fundamental restructuring of the patriarchal system. Prominent figures like Gloria Steinem, Bella Abzug, and Shirley Chisholm played pivotal roles in raising awareness, organizing marches and protests, and advocating for legislative reforms to address issues such as reproductive rights, workplace discrimination, and violence against women.

The diversity of approaches within the second wave of feminism reflected the complex and multifaceted nature of the challenges women faced. Liberal feminists, such as Betty Friedan and the National Organization for Women (NOW), focused on achieving legal and policy reforms to ensure equal rights and opportunities within existing societal frameworks. In contrast, radical feminists, like Shulamith Firestone and the Redstockings collective, called for a more revolutionary overhaul of societal structures and power dynamics, challenging the very foundations of patriarchy.

In the arena of legislation, the passing of the Equal Pay Act of 1963 in the United States represented a significant stride toward economic justice, decreeing that men and women should receive equal pay for equal work. This law aimed to dismantle the systemic discrimination that had long deprived women of fair compensation and hindered their financial independence. However, even today, the gender pay gap persists across various industries and professions, reminding us that laws alone are not enough to uproot deep-seated inequities and biases.

The Equal Pay Act of 1963 was a landmark achievement in addressing wage discrimination, but its implementation and enforcement have faced significant challenges. Despite the law's prohibition of unequal pay for equal work, loopholes and ambiguities have allowed pay disparities to persist. Additionally, the law does not account for occupational segregation, where women are often concentrated in lower-paying industries and positions, contributing to the overall gender pay gap.

Despite the Equal Pay Act, data from the U.S. Census Bureau in 2020 revealed that women earned approximately 82 cents for every dollar earned by men, with the gap being even wider for women of color. This persistent wage disparity not only reflects ongoing discrimination but also contributes to the economic disadvantages and financial insecurity faced by many women, highlighting the need for stronger enforcement mechanisms and comprehensive policy solutions to address the root causes of this inequality.

The persistence of the gender pay gap has far-reaching consequences beyond individual income disparities. It contributes to the perpetuation of poverty, particularly for single mothers and women-headed households, and limits women's economic independence and decision-making power within households and communities. Furthermore, the compounded effect of lower earnings over a lifetime can significantly impact women's long-term financial security, including their ability to save for retirement and build wealth.

The year 1973 brought forth a decision that would reverberate through the decades: Roe v. Wade. The United States Supreme Court ruled that the Constitution protects a woman's right to an abortion, a pronouncement that was both celebrated and contested, reflecting the nation's divided views on reproductive rights. This landmark decision recognized a woman's autonomy over her own body and sparked intense debates about the intersection of women's rights, ethics, and religious beliefs – debates that continue to shape the political landscape to this day.

The Roe v. Wade decision was a pivotal moment in the fight for reproductive rights, but it also sparked a fierce backlash from anti-abortion advocates and conservative groups. In the years following the ruling, numerous states enacted restrictive abortion laws, creating barriers to access and fueling ongoing legal battles over the interpretation and scope of the decision. The ongoing debates surrounding abortion rights highlight the complex interplay between personal autonomy, societal values, and the role of the state in regulating reproductive choices.

The Roe v. Wade decision was a watershed moment for reproductive rights, but it also ignited a fierce backlash from anti-abortion advocates and conservative groups. In the years that followed, numerous states enacted restrictive abortion laws, creating barriers to access and fueling ongoing legal battles over the scope and limitations of the ruling. The ongoing debates surrounding abortion rights highlight the complex interplay between personal autonomy, societal values, and the role of the state in regulating reproductive choices.

The aftermath of Roe v. Wade saw a wave of legislative efforts aimed at restricting access to abortion services. According to the Guttmacher Institute, a reproductive health research organization, between 1973 and 2022, states enacted over 1,300 abortion restrictions, ranging from mandatory waiting periods and parental involvement requirements to outright bans in certain states. These restrictions disproportionately impacted low-income women, women of color, and those living in rural areas, further exacerbating existing disparities in access to reproductive healthcare.

Around the globe, women were making their presence felt through bold acts of solidarity and resistance. On October 24, 1975, Icelandic women orchestrated a monumental strike known as "Women's Day Off." An astounding 90% of the country's women refused to work, cook, or care for children, bringing the nation to a standstill. This powerful demonstration highlighted the indispensable role women play in society and the economic disruption caused by their absence, sending shockwaves across the world and inspiring similar actions in other countries.

The impact of the Icelandic women's strike was profound and far-reaching. According to a report by the United Nations, the strike led to the establishment of the Gender Equality Council in Iceland and the adoption of new laws and policies aimed at promoting gender equality in the workplace, including the world's first law mandating equal pay for equal work. The strike's success demonstrated the power of collective action and solidarity in catalyzing systemic change and served as an inspiration for similar women's strikes and protests globally.

The Icelandic women's strike was a groundbreaking act of collective action, underscoring the power of solidarity and nonviolent resistance in advancing women's rights. It showcased the profound impact that women's labor, both paid and unpaid, has on the functioning of society and the economy. The strike's success also demonstrated the effectiveness of direct action in drawing attention to issues of gender inequality and prompting societal and policy changes.

The strike's impact extended beyond Iceland, inspiring women's movements around the world to adopt similar tactics of nonviolent resistance and direct action. In Spain, for example, the International Women's Strike, which began in 2018, brought millions of women into the streets to protest gender-based violence, pay disparities, and the disproportionate burden of unpaid domestic labor. These collective actions highlighted the intersectional nature of women's struggles and the need for a unified, global movement to address systemic gender inequalities.

In 1979, the United Nations General Assembly adopted the Convention on the Elimination of All Forms of Discrimination against Women (CEDAW), often described as an international bill of rights for women. This landmark treaty provided a comprehensive framework for combating discrimination against women in all spheres of life, including political, economic, social, and cultural realms. CEDAW was a clarion call to nations to dismantle discriminatory laws and practices that hindered women's progress, and to actively promote gender equality through policy and legislative reforms.

CEDAW has been instrumental in setting international standards and norms for women's rights, serving as a guide for national legislation and policy reforms. For example, the convention's provisions on political participation and representation have been cited by countries seeking to increase women's representation in decision-making bodies through measures such as gender quotas or reserved seats. Additionally, CEDAW has provided a framework for addressing issues such as gender-based violence, reproductive rights, and discriminatory practices in areas like education and employment.

CEDAW has been ratified by 189 countries, making it one of the most widely adopted international human rights treaties. However, its implementation has faced challenges, as some countries have entered reservations or failed to fully comply with its provisions. Monitoring and enforcement mechanisms, such as periodic reporting and review processes, have been crucial in holding signatory nations accountable and ensuring that the treaty's principles are translated into tangible actions and policy changes.

While the ratification of CEDAW is a significant step, its effective implementation remains a challenge in many countries. According to the United Nations, as of 2022, over 100 countries have entered reservations to certain provisions of the convention, often citing conflicts with national laws, customs, or religious traditions. Additionally, the lack of effective monitoring and enforcement mechanisms has allowed some countries to ratify the convention without fully translating its principles into tangible policies and actions.

The 1980s and 1990s witnessed a surge in the number of women occupying positions of power within political realms, shattering glass ceilings that had long seemed impenetrable. Leaders like Margaret Thatcher in the United Kingdom, Gro Harlem Brundtland in Norway, and Benazir Bhutto in Pakistan defied societal norms and paved the way for future generations of women to aspire to the highest echelons of leadership. Thatcher, Britain's first female prime minister, faced immense opposition and criticism, but her tenure demonstrated that women were equally capable of wielding power and influencing global affairs. Brundtland, Norway's first female prime minister, championed environmental causes and sustainable development, while Bhutto's election as Pakistan's prime minister challenged patriarchal traditions and inspired women across the Muslim world.

The rise of these pioneering women leaders was not without controversy and resistance. Their ascent to power often faced opposition from entrenched patriarchal structures and cultural norms that questioned women's ability to lead. For instance, Margaret Thatcher's leadership style was frequently criticized as overly aggressive and "unfeminine," highlighting the double standards and biases that women in power often face. Similarly, Benazir Bhutto's political career was marked by allegations of corruption and instability, with some observers attributing these challenges to the patriarchal resistance she faced as a woman leader in a deeply conservative society.

While the ascent of these pioneering women leaders was a significant milestone, their experiences also highlighted the unique challenges and biases faced by women in positions of power. They often encountered heightened scrutiny, double standards, and unfair criticism regarding their leadership styles, physical appearance, and personal lives – biases that their male counterparts rarely faced. Their stories underscored the need for ongoing efforts to dismantle deep-rooted gender stereotypes and create more inclusive and equitable environments for women leaders.

The experiences of these trailblazing women leaders also shed light on the intersectional nature of the challenges they faced. For instance, as a woman of color from a developing nation, Benazir Bhutto's leadership was often scrutinized through the lens of racial and cultural biases, in addition to gender-based discrimination. This underscores the importance of an intersectional approach that recognizes the compounded barriers faced by women who belong to multiple marginalized groups.

However, the ascent of these trailblazers was not without obstacles and backlash. Their experiences highlighted the persistent barriers and gender biases that women in positions of authority continue to face, from double standards in scrutiny and criticism to the disproportionate burdens of balancing professional and personal responsibilities.

One of the persistent barriers faced by women in leadership positions is the challenge of balancing professional and personal responsibilities. Research has consistently shown that women, regardless of their career or leadership roles, often bear a disproportionate share of household and caregiving duties compared to their male counterparts. This "second shift" can lead to burnout, stress, and difficulties in advancing their careers, further entrenching gender inequalities in leadership positions.

The Beijing Declaration and Platform for Action, a blueprint for women's rights, emerged from the Fourth World Conference on Women in 1995. This landmark document outlined a visionary agenda for the empowerment of women, addressing issues such as poverty, education, health, violence against women, and decision-making roles. The Beijing Declaration called upon governments, civil society, and the international community to take concrete actions to advance gender equality, recognizing that women's rights are integral to achieving sustainable development and fostering peaceful, prosperous societies.

The Beijing Declaration and Platform for Action set forth a comprehensive and ambitious agenda for achieving gender equality, with specific targets and commitments across 12 critical areas of concern. These areas included women's poverty, education and training, health, violence against women, armed conflict, economic structures and policies, power and decision-making, institutional mechanisms for the advancement of women, human rights, media, environment, and the girl child. By identifying these intersecting issues, the Beijing Platform recognized the multidimensional nature of gender inequality and the need for a holistic approach to address it.

The Beijing Declaration and Platform for Action was a groundbreaking document that recognized the intersectional nature of women's rights and the need to address the diverse challenges faced by women from different backgrounds, cultures, and socio-economic statuses. It emphasized the importance of mainstreaming gender perspectives into all areas of policymaking and development, and called for the elimination of all forms of violence against women, including harmful practices such as female genital mutilation and child marriage.

The Beijing Platform for Action was groundbreaking in its recognition of the intersectional nature of women's oppression and the diverse challenges faced by different groups of women. It acknowledged that women's experiences are shaped by multiple, intersecting systems of oppression, including race, ethnicity, class, age, disability, and other factors. This intersectional approach challenged the notion of a monolithic "women's experience" and highlighted the need for nuanced strategies tailored to the specific needs and challenges faced by different groups of women.

As the 21st century dawned, the fight for gender equality diversified and digitized, harnessing the power of technology and social media to amplify voices and mobilize global movements. The #MeToo movement, which exploded onto the digital landscape in 2017, exposed the pervasive nature of sexual harassment and assault, sparking a worldwide conversation and holding perpetrators accountable across industries and socio-economic strata. This movement transcended borders and socio-economic status, proving that the thirst for justice and the demand for safer, more equitable workplaces and public spaces was universal.

The #MeToo movement was a watershed moment in the fight against sexual harassment and assault, but it also highlighted the intersectional nature of these issues. While the movement brought much-needed attention to the experiences of women in the entertainment industry and corporate settings, it also shed light on the unique challenges faced by marginalized women, such as those in low-wage industries, undocumented workers, and women in the military. These groups often face additional barriers to reporting and seeking justice due to factors such as economic insecurity, fear of retaliation, and lack of access to resources.

The #MeToo movement demonstrated the power of social media and digital activism in amplifying marginalized voices and catalyzing social change. By sharing personal stories and experiences, the movement helped to break the silence around sexual harassment and assault, challenging the culture of victim-blaming and impunity that had long prevailed. While the movement faced criticism and backlash, it also prompted institutional reforms, policy changes, and a broader cultural shift in how society perceives and addresses issues of sexual misconduct and gender-based violence.

While the #MeToo movement was a powerful catalyst for change, it also faced criticism and backlash, particularly from those who viewed it as a threat to established power structures and gender norms. Critics argued that the movement went too far, unfairly targeting individuals without due process, and creating a "witch hunt" mentality. However, proponents of the movement argued that it was a necessary and long-overdue reckoning with the pervasive nature of sexual harassment and assault, and that the backlash was a symptom of the deep-rooted cultural resistance to addressing these issues.

In the heat of these movements, new challenges emerged, underscoring the intersectionality of women's rights with other human rights struggles. Malala Yousafzai, the Pakistani advocate for girls' education, who survived an assassination attempt simply for attending school, became the youngest Nobel Prize laureate in 2014 at the age of 17. Her story is a solemn reminder that the quest for gender equality is inextricably linked to the fight for basic human rights, education, and freedom from violence in many parts of the world.

Malala Yousafzai's story highlighted the intersections between gender discrimination, poverty, extremism, and the denial of fundamental human rights, particularly in the context of armed conflict and displacement. According to the United Nations, girls living in conflict-affected areas are 2.5 times more likely to be out of school than their counterparts in stable regions. This stark reality underscores the need for a holistic approach to addressing the multifaceted barriers to girls' education and empowerment, including efforts to promote peace, security, and sustainable development.

Malala Yousafzai's courageous advocacy for girls' education and her resilience in the face of adversity inspired a global movement for education rights and gender equality. Her story highlighted the intersections between gender discrimination, poverty, extremism, and the denial of fundamental human rights, emphasizing the need for a holistic approach to address these interconnected challenges. Yousafzai's work continues to raise awareness and mobilize efforts to ensure access to quality education for girls, particularly in regions where cultural and socio-economic barriers persist.

Malala Yousafzai's tireless advocacy has not only raised global awareness about the importance of girls' education but has also led to tangible initiatives and policy changes. The Malala Fund, a non-profit organization she co-founded, works to provide educational opportunities for girls in developing countries, with a focus on regions affected by conflict, poverty, and gender discrimination. The fund has invested in programs that address the multifaceted barriers to girls' education, such as building schools, training teachers, and providing resources for safe and inclusive learning environments.

As the gender equality movement evolved, it intersected with other social and civil rights movements, such as the fight for racial equality, LGBTQ+ rights, and disability rights. These intersections highlighted the complex layers of oppression and discrimination faced by women from diverse backgrounds and identities, and the need for an intersectional approach to address the multifaceted barriers they encountered. Figures like bell hooks, Audre Lorde, and the Combahee River Collective played pivotal roles in advancing intersectional feminism, advocating for the recognition of the unique experiences and perspectives of women of color, queer women, and other marginalized groups within the broader feminist discourse.

The contributions of intersectional feminists like bell hooks, Audre Lorde, and the Combahee River Collective were instrumental in reshaping the feminist movement and challenging its historical exclusions and biases. These thinkers and activists emphasized the need to understand and address the intersections of gender, race, class, sexuality, and other systems of oppression, and to center the voices and experiences of marginalized women who had long been sidelined within mainstream feminist discourse.

The intersectional approach to feminism recognizes that women's experiences are shaped by multiple, intersecting systems of oppression, including race, class, sexuality, ability, and other identity markers. By acknowledging these intersections, intersectional feminism aims to create a more inclusive and representative movement that addresses the diverse needs and challenges faced by women from different backgrounds. This approach has challenged the notion of a monolithic "women's experience" and has sought to amplify the voices and perspectives of marginalized women who have historically been sidelined or overlooked within mainstream feminist discourse.

The concept of intersectionality has been instrumental in reframing the feminist discourse and challenging the notion of a universal "women's experience." Intersectional feminists argue that the experiences of women cannot be understood through a singular lens of gender alone, as factors such as race, class, sexuality, and ability intersect to create unique and multifaceted experiences of oppression and marginalization. This perspective has been crucial in acknowledging and addressing the diverse needs and challenges faced by women from different backgrounds, and in building a more inclusive and representative feminist movement.

Technological advancements and the rise of social media also reshaped the landscape of contemporary feminist movements, facilitating global solidarity and activism through digital platforms. Online campaigns, hashtag activism, and the sharing of personal stories enabled women to connect, organize, and mobilize in unprecedented ways, transcending geographical boundaries and amplifying marginalized voices.

The rise of digital feminism has not been without its challenges and critiques. While social media and online platforms have enabled unprecedented global connectivity and amplification of marginalized voices, they have also exposed the digital divide that exists between women in different socio-economic and geographical contexts. Critics have argued that online feminist activism often reflects the perspectives and priorities of women in the Global North, potentially overshadowing or marginalizing the experiences and struggles of women in the Global South and other under-represented regions.

Despite the remarkable progress achieved, the journey towards gender equality remains an ongoing struggle, punctuated by setbacks and resistance. Persistent gender-based violence, discrimination in the workplace and education, unequal access to healthcare and economic opportunities, and the backlash against feminist ideals in some regions or communities serve as stark reminders that complacency is not an option.

The backlash against feminist ideals and gender equality efforts has taken various forms across different regions and communities. In some contexts, this backlash manifests as a resurgence of conservative or traditionalist ideologies that seek to reinforce patriarchal norms and gender roles. In others, it takes the form of organized opposition to specific policies or initiatives aimed at promoting women's rights and empowerment, such as reproductive rights, gender-based violence prevention, or anti-discrimination measures.

According to UN Women, one in three women worldwide experiences physical or sexual violence in their lifetime, often perpetrated by an intimate partner. This staggering statistic underscores the pervasive nature of gender-based violence and the urgent need for comprehensive prevention and protection measures, including legal reforms, access to support services, and efforts to address the underlying sociocultural norms and attitudes that enable such violence.

Within the feminist movement itself, a diversity of perspectives and approaches has emerged, reflecting the multifaceted nature of the challenges faced by women across different cultures, socio-economic backgrounds, and life experiences. Liberal feminism advocates for equal rights and opportunities within existing societal structures, while radical feminism challenges the patriarchal foundations of society and calls for a complete restructuring of power dynamics. Intersectional feminism, rooted in the recognition of the interconnected systems of oppression, seeks to address the unique experiences of women who face multiple, intersecting forms of discrimination based on race, class, sexuality, ability, and other identities.

The diversity of perspectives within feminism has sparked debates and tensions, as different approaches prioritize different strategies and goals. However, this diversity can also be seen as a strength, reflecting the richness and complexity of women's experiences and the multidimensional nature of the challenges they face. By embracing an intersectional and inclusive approach, the feminist movement can better address the diverse needs and aspirations of women across various contexts, while remaining united in the common pursuit of gender equality and social justice.

As we forge ahead, it's crucial to celebrate the incremental but significant progress, such as the increasing number of countries enacting laws against domestic violence, or the steady climb in female representation within governmental and corporate leadership roles. However, these achievements should not obscure the ongoing struggle for true gender parity, where women are not only present at the table but empowered to shape the narrative and influence decision-making processes without facing systemic barriers or discrimination.

The role of men and allies in supporting and advancing the cause of gender equality cannot be understated. Engaging all genders in dismantling patriarchal structures and fostering a culture of respect, empathy, and shared responsibility is essential for creating a more equitable society. Men who leverage their privilege and platforms to amplify women's voices, challenge toxic masculinity norms, and champion gender-inclusive policies and practices are invaluable allies in the pursuit of lasting change.

The engagement of men and allies in the gender equality movement is not only a matter of solidarity but also a recognition that gender inequality is a societal issue that affects everyone. When women are empowered and free from discrimination, entire communities and societies benefit from increased economic growth, improved health outcomes, and greater social cohesion. By challenging harmful gender norms and stereotypes, men can play a crucial role in transforming cultural attitudes and creating more inclusive and equitable environments for all.

Looking toward the future, the gender equality movement must remain adaptable and responsive to emerging challenges and priorities. The disproportionate impact of climate change on women, particularly in developing nations, underscores the need for a gender-conscious approach to environmental policies and disaster risk reduction strategies. The integration of gender perspectives in fields like technology and artificial intelligence is crucial to mitigate the perpetuation of biases and ensure that these rapidly evolving domains do not exacerbate existing inequalities.

The impact of climate change on women is a pressing issue that requires immediate attention and action. According to the United Nations Framework Convention on Climate Change (UNFCCC), women and girls are disproportionately affected by climate-related disasters, due to factors such as entrenched gender inequalities, limited access to resources, and their traditional roles as primary caregivers and providers of food, water, and fuel for their families. Addressing this issue requires a multi-pronged approach that involves empowering women as decision-makers and leaders in climate change adaptation and mitigation efforts, as well as incorporating gender perspectives into climate policies and disaster risk reduction strategies.

The COVID-19 pandemic has also highlighted the gendered impacts of global crises, with women disproportionately bearing the burden of unpaid care work, job losses, and increased vulnerability to domestic violence. As the world grapples with the long-term consequences of the pandemic, it is crucial to incorporate gender-responsive measures into recovery efforts, addressing the unique challenges faced by women and ensuring that they are not left behind in the pursuit of economic and social resilience.

The COVID-19 pandemic has exposed and exacerbated existing gender inequalities, with women bearing the brunt of the economic and social fallout. According to the International Labour Organization (ILO), women have been disproportionately affected by job losses and economic insecurity during the pandemic, with sectors that employ a high proportion of women, such as hospitality, retail, and informal sectors, being among the hardest hit. Additionally, the increased burden of unpaid care work, such as caring for children and elderly family members, has fallen disproportionately on women, further hindering their economic opportunities and well-being.

One cannot help but pause and reflect: How far have we come, and what else must we achieve to ensure that gender equality is not just a theoretical concept but a lived reality for all? The story of women's rights is one of resilience, of voices rising in unison to declare that equality is not a privilege but a fundamental human right.

Despite the significant progress made in advancing women's rights and gender equality, the road ahead remains long and arduous. Achieving true gender equality requires a sustained and multifaceted approach that addresses the deep-rooted structural, cultural, and socio-economic barriers that perpetuate gender-based discrimination and oppression. It also requires a commitment to intersectionality, recognizing and addressing the unique challenges faced by women who experience multiple, intersecting forms of marginalization based on race, class, sexual orientation, disability, and other identities.

One of the key structural barriers to gender equality is the persistent gender gap in access to economic resources and opportunities. According to the World Bank, women have less access to productive resources such as land, credit, and technology than men, which hinders their ability to generate income and achieve financial independence. This economic disadvantage not only perpetuates poverty and vulnerability for women but also has broader implications for economic growth and development at the societal level.

Despite the significant milestones achieved, the path towards true gender equality remains long and arduous. According to the World Economic Forum's Global Gender Gap Report 2022, it will take another 132 years to close the global gender gap at the current rate of progress. This staggering statistic underscores the urgency of accelerating efforts and tackling the deep-rooted systemic barriers that perpetuate gender inequalities across all sectors and societies.

The Global Gender Gap Report, published annually by the World Economic Forum, provides a comprehensive assessment of gender disparities across four key dimensions: economic participation and opportunity, educational attainment, health and survival, and political empowerment. The report highlights the persistent gaps and challenges across these areas, serving as a call to action for governments, organizations, and civil society to intensify their efforts toward achieving gender parity.

The milestones mentioned here are but a few threads in the rich constellation of the gender equality movement. Each achievement, no matter how small, is a building block towards a world where gender does not dictate one's opportunities or rights. Though the journey is far from complete, and the path ahead is riddled with obstacles, the relentless spirit of those who have fought for equality continues to inspire action and propel the movement forward.

Despite the challenges and obstacles, the relentless spirit of women's rights advocates and the unwavering commitment to the cause of gender equality have been instrumental in driving progress. From the early suffragettes to contemporary activists, each generation has built upon the foundations laid by those who came before, adapting strategies and tactics to address the evolving needs and challenges of their times. This intergenerational transfer of knowledge, experience, and activism has been a driving force behind the movement's momentum and resilience.

As the gender equality movement progresses, it must also grapple with emerging challenges and intersectional issues. The impact of climate change on women, particularly in developing nations, is one such area of concern. Women are often disproportionately affected by natural disasters, resource scarcity, and environmental degradation, exacerbating existing vulnerabilities and perpetuating cycles of poverty and marginalization. Addressing these intersections through gender-responsive climate policies and disaster risk reduction strategies is crucial for achieving sustainable and equitable development.

The disproportionate impact of climate change on women is not only a humanitarian concern but also a barrier to achieving gender equality and sustainable development goals. According to the United Nations Development Programme (UNDP), women's vulnerability to climate change is exacerbated by factors such as limited access to resources, restricted decision-making power, and gender-based discrimination. Addressing this issue requires a holistic approach that incorporates gender perspectives into climate change mitigation and adaptation strategies, empowers women as active participants and decision-makers, and promotes gender-responsive disaster risk reduction measures.

As we look to the horizon, let us carry forth the legacy of these trailblazers with unwavering resolve. In the final analysis, the narrative of gender equality is intricately linked to the narrative of humanity, a story we must collectively strive to craft, constructing strands of justice, empowerment, and inclusive prosperity for all.

Carrying forth the legacy of trailblazers in the gender equality movement requires not only honoring their sacrifices and achievements but also embracing their spirit of resilience, courage, and unwavering commitment to justice. It means recognizing that the struggle for gender equality is an ongoing journey, one that demands constant vigilance, activism, and a willingness to adapt to new challenges and contexts. By drawing inspiration from the pioneers who paved the way, the current and future generations of advocates can continue to push boundaries, challenge entrenched norms, and work towards creating a world where every individual, regardless of gender, can thrive and reach their full potential.

The pursuit of gender equality is not merely a women's issue but a human rights issue that affects us all. By fostering inclusive and equitable societies, where individuals of all genders have equal opportunities to thrive and contribute, we unlock the full potential of humanity. It is a journey that requires sustained commitment, intersectional approaches, and a willingness to challenge and dismantle deeply entrenched systems of oppression and discrimination. Only through collective action, solidarity, and a shared vision of a more just and equitable world can we truly achieve the transformative change we seek.

The transformative change envisioned by the gender equality movement requires a collective and collaborative effort that transcends gender, racial, ethnic, and cultural boundaries. It necessitates the active involvement and allyship of individuals from all walks of life, united in their shared commitment to creating a more just and equitable world. By fostering solidarity, understanding, and a willingness to listen and learn from diverse perspectives and experiences, we can build a movement that is truly inclusive, representative, and capable of effecting lasting and meaningful change.

The pursuit of gender equality is inextricably linked to the broader struggle for human rights, social justice, and the realization of a more equitable and inclusive world. By challenging gender-based oppression and discrimination, we not only empower women and girls but also confront the systemic barriers and prejudices that perpetuate marginalization and inequality across various sectors of society. As such, the fight for gender equality is a fight for the universal values of dignity, respect, and equal opportunity for all individuals, regardless of their gender identity or expression.

Achieving true gender equality requires a multifaceted and sustained approach that addresses the complex intersections of various forms of oppression and marginalization. It necessitates challenging deeply entrenched cultural norms, societal biases, and discriminatory practices that have historically disadvantaged women and other marginalized groups. This process involves not only legal and policy reforms but also a fundamental shift in attitudes, mindsets, and behaviors at both individual and collective levels.

Section C. Impact of Past Movements on Shaping the Current Landscape of Women's Rights

The relentless waves of feminism that have washed over the shores of history have not receded without leaving indelible marks upon the sand. How has the tireless advocacy of the past sculpted the society we navigate today? The current landscape of women's rights, undeniably, owes much of its contours to the pioneering movements that preceded it, their legacy woven into the very fabric of contemporary struggle and progress.

The origins of feminist thought can be traced back even further, to ancient philosophers and thinkers who challenged patriarchal norms and advocated for the equality of women. In ancient Greece, Plato's student Aristotle argued against the subjugation of women, stating that "the male is by nature superior and the female inferior; and the one rules and the other is ruled; this principle, of necessity, extends to all mankind." Such early voices, though often marginalized, planted the seeds for future feminist movements.

The origins of the feminist movement can be traced back to the late 18th century and the works of pioneering thinkers like Mary Wollstonecraft. Her seminal work, "A Vindication of the Rights of Woman," challenged the patriarchal norms of the time and advocated for equal educational opportunities for women. This laid the intellectual foundations for subsequent feminist movements and forever altered the discourse surrounding gender equality.

Wollstonecraft's work was groundbreaking in its critique of the societal and legal subjugation of women. She argued that women were not inherently inferior to men, but rather that their perceived inferiority was a result of their lack of access to education and societal restrictions. Her call for the equal education of women was a radical idea at the time, and her work inspired generations of feminists to come.

Although the origins of feminist thought can be traced back centuries, the late 18th century Enlightenment period marked a significant juncture in the formalization of women's rights movements. Pioneering thinkers like Mary Wollstonecraft, through her seminal work "A Vindication of the Rights of Woman," challenged the pervasive patriarchal norms and advocated for equal educational opportunities for women. These early voices laid the intellectual foundations upon which subsequent movements would build, forever altering the discourse surrounding gender equality.

The Enlightenment period, with its emphasis on reason, individualism, and natural rights, provided fertile ground for the growth of feminist thought. Thinkers like Olympe de Gouges, a French playwright and activist, built upon the ideas of Wollstonecraft and called for the extension of the revolutionary ideals of "liberty, equality, and fraternity" to women. De Gouges' "Declaration of the Rights of Woman and the Female Citizen," published in 1791, was a direct response to the French Revolution's exclusion of women from its promises of equality and universal rights.

The impact of the women's suffrage movement, which began in the mid-19th century, cannot be overstated. By advocating for and eventually securing the right to vote for women, this movement challenged the patriarchal notion that women were unfit for political participation and decision-making. The 19th Amendment to the U.S. Constitution, granting women the right to vote, was a landmark victory that paved the way for greater political representation and influence for women in shaping policies and laws that affect their lives.

The suffrage movement was a decades-long struggle that spanned multiple generations of activists and involved various tactics, including civil disobedience, lobbying, and public demonstrations. Figures like Susan B. Anthony, Elizabeth Cady Stanton, and Ida B. Wells-Barnett played pivotal roles in this movement, often facing harassment, arrest, and violence for their advocacy. The 19th Amendment's ratification in 1920 was a hard-won victory that marked a significant milestone in the quest for women's equality and political empowerment.

As the echoes of women's suffrage resonate through the years, one may ponder how the acquisition of the vote has, in essence, reconfigured the dynamics of power. The ballot box, once an instrument of patriarchal governance, has been transformed into a tool of influence for women, facilitating their entry into the political arena. This seismic shift has allowed for the introduction of legislations that seek to protect and promote women's rights, such as the Violence Against Women Act in the United States, which criminalized domestic violence and provided funding for support services, thanks in part to the advocacy of newly elected female representatives.

The impact of the 19th Amendment, however, was not felt equally by all women. Women of color, particularly Black women, faced additional barriers to exercising their right to vote due to discriminatory laws and practices, such as poll taxes, literacy tests, and outright violence. Figures like Ida B. Wells-Barnett and Mary

Church Terrell, who were active in both the women's suffrage and civil rights movements, fought tirelessly to ensure that the promise of the 19th Amendment extended to all women, regardless of race.

The impact of female political representation extends beyond specific legislations. According to a study by the Inter-Parliamentary Union, countries with higher percentages of women in parliament tend to prioritize issues related to gender equality, child welfare, and social welfare programs. For example, in Rwanda, where women hold 61.3% of parliamentary seats, legislation has been passed to promote gender equality in education, employment, and land ownership.

The correlation between increased female representation and prioritization of gender equality and social welfare policies is not limited to Rwanda. A 2019 study by the World Bank analyzed data from over 100 countries and found that higher levels of female political representation were associated with increased investments in education, healthcare, and social protection programs. This suggests that women in leadership positions are more likely to champion policies that address the unique needs and challenges faced by women and families.

The impact of women's political empowerment extends far beyond legislative changes. According to a study by the United Nations Development Programme, countries with higher levels of female parliamentary representation are more likely to ratify international treaties advancing gender equality and allocate more resources to social services that benefit women and children. Furthermore, research by the World Bank suggests that increasing the share of women in parliament by just 10% can boost economic growth by up to 2 percentage points, highlighting the profound implications of women's participation in governance.

The economic benefits of increased female political participation are not limited to GDP growth. A 2018 study by the International Monetary Fund found that greater inclusion of women in leadership roles, including in politics, is associated with higher levels of income equality and lower levels of income inequality within a country. This suggests that women in positions of power are more likely to advocate for policies and programs that promote economic empowerment and redistribute resources more equitably.

The second wave of feminism, which emerged in the 1960s and 1970s, brought attention to a wide range of issues related to women's personal and professional lives. Activists like Betty Friedan, author of "The Feminine Mystique," challenged the societal expectations and limitations placed on women, particularly in the realms of domestic life and career opportunities. This movement played a pivotal role in shaping discussions around reproductive rights, workplace equality, and the overall autonomy and freedom of women.

The impact of the second wave of feminism was not limited to the United States. In Europe, activists like Simone de Beauvoir, author of "The Second Sex," and Germaine Greer, author of "The Female Eunuch," challenged traditional gender roles and patriarchal structures. Their works inspired women across the continent to demand greater autonomy, equal opportunities in the workplace, and control over their bodies and reproductive choices. The second wave's influence extended to Latin America, Africa, and Asia, where local feminist movements emerged, often adapting and contextualizing the movement's themes to their specific cultural and socio-economic realities.

Could the ripples of the second wave of feminism, with its expansion of the discourse to the personal realms of reproductive rights, sexuality, and workplace equality, be felt in the current dialogues surrounding women's autonomy and freedom? The answer is a resounding yes. The very language we use to discuss harassment, discrimination, and bodily autonomy has been shaped by the groundbreaking work of activists like Gloria Steinem and the National Organization for Women, who refused to be silenced and challenged the pervasive sexism and gender-based inequalities that permeated every aspect of society.

The impact of the second wave's focus on reproductive rights cannot be overstated. In the United States, the landmark Roe v. Wade decision in 1973 recognized a woman's constitutional right to have an abortion, a victory that many attribute to the tireless advocacy of second-wave feminists. While this ruling has faced numerous legal challenges over the decades, it remains a cornerstone of the ongoing fight for bodily autonomy and reproductive justice. Furthermore, the introduction of birth control pills and the destigmatization of family planning have empowered women to exercise greater control over their reproductive choices, a fundamental aspect of gender equality.

Consider the vibrant constellation of today's feminist movement, enriched by the diversity of voices that have emerged from the margins. The intersectionality that characterizes contemporary activism is inseparable from the lessons learned during the civil rights movement and the subsequent waves of feminism. It is through understanding the interconnectedness of various forms of oppression that the cause of women's rights has grown more inclusive and powerful, amplifying the voices of women of color, LGBTQ+ women, and other marginalized groups who were often sidelined in earlier iterations of the movement.

The concept of intersectionality, coined by legal scholar Kimberlé Crenshaw, has been instrumental in shaping contemporary feminist discourse and activism. Intersectional feminists recognize that women's experiences are shaped by multiple, overlapping identities and systems of oppression, such as race, class, sexuality, and disability. This approach has highlighted the unique challenges faced by marginalized women and has advocated for inclusive policies and strategies that address the diverse needs and experiences of all women.

The contributions of intersectional feminists like bell hooks, Audre Lorde, and Kimberlé Crenshaw have been instrumental in broadening the scope of the feminist movement. By highlighting the unique experiences of women facing multiple, overlapping forms of discrimination, they have challenged the notion of a monolithic "woman's experience" and advocated for an approach that acknowledges the complexities of identity and power structures. This has led to a more nuanced understanding of how race, class, sexuality, and other factors intersect with gender, shaping the lived realities of women from diverse backgrounds.

The impact of intersectional feminism can be seen in contemporary activism and policy efforts aimed at addressing the specific needs and challenges faced by diverse groups of women. For example, the Movement for Black Lives, a coalition of organizations fighting for racial justice, has prioritized issues such as reproductive justice, LGBTQ+ rights, and economic equity for Black women, highlighting the intersections of race, gender, and other identities.

In what ways have the legal victories of yesteryears laid the groundwork for modern advocacy? The passage of the Equal Pay Act of 1963 in the United States provided a framework for addressing gender-based wage discrimination, paving the way for subsequent efforts to close the persistent pay gap through legislation, litigation, and policy reforms. Similarly, the landmark decision of Roe v. Wade in 1973, while highly contested and subject to ongoing challenges, established a constitutional right to abortion that has been a cornerstone of the fight for reproductive rights and bodily autonomy.

While the Equal Pay Act of 1963 was a significant step forward, the gender pay gap persists, with women in the United States earning approximately 82 cents for every dollar earned by men, according to data from the U.S. Census Bureau in 2020. This disparity is even more pronounced for women of color, with Black women earning 63 cents and Hispanic women earning 57 cents for every dollar earned by white, non-Hispanic men. Ongoing efforts to address this issue include regular re-evaluations of pay practices, pay transparency laws, and litigation against discriminatory pay practices.

Despite these significant milestones, the battle for economic equality and reproductive rights remains an uphill struggle. According to data from the U.S. Census Bureau, women still earn only 82 cents for every dollar earned by men, a disparity that widens further for women of color. Meanwhile, access to safe and legal abortion services continues to be curtailed in many parts of the United States and around the world, with numerous states enacting restrictive laws that undermine the principles established by Roe v. Wade. These ongoing challenges underscore the need for sustained activism and a commitment to building upon the foundations laid by past movements.

The ongoing legal battles surrounding abortion rights in the United States highlight the fragility of hard-won victories and the importance of sustained activism. In June 2022, the Supreme Court overturned Roe v. Wade, eliminating the federal constitutional right to abortion and allowing individual states to regulate or ban the procedure. This decision has led to a patchwork of laws across the country, with some states moving to protect abortion access while others have implemented restrictive or outright bans. Pro-choice advocates continue to fight for reproductive rights through legal challenges, legislative efforts, and grassroots activism.

The global impact of CEDAW and the Beijing Declaration cannot be overstated. These international agreements have acted as blueprints for nations to construct more equitable societies, serving as rallying points for local and grassroots activism. One must applaud the tenacity of women around the world who have utilized these tools to challenge and change oppressive laws, leading to advancements such as the proliferation of policies against domestic violence, the criminalization of marital rape, and the steady increase in female representation in leadership roles across various sectors.

The Convention on the Elimination of All Forms of Discrimination Against Women (CEDAW), adopted by the UN General Assembly in 1979, has been instrumental in establishing international standards for women's rights. As of 2022, 189 countries have ratified CEDAW, committing to implement policies and legislation to promote gender equality and eliminate discrimination against women. However, some countries have entered reservations or failed to fully implement the provisions of CEDAW, underscoring the ongoing need for advocacy and accountability.

However, the implementation of these international agreements has been uneven, with significant disparities across regions and countries. According to UN Women, only 25% of national parliaments have achieved the critical minority representation of 30% women, while in some regions, such as the Pacific Islands and the Arab States, the average representation remains below 20%. Additionally, data from the World Health Organization suggests that one in three women worldwide still experiences physical or sexual violence, highlighting the urgent need for stronger enforcement of laws and policies aimed at protecting women's safety and dignity.

Should we consider the digital age as a mere continuation of past struggles, or as a novel frontier in the fight for equality? The #MeToo movement, born out of the ability to share experiences instantaneously across the globe, demonstrates how technology has revolutionized activism and amplified marginalized voices. It has brought to light the ubiquity of gender-based violence, creating a solidarity that transcends geographical boundaries and sparking widespread efforts to address workplace harassment, hold perpetrators accountable, and implement comprehensive policies and training programs.

The power of digital activism lies not only in its ability to raise awareness but also in its potential to drive tangible change. For instance, the #MeToo movement has led to the creation of organizations like Time's Up, which provides legal and financial support to survivors of sexual harassment and assault, and has influenced corporate policies and training programs worldwide. Furthermore, social media platforms have enabled grassroots mobilization on a global scale, allowing activists to coordinate protests, share resources, and build transnational networks of support and advocacy.

The stories of courageous figures like Malala Yousafzai, the Pakistani advocate for girls' education who survived an assassination attempt, inspire a new generation of activists and serve as powerful reminders that the quest for educational equity is a battle still being waged. Victories in this arena, such as increased access to education for girls in developing nations and the promotion of STEM fields for women, are vital for the empowerment of women and girls worldwide. The fight for gender equality in education is a testament to the enduring influence of past movements that have always held education as a key to liberation.

The strides made in women's rights are not merely historical anecdotes; they are the building blocks of the freedoms and opportunities women experience today. The increasing number of laws against domestic violence, the rising tide of women in governance and corporate spheres, and the growing recognition of the need for paid family leave and affordable childcare are direct outcomes of the advocacy and sacrifices made by those who came before us.

Yet, the successes of past movements do not compel us to rest on our laurels but rather challenge us to continue the pursuit of justice with renewed fervor and dedication. The ongoing disparities and injustices that women face, such as persistent pay gaps, underrepresentation in leadership roles, and the disproportionate burden of unpaid labor, serve as stark reminders that the story of women's rights is far from over; it is an epic still being written, with each chapter calling for collective action and unwavering commitment.

As we stand on the shoulders of giants, let us not forget that the work of past movements is not a relic to be admired from afar but a torch to be carried forward. Each victory, each challenge overcome, serves as a stepping stone toward a future where gender equality is not a distant dream but a tangible reality. The lessons learned from the struggles and strategies employed by past movements have informed and shaped the tactics, approaches, and philosophies of contemporary feminist activism, fostering a rich continuum of knowledge and experience.

The intergenerational connections and knowledge transfer between earlier generations of feminist activists and contemporary leaders have been crucial in maintaining this continuity and ensuring that the hard-won gains of the past are not only preserved but expanded upon. Mentorship programs, oral histories, and academic research have played a vital role in documenting and disseminating the impact of past movements, allowing for a deeper understanding of the sacrifices made and the obstacles overcome.

Moreover, the global nature of past movements, such as CEDAW and the Beijing Declaration, has fostered international cooperation and solidarity in advancing women's rights across different cultural and socio-economic contexts. This cross-border collaboration has facilitated the exchange of best practices, shared learning, and collective advocacy efforts, recognizing that gender equality is not a localized issue but a universal human rights imperative.

In the grand narrative of women's rights, the significance of past movements cannot be overstated. They are the architects of the present, the harbingers of the future, and the legacy that we have the privilege and responsibility to enhance. With gratitude for the paths carved by our predecessors, we march onward, knowing that the barriers broken have laid the foundation for a world where every woman can rise to her full potential, free from the shackles of discrimination and oppression.

Chapter 3
Legal and Political Advances

Section A: Overview of legislative and policy advancements promoting women's rights

The march towards gender equality has been paved by the tireless efforts of activists, lawmakers, and everyday champions who have fought to enshrine women's rights in the halls of power. Through the lens of legislative and policy advancements, we witness the transformative impact of these efforts on the lives of women across the globe. From the classroom to the boardroom, from the doctor's office to the courtroom, the landscape of women's rights has been reshaped by the power of the pen and the gavel.

The journey towards legislative and policy advancements in women's rights has been a long and arduous one, marked by both triumphs and setbacks. Throughout history, women have had to overcome immense barriers and resistance to assert their fundamental rights and equality. From the early suffragette movements demanding the right to vote to the more recent struggles for reproductive autonomy and workplace equity, the fight for women's rights has been a testament to the resilience and determination of countless activists, advocates, and ordinary women who refused to accept the status quo.

The path to legislative and policy advancements in women's rights has been fraught with challenges and setbacks, as deeply entrenched cultural norms, patriarchal structures, and resistance to change have often impeded progress. However, the unwavering determination and collective action of women's rights advocates have consistently pushed the boundaries, creating ripples of change that have reverberated across societies and generations. Each legal and policy victory, no matter how small, has served as a stepping stone towards a more equitable and just world for women.

One of the most significant legislative advancements in women's rights was the adoption of the Convention on the Elimination of All Forms of Discrimination Against Women (CEDAW) by the United Nations General Assembly in 1979. This landmark international treaty, often referred to as the "Bill of Rights for Women," established a comprehensive framework for addressing gender-based discrimination and promoting women's rights in various spheres, including political, economic, social, and cultural life. CEDAW provided a powerful legal instrument for holding governments accountable and served as a catalyst for numerous national laws and policies aimed at advancing gender equality.

In the sphere of education, laws like Title IX in the United States and the Right to Education Act in India have been instrumental in promoting gender parity in educational access and opportunities. These legal frameworks have opened doors that were once closed, allowing generations of girls and women to pursue their dreams and reach their full potential. However, the journey towards educational equity is far from complete, as disparities persist, particularly in developing nations where deep-rooted cultural norms, poverty, and lack of infrastructure continue to hinder girls' access to quality education. Grassroots movements like Camfed (Campaign for Female Education) and community-led initiatives have played a crucial role in bridging these gaps, working tirelessly to empower girls through education while addressing intersectional issues like poverty and gender-based violence.

Despite the progress made in promoting girls' education through legislative and policy measures, challenges persist in ensuring effective implementation and addressing systemic barriers. In many regions, cultural and religious norms, as well as safety concerns, continue to discourage families from investing in their daughters' education. Additionally, issues such as child marriage, gender-based violence, and the lack of adequate sanitation facilities in schools further impede girls' access to quality education. Addressing these multifaceted challenges requires a holistic approach that combines legal reforms with community engagement, awareness campaigns, and the provision of essential support services.

The impact of education laws and policies on women's empowerment cannot be overstated. According to UNESCO, each additional year of schooling for girls can increase their future earnings by up to 20%. Furthermore, educated women are more likely to participate in decision-making processes within their households and communities, contributing to the overall development and progress of society. However, it is essential to recognize that access to education alone is not enough; the quality of education, inclusive curricula, and safe learning environments are equally crucial in ensuring that girls and women can fully benefit from educational opportunities.

The quality of education is a critical factor in ensuring that girls and women can translate their educational opportunities into meaningful outcomes. In many parts of the world, girls in school face challenges such as gender-biased curricula, lack of female teachers and role models, and inadequate resources and infrastructure. Addressing these issues requires a concerted effort to develop gender-sensitive curricula, train and support female educators, and invest in educational infrastructure, particularly in rural and underserved areas. By prioritizing the quality of education alongside access, policymakers can better equip girls and women with the knowledge, skills, and confidence needed to thrive in various spheres of life.

In the workplace, legislative milestones like the Equal Pay Act and the Lilly Ledbetter Fair Pay Act in the United States, the Equal Remuneration Act in India, and the Gender Equality Act in Sweden, have been instrumental in combating wage discrimination and promoting fairness in compensation. These laws have paved the way for women to demand their rightful place in the workforce and to be recognized for their contributions. However, the gender pay gap remains a persistent reality, with women often earning less than their male counterparts for the same work, compounded by the intersections of race, ethnicity, and other identities. The fight for pay equity continues, bolstered by the efforts of trade unions, women's rights organizations, civil society groups, and individual advocates who refuse to accept anything less than full equality.

In addition to legal measures, addressing the gender pay gap requires a multifaceted approach that tackles the underlying causes of wage inequality. This includes challenging occupational segregation, where women are concentrated in lower-paying sectors and industries, as well as promoting equal opportunities for career advancement and leadership positions. Furthermore, policies that support work-life balance, such as paid parental leave and affordable childcare, can help reduce the "motherhood penalty" that often contributes to the gender pay gap. By addressing these systemic issues, policymakers can create an enabling environment for women to fully participate in the workforce and achieve their economic potential.

Despite the existence of equal pay laws, the gender pay gap persists due to a multitude of factors, including occupational segregation, discrimination in hiring and promotion practices, and the undervaluation of work traditionally performed by women. According to a report by the International Labour Organization (ILO), the global gender pay gap stands at around 20%, with significant variations across regions and industries. Addressing this issue requires a comprehensive approach that includes strengthening legal protections, promoting pay transparency, and challenging societal attitudes and biases that perpetuate the undervaluation of women's work.

The persistence of the gender pay gap is not only an issue of economic inequality but also a manifestation of deeply rooted societal attitudes and biases. Often, work traditionally associated with women, such as caregiving, teaching, and nursing, is undervalued and underpaid compared to male-dominated professions. Challenging these biases and promoting the recognition and fair compensation of "women's work" is crucial in addressing the gender pay gap. This may involve initiatives such as conducting gender-neutral job evaluations, raising awareness about the value of traditionally female-dominated professions, and advocating for equal pay in sectors where women are concentrated.

Reproductive rights have been at the forefront of the struggle for women's autonomy and bodily integrity. Landmark legislation like the Abortion Act of 1967 in the United Kingdom, the Roe v. Wade decision in the United States (later overturned by Dobbs v. Jackson), and the María Eugenia Morales de Sierra case in Guatemala, which decriminalized abortion in cases of rape, have affirmed women's right to make decisions about their own bodies and reproductive health. However, these hard-won victories are under constant threat, with conservative forces seeking to roll back progress and restrict access to reproductive healthcare. The ongoing battle for reproductive justice is a testament to the resilience and determination of women's rights advocates, who continue to fight for the fundamental right to choose, often in the face of formidable legal, social, and cultural obstacles.

The struggle for reproductive rights is intrinsically linked to broader issues of gender equality, women's empowerment, and human rights. Access to comprehensive reproductive healthcare services, including contraception, safe abortion services, and maternal care, is essential for women to exercise bodily autonomy and make informed choices about their lives and futures. Furthermore, restrictive reproductive policies disproportionately impact marginalized and vulnerable women, such as those living in poverty, women with disabilities, and those in conflict-affected areas, further exacerbating existing inequalities and human rights violations.

The fight for reproductive rights is intrinsically linked to the broader struggle for women's bodily autonomy, human rights, and gender equality. According to a report by the World Health Organization (WHO), restrictive abortion laws do not reduce the need for abortion but rather lead to unsafe abortion practices, putting women's lives and health at risk. Furthermore, access to comprehensive reproductive healthcare services, including contraception and maternal care, is essential for women's empowerment and the realization of their full potential in all spheres of life.

The legal battles surrounding reproductive rights have extended beyond national borders, with international human rights bodies and courts playing an increasingly important role. For instance, the European Court of Human Rights has issued landmark rulings recognizing the denial of safe and legal abortion services as a violation of human rights, setting precedents that have influenced national laws and policies. Additionally, the United Nations Human Rights Committee has affirmed that restrictive abortion laws can amount to cruel, inhuman, and degrading treatment, further solidifying the link between reproductive rights and fundamental human rights principles.

The scourge of gender-based violence has been met with a growing arsenal of legal protections and support services for survivors. Laws like the Violence Against Women Act in the United States, the Domestic Violence Act in South Africa, and the Maria da Penha Law in Brazil have provided a framework for addressing and preventing abuse, empowering survivors to seek justice and rebuild their lives. However, the implementation of these laws often falls short, with many women still facing barriers to accessing support due to underfunding, lack of resources, or ineffective law enforcement. Grassroots organizations, women's shelters, and community-based initiatives have stepped in to fill these gaps, providing vital services and advocacy for survivors of violence.

The effectiveness of legal protections against gender-based violence is often hindered by deeply entrenched sociocultural attitudes and norms that normalize or trivialize such violence. In many contexts, victims of domestic violence, sexual assault, or intimate partner violence face stigma, victim-blaming, and a lack of support from their communities and institutional systems. Addressing these cultural barriers requires a comprehensive approach that combines legal reforms with awareness campaigns, community engagement, and the involvement of influential stakeholders such as religious and community leaders in promoting gender equality and challenging harmful attitudes toward violence against women.

The impact of gender-based violence extends far beyond the physical and emotional trauma experienced by individual survivors. It has profound societal and economic consequences, hindering women's participation in the workforce, limiting their educational opportunities, and perpetuating cycles of poverty and marginalization. According to the World Bank, the economic costs of intimate partner violence alone are estimated to range from 1.2% to 3.7% of global GDP. Addressing this issue requires a comprehensive and multi-sectoral approach that combines legal reforms, community engagement, and the provision of essential support services for survivors.

Addressing gender-based violence requires a coordinated and multidisciplinary response that involves various sectors, including law enforcement, healthcare, social services, and the justice system. This approach, often referred to as a "coordinated community response," aims to provide comprehensive support to survivors while also addressing the root causes of violence and promoting prevention efforts. Effective implementation of this approach requires adequate funding, training for frontline responders, and strong collaboration among stakeholders to ensure a victim-centered and trauma-informed approach to service delivery.

On the international stage, legally binding agreements like the Convention on the Elimination of All Forms of Discrimination Against Women (CEDAW) and regional instruments like the Maputo Protocol in Africa have set global standards for women's rights and gender equality. Ratified by 189 countries, CEDAW provides a comprehensive framework for addressing discrimination and promoting women's empowerment across all spheres of life, while the Maputo Protocol specifically focuses on issues like women's bodily autonomy, harmful traditional practices, and gender-based violence. However, the implementation of these agreements varies widely across countries, with some nations making significant strides towards gender equality while others lag behind, often due to cultural resistance, lack of political will, or limited resources. The work of international organizations like UN Women, as well as local and grassroots women's rights groups, has been crucial in holding governments accountable and pushing for the full realization of these agreements' promises.

International legal frameworks like CEDAW and the Maputo Protocol have played a crucial role in setting normative standards and providing a roadmap for national legislative and policy reforms. However, their effective implementation requires sustained political commitment, adequate resource allocation, and robust monitoring and accountability mechanisms. Civil society organizations, women's rights advocates, and international bodies play a vital role in holding governments accountable to their commitments under these treaties, through activities such as shadow reporting, advocacy campaigns, and strategic litigation.

The importance of international legal frameworks like CEDAW and the Maputo Protocol cannot be overstated, as they provide a universal set of standards and principles that can guide national legislation and policies towards gender equality. However, their effective implementation requires sustained political commitment, adequate resource allocation, and the active involvement of civil society organizations in monitoring and holding governments accountable. Furthermore, these instruments must be complemented by efforts to address the underlying social and cultural norms that perpetuate gender discrimination, through education, awareness campaigns, and the promotion of positive role models and narratives that challenge gender stereotypes.

The impact of international legal frameworks on advancing women's rights is not limited to their influence on national laws and policies. These instruments have also played a vital role in shaping global norms and discourse around gender equality, providing a common language and set of principles for advocacy efforts and collective action across borders. By ratifying and adhering to these treaties, governments signal their commitment to upholding women's rights and can be held accountable by the international community for their progress or lack thereof.

The impact of legislative and policy advancements on women's lives cannot be overstated. From granting women the right to vote to protecting them from discrimination and violence, these measures have been instrumental in reshaping societies and challenging entrenched gender inequalities. However, the work is far from finished. The full implementation and enforcement of gender equality laws remain a challenge, particularly in the face of cultural resistance, inadequate funding, and the intersectional barriers faced by marginalized groups of women. The road ahead requires a sustained commitment from governments, civil society, and individuals alike to ensure that the promise of equality becomes a lived reality for all women, regardless of their race, class, ethnicity, or other intersecting identities.

Despite the significant progress made through legislative and policy advancements, the full realization of women's rights and gender equality remains elusive in many parts of the world. Persistent challenges include the lack of effective implementation and enforcement mechanisms, inadequate resource allocation, and the influence of regressive cultural norms and practices that undermine the spirit and intent of gender equality laws. Overcoming these obstacles requires a concerted effort from all stakeholders, including governments, civil society organizations, international bodies, and individuals, to hold duty-bearers accountable, mobilize resources, and challenge harmful sociocultural attitudes and practices that perpetuate gender discrimination.

The ongoing challenges in fully realizing the promises of gender equality laws and policies highlight the need for a multi-pronged approach that combines legal reforms with grassroots activism, community engagement, and efforts to address the underlying sociocultural factors that perpetuate gender discrimination. This may involve initiatives such as gender-sensitive education and awareness campaigns, capacity-building programs for law enforcement and judicial officials, and the meaningful inclusion of women's voices and perspectives in policy formulation and decision-making processes. Additionally, it is crucial to recognize the intersectional nature of gender inequality and tailor interventions to address the unique challenges faced by marginalized groups of women, such as those from minority ethnic or religious backgrounds, women with disabilities, or those living in conflict-affected areas.

Addressing the intersectional nature of gender inequality requires a nuanced and context-specific approach that recognizes the diverse experiences and challenges faced by different groups of women. This may involve targeted interventions, such as providing accessible and culturally appropriate services for women with disabilities, addressing language barriers and promoting cultural sensitivity in service delivery for indigenous or ethnic minority women, or tailoring programs to meet the specific needs of women in conflict-affected or post-conflict settings. By acknowledging and addressing these intersectional challenges, policymakers and stakeholders can ensure that legislative and policy advancements are truly inclusive and benefit all women, regardless of their diverse backgrounds and identities.

As we reflect on the legislative and policy advancements that have brought us to this point, we must recognize the role of grassroots movements, activism, and ongoing advocacy in driving transformative change. From the suffragettes who fought for the right to vote to the #MeToo movement that exposed sexual harassment and assault, women have been at the forefront of the struggle for their own liberation. These movements have been the driving force behind many legal and policy changes, pushing the boundaries of what is possible while amplifying marginalized voices and experiences.

The power of grassroots movements and activism lies in their ability to raise awareness, mobilize public opinion, and exert pressure on policymakers and institutions to enact meaningful change. By amplifying the voices and experiences of those directly affected by gender inequality and discrimination, these movements have challenged dominant narratives, exposed systemic injustices, and demanded accountability from those in positions of power. From the Women's March to the Ni Una Menos movement in Latin America, the collective action of women and their allies has been instrumental in shaping the discourse on women's rights and driving legislative and policy reforms.

One powerful example of grassroots activism leading to legal change is the movement to ratify the Equal Rights Amendment (ERA) in the United States. First proposed in 1923, the ERA aimed to enshrine equal rights for women in the U.S. Constitution. Despite failing to gain the required number of state ratifications by the original 1982 deadline, the grassroots activism of organizations like the National Organization for Women (NOW) kept the issue alive. Their efforts led to the re-introduction of the ERA in Congress in recent years, with some states continuing to ratify it. This ongoing movement demonstrates the tenacity of grassroots organizers in pushing for transformative legal changes, even in the face of setbacks and delays.

Looking to the future, the work of advancing women's rights through legislation and policy must remain responsive to emerging challenges and priorities. The disproportionate impact of climate change, armed conflicts, and economic crises on women underscores the need for gender-inclusive policies that address these intersectional vulnerabilities. The integration of gender perspectives in fields like technology, artificial intelligence, and STEM is crucial to mitigate the perpetuation of biases and ensure equitable access and opportunities.

As the world grapples with the escalating climate crisis, it is imperative that policies and strategies to address this global challenge incorporate a gender lens. Women, particularly in developing nations and indigenous communities, are disproportionately affected by the impacts of climate change due to existing gender inequalities, limited access to resources, and their traditional roles as primary caregivers and providers of food and fuel. Integrating women's perspectives, knowledge, and leadership in climate action plans can lead to more effective and sustainable solutions tailored to local contexts. Legal and policy frameworks that mandate gender mainstreaming in climate initiatives, as well as support for women's participation in decision-making processes, can help mitigate the gendered impacts of climate change.

As technology continues to reshape various aspects of society, it is essential to ensure that gender equality principles are embedded in the development and deployment of emerging technologies. This includes addressing issues such as algorithmic bias in AI systems, promoting gender diversity in STEM fields, and ensuring that women have equal access to and control over digital resources and platforms. Failure to address these issues could exacerbate existing gender inequalities and create new barriers for women's empowerment in the digital age.

The rapid advancement of artificial intelligence (AI) and its increasing integration into various sectors, from healthcare to finance and beyond, has raised concerns about the potential perpetuation and amplification of gender biases. AI systems trained on historical data that reflects societal biases can reinforce and perpetuate harmful stereotypes and discrimination against women. Addressing this issue requires a concerted effort to ensure diverse and inclusive data sets, algorithmic audits for bias, and the involvement of women and gender experts in the development and deployment of AI technologies. Legal and regulatory frameworks that mandate fairness, accountability, and transparency in AI can help mitigate algorithmic bias and promote gender equality in the digital age.

At the same time, legal and policy change alone is not enough. Transforming the underlying attitudes, beliefs, and systems that perpetuate gender inequality requires a sustained effort from all spheres of society. It necessitates dismantling patriarchal structures, challenging toxic masculinity norms, and fostering a culture that values and respects the rights and dignity of all women, in all their diversity.

Efforts to dismantle patriarchal structures and challenge toxic masculinity norms must involve a multi-pronged approach that addresses socialization processes, institutional cultures, and media representations. From an early age, children are exposed to gender stereotypes and expectations that reinforce harmful patriarchal ideologies and perpetuate toxic masculinities. Countering these influences requires the development of gender-sensitive curricula in educational settings, initiatives to promote positive and diverse representations of masculinities in media and popular culture, and the fostering of more inclusive and equitable institutional environments, particularly in traditionally male-dominated spheres such as the military, law enforcement, and certain corporate sectors.

Addressing the deep-rooted cultural and societal norms that perpetuate gender inequality requires a long-term, multi-generational approach that involves education, media representation, and the promotion of positive role models and narratives. This can include initiatives such as gender-sensitive curricula in schools, media campaigns challenging harmful stereotypes, and the amplification of diverse stories and perspectives that celebrate the achievements and contributions of women from all walks of life. By challenging and transforming the cultural narratives that shape societal attitudes, we can create a more enabling environment for the full realization of gender equality and women's rights.

The role of education in challenging harmful gender norms and fostering a culture of respect and equality cannot be overstated. Gender-sensitive curricula that deconstruct stereotypes, promote critical thinking, and encourage inclusive perspectives can help shape the attitudes and beliefs of future generations. Additionally, initiatives that promote positive role models and highlight the contributions of diverse women leaders across various fields can inspire and empower young girls and boys alike to challenge traditional gender roles and pursue their aspirations without limitations. By investing in gender-transformative education, we can lay the foundation for a more equitable and inclusive society.

The legislative and policy advancements in the fight for women's rights are a testament to the power of collective action, resilience, and the unwavering pursuit of justice. They remind us that change is possible, even in the face of formidable odds. As we continue to push forward, let us draw strength from the victories of the past while remaining steadfast in our commitment to creating a more just, equitable, and inclusive world for all.

As we reflect on the progress made and the challenges that lie ahead, it is crucial to recognize the intersectional nature of the struggle for women's rights. The experiences and needs of women are shaped by multiple, intersecting factors such as race, ethnicity, socioeconomic status, disability, and sexual orientation. Addressing these intersectional challenges requires a nuanced and inclusive approach that amplifies the voices and perspectives of marginalized groups and addresses the compounded forms of discrimination they face. By embracing intersectionality and fostering solidarity across diverse communities and movements, we can build a more powerful and united front for advancing women's rights and achieving true gender equality for all.

Embracing intersectionality in the pursuit of gender equality requires a willingness to confront and dismantle systems of privilege and oppression that exist within our own movements and organizations. It necessitates actively listening to and uplifting the voices of marginalized women, ceding spaces and platforms when necessary, and engaging in continuous self-reflection and learning. By acknowledging and addressing our own biases, blind spots, and complicity in perpetuating intersectional forms of oppression, we can build more inclusive and effective movements that truly represent and serve the diverse experiences and needs of all women.

Section B: Analysis of landmark legal cases and rulings pertaining to gender equality

In the halls of justice, landmark legal cases and rulings have etched indelible marks on the constellation of gender equality. These momentous decisions, born from the courage and tenacity of those who dared to challenge the status quo, have not only transformed the legal landscape but also reshaped societal norms and perceptions. As we delve into the annals of legal history, we uncover a narrative of progress, setbacks, and unwavering determination in the fight for women's rights.

The legal battles for gender equality have been fought on many fronts, spanning diverse regions, cultures, and legal systems. While some cases have set precedents at the national level, others have had a global impact, influencing international human rights jurisprudence and shaping the discourse on women's rights worldwide. These landmark cases not only reflect the specific sociocultural contexts in which they arose but also highlight the universal nature of the struggle for gender justice and the shared aspirations of women across borders.

The legal battles for gender equality have been fought on many fronts, spanning diverse regions, cultures, and legal systems. While some cases have set precedents at the national level, others have had a global impact, influencing international human rights jurisprudence and shaping the discourse on women's rights worldwide. These landmark cases not only reflect the specific sociocultural contexts in which they arose but also highlight the universal nature of the struggle for gender justice and the shared aspirations of women across borders.

The legal battles for gender equality have often been catalysts for broader social movements and collective action. The courageous individuals and organizations who have taken on these legal challenges have not only sought redress through the judicial system but have also worked to mobilize public opinion, raise awareness, and inspire others to join the fight for justice. Their efforts have transcended the courtroom, sparking important dialogues and debates that have helped shift societal attitudes and norms over time. These landmark cases serve as powerful reminders of the transformative potential of strategic litigation when combined with grassroots organizing and sustained advocacy efforts.

One of the most pivotal cases in the struggle for reproductive autonomy is Roe v. Wade, the 1973 U.S. Supreme Court decision that affirmed a woman's right to choose. This landmark ruling recognized that the constitutional right to privacy extended to a woman's decision to terminate a pregnancy, striking down restrictive state laws that had criminalized abortion. The impact of Roe v. Wade reverberated far beyond the United States, setting a precedent for reproductive rights advocacy worldwide. However, the battle for bodily autonomy remains far from over, as evidenced by the ongoing efforts to erode abortion access and the recent overturning of Roe v. Wade in the Dobbs v. Jackson Women's Health Organization decision. This setback serves as a stark reminder that the fight for reproductive justice is an ongoing struggle, demanding vigilance, legal advocacy, and unwavering commitment from human rights organizations, women's rights groups, and individual litigants.

The legal battle over Roe v. Wade and abortion rights in the United States has highlighted the critical role of state legislatures and state courts in shaping the landscape of reproductive rights. In the wake of the Dobbs v. Jackson decision, several states have moved swiftly to enact stringent abortion restrictions or outright bans, while others have taken steps to enshrine and protect abortion access. This patchwork of state laws has led to a complex legal terrain, with advocates on both sides of the issue pursuing strategic litigation and legislative efforts at the state level. This evolving legal landscape underscores the importance of multi-pronged advocacy strategies that combine national, state, and local efforts to safeguard reproductive rights.

The overturning of Roe v. Wade has reignited a fierce debate around reproductive rights in the United States, with several states moving swiftly to enact restrictive abortion laws, while others have taken steps to enshrine and protect abortion access. This legal and political polarization underscores the fragility of hard-won rights and the need for sustained advocacy and legal efforts to safeguard women's bodily autonomy. Furthermore, it highlights the importance of intersectional approaches that recognize the disproportionate impact of restrictive reproductive policies on marginalized communities, including low-income women, women of color, and those in rural or underserved areas.

The legal battles surrounding reproductive rights have highlighted the critical importance of intersectional approaches that recognize the compounded barriers and challenges faced by marginalized women. For example, women living in poverty, immigrant women, and women of color often face significant obstacles in accessing reproductive healthcare services, including financial barriers, language and cultural barriers, and systemic discrimination within the healthcare system. Legal advocacy efforts that incorporate these intersectional perspectives are essential to ensure that reproductive rights are protected and accessible to all women, regardless of their socioeconomic status, race, ethnicity, or immigration status.

The overturning of Roe v. Wade has reignited a fierce debate around reproductive rights in the United States, with several states moving swiftly to enact restrictive abortion laws, while others have taken steps to enshrine and protect abortion access. This legal and political polarization underscores the fragility of hard-won rights and the need for sustained advocacy and legal efforts to safeguard women's bodily autonomy. Furthermore, it highlights the importance of intersectional approaches that recognize the disproportionate impact of restrictive reproductive policies on marginalized communities, including low-income women, women of color, and those in rural or underserved areas.

Across the Atlantic, the European Court of Justice made history with the Defrenne v. Sabena case in 1976. Gabrielle Defrenne, a Belgian flight attendant, challenged her employer's discriminatory policies that forced female cabin crew members to retire at an earlier age than their male counterparts. The court's ruling established the principle of equal pay for equal work as a fundamental right under

European Community law, setting the stage for further advances in workplace gender equality, such as the Equal Pay Directive and the Pregnant Workers Directive. The Defrenne case paved the way for subsequent litigation and advocacy efforts aimed at dismantling structural barriers and discriminatory practices in employment, with organizations like the European Women's Lobby playing a pivotal role in shaping the legal landscape.

The Defrenne v. Sabena case was a groundbreaking victory that extended beyond the immediate issue of equal pay and retirement ages. By recognizing gender-based discrimination in employment as a violation of fundamental rights under European Community law, the court set a powerful precedent for challenging a wide range of discriminatory practices against women in the workplace. This legal principle has been instrumental in subsequent cases addressing issues such as pregnancy discrimination, sexual harassment, and the underrepresentation of women in leadership positions, paving the way for a more equitable and inclusive work environment for women across the European Union.

The impact of the Defrenne v. Sabena case went beyond the issue of equal pay, as it set a precedent for challenging gender-based discrimination in employment practices and policies across various sectors. This landmark ruling played a crucial role in advancing women's economic rights and empowerment within the European Union, paving the way for subsequent legal challenges to discriminatory practices related to recruitment, promotion, and workplace conditions. However, despite these legal advances, the gender pay gap persists in many European countries, highlighting the need for continued efforts to ensure effective implementation and enforcement of equal pay legislation.

The impact of the Defrenne v. Sabena case went beyond the issue of equal pay, as it set a precedent for challenging gender-based discrimination in employment practices and policies across various sectors. This landmark ruling played a crucial role in advancing women's economic rights and empowerment within the European Union, paving the way for subsequent legal challenges to discriminatory practices related to recruitment, promotion, and workplace conditions. However, despite these legal advances, the gender pay gap persists in many European countries, highlighting the need for continued efforts to ensure effective implementation and enforcement of equal pay legislation.

Despite the legal victories achieved through cases like Defrenne v. Sabena, addressing the persistent gender pay gap in Europe requires a multidimensional approach that goes beyond legislative measures. Efforts must be made to challenge deeply ingrained societal attitudes and biases that undervalue women's work, promote gender-neutral job evaluations and pay structures, and address the underlying factors that contribute to occupational segregation and the concentration of women in lower-paying sectors. Additionally, policies that support work-life balance and enable women to fully participate in the workforce, such as accessible childcare and family leave provisions, are crucial in closing the gender pay gap and promoting women's economic empowerment.

In India, the Vishaka v. State of Rajasthan case in 1997 marked a watershed moment in the fight against sexual harassment. The Supreme Court of India, in response to a gang rape of a social worker, laid down comprehensive guidelines for preventing and redressing sexual harassment in the workplace. The Vishaka Guidelines, as they came to be known, defined sexual harassment, mandated the creation of complaint committees, and outlined the responsibilities of employers in creating a safe and inclusive work environment. The case catalyzed a national conversation about the pervasiveness of sexual harassment and the urgent need for robust legal protections, leading to the enactment of the Sexual Harassment of Women at Workplace (Prevention, Prohibition and Redressal) Act in 2013. The Vishaka case exemplifies the transformative power of strategic litigation in driving social change and influencing policy reform, while also highlighting the intersectional nature of gender-based discrimination and its compounding effects on marginalized women.

The Vishaka case not only had legal implications but also carried significant sociocultural resonance in India. By addressing the pervasive issue of sexual harassment in the workplace, the case challenged deeply entrenched patriarchal attitudes and power dynamics that had long enabled and normalized such behavior. The guidelines and subsequent legislation prompted a national conversation about women's safety, dignity, and equal rights in the workplace, serving as a catalyst for broader cultural shifts and empowerment efforts. Additionally, the case highlighted the importance of intersectional approaches, as marginalized women, such as those from lower socioeconomic backgrounds or in informal employment sectors, often face heightened risks and barriers to reporting sexual harassment.

The Vishaka case exemplified the power of strategic litigation to not only establish legal precedents but also catalyze broader societal transformations. By bringing to light the pervasive issue of workplace sexual harassment, the case challenged long-held cultural norms and power structures that had perpetuated gender-based violence and discrimination. The resulting national dialogue and awareness-raising efforts helped to shift societal attitudes, empowering women to speak out against harassment and assert their fundamental rights to safety and dignity in the workplace.

The Vishaka Guidelines and subsequent legislation have played a crucial role in raising awareness about sexual harassment in the workplace and providing legal recourse for survivors. However, the effectiveness of these measures has been hindered by several factors, including inadequate implementation, lack of awareness among employees and employers, and the persistence of sociocultural attitudes that normalize or trivialize sexual harassment. Addressing these challenges requires sustained efforts in areas such as education, capacity-building for complaint committees, and fostering a culture of zero tolerance for harassment in workplaces across India.

Despite the landmark Vishaka Guidelines and subsequent legislation, the implementation and enforcement of these measures have faced significant obstacles. According to a report by the International Labour Organization (ILO), many Indian workplaces lack functional internal complaints committees or adequate grievance redressal mechanisms for addressing sexual harassment cases. This gap in implementation is often exacerbated by a lack of awareness and sensitivity among employers, as well as the persistence of sociocultural attitudes that trivialize or normalize harassment, deterring survivors from reporting incidents.

The struggle for gender equality has often intersected with the fight against discrimination based on race, ethnicity, and class. In South Africa, the Bhe v. Magistrate, Khayelitsha case in 2005 challenged the customary law of male primogeniture, which excluded women from inheriting property. The Constitutional Court struck down this discriminatory practice, affirming the right of women to inherit and own property on an equal basis with men. The Bhe case was a landmark victory for women's economic rights and a powerful statement against the subordination of customary law to constitutional principles of equality and non-discrimination. It also highlighted the importance of an intersectional approach to gender justice, recognizing the compounded marginalization faced by women who experience multiple forms of discrimination based on gender, race, and socioeconomic status.

The Bhe v. Magistrate, Khayelitsha case was significant not only for its legal implications but also for its role in advancing broader societal discussions and debates around the intersection of gender, culture, and human rights. The case highlighted the complex interplay between customary practices, which are deeply rooted in cultural traditions, and constitutional principles of equality and non-discrimination. By affirming the supremacy of constitutional rights, the ruling challenged traditional patriarchal norms and sparked important dialogues about the need to reform or reinterpret cultural practices that perpetuate gender-based discrimination.

The Bhe v. Magistrate, Khayelitsha case not only had legal implications but also carried significant sociocultural significance in challenging deeply rooted patriarchal traditions and gender norms within South African society. The ruling sparked a broader dialogue about the need to harmonize customary laws and practices with constitutional principles of equality, addressing the tensions between cultural traditions and human rights. This case underscored the importance of recognizing the intersectional nature of discrimination and the need for a nuanced approach that respects cultural diversity while upholding fundamental rights and principles of non-discrimination.

The Bhe case highlighted the complex and often contentious intersection of gender, culture, and human rights in post-apartheid South Africa. While the ruling was celebrated as a victory for women's rights and gender equality, it also sparked debates and resistance from certain cultural and traditional leaders who viewed the decision as an erosion of customary practices and an imposition of Western values. These tensions underscored the need for inclusive and consultative approaches that involve traditional authorities and communities in the process of harmonizing cultural practices with constitutional principles, fostering greater understanding and buy-in for reforms aimed at advancing gender equality.

The United States v. Virginia case in 1996 was another groundbreaking decision that challenged the exclusion of women from male-only educational institutions. The U.S. Supreme Court ruled that the Virginia Military Institute's male-only admissions policy violated the Equal Protection Clause of the Fourteenth Amendment, paving the way for greater gender integration in higher education and challenging deep-rooted gender stereotypes and biases. The case reaffirmed the principle that gender stereotypes and generalizations cannot justify the denial of equal opportunities, setting a precedent for future challenges to discriminatory policies in education and beyond. However, the persistence of gender disparities in STEM fields, leadership positions in academia, and the overall underrepresentation of women in certain academic domains underscores the need for continued legal advocacy, policy reforms, and institutional changes to dismantle the intersectional barriers that impede women's full participation and advancement.

The United States v. Virginia case was a pivotal moment in the fight for gender equality in education, as it challenged the deeply entrenched notion that certain educational institutions and fields of study were inherently "masculine" and therefore unsuitable for women. By striking down the exclusionary policies of the Virginia Military Institute, the Supreme Court sent a powerful message that gender stereotypes and biases cannot be used to justify discrimination and the denial of equal opportunities in education.

While the United States v. Virginia case was a significant victory for gender equality in education, its impact has been tempered by the ongoing challenges faced by women in academia. According to a report by the American Association of University Women (AAUW), women continue to face a range of barriers, including gender discrimination in hiring and promotion, sexual harassment, and a lack of family-friendly policies and support systems. Addressing these issues requires a multi-pronged approach that combines legal advocacy, institutional reforms, and efforts to challenge the ingrained biases and stereotypes that perpetuate gender disparities in academic settings.

Despite the legal precedent set by the United States v. Virginia case, the underrepresentation of women in certain academic fields and leadership positions persists. This is particularly evident in the STEM (Science, Technology, Engineering, and Mathematics) fields, where women continue to face significant barriers to entry and advancement, including gender stereotypes, lack of role models and mentors, and a culture that often marginalizes or excludes women. Addressing these challenges requires a concerted effort from educational institutions, policymakers, and industry partners to foster inclusive and supportive environments, challenge gender biases, and promote equal opportunities for women in STEM education and careers.

In recent years, the #MeToo movement has catalyzed a new wave of legal challenges to sexual harassment and assault. The Harvey Weinstein case, which resulted in the conviction of the Hollywood mogul for rape and sexual assault, was a landmark moment in the fight against sexual violence and gender-based discrimination. The case not only held a powerful abuser accountable but also sent a message that no one is above the law, no matter their wealth, status, or influence. The Weinstein case has inspired a global reckoning with the pervasiveness of sexual violence and the urgent need for systemic change, leading to a surge in legal reforms, policy initiatives, and civil lawsuits aimed at strengthening protections for survivors, preventing abuse, and challenging toxic workplace cultures that enable harassment and discrimination.

The Harvey Weinstein case and the broader #MeToo movement have brought to light the systemic nature of sexual harassment and assault, particularly in industries and workplaces where power imbalances and a culture of silence have enabled abusive behavior to persist unchecked. The case highlighted the need for comprehensive legal and institutional reforms to address the underlying power dynamics, lack of accountability mechanisms, and sociocultural attitudes that have enabled perpetrators to operate with impunity. Beyond individual cases, the #MeToo movement has sparked a broader reckoning with workplace cultures, calling for transformative changes in policies, reporting structures, and institutional practices to create safer and more equitable environments for all.

The impact of the #MeToo movement and the Weinstein case has extended far beyond the legal realm, sparking a cultural shift in how society perceives and responds to sexual harassment and assault. The widespread sharing of survivors' stories has helped to destigmatize the issue, encouraging more individuals to come forward and seek justice. Moreover, the movement has prompted companies and organizations to reevaluate their policies and procedures, with many implementing mandatory training, establishing clear reporting mechanisms, and adopting a zero-tolerance approach to sexual misconduct.

The cultural impact of the #MeToo movement cannot be overstated. By amplifying the voices and experiences of survivors across various industries and backgrounds, the movement has challenged societal myths, victim-blaming narratives, and the normalization of sexual harassment and assault. This collective voice has not only empowered individuals to speak out but has also put pressure on institutions, companies, and policymakers to take concrete steps to address these issues and create safer environments for everyone. The movement has also highlighted the need for a more trauma-informed and survivor-centric approach to addressing sexual violence, prioritizing the well-being and empowerment of those who have experienced harm.

The Opuz v. Turkey case at the European Court of Human Rights in 2009 was a significant victory in addressing domestic violence as a human rights violation and holding states accountable for failing to protect victims. The court ruled that Turkey had violated the European Convention on Human Rights by failing to protect the applicant and her mother from repeated acts of violence by the applicant's husband, despite their numerous attempts to seek protection from the authorities. This landmark decision recognized domestic violence as a form of gender-based discrimination and set a precedent for state responsibility in preventing and addressing violence against women.

The Opuz v. Turkey case was groundbreaking in its recognition of domestic violence as a human rights issue and a form of discrimination against women. By holding the state accountable for failing to protect victims, the European Court of Human Rights sent a powerful message that domestic violence is not a private matter but a violation of fundamental rights that requires state intervention and prevention efforts. This ruling has served as a catalyst for legal and policy reforms across Europe, pushing governments to strengthen their domestic violence laws, improve victim support services, and implement comprehensive strategies to combat this pervasive issue.

The Opuz v. Turkey case not only had implications for the legal response to domestic violence but also highlighted the broader societal and cultural factors that contribute to gender-based violence. The court's ruling underscored the need for a comprehensive approach that addresses the root causes of violence against women, including patriarchal attitudes, gender stereotypes, and the lack of effective prevention and support mechanisms. This case served as a catalyst for further legal reforms and policy initiatives aimed at combating domestic violence, while also emphasizing the importance of education, awareness campaigns, and the involvement of civil society organizations in addressing this pervasive human rights issue.

The Opuz v. Turkey case highlighted the critical role that sociocultural factors play in perpetuating and normalizing gender-based violence. The court's recognition of the state's failure to protect victims was rooted in an understanding of the deeply entrenched patriarchal attitudes and gender stereotypes that often minimize or justify violence against women. Addressing these underlying sociocultural drivers requires a comprehensive approach that involves educational initiatives, media campaigns, and the engagement of community leaders and influencers in challenging harmful attitudes and promoting gender equality and respect for women's rights.

As we reflect on these landmark cases and the many others that have shaped the legal landscape of gender equality, we are reminded of the power of the law as a tool for social change. These decisions have not only provided redress for individual plaintiffs but have also set precedents that have had far-reaching impacts on society as a whole. They have challenged entrenched gender stereotypes, affirmed women's fundamental rights and freedoms, and catalyzed broader social and political movements for gender justice.

However, we must also recognize that legal victories alone are not enough to achieve true gender equality. The law is a necessary but insufficient condition for social change, and must be accompanied by shifts in attitudes, behaviors, and social norms. The landmark cases we have explored are but stepping stones on the long and winding path towards a more just and equitable world. They remind us of the progress we have made, but also of the work that remains to be done.

While landmark legal cases have played a crucial role in advancing gender equality, their impact is often contingent upon broader societal change and the dismantling of systemic barriers. Legal victories can set important precedents and provide a framework for reform, but their full realization requires sustained efforts to challenge deeply ingrained sociocultural attitudes, institutional biases, and structural inequalities. This underscores the need for a holistic approach that combines legal strategies with grassroots activism, educational initiatives, and efforts to promote cultural shifts that embrace gender equality as a fundamental value.

The effective implementation and enforcement of legal precedents and rulings pertaining to gender equality require a multifaceted approach that involves collaboration between various stakeholders, including government agencies, the judiciary, civil society organizations, and the broader public. This may involve initiatives such as capacity-building programs for law enforcement and judicial officials, public education campaigns to raise awareness about legal rights and protections, and the establishment of robust monitoring and accountability mechanisms to ensure compliance with court rulings and legal frameworks.

Ensuring effective implementation and enforcement of legal precedents related to gender equality often requires a multi-stakeholder approach that engages government agencies, the judiciary, civil society organizations, and the broader public. One promising strategy is the establishment of dedicated gender equality commissions or ombudspersons tasked with monitoring compliance, receiving and investigating complaints, and advocating for policy reforms. These bodies can serve as crucial intermediaries between the legal system, state institutions, and civil society, working to bridge gaps and ensure that legal protections are translated into tangible outcomes for women and marginalized groups.

The impact of these landmark cases on subsequent legislation, policies, and societal attitudes has been profound, yet the challenges in enforcing legal precedents and ensuring compliance with court rulings persist. In many instances, cultural resistance, lack of resources, and institutional biases have hindered the full implementation of these legal victories, highlighting the need for ongoing advocacy, education, and systemic reforms to bridge the gap between legal protections and lived realities.

One significant challenge in the enforcement of legal precedents and rulings related to gender equality is the lack of comprehensive data and monitoring mechanisms. Many countries lack robust data collection systems that track the implementation of court rulings, the prevalence of gender-based discrimination, and the effectiveness of legal remedies. Addressing this data gap is crucial for informing evidence-based policies, identifying areas that require targeted interventions, and holding relevant stakeholders accountable for upholding the principles of gender equality enshrined in legal frameworks.

Addressing the data and monitoring gaps related to gender equality requires a concerted effort from governments, international organizations, and civil society actors. This may involve initiatives such as developing standardized indicators and data collection methodologies, strengthening national statistical systems, and fostering collaboration between government agencies, research institutions, and grassroots organizations. Additionally, leveraging new technologies and digital platforms can enable more efficient and participatory data collection processes, empowering marginalized communities to document and report instances of gender-based discrimination and human rights violations.

As we move forward, we must continue to use the law as a tool for advancing gender equality, while also working to transform the underlying structures and systems that perpetuate inequality. We must support the brave individuals and organizations who take on the mantle of legal advocacy, and work to create a more inclusive and representative legal system that reflects the diversity of our societies and the intersectional experiences of women from various backgrounds.

Building a more inclusive and representative legal system requires a concerted effort to increase the diversity of legal professionals, including judges, lawyers, and policymakers. Diverse perspectives and lived experiences within the legal profession can contribute to a more nuanced understanding of gender-based discrimination and the intersectional challenges faced by marginalized groups of women. This can be achieved through initiatives such as targeted recruitment and retention programs, mentorship opportunities, and the promotion of legal education and career paths among underrepresented communities.

Increasing diversity and representation within the legal profession is not only a matter of fairness and equity but also a strategic imperative for ensuring that the legal system is responsive to the diverse needs and experiences of all members of society. A more diverse bench and legal workforce can help to challenge ingrained biases, promote greater understanding of intersectional issues, and foster public trust and confidence in the justice system. This requires a concerted effort from legal institutions, educational establishments, and professional associations to actively recruit, support, and retain diverse talent, while also addressing systemic barriers and creating inclusive environments that value and celebrate diversity.

In the end, the landmark legal cases and rulings pertaining to gender equality are a testament to the resilience, courage, and determination of those who have fought for justice in the face of overwhelming odds. They remind us that change is possible, even in the darkest of times, and that the arc of the moral universe, though long, bends towards justice. As we continue to bend that arc, let us draw strength from the victories of the past and the knowledge that a more just and equitable future is within our reach, one where the rights and dignity of all women are respected and upheld, regardless of their intersecting identities and experiences.

The journey towards gender equality through legal means has been marked by countless acts of bravery and sacrifice by individuals who have risked their safety, livelihoods, and even their lives to challenge systemic oppression and discrimination. From the brave plaintiffs who have put their personal stories and experiences at the forefront of landmark cases to the tireless advocates and lawyers who have devoted their careers to advancing gender justice, the progress we have made is a testament to the power of collective action and unwavering commitment to human rights.

As we look towards the future, it is essential to recognize that the pursuit of gender equality through legal means is an ongoing journey that will require sustained commitment, collaboration, and a willingness to adapt to emerging challenges and evolving societal contexts. The landmark cases we have explored serve as milestones in this journey, but they are not the final destination. By learning from the lessons of the past, embracing intersectionality, and fostering a culture of human rights and respect for all, we can continue to forge a path towards a more just and equitable world for women in all their diversity.

As we look to the future, it is critical to anticipate and address emerging challenges that could threaten hard-won gains in gender equality or create new barriers for women's empowerment. One such challenge is the rapid advancement of emerging technologies, such as artificial intelligence (AI) and machine learning algorithms, which have the potential to perpetuate and amplify existing biases and discrimination if not developed and deployed with a gender lens. Proactive legal and policy measures are needed to ensure that these technologies are designed and implemented with principles of fairness, transparency, and non-discrimination, and that they do not exacerbate gender-based inequalities or create new forms of marginalization.

Another emerging challenge that demands our attention is the disproportionate impact of climate change and environmental degradation on women, particularly in developing and marginalized communities. As the effects of climate change intensify, women face increased risks of displacement, loss of livelihoods, and gender-based violence, exacerbating existing inequalities and vulnerabilities. Legal frameworks and policies must incorporate gender-responsive approaches to climate action, ensuring that women's voices, experiences, and leadership are central to developing sustainable and equitable solutions to this global crisis.

"The pursuit of gender equality through legal means is not a sprint, but a marathon," says Phumzile Mlambo-Ngcuka, former Executive Director of UN Women. "It requires sustained commitment, perseverance, and a willingness to adapt our strategies to meet evolving challenges. As we look to the future, we must be prepared to confront new frontiers of discrimination and inequality, and to leverage the power of the law as a tool for transformative change."

In addition to addressing emerging challenges, the pursuit of gender equality through legal means must also prioritize the meaningful inclusion and empowerment of marginalized and underrepresented groups. This includes amplifying the voices and perspectives of women of color, indigenous women, women with disabilities, and LGBTQIA+ individuals, ensuring that their unique experiences and intersectional identities inform legal strategies, policies, and decision-making processes. By embracing intersectionality and centering the voices of those who have been historically marginalized, we can build a more inclusive, representative, and effective movement for gender justice.

"Achieving true gender equality requires us to acknowledge and dismantle the multiple, intersecting systems of oppression that impact marginalized communities," says Kimberlé Crenshaw, legal scholar and pioneering theorist of intersectionality. "We cannot simply address gender discrimination in isolation; we must confront the ways in which race, class, disability, sexuality, and other identities intersect with gender to create compounded forms of marginalization and discrimination."

As we forge ahead, it is crucial to recognize that the pursuit of gender equality is not just a legal battle, but a broader socio-cultural struggle that requires a multifaceted approach. While legal reforms and precedents are essential, they must be accompanied by concerted efforts to challenge deeply ingrained societal attitudes, beliefs, and practices that perpetuate gender discrimination and inequality. This may involve initiatives such as gender-sensitive education and media campaigns, community engagement programs, and collaborations with religious and traditional leaders to foster a culture of respect, inclusion, and equal opportunities for all.

"Legal victories are important, but they are not enough," says Kolhi Naidoo, Director of CIVICUS, a global alliance dedicated to strengthening citizen participation and civil society. "Transformative change requires a holistic approach that addresses the root causes of gender inequality, including patriarchal structures, harmful social norms, and systemic barriers that prevent women from fully participating in all spheres of life. We must engage with communities, challenge outdated belief systems, and create enabling environments where women's rights are respected and celebrated.

By learning from the lessons of the past, embracing intersectionality, and fostering a culture of human rights and respect for all, we can continue to forge a path towards a more just and equitable world for women in all their diversity.

As we chart the course towards a more equitable future, it is essential to recognize the power of intergenerational collaboration and knowledge-sharing. By engaging and empowering younger generations as agents of change, we can ensure that the struggles and sacrifices of those who came before us are not forgotten, and that the lessons learned from landmark legal battles inform and inspire future efforts to advance gender equality. Simultaneously, we must remain open to the fresh perspectives, innovative ideas, and bold visions of young activists and advocates, who are poised to carry the torch of gender justice into new frontiers.

"The fight for gender equality is a multi-generational struggle," says Malala Yousafzai, activist for female education and the youngest Nobel Prize laureate. "It is our responsibility to learn from the triumphs and setbacks of the past, while also embracing new strategies and approaches that are relevant to the challenges of our time. By fostering intergenerational solidarity and amplifying the voices of young women and girls, we can create a more inclusive, sustainable, and transformative movement for gender justice."

As we reflect on the path ahead, it is essential to approach the pursuit of gender equality with a spirit of hope, resilience, and unwavering commitment to justice. While the challenges may seem daunting, the victories achieved through landmark legal cases and rulings serve as a testament to the power of collective action and the indomitable human spirit. By drawing inspiration from the courage and perseverance of those who have paved the way, and by embracing a vision of a more just and equitable world, we can continue to bend the arc of the moral universe towards a future where the rights and dignity of all women are respected and upheld.

Section C: Examination of women's representation in political leadership roles and government institutions

The halls of power have long been dominated by men, with women's voices and perspectives often relegated to the margins. However, as the tides of social change have swept across the globe, women have increasingly claimed their rightful place in the corridors of political leadership and government institutions. From the grassroots to the highest echelons of power, women are breaking down barriers and transforming the face of governance. As we examine the state of women's representation in these spheres, we uncover a story of progress, perseverance, and the ongoing fight for gender parity in decision-making.

The underrepresentation of women in political leadership and decision-making roles has deep historical roots, stemming from patriarchal power structures and sociocultural norms that have traditionally confined women to domestic and caregiving roles. In many societies, women have been systematically excluded from the spheres of power and influence, denied access to education and economic opportunities, and deprived of the fundamental right to participate in political processes. Overcoming these deeply entrenched barriers has required a sustained struggle, with women activists and advocates challenging the status quo through collective action, legal battles, and grassroots mobilization.

The significance of women's representation in political leadership and government institutions goes beyond symbolic gestures or numerical targets. It is a fundamental issue of democracy, justice, and the realization of human rights. When women are excluded from decision-making processes, their perspectives, experiences, and priorities are often overlooked, leading to policies and programs that fail to address their specific needs and concerns. Furthermore, the underrepresentation of women in these spheres perpetuates gender-based discrimination, undermines the principles of equality and non-discrimination, and hinders the achievement of sustainable and inclusive development.

"Women's equal participation in decision-making is not only a demand for simple justice or democracy, but can also be seen as a necessary condition for women's interests to be taken into account," notes the United Nations' report on the "Participation of Women in Public and Political Life." When women are excluded from the halls of power, their unique perspectives, experiences, and priorities are often overlooked or marginalized, leading to policies and programs that fail to address the specific challenges and needs faced by women and girls.

One need look no further than the inspiring examples of women who have shattered the glass ceiling of political leadership to see the transformative impact of women's representation. In Germany, Angela Merkel's 16-year tenure as Chancellor was marked by steady leadership, pragmatism, and a commitment to consensus-building. Her leadership during times of crisis, from the global financial meltdown to the COVID-19 pandemic, has been a testament to the strength and resilience of women in power. Similarly, in New Zealand, Prime Minister Jacinda Ardern has been hailed as a model of compassionate and effective leadership, deftly steering her country through the challenges of a terrorist attack, a natural disaster, and a global pandemic. Her leadership has been characterized by empathy, clear communication, and a commitment to inclusive decision-making, qualities that have resonated with people around the world.

The examples of Merkel and Ardern highlight not only the transformative potential of women's leadership but also the unique strengths and perspectives that women can bring to the table. As noted by Melanne Verveer, former U.S. Ambassador for Global Women's Issues, "When women participate in the political process, they raise issues that others may not prioritize, such as children's health and education, women's economic empowerment, and gender-based violence." By bringing these perspectives to the forefront, women leaders can help shape policies and programs that better address the diverse needs and challenges faced by communities.

The examples of Merkel and Ardern highlight the unique strengths and leadership styles that women can bring to the table, often challenging traditional notions of power and authority. Their successful tenures have dispelled long-held myths about women's ability to lead effectively, particularly in times of crisis. However, it is important to recognize that these women's experiences are not monolithic, and that women leaders come from diverse backgrounds, hold different ideologies, and employ a range of leadership approaches. The key is to create an enabling environment where women from all walks of life can access political leadership roles and contribute their diverse perspectives and experiences to the decision-making process.

While the examples of Merkel and Ardern demonstrate the transformative potential of women's leadership, it is crucial to recognize that their experiences are not monolithic or representative of all women leaders. Women in political leadership roles come from diverse backgrounds, hold varied ideological positions, and employ a range of leadership styles and approaches. This diversity is a strength, as it ensures that a wide range of perspectives and experiences are brought to the decision-making table, fostering more inclusive and responsive governance.

However, the road to political leadership is often strewn with obstacles and barriers that women must navigate. From gender stereotypes and bias to the unequal distribution of domestic and caregiving responsibilities, women face a myriad of challenges in their quest for political office. The pervasive culture of misogyny and sexism in politics, coupled with the lack of institutional support for women candidates, has meant that women must often work twice as hard to prove their competence and legitimacy as leaders. The threat of gender-based violence, harassment, and online abuse further compounds the challenges faced by women in politics, deterring many from pursuing or remaining in public office. The media's tendency to focus on women politicians' appearance, personal lives, and emotional responses, rather than their policies and accomplishments, is another manifestation of the gender bias that pervades the political sphere.

The challenges faced by women in politics extend beyond the electoral process and into the realm of governance and decision-making. A study by the Inter-Parliamentary Union (IPU) and the Parliamentary Assembly of the Council of Europe (PACE) found that women parliamentarians often face marginalization, harassment, and a lack of access to informal networks and power structures within their institutions. This can manifest in various forms, such as being assigned to less influential committees, having their contributions and expertise overlooked or undervalued, and facing backlash or retaliation for advocating for gender-related issues.

The challenges faced by women in politics are not limited to the electoral process or their time in office. Women politicians often confront unique barriers in their ability to effectively participate in and influence decision-making processes within their respective institutions. This can include being excluded from informal networks and power circles, having their contributions and expertise overlooked or undervalued, and facing backlash or retaliation for challenging the status quo or advocating for gender-related issues. Addressing these systemic barriers is crucial for ensuring that women's representation in political leadership translates into meaningful and substantive participation in governance.

The challenges faced by women in political leadership are not limited to the electoral process or their time in office but extend to their ability to effectively participate in and influence decision-making processes within their respective institutions. A study by the International Institute for Democracy and Electoral Assistance (IDEA) found that even when women are elected to political office, they often face marginalization, exclusion from informal power networks, and limited access to resources and support systems essential for effective governance.

Despite these challenges, women have made significant strides in political representation in recent years. According to the Inter-Parliamentary Union, the global average of women in national parliaments reached 26.1% as of January 2023, a significant increase from just 11.3% in 1995. Countries like Rwanda, Cuba, and the United Arab Emirates have led the way in achieving gender parity in their legislative bodies, thanks in part to the adoption of gender quotas and other affirmative action measures. These policies have been instrumental in ensuring that women's voices are heard in the halls of power and that their perspectives are taken into account in decision-making processes.

The progress made in increasing women's political representation, while significant, is not evenly distributed across regions and countries. According to UN Women, as of January 2023, only three countries (Rwanda, Cuba, and the United Arab Emirates) have achieved 50% or higher representation of women in their national parliaments. Additionally, several countries, particularly in the Middle East and North Africa regions, continue to have alarmingly low levels of women's representation, with some national legislatures having less than 10% female representation.

The success of gender quotas in increasing women's political representation has been the subject of much research and debate. While some argue that quotas are a necessary temporary measure to address systemic barriers and accelerate progress towards gender parity, others contend that they may perpetuate the perception that women are less qualified or have achieved their positions through preferential treatment rather than merit. Regardless of the debate, the experiences of countries like Rwanda, which has consistently ranked among the top nations for women's representation in parliament, suggest that quotas can be an effective tool when combined with broader efforts to address sociocultural norms, promote women's leadership development, and create an enabling environment for their political participation.

The debate surrounding gender quotas in politics highlights the complex interplay of legal, institutional, and sociocultural factors that shape women's political participation. While quotas can be an effective tool for increasing numerical representation, they must be accompanied by broader efforts to challenge deeply rooted gender norms, promote women's leadership development, and create an enabling environment for their meaningful participation in decision-making processes. As noted by UN Women, "Quotas alone are not enough to create a critical mass of women in parliament or government, but they can be an important first step in opening up opportunities for women in politics."

However, the picture is not always so rosy. In many countries, women's representation in political leadership remains abysmally low, with women holding only a small fraction of seats in national parliaments and other decision-making bodies. For instance, as of January 2023, women occupied only 25% of parliamentary seats globally, with significant regional disparities, such as the Pacific Islands region having the lowest representation at 20.8%.

The persistent underrepresentation of women in political leadership is particularly concerning in regions and countries affected by conflict, fragility, and humanitarian crises. According to a report by the Georgetown Institute for Women, Peace and Security, women's political representation in conflict-affected countries is often significantly lower than the global average, with numerous barriers and challenges hindering their participation. These include displacement, insecurity, lack of access to resources and support networks, and the breakdown of traditional governance structures. Addressing these challenges requires a comprehensive approach that prioritizes women's political empowerment as an integral component of peacebuilding and conflict resolution efforts.

The persistent underrepresentation of women in political leadership in some regions can be attributed to a confluence of factors, including deeply entrenched patriarchal norms, legal and constitutional barriers, lack of access to education and economic opportunities, and the prevalence of gender-based violence and insecurity. In conflict-affected areas and fragile states, the challenges are often compounded by the breakdown of traditional governance structures, displacement, and the prioritization of security concerns over gender equality initiatives. Addressing these complex and multifaceted challenges requires a comprehensive and context-specific approach that addresses the root causes of gender inequality while also providing targeted support and resources for women's political participation.

One of the key barriers to women's political participation in many regions is the lack of access to education and economic opportunities. According to a report by the World Bank, greater access to education and economic resources can increase women's likelihood of participating in political processes and decision-making. This highlights the importance of addressing intersectional issues such as poverty, illiteracy, and economic marginalization as part of a holistic strategy to promote women's political empowerment.

In some cases, the underrepresentation stems from entrenched cultural attitudes and practices that discourage women's political participation, such as the belief that politics is a man's domain or the expectation that women should prioritize their domestic responsibilities over their political ambitions. In other cases, it is the result of systemic barriers and institutional biases that make it difficult for women to access the resources, networks, and support they need to run for office and succeed in politics.

Cultural and societal norms that reinforce traditional gender roles and discourage women's political participation can pose significant barriers to progress. In some contexts, women who seek political office or leadership positions may face stigma, social ostracization, or even threats of violence from their communities or families. Addressing these deeply rooted cultural barriers requires a multifaceted approach that combines legal and institutional reforms with community engagement, public awareness campaigns, and the involvement of influential leaders and role models in promoting gender equality and women's political empowerment.

One of the key systemic barriers to women's political participation is the lack of access to financial resources and campaign funding. Women candidates often face significant challenges in securing the necessary funds to mount effective political campaigns, as they may have limited access to traditional sources of funding, such as corporate donors or wealthy individuals. This financial disadvantage can have a cascading effect, hindering women's ability to hire staff, conduct outreach, and effectively communicate their messages and platforms to voters. Initiatives aimed at providing financial support and training for women candidates, as well as reforms to campaign finance laws and regulations, can play a crucial role in leveling the playing field and creating a more inclusive political landscape.

The lack of access to financial resources and campaign funding for women candidates is a critical barrier that often perpetuates gender disparities in political representation. According to a report by the National Democratic Institute (NDI), women candidates often face significant disadvantages in fundraising due to a range of factors, including gender-based discrimination, limited access to traditional funding networks, and the disproportionate burden of unpaid care work that limits their ability to engage in fundraising activities. Addressing this challenge requires concerted efforts to provide financial support, training, and networking opportunities for women candidates, as well as reforms to campaign finance laws and regulations to promote transparency and level the playing field.

The challenges faced by women in politics are further compounded by the intersections of gender with other identities, such as race, ethnicity, disability, or socioeconomic status. Women from marginalized communities often face multiple and intersecting forms of discrimination, limiting their opportunities for political participation and representation. For instance, Indigenous women, women of color, and women with disabilities are significantly underrepresented in political leadership roles across various regions.

The intersectional challenges faced by marginalized women in politics are multifaceted and deeply rooted in systemic inequalities and discrimination. For example, women with disabilities may face physical barriers that hinder their ability to participate in political activities, such as inaccessible campaign venues or lack of accommodations for mobility or sensory impairments. Indigenous women and women from ethnic minority groups may confront language barriers, cultural biases, and the marginalization of their communities within broader political structures. Addressing these intersectional challenges requires targeted interventions, inclusive policies, and the meaningful involvement of marginalized women in shaping solutions and strategies for their political empowerment.

The intersectional challenges faced by marginalized women in politics are multifaceted and deeply rooted in systemic inequalities and discrimination. For example, Indigenous women may face barriers such as language barriers, lack of access to education and resources, and the marginalization of their communities within broader political structures. Women with disabilities may encounter physical and attitudinal barriers that limit their ability to participate effectively in political processes, such as inaccessible campaign events, lack of accommodations, and stigma or bias against their capabilities. Addressing these intersectional challenges requires targeted interventions, inclusive policies, and the meaningful involvement of marginalized women in shaping solutions and strategies for their political empowerment.

The intersectional barriers faced by marginalized women in politics are not limited to the electoral process but extend to their ability to effectively participate and influence decision-making processes once in office. A study by the United Nations Development Programme (UNDP) found that women from marginalized groups often face additional challenges within political institutions, such as limited access to informal power networks, exclusion from key decision-making processes, and a lack of support systems and resources to effectively carry out their roles. Addressing these intersectional challenges requires a multi-pronged approach that combines institutional reforms, capacity-building initiatives, and efforts to promote inclusive and representative political environments.

The underrepresentation of women in political leadership has far-reaching consequences for the quality and effectiveness of governance. Research has shown that when women are included in decision-making processes, the resulting policies are more likely to be inclusive, equitable, and responsive to the needs of all citizens. Women politicians are more likely to prioritize issues like healthcare, education, social welfare, and environmental protection, and to advocate for policies that benefit marginalized and vulnerable populations. Moreover, the presence of women in leadership positions can have a powerful symbolic impact, inspiring future generations of women to pursue their own political ambitions and challenging traditional gender norms and expectations.

The positive impact of women's political representation on governance and policymaking is supported by extensive research and empirical evidence. A study by the World Bank found that increasing women's representation in national parliaments by just 10% can lead to higher expenditures on education, health, and social services, reflecting the tendency of women legislators to prioritize issues that directly impact the well-being of their communities. Additionally, research by the International Monetary Fund (IMF) suggests that greater gender diversity in leadership and decision-making roles can contribute to more sustainable economic growth and development outcomes.

The positive impact of women's political representation on governance and policymaking has been demonstrated in various contexts. For instance, studies have shown that in countries with higher levels of women's representation in parliament, there is a greater likelihood of ratifying international treaties related to women's rights, such as the Convention on the Elimination of All Forms of Discrimination Against Women (CEDAW). Additionally, research has found that when women are involved in peace negotiations and conflict resolution processes, the resulting agreements are more likely to be sustainable and address issues related to gender-based violence, human rights, and the specific needs of women and children affected by conflict.

The link between women's political representation and the advancement of gender equality policies is further supported by a study conducted by the World Bank. The study found that countries with higher percentages of women in parliament were more likely to adopt legislation addressing issues such as domestic violence, sexual harassment, and human trafficking. This highlights the critical role that women leaders play in advocating for and prioritizing policies that address the unique challenges and vulnerabilities faced by women and girls.

The challenges of women's underrepresentation are not limited to national politics but extend to other spheres of government as well. In the judiciary, for example, women are often underrepresented in the highest courts of the land, despite the critical role that these institutions play in shaping laws and policies that affect women's lives. As of 2021, only 28.6% of judges in constitutional courts worldwide were women, according to data from the World Bank. This gender imbalance has significant implications for the quality and impartiality of judicial decision-making, as well as for the legitimacy and credibility of the judiciary in the eyes of the public.

The underrepresentation of women in the judiciary is particularly concerning given the pivotal role that courts play in interpreting and upholding constitutional rights and protections related to gender equality, such as non-discrimination, reproductive rights, and protection against gender-based violence. A lack of gender diversity on the bench can lead to a narrower interpretation of these rights and a failure to fully consider the unique experiences and perspectives of women. As noted by former U.S. Supreme Court Justice Sandra Day O'Connor, "A wise old man and wise old woman will reach the same conclusion in deciding cases."

The underrepresentation of women in the judiciary is particularly concerning given the pivotal role that courts play in interpreting and upholding constitutional rights and protections, including those related to gender equality and non-discrimination. A diverse and representative judiciary is essential for ensuring that legal decisions reflect the experiences and perspectives of all members of society, and for promoting public trust and confidence in the judicial system. Efforts to increase gender diversity in the judiciary must address barriers such as gender bias in judicial appointments, lack of mentorship and support networks for women lawyers and judges, and the need to create a more inclusive and family-friendly culture within the legal profession.

Addressing the underrepresentation of women in the judiciary requires a multi-pronged approach that targets various stages of the legal profession. This may include initiatives to encourage and support more women to enter and persist in legal education, mentorship and sponsorship programs for women lawyers, and the establishment of transparent and merit-based judicial appointment processes that actively seek to identify and consider qualified women candidates. Additionally, efforts to create more family-friendly policies and cultures within the legal profession can help retain and promote women's advancement to leadership positions, including judgeships.

Similarly, in international organizations like the United Nations, women have historically been underrepresented in leadership positions, despite the organization's stated commitment to gender equality. As of January 2022, only 30.9% of senior leadership positions in the United Nations Secretariat were held by women, falling short of the goal of gender parity. The lack of women's representation in these influential bodies can have far-reaching consequences for global policymaking and the advancement of women's rights worldwide.

The underrepresentation of women in leadership positions within the United Nations and other international organizations is particularly concerning given the global scope and impact of these institutions' policies and programs. As noted by UN Women, "When women are equally represented in decision-making processes, their perspectives and experiences are better reflected in policies, priorities and resource allocation." This is critical in addressing global challenges that disproportionately impact women, such as poverty, climate change, and armed conflict.

The underrepresentation of women in international organizations like the United Nations is particularly concerning given the global nature of the challenges facing humanity, such as climate change, conflict, and human rights violations. Women's perspectives and experiences are crucial in shaping effective and inclusive solutions to these complex issues, as they often bear the brunt of the consequences and are at the forefront of grassroots efforts to address them. Increasing women's representation in the leadership and decision-making structures of international organizations is not only a matter of gender equality but also a strategic imperative for achieving sustainable and equitable global development outcomes.

The lack of gender parity in leadership positions within international organizations like the United Nations is symptomatic of broader systemic barriers and biases that prevent women from advancing to higher echelons of power and decision-making. These barriers include entrenched patriarchal attitudes, gender-based discrimination in recruitment and promotion processes, and the lack of family-friendly policies and support systems that enable women to balance professional and personal responsibilities. Addressing this issue requires a comprehensive approach that combines policy reforms, targeted training and development programs, and efforts to foster more inclusive and equitable organizational cultures.

Efforts to increase women's representation in political leadership and government institutions have taken many forms, from the adoption of quotas and affirmative action policies to the creation of mentorship and training programs for women candidates. Civil society organizations, women's political networks, and international bodies like UN Women have played a crucial role in promoting women's political empowerment through capacity-building, advocacy, and supporting grassroots initiatives.

One notable initiative aimed at increasing women's political participation is the iKNOW Politics platform, a joint initiative of the United Nations, International Knowledge Network of Women in Politics, and several partner organizations. This online resource provides a global hub for knowledge sharing, capacity-building, and networking opportunities for women in political leadership roles. Through forums, webinars, and access to expert resources, the platform aims to equip women with the skills, knowledge, and support networks necessary to navigate the complexities of political processes and decision-making.

One noteworthy initiative aimed at advancing women's political representation is the Global Parliamentary Report, a joint effort by the Inter-Parliamentary Union (IPU) and UN Women. This report provides a comprehensive analysis of women's participation in national parliaments, tracking progress, identifying challenges, and sharing best practices from around the world. By highlighting data and trends, the report serves as a powerful advocacy tool for promoting gender-sensitive policies and reforms, as well as a resource for policymakers, civil society organizations, and other stakeholders working to increase women's political participation and leadership.

In addition to data and analysis, the Global Parliamentary Report also highlights innovative strategies and initiatives from various countries aimed at increasing women's political representation. For example, the report showcases the efforts of the Rwandan Women Parliamentary Forum, which has played a crucial role in advancing gender-sensitive legislation and promoting the participation and leadership of women in Rwanda's political processes. By sharing such best practices and success stories, the report serves as a source of inspiration and guidance for policymakers, civil society organizations, and women's rights advocates worldwide.

One notable success story is the Women's Reservation Bill in India, which mandates that one-third of seats in the national parliament and state legislative assemblies be reserved for women. While the bill has faced considerable resistance and delays in its implementation, it has nonetheless facilitated the entry of more women into the political arena and challenged traditional gender norms.

Despite the challenges in implementing the Women's Reservation Bill in India, its impact has been significant in terms of increasing women's representation at various levels of government. According to data from the Election Commission of India, the percentage of women elected to state legislative assemblies has increased from around 5% in the early 1990s to over 14% in recent elections. This highlights the potential of gender quotas and affirmative action measures to create a critical mass of women in political leadership positions, which can then contribute to shifting societal norms and perceptions.

The experience of the Women's Reservation Bill in India highlights the complex interplay of legislative reforms, political will, and sociocultural factors in advancing women's political representation. While the bill has faced challenges in implementation, it has also sparked important debates and conversations about the role of women in politics, the need for affirmative action measures, and the broader issue of gender equality in Indian society. The journey towards full implementation and the realization of the bill's intended impact underscores the importance of sustained advocacy, capacity-building efforts, and the involvement of diverse stakeholders, including women's rights organizations, political parties, and community leaders.

The experience of the Women's Reservation Bill in India also highlights the importance of addressing the intersectional challenges faced by marginalized women in their pursuit of political representation. Women from disadvantaged communities, such as Dalits, Adivasis, and religious minorities, often face compounded forms of discrimination and barriers to political participation. Initiatives aimed at increasing women's representation must be accompanied by targeted efforts to amplify the voices and address the unique needs of these marginalized groups, ensuring that the benefits of increased representation are inclusive and equitable.

However, quotas and affirmative action policies alone are not a panacea for achieving gender parity in political representation. Addressing the root causes of women's underrepresentation, such as gender-based violence, lack of access to education and economic opportunities, and restrictive social norms, is equally crucial. Additionally, efforts must be made to ensure that women's political participation is not tokenistic but translates into substantive influence and decision-making power.

Ensuring that women's political representation translates into substantive influence and decision-making power requires a multi-pronged approach that addresses various institutional and sociocultural barriers. This may involve initiatives to promote gender-sensitive parliamentary practices and procedures, such as ensuring that women are represented in key committees and leadership positions. Additionally, efforts to challenge and dismantle patriarchal power structures and informal networks that often exclude or marginalize women's voices are crucial. By creating more inclusive and equitable political environments, women can effectively shape policies and decisions that reflect their experiences and priorities.

Beyond numerical representation, it is essential to create an enabling environment that empowers women to effectively participate in and influence decision-making processes. This may involve initiatives such as capacity-building programs that equip women politicians with the skills and knowledge needed to navigate complex policy landscapes, as well as efforts to foster gender-sensitive parliamentary practices and procedures. Additionally, addressing the intersectional challenges faced by marginalized women in politics requires targeted interventions that address their specific needs and experiences, such as language support, disability accommodations, and efforts to combat discrimination and bias based on race, ethnicity, or other identities.

The creation of an enabling environment for women's effective participation in political decision-making also requires efforts to address the barriers and challenges they face outside of formal political institutions. This may involve initiatives to combat gender-based violence and harassment in the political sphere, as well as measures to support women in balancing their political roles with familial and caregiving responsibilities. By addressing these intersecting challenges, policymakers and stakeholders can ensure that women's representation in political leadership translates into meaningful and substantive influence over the policies and decisions that shape their communities and societies.

As we look to the future, it is clear that achieving gender parity in political leadership and government institutions is not only a matter of representation but also a prerequisite for fostering inclusive, sustainable, and just societies. The voices and perspectives of women, in all their diversity, must be at the forefront of decision-making processes to ensure that policies and programs are responsive to the needs and aspirations of all citizens.

As we look towards achieving gender parity in political leadership and decision-making, it is essential to recognize the intersectional nature of gender inequality and the compounded barriers faced by women from marginalized communities. Efforts to increase women's representation must be accompanied by targeted measures to address the unique challenges faced by indigenous women, women with disabilities, LGBTQ+ women, and those from ethnic or religious minority groups. By embracing an intersectional approach and amplifying diverse voices, we can ensure that the benefits of increased representation are truly inclusive and reflective of the diverse experiences and perspectives within societies.

The COVID-19 pandemic has further underscored the importance of inclusive and gender-responsive governance, as the crisis has disproportionately impacted women in various ways, including increased economic insecurity, heightened risks of gender-based violence, and the exacerbation of existing inequalities in healthcare access and caregiving responsibilities. As countries and communities navigate the path to recovery, it is essential that women's voices and leadership are at the forefront, shaping policies and programs that address the gendered impacts of the pandemic and build more resilient and equitable societies.

The COVID-19 pandemic has highlighted the critical importance of gender-responsive governance and the pivotal role that women's leadership can play in addressing crises and shaping effective recovery efforts. A study by the United Nations Development Programme (UNDP) found that countries with higher levels of women's political representation had better responses to the pandemic, including more investment in social protection measures and better communication and trust-building with citizens. This underscores the need to actively promote and support women's leadership in all spheres of decision-making, not only during times of crisis but as a foundational principle for building more resilient and equitable societies.

The path ahead is not without challenges, but the resilience and determination of women leaders and advocates around the world offer a beacon of hope. From grassroots movements to international advocacy efforts, the push for greater women's representation in political leadership and government institutions continues to gain momentum.

As we forge ahead, it is crucial to recognize the intersectionality of gender with other identities and to ensure that the experiences and perspectives of women from diverse backgrounds are reflected in decision-making processes. Intersectional approaches that address the compounded barriers faced by marginalized women must be at the heart of efforts to achieve true gender parity and inclusive governance.

As the global movement for gender equality and women's empowerment continues to gain momentum, it is essential to foster intergenerational collaboration and knowledge-sharing. By engaging and amplifying the voices of young women leaders, activists, and advocates, we can ensure that the struggles and lessons of the past inform and inspire future efforts to create more inclusive and equitable political systems. Simultaneously, we must remain open to the fresh perspectives and innovative approaches brought forth by younger generations, who have the potential to challenge entrenched power structures and drive transformative change.

One promising approach to advancing intersectional representation is the adoption of comprehensive gender and diversity policies within political institutions and governing bodies. These policies can include measures such as targeted recruitment and mentorship programs for women from marginalized communities, the establishment of dedicated seats or quotas for underrepresented groups, and the integration of diversity and inclusion training for all members and staff. By actively promoting and valuing diversity within their ranks, political institutions can better reflect the communities they serve and foster more inclusive and responsive decision-making processes.

The adoption of comprehensive gender and diversity policies within political institutions and governing bodies is not only a matter of representation but also a strategic imperative for fostering more inclusive, responsive, and effective governance. As noted by the Organization for Security and Co-operation in Europe (OSCE), "Diverse and inclusive parliaments better reflect the societies they represent, enhancing their legitimacy and credibility, and contributing to more responsive and effective policymaking." By embracing diversity and promoting the meaningful participation of underrepresented groups, political institutions can tap into a wealth of perspectives, experiences, and knowledge, ultimately leading to more informed and equitable decision-making processes.

The journey towards gender equality in political leadership and government institutions is not just a matter of numbers but a transformative process that challenges entrenched power structures, dismantles systemic biases, and empowers women to shape the course of their communities and nations. It is a journey that requires collective action, sustained commitment, and a unwavering belief in the transformative power of women's leadership.

As we navigate this path, let us draw inspiration from the trailblazers who have paved the way, and let us continue to build upon their legacy. For in the end, the representation of women in positions of power is not merely a matter of equity but a catalyst for creating a more just, inclusive, and sustainable world for all.

As we forge ahead on the journey towards gender parity in political leadership and decision-making, it is essential to recognize the transformative power of women's leadership not only in terms of advancing gender equality but also in addressing the myriad global challenges facing humanity. From climate change and environmental degradation to conflict resolution and peacebuilding, women's perspectives and experiences are invaluable in shaping innovative and sustainable solutions. By actively promoting and supporting women's leadership across all spheres of governance, we can tap into a wellspring of knowledge, resilience, and creativity that can help build a more just, equitable, and sustainable world for all.

155

Chapter 4
Economic Empowerment and Workplace Equality

Section A: Discussion of advancements in women's economic rights and opportunities

Women's economic empowerment represents a crucial cornerstone for the facilitation of societal advancement. Have you stopped to consider the magnitude of change in women's economic rights and opportunities in modern society? This chapter delves into the heart of this transformation, exploring the strides made and the challenges that lie ahead, weaving a narrative of resilience, innovation, and the relentless pursuit of equality.

Imagine a time not so distant when women's financial independence was a notion met with skepticism, even disdain. Yet, today, we stand in an era where women are not only active participants in the workforce but are also influential leaders in business and entrepreneurship. How did we arrive at this juncture, and what does it mean for the fabric of our economies and societies?

The journey toward economic empowerment has been a testament to resilience and tenacity, fueled by legislative reforms that have paved the way for greater gender equality. Laws such as the Equal Pay Act and the Lilly Ledbetter Fair Pay Act in the United States, the Equal Remuneration Act in India, and the Gender Equality Act in Sweden serve as milestones in a long march toward wage parity. While the gender pay gap persists, these laws lay the groundwork for a more equitable workforce, providing women with the legal tools to challenge discriminatory practices and demand fair compensation.

Despite these legal frameworks, the implementation and enforcement of these laws remain a challenge in many parts of the world. Cultural and social norms, deeply entrenched biases, and a lack of awareness and accountability mechanisms often undermine the effectiveness of these laws. Addressing these obstacles requires a multi-stakeholder approach, involving governments, private sector organizations, civil society, and communities themselves. Awareness campaigns, training programs, and robust monitoring and reporting mechanisms are essential to ensure that these laws translate into tangible changes in workplace practices and societal attitudes towards gender equality.

Despite the progress made, the global gender pay gap remains a persistent challenge. According to the World Economic Forum's Global Gender Gap Report 2023, the economic participation and opportunity gap between men and women stands at 60.3% globally. This means that for every dollar earned by a man, a woman earns only 63 cents on average. The reasons behind this disparity are multifaceted, ranging from occupational segregation and lack of access to high-paying fields to unconscious biases and discrimination in hiring and promotion practices. Addressing this issue requires a multi-pronged approach, including pay transparency measures, equal opportunity policies, and targeted initiatives to support women's advancement in male-dominated industries.

The gender pay gap is not just a moral issue but also a significant economic concern. According to a report by the International Labour Organization (ILO), closing the gender pay gap could increase global wealth by $16.8 trillion, highlighting the economic imperative of achieving pay parity. Additionally, research has shown that organizations with greater gender diversity and equal pay practices tend to outperform their counterparts in terms of profitability, innovation, and employee retention. By failing to address the gender pay gap, businesses and economies are missing out on a significant opportunity to unlock the full potential of their workforce and drive sustainable growth.

In the corporate arena, the glass ceiling is showing cracks, thanks to the relentless efforts of trailblazers who defy the odds. Women like

Indra Nooyi, former CEO of PepsiCo, and Mary Barra of General Motors, exemplify the changing tides in corporate leadership. Their ascension to the apex of corporate power is emblematic of a broader trend: the surge of women occupying boardroom seats and executive positions. This shift does not merely add a feminine presence; it brings a diversity of thought that enriches decision-making and drives innovation, fostering a more inclusive and dynamic business environment.

However, the path to the top remains fraught with challenges for many women. A study by McKinsey & Company found that women are more likely to face microaggressions, experience greater scrutiny and higher performance standards, and receive less support and sponsorship than their male counterparts. These challenges often result in a "broken rung" on the corporate ladder, where women are underrepresented in entry-level and mid-level management roles, making it more difficult for them to advance to senior leadership positions. Addressing this issue requires a multi-faceted approach, including unconscious bias training, mentorship and sponsorship programs, and a commitment to creating an inclusive and supportive corporate culture that values diversity and empowers women to thrive.

However, the representation of women in top leadership roles remains low. According to a 2022 report by Catalyst, women held only 6.4% of CEO positions in S&P 500 companies. The numbers are even lower for women of color, who held only 0.8% of these top roles. Breaking through the glass ceiling often requires navigating a complex web of biases, stereotypes, and systemic barriers. Initiatives like leadership development programs, sponsorship opportunities, and policies that promote work-life balance can help pave the way for more women to ascend to leadership positions and shatter the glass ceiling once and for all.

The lack of diversity in leadership roles is not just a missed opportunity for women but also a detriment to organizational performance and innovation. Research by McKinsey & Company has consistently shown that companies in the top quartile for gender diversity on executive teams are 25% more likely to outperform their peers in profitability. Diverse leadership teams bring a broader range of perspectives, experiences, and problem-solving approaches, which can lead to better decision-making, increased creativity, and a deeper understanding of diverse customer bases. By failing to promote and retain diverse talent, organizations risk stifling their potential for growth and innovation.

Consider, too, the rise of female entrepreneurship, facilitated by initiatives that have expanded access to capital, mentorship, and networks for women-owned businesses. Women are starting businesses at an unprecedented rate, bringing forth a kaleidoscope of services and products that reflect their unique perspectives and experiences. From tech startups to sustainable fashion brands, these ventures contribute significantly to economic growth, job creation, and the empowerment of women within their communities.

However, the entrepreneurial landscape is not without its challenges for women. According to a report by the Harvard Business Review, women entrepreneurs face significant biases and skepticism when seeking funding, often being asked more preventive and risk-averse questions than their male counterparts. This bias, coupled with limited access to networks and mentorship opportunities, can hinder the growth and scalability of women-owned businesses. Addressing these challenges requires targeted support programs, such as accelerators and incubators specifically designed for women entrepreneurs, as well as initiatives to increase the representation of women in venture capital and angel investor networks. By fostering a more inclusive and supportive ecosystem for women entrepreneurs, we can unlock their full potential and harness the economic benefits of their innovative ideas and ventures.

The impact of women-owned businesses on economic growth is undeniable. According to a 2019 report by the Boston Consulting Group, if women and men participated equally as entrepreneurs, global GDP could rise by up to 6% or $5 trillion. However, access to funding remains a significant barrier for many women entrepreneurs. Data from Pitchbook shows that in 2022, only 2% of venture capital funding went to companies founded solely by women. Initiatives like gender-lens investing, which evaluates investment opportunities through a gender lens, and dedicated funding programs for women-led businesses can help bridge this gap and unlock the economic potential of female entrepreneurs.

In addition to funding challenges, women entrepreneurs often face unique obstacles in balancing their business and personal responsibilities. A study by the National Women's Business Council found that women entrepreneurs are more likely to prioritize family obligations over business growth, citing challenges such as a lack of affordable childcare and inflexible work arrangements. Addressing these barriers requires a multi-stakeholder approach, involving policymakers, business leaders, and community organizations. Initiatives such as subsidized or on-site childcare facilities, flexible work arrangements, and mentorship programs that provide guidance on work-life integration can help create a more supportive environment for women entrepreneurs to thrive.

What drives these women to embrace the challenges of entrepreneurship? It is a blend of necessity, opportunity, and a desire to carve out spaces where their voices and ideas can thrive. Initiatives such as microfinance programs and targeted business development support have played a crucial role in nurturing this entrepreneurial spirit, particularly in developing economies where women face significant barriers to economic participation.

While microfinance initiatives have been instrumental in providing access to capital for women entrepreneurs in developing economies, their impact has been limited by a lack of complementary support services. Many women entrepreneurs lack access to business training, mentorship, and market linkages, which are essential for scaling their ventures and achieving long-term sustainability. To address this gap, organizations like the Cherie Blair Foundation for Women and the Aspen Network of Development Entrepreneurs (ANDE) have focused on providing holistic support services, including business skills training, access to networks, and market facilitation. By taking a comprehensive approach, these initiatives aim to empower women entrepreneurs not only with financial resources but also with the knowledge and connections needed to navigate the complexities of starting and growing a successful business.

According to a report by the Global Entrepreneurship Monitor, women in developing economies are more likely to pursue entrepreneurship out of necessity rather than opportunity, driven by factors such as unemployment, limited job prospects, and the need to generate income for their families. Microfinance initiatives, like those pioneered by organizations such as Grameen Bank, have been instrumental in providing access to small loans and financial services, enabling women to start and grow their own businesses. These programs not only empower women economically but also foster social and community development, as women entrepreneurs often reinvest their profits into their families and communities.

The impact of microfinance initiatives on women's economic empowerment extends beyond the individual level. By fostering entrepreneurship and financial inclusion, these programs contribute to the overall economic development of communities and nations. A study by the World Bank found that an increase in women's labor force participation can lead to significant reductions in poverty and improved human development outcomes, including better health and education for children. Furthermore, women entrepreneurs often prioritize socially responsible and sustainable business practices, contributing to the overall well-being of their communities and the environment. By investing in women's economic empowerment through microfinance and entrepreneurship support, we not only unlock individual potential but also drive broader social and economic progress.

Financial inclusion is another arena where significant progress has been made. Access to banking services, credit, and financial literacy programs has empowered women to take control of their economic destinies. Organizations like Women's World Banking and initiatives such as the Denarau Action Plan have been instrumental in promoting financial inclusion for women, recognizing that economic empowerment is inextricably linked to access to financial resources and education.

Digital financial services have emerged as a game-changer in promoting financial inclusion for women, particularly in remote and underserved areas. Mobile money platforms, digital banking, and fintech solutions have the potential to overcome barriers such as limited physical access to financial institutions and socio-cultural norms that may restrict women's mobility. However, the gender digital divide remains a significant challenge, with women being less likely to own or have access to mobile phones and the internet. Addressing this divide through initiatives such as the GSMA Connected Women program, which aims to increase women's access to and use of mobile internet, is crucial for ensuring that the benefits of digital financial services are accessible to all women.

Despite the progress, there is still a significant gender gap in financial inclusion. According to the World Bank's Global Findex Database, around 1 billion women remain unbanked, lacking access to formal financial services. This exclusion perpetuates economic marginalization and hinders women's ability to participate fully in economic activities. Closing this gap requires a multifaceted approach that addresses cultural and social barriers, as well as promoting digital financial services and tailored financial products that cater to the unique needs of women. Experts like Inez Murray, CEO of the Global Banking Alliance for Women, emphasize the importance of gender-intelligent product design and targeted marketing strategies to increase women's financial inclusion.

Moreover, the contributions of women-led businesses and industries cannot be overstated. From the vibrant world of fashion and design, where women entrepreneurs have disrupted traditional models, to the rapidly growing green economy, where women are at the forefront of sustainable innovation, the impact of women's economic participation is evident. These enterprises not only generate wealth and employment but also serve as beacons of inspiration, challenging stereotypes and showcasing the transformative power of women's leadership.

The care economy, which encompasses sectors such as healthcare, education, and social services, is another area where women's contributions have been significant. According to the International Labour Organization (ILO), women make up nearly 70% of the global workforce in the care economy. While often undervalued and underpaid, these sectors play a vital role in supporting human development and economic productivity. Recognizing and valuing the contributions of women in the care economy is essential for creating more equitable and sustainable economic systems. Initiatives such as the ILO's Care Work and Care Jobs for the Future of Decent Work programme aim to promote decent work conditions and social protection for care workers, while also highlighting the importance of investing in the care economy as a driver of inclusive and sustainable economic growth.

Women-led businesses are not only contributing to economic growth but also driving innovation and addressing societal challenges. In the fashion industry, companies like Reformation and Rent the Runway, founded by women, have pioneered sustainable and circular business models, challenging the traditional fast-fashion paradigm. In the renewable energy sector, women entrepreneurs like Inga Wetzer, founder of Wair, are developing innovative solutions to provide clean air and water in underserved communities. These examples demonstrate the potential of women-led enterprises to create positive social and environmental impact while generating economic value.

The intersection of women's economic empowerment and environmental sustainability is becoming increasingly important in the face of climate change and environmental degradation. Women, particularly in developing countries, are often disproportionately affected by the impacts of climate change due to their reliance on natural resources and vulnerability to extreme weather events. At the same time, women are emerging as leaders in the fight against climate change, driving sustainable practices and advocating for climate action. Organizations like the Women's Earth Alliance and the Global Alliance for Clean Cookstoves are supporting women-led initiatives that address environmental challenges while creating economic opportunities. By promoting women's leadership in the green economy, we can unlock innovative solutions that address both environmental and economic challenges simultaneously.

Education and vocational training have been cornerstones of economic advancement for women, equipping them with the necessary skills and knowledge to compete in the global marketplace. Initiatives like the United Nations Girls' Education Initiative (UNGEI) and the World Bank's Skills Development and Opportunities for Work for Women program have focused on providing education and training opportunities, particularly in fields traditionally dominated by men, such as STEM (Science, Technology, Engineering, and Mathematics).

Beyond access to education, the quality and relevance of curricula and teaching methods play a crucial role in preparing women for the workforce of the future. Initiatives like the STEM and Gender Advancement (SAGA) project by the United Nations Educational, Scientific and Cultural Organization (UNESCO) aim to develop gender-responsive STEM curricula and pedagogies, addressing gender biases and stereotypes that often discourage girls and women from pursuing STEM careers. By fostering inclusive and engaging learning environments, these initiatives aim to nurture the next generation of female scientists, engineers, and innovators, who will drive economic growth and address global challenges through their skills and expertise.

However, significant gender disparities persist in access to quality education and training opportunities. According to UNESCO, around 130 million girls worldwide are out of school, and women represent only 28% of graduates in STEM fields. Addressing these gaps is crucial for unlocking women's economic potential and fostering a diverse and skilled workforce. Initiatives like the African Development Bank's Coding for Employment program, which provides digital skills training to young African women, are examples of targeted efforts to bridge this gap and create pathways for women's economic empowerment through education and skill development.

The COVID-19 pandemic has further exacerbated existing educational disparities, with school closures and disruptions disproportionately affecting girls and women. According to a report by the Malala Fund, 20 million more secondary school-aged girls could be out of school after the pandemic, putting them at higher risk of early marriage, violence, and economic insecurity. Addressing this setback requires targeted interventions, such as remote learning initiatives, catch-up programs, and support services that address the unique challenges faced by girls and young women during the pandemic. By prioritizing gender-responsive educational recovery efforts, we can ensure that the gains made in women's education and economic empowerment are not reversed, and that future generations of women have access to the skills and opportunities necessary for their full economic participation.

Technology and digitalization have also played a pivotal role in creating new economic opportunities for women. The rise of remote work, e-commerce platforms, and the gig economy has opened doors for women to participate in the workforce while balancing other responsibilities. Digital literacy and access to technology have become crucial enablers, empowering women to leverage online platforms for entrepreneurship, skill development, and financial services.

The power of digital technologies in promoting women's economic empowerment is multifaceted. E-commerce platforms, for instance, have lowered barriers to entry for women entrepreneurs, allowing them to reach global markets and bypass traditional distribution channels that may be dominated by men. Online marketplaces like Etsy and Shopify have enabled women to turn their skills and hobbies into thriving businesses, providing them with economic opportunities and financial independence. Additionally, the gig economy, facilitated by platforms like Upwork and Fiverr, has opened up new avenues for women to freelance and offer their services, providing flexibility and control over their work schedules.

The COVID-19 pandemic has further accelerated the adoption of digital technologies and remote work, presenting both opportunities and challenges for women's economic participation. On one hand, the increased flexibility and accessibility of remote work have enabled many women to maintain employment and balance caregiving responsibilities. On the other hand, the digital divide and lack of access to technology and digital skills have exacerbated existing inequalities, leaving many women behind. Bridging this digital divide through initiatives like the EQUALS Global Partnership, which aims to close the gender digital divide, is crucial for ensuring that women can fully benefit from the economic opportunities presented by technological advancements.

The COVID-19 pandemic has also highlighted the importance of digital skills for women's economic resilience. As businesses and services moved online, those with strong digital literacy and remote work capabilities were better positioned to adapt and maintain their economic activities. However, many women, particularly in developing countries and rural areas, lack access to digital training and resources, hindering their ability to navigate the digital economy. Initiatives like the WorldBank's Digital Skills for Girls and Women program, which provides training in areas such as coding, digital marketing, and cybersecurity, are crucial for equipping women with the skills they need to thrive in the digital age and build economic resilience in the face of future disruptions.

Yet, despite these advancements, the landscape is not devoid of obstacles. Women still face disproportionate hurdles in accessing capital, mentoring, and networks that are critical for scaling their businesses. Societal biases, gender norms, and the unequal distribution of unpaid care work continue to hinder women's economic participation and advancement. The COVID-19 pandemic has further exacerbated these challenges, with women disproportionately impacted by job losses, increased caregiving responsibilities, and the disruption of women-owned businesses.

One of the significant challenges faced by women entrepreneurs is the lack of access to mentorship and networks. According to a study by the Boston Consulting Group, women entrepreneurs often lack access to role models and mentors who can provide guidance, support, and connections to resources and opportunities. This lack of mentorship can lead to feelings of isolation and hinder the growth and scalability of women-owned businesses. Initiatives like the Global Mentorship Initiative by Vital Voices, which connects women entrepreneurs with experienced mentors from around the world, are addressing this gap and providing women with the support and guidance they need to navigate the complexities of entrepreneurship.

The burden of unpaid care work, such as childcare and household duties, disproportionately falls on women, hindering their economic opportunities and advancement. According to a report by Oxfam, women globally perform at least 12.5 billion hours of unpaid care work each day, equivalent to a staggering $10.8 trillion in annual economic value. Addressing this issue requires a multi-faceted approach, including promoting shared responsibility within households, providing affordable and accessible childcare services, and implementing family-friendly workplace policies that support work-life balance for working mothers.

The unequal distribution of unpaid care work not only hinders women's economic participation but also perpetuates gender inequalities and reinforces traditional gender roles. Women who shoulder a disproportionate share of care work often face challenges in advancing their careers, starting businesses, or pursuing educational opportunities. This burden can also have negative impacts on their physical and mental well-being, further exacerbating existing inequalities. Addressing this issue requires a multi-stakeholder approach involving governments, employers, and communities to promote cultural shifts, implement supportive policies, and invest in accessible and affordable care infrastructure.

The intersection of women's economic rights with other social and cultural factors, such as gender norms, access to childcare, and work-life balance policies, cannot be ignored. Efforts to promote women's economic empowerment must be holistic, addressing the multidimensional barriers that women face. This includes challenging deeply rooted gender stereotypes, providing affordable and accessible childcare solutions, and implementing family-friendly workplace policies that support working mothers.

One of the key social and cultural factors that impact women's economic empowerment is the lack of decision-making power within households and communities. In many contexts, women have limited agency and autonomy in making decisions about their education, employment, and financial resources. This lack of decision-making power can perpetuate gender inequalities and hinder women's ability to fully participate in economic activities. Addressing this issue requires a multifaceted approach that involves engaging with local communities, challenging traditional gender norms, and promoting women's leadership and participation in decision-making processes at all levels.

Gender stereotypes and social norms play a significant role in shaping societal attitudes and expectations towards women's economic participation. Traditional gender roles and the perception of women as primary caregivers often create biases and barriers in the workplace, limiting their opportunities for advancement and leadership roles. Dismantling these deeply ingrained stereotypes requires a concerted effort from all stakeholders, including policymakers, educational institutions, media, and the private sector. Initiatives like the UN Women's HeForShe campaign, which engages men and boys as allies in promoting gender equality, can help shift mindsets and create a more inclusive and supportive environment for women's economic empowerment.

The media plays a crucial role in shaping and reinforcing gender stereotypes and social norms. Negative portrayals of women in media, advertising, and popular culture can perpetuate harmful stereotypes and reinforce traditional gender roles. On the other hand, positive representations of women as leaders, entrepreneurs, and breadwinners can challenge these stereotypes and inspire change. Initiatives like the Unstereotype Alliance, a coalition of organizations committed to promoting positive and non-stereotypical portrayals of women in media and advertising, are working to change the narrative and create a more inclusive and empowering media landscape for women.

International organizations like the World Bank, the International Labour Organization (ILO), and UN Women have played a crucial role in promoting women's economic empowerment through policies, funding, and capacity-building initiatives. The World Bank's Gender Strategy, for instance, aims to remove barriers to women's ownership of productive assets, increase their access to quality jobs, and promote their participation in decision-making roles. These global efforts have fostered international cooperation and knowledge-sharing, recognizing that gender equality is not only a moral imperative but also a key driver of sustainable economic growth and development.

While international organizations have made significant contributions, the private sector also has a critical role to play in promoting women's economic empowerment. Companies that prioritize gender diversity, equal pay, and inclusive workplace policies not only contribute to social progress but also benefit from increased productivity, innovation, and employee retention. Initiatives like the United Nations Global Compact's Women's Empowerment Principles provide a framework for businesses to promote gender equality and support women's economic participation through policies and practices such as non-discrimination, equal pay, and leadership development programs. By aligning their practices with these principles, companies can create more equitable and inclusive workplaces, while also contributing to the broader goal of sustainable economic development.

While international organizations have made significant contributions, the involvement of national governments and local stakeholders is equally crucial for driving sustainable change. Countries like Rwanda and Iceland have emerged as global leaders in promoting gender equality and women's economic empowerment through comprehensive policy frameworks and targeted initiatives. Rwanda, for instance, has implemented gender-responsive budgeting and has one of the highest rates of women's participation in parliament, while Iceland has consistently ranked among the top countries in the World Economic Forum's Global Gender Gap Report, thanks to its robust policies and commitment to gender equality.

In addition to national governments, local civil society organizations and grassroots movements play a critical role in driving change and advocating for women's economic empowerment. These organizations often have a deep understanding of the specific challenges and contexts faced by women in their communities and can tailor their interventions accordingly. For example, organizations like SEWA (Self-Employed Women's Association) in India have been instrumental in organizing and empowering women in the informal sector, providing them with access to resources, training, and advocacy support. By engaging with local stakeholders and amplifying the voices of women themselves, these grassroots efforts can drive sustainable and context-specific change.

As we reflect on the advancements in women's economic rights and opportunities, it is essential to recognize that progress is a mosaic, with each strand representing the diverse experiences and challenges faced by women across different regions, cultures, and socio-economic contexts. The overarching trend is one of forward momentum, punctuated by the determination and achievements of women from all walks of life who have defied odds, challenged norms, and carved out spaces for themselves in the economic landscape.

It is also important to recognize that women's economic empowerment is not just a women's issue; it is a societal issue that affects us all. When women are economically empowered, they can contribute more to their families, communities, and the overall economic growth of their countries. Studies have shown that increased income in the hands of women leads to better investments in education, health, and nutrition, creating a ripple effect that benefits entire communities. By promoting women's economic empowerment, we are not only advancing gender equality but also fostering inclusive and sustainable development that benefits society as a whole.

The experiences of women in conflict-affected regions and fragile states present unique challenges that require targeted interventions. In these contexts, women often face heightened vulnerabilities, including displacement, gender-based violence, and limited access to education and economic opportunities. Organizations like the International Rescue Committee (IRC) and the Women's Refugee Commission have focused on providing livelihood support, vocational training, and entrepreneurship programs to empower women in these settings, recognizing that economic empowerment is a crucial pathway to rebuilding lives and communities.

In conflict-affected regions and fragile states, women's economic empowerment is not only a means for individual advancement but also a critical component of peacebuilding and post-conflict reconstruction efforts. When women are economically empowered, they are better equipped to participate in decision-making processes, advocate for their rights, and contribute to the rebuilding of their communities. Initiatives like the United Nations Trust Fund to End Violence against Women have supported projects that combine economic empowerment with efforts to address gender-based violence and promote women's leadership in peacebuilding processes. By taking a holistic approach that integrates economic empowerment with other aspects of women's rights and well-being, these interventions can contribute to sustainable and lasting peace and security.

However, the path ahead is not without obstacles. Persistent gender disparities in access to education, financial resources, and leadership opportunities continue to impede women's full economic potential. Addressing these challenges requires a multifaceted approach that involves policy reforms, targeted investments, and a fundamental shift in societal attitudes and cultural norms that have historically marginalized women's economic participation.

One of the persistent obstacles to women's economic empowerment is the lack of legal and property rights in many parts of the world. According to the World Bank, over 90 countries have at least one law that restricts women's economic opportunities, including limitations on their ability to own and inherit property, access credit, or pursue certain occupations. These legal barriers not only hinder women's economic participation but also perpetuate gender inequalities and reinforce patriarchal power structures. Addressing these issues requires comprehensive legal reforms, coupled with awareness campaigns and enforcement mechanisms to ensure that women's economic rights are protected and upheld.

Climate change and environmental degradation are emerging as significant threats to women's economic empowerment, particularly in regions where women's livelihoods are closely tied to natural resources and agriculture. The disproportionate impact of climate change on women, exacerbated by existing gender inequalities, highlights the need for gender-responsive climate action and policies that support women's resilience and economic opportunities in the face of environmental challenges. Initiatives like the Green Climate Fund's Gender Policy, which aims to mainstream gender considerations into climate finance and project design, are crucial steps in this direction.

In addition to the direct impacts of climate change on women's livelihoods, there is also a need to address the gendered impacts of environmental degradation and resource scarcity. In many parts of the world, women are responsible for collecting water, firewood, and other natural resources for their households. As these resources become scarcer due to environmental degradation, women often bear the brunt of the burden, spending more time and energy on these tasks, which can hinder their ability to engage in economic activities or pursue educational opportunities. Initiatives that promote sustainable resource management, access to clean energy, and water security not only address environmental concerns but also contribute to women's economic empowerment by reducing their unpaid labor burdens.

Let this chapter serve as a testament to the progress made and an acknowledgment of the work that remains. For every barrier broken, new opportunities blossom—opportunities that hold the promise of a world where women's economic empowerment is not an aspiration but a reality. Our collective efforts to nurture and expand these gains will determine the pace at which we move toward that equitable future, where the economic rights and opportunities of women are woven into the very fabric of our societies, strengthening and enriching our economies and communities.

While the path ahead is challenging, it is essential to remember that the pursuit of women's economic empowerment is not merely a moral imperative but also a catalyst for sustainable development and economic growth. Studies have consistently shown that empowering women and promoting gender equality can lead to higher productivity, increased household income, and improved health and educational outcomes for families and communities. By investing in women's economic empowerment, we are not only upholding fundamental human rights but also unlocking the untapped potential of half the world's population, driving innovation, and fostering more inclusive and prosperous societies.

As we move forward, it is essential to celebrate the achievements and resilience of women who have broken barriers and paved the way for future generations. Their stories of courage, determination, and excellence serve as inspiration and a reminder that change is possible when we work together towards a common goal. By amplifying the voices and experiences of these trailblazers, we can inspire others to follow in their footsteps and continue the momentum for women's economic empowerment, creating a ripple effect that transcends borders and generations.

The pursuit of women's economic empowerment is not merely a journey towards gender equality; it is a transformative force that has the power to reshape entire societies and economies. By unlocking the full potential of women, we create a world where diverse perspectives and talents are celebrated, where innovation thrives, and where no one is left behind. It is a journey that requires collective action, unwavering commitment, and a shared vision of a more just and equitable world for all. As we embark on this journey together, let us be guided by the principles of inclusivity, resilience, and a steadfast belief in the power of women to shape a better future for themselves, their families, and their communities.

Section B: Analysis of gender wage gap trends and efforts to achieve pay equity

As we delve into the intricacies of the gender wage gap, we must ask ourselves: How far have we come in bridging this economic divide, and what catalysts are driving us toward the elusive goal of pay equity? This chapter seeks to unravel the complex web of wage disparities, charting the trends and highlighting the concerted efforts to balance the scales of economic justice.

The persistence of the gender wage gap is a global phenomenon, with variations across regions and countries. According to the International Labour Organization (ILO), the global gender pay gap stands at 20%, with women earning approximately 80% of what men earn for work of equal value. In some regions, the gap is even wider, such as in South Asia, where women earned only 62% of men's earnings in 2019. These disparities not only undermine women's economic empowerment but also hinder overall economic growth and development, as women's earning potential and purchasing power are suppressed.

The global prevalence of the gender wage gap is not only an economic issue but also a reflection of deeply rooted systemic inequalities and gender discrimination that persist across societies.

Despite international commitments and efforts to achieve gender equality, such as the United Nations Sustainable Development Goals and the Convention on the Elimination of All Forms of Discrimination Against Women (CEDAW), the wage gap remains a persistent challenge, highlighting the need for sustained and concerted action at all levels to address the underlying structural barriers and biases that perpetuate this economic disparity.

The persistence of the gender wage gap is not only an economic issue but also a reflection of deeply rooted social and cultural norms that perpetuate gender discrimination and inequality. In many societies, traditional gender roles and expectations continue to shape perceptions about women's role in the workforce, leading to biases and discrimination that contribute to the wage gap. Addressing this issue requires a comprehensive approach that challenges societal attitudes, promotes gender equality in education and employment, and fosters an inclusive and enabling environment for women's economic participation.

The economic consequences of the gender wage gap are far-reaching and extend beyond individual earnings. According to a report by the McKinsey Global Institute, closing the gender pay gap could add $13 trillion to global GDP by 2030. This highlights the significant economic opportunities that are being missed due to the underutilization and undervaluation of women's labor and contributions. By addressing the gender wage gap, economies can unlock this untapped potential and drive sustainable growth, benefiting individuals, businesses, and societies as a whole.

The gender wage gap, a stubborn and pervasive issue, is the differential in earnings between women and men. Despite considerable progress, the chasm persists, varying in depth across different industries, regions, and demographics. In the United States, for instance, women earned approximately 83 cents for every dollar earned by men in 2022, according to data from the U.S. Census Bureau. However, this national average masks significant variations across different racial and ethnic groups, with Black and Hispanic women facing even wider wage gaps compared to their white counterparts.

The persistence of the gender wage gap across industries and regions highlights the complex and multifaceted nature of this issue. While some sectors, such as finance and technology, have made strides in addressing pay disparities, others, like the service industry and manufacturing, continue to grapple with significant wage gaps. Similarly, certain regions and countries have been more proactive in implementing policies and initiatives to promote pay equity, while others lag behind. Addressing these variations requires a nuanced understanding of the specific factors contributing to the wage gap in different contexts and tailoring strategies accordingly.

The gender wage gap is not a static phenomenon but rather a dynamic issue that evolves over the course of a woman's career. Research has shown that the wage gap often widens as women progress in their careers, particularly in fields and industries where gender biases and discrimination are more prevalent. This "career wage gap" reflects the cumulative impact of various factors, including occupational segregation, the "motherhood penalty," and the persistent undervaluation of traditionally female-dominated occupations. Addressing this dynamic aspect of the wage gap requires a holistic approach that addresses the systemic barriers and biases women face at different stages of their careers.

The gender wage gap is not just a static statistic but a dynamic phenomenon that evolves over the course of a woman's career. Research has shown that the wage gap often widens as women progress in their careers, with the disparity becoming more pronounced at higher levels of management and leadership roles. This phenomenon, known as the "glass ceiling effect," reflects the persistent barriers and biases that hinder women's advancement and equal compensation as they climb the corporate ladder. Addressing this issue requires targeted efforts to promote women's leadership development, mentorship, and a commitment to pay transparency at all levels of an organization.

Intersectionality plays a crucial role in understanding the nuances of the gender wage gap. The experiences of women from marginalized communities, such as women of color, LGBTQ+ women, and women with disabilities, are often compounded by multiple forms of discrimination and systemic barriers. For example, according to the National Women's Law Center, Black women in the United States earned only 64 cents for every dollar earned by white, non-Hispanic men in 2021. This intersectional lens highlights the need for tailored strategies that address the unique challenges faced by diverse groups of women in the pursuit of pay equity.

The intersectional nature of the gender wage gap is further compounded by factors such as socioeconomic status, educational attainment, and family status. Women from low-income backgrounds, those with lower levels of education, and single mothers often face heightened economic vulnerabilities and barriers to equal pay, reflecting the intersecting forms of marginalization and discrimination they experience. Addressing this intersectionality requires a comprehensive approach that acknowledges and addresses the multiple and overlapping systems of oppression that contribute to wage disparities for diverse groups of women.

The intersectional nature of the gender wage gap is further compounded by factors such as immigration status, age, and geographic location. Immigrant women, particularly those from developing countries, often face significant barriers to economic integration, including language barriers, lack of recognition of foreign credentials, and limited access to professional networks. Similarly, older women and women living in rural or remote areas may encounter additional obstacles, such as age discrimination, limited job opportunities, and restricted access to resources and support services. Addressing these intersectional challenges requires a nuanced and context-specific approach that considers the unique experiences and needs of diverse groups of women.

The intersectional nature of the gender wage gap extends beyond race and ethnicity, encompassing various other identities and social factors. For instance, women with disabilities often face compounded barriers to employment, lower wages, and limited opportunities for advancement due to the intersection of gender discrimination and ableism. Similarly, LGBTQ+ women may confront additional challenges and biases related to their sexual orientation or gender identity, further exacerbating the wage disparities they experience.

Addressing these intersectional wage gaps requires a holistic approach that recognizes and addresses the multiple and overlapping forms of discrimination and marginalization that diverse groups of women face.

Statistics speak volumes, but the stories behind the numbers reveal the nuanced reality of this economic imbalance. What factors contribute to this wage gap, and how do they intertwine with the broader narrative of women's rights?

One significant factor contributing to the gender wage gap is the unequal distribution of unpaid care work, which disproportionately falls on women. According to a report by Oxfam, women globally perform at least 12.5 billion hours of unpaid care work each day, equivalent to a staggering $10.8 trillion in annual economic value. This unpaid labor, often overlooked and undervalued, can lead to career interruptions, reduced work hours, and limited opportunities for advancement, ultimately impacting women's earning potential and perpetuating the wage gap.

The burden of unpaid care work is not only an economic issue but also a reflection of deeply ingrained gender norms and societal expectations that place the responsibility for caregiving disproportionately on women. These norms are reinforced across various institutions and domains, including families, communities, and workplaces, perpetuating the notion that caregiving is primarily a woman's responsibility. Challenging these norms and promoting a more equitable distribution of care work requires a multifaceted approach that involves transformative policies, public awareness campaigns, and a fundamental shift in societal attitudes toward gender roles and caregiving responsibilities.

The burden of unpaid care work is not evenly distributed across all women, with women from lower socioeconomic backgrounds and women of color often shouldering a disproportionate share of this invisible labor. This unequal distribution of care responsibilities is rooted in intersecting forms of discrimination and systemic inequalities, including poverty, lack of access to affordable childcare and elder care services, and deeply ingrained cultural norms and gender stereotypes. Addressing this issue requires a comprehensive and intersectional approach that tackles the root causes of these inequalities and promotes a more equitable distribution of care responsibilities within households, communities, and society as a whole.

The burden of unpaid care work is not evenly distributed across all women, with women from lower socioeconomic backgrounds and women of color often shouldering a disproportionate share of this invisible labor. This unequal distribution of care responsibilities not only exacerbates existing economic inequalities but also reinforces gender norms and stereotypes about women's roles as primary caregivers. Addressing this issue requires a multifaceted approach that includes promoting more equitable distribution of care work within households, investing in accessible and affordable childcare and elder care services, and challenging societal attitudes that perpetuate the devaluation of care work.

To paint a vivid picture, let us consider a day in the life of a working woman. Dawn breaks, and with it comes the balancing act of professional responsibilities and, often, unpaid care duties. A mother readies her children for school before she herself heads to work, where her salary does not reflect her equal contribution to that of her male counterparts. Why is her paycheck lighter? Is it the echo of historical undervaluation of women's work, or perhaps the consequence of a career interrupted by maternity leaves or part-time work to tend to family needs?

The challenges faced by working mothers in balancing career and caregiving responsibilities are not just a personal struggle but a manifestation of broader systemic issues. The lack of affordable and accessible childcare options, inadequate family-friendly policies in the workplace, and societal expectations around gender roles all contribute to the "second shift" of unpaid labor that many working mothers face. This double burden not only hinders women's economic advancement but also perpetuates the devaluation of caregiving work, reinforcing the cycle of gender inequality in both the public and private spheres.

The challenges faced by working mothers in balancing career and caregiving responsibilities are exacerbated by the lack of supportive workplace policies and practices. In many countries, insufficient paid parental leave provisions, limited access to affordable and high-quality childcare, and the prevalence of inflexible work arrangements create significant barriers for women trying to maintain their careers while raising families. These systemic obstacles not only contribute to the gender wage gap but also reinforce the perception that caregiving responsibilities are primarily a woman's burden, perpetuating gender stereotypes and norms that ultimately hinder women's economic empowerment and gender equality in the workplace.

The challenges faced by working mothers in managing the "second shift" of unpaid care work and household responsibilities can have a profound impact on their career trajectories and earning potential. Research has shown that women are more likely than men to take career breaks or reduce their working hours to accommodate caregiving responsibilities, resulting in lower lifetime earnings and reduced opportunities for advancement. Moreover, the lack of affordable and accessible childcare options can further limit women's ability to participate fully in the workforce, exacerbating the wage gap. Addressing this issue requires a multi-stakeholder approach that involves employers, policymakers, and societal shifts in attitudes towards shared caregiving responsibilities.

The impact of motherhood on the wage gap is well-documented. According to a study by the National Bureau of Economic Research, women in the United States experience a "motherhood penalty" in earnings, with mothers earning around 5% less per child compared to childless women. This penalty can be attributed to factors such as reduced work hours, career interruptions, and discrimination in hiring and promotion practices. Conversely, men often experience a "fatherhood premium," with their earnings increasing after having children, reflecting societal biases and assumptions about gender roles and breadwinning responsibilities.

The "motherhood penalty" and the "fatherhood premium" are not just economic phenomena but also reflect deeply entrenched societal attitudes and expectations about gender roles and caregiving responsibilities. These societal biases often manifest in workplace policies and practices that privilege men's career advancement while penalizing women for taking on caregiving responsibilities. Addressing this issue requires a comprehensive approach that challenges traditional gender norms, promotes shared caregiving responsibilities, and fosters inclusive and family-friendly workplace cultures that support both working mothers and fathers.

The "motherhood penalty" and the "fatherhood premium" are not merely statistical observations but reflect deeply ingrained societal attitudes and expectations about gender roles and caregiving responsibilities. These societal biases often manifest in workplace policies and practices that privilege men's career advancement while penalizing women for taking on caregiving responsibilities. Addressing this issue requires a comprehensive approach that challenges traditional gender norms, promotes shared caregiving responsibilities, and fosters inclusive and family-friendly workplace cultures that support both working mothers and fathers. This includes measures such as paid parental leave for all genders, accessible and affordable childcare options, and flexible work arrangements that enable both parents to balance work and family responsibilities.

The "motherhood penalty" is not a uniform experience for all women, as the severity of the wage gap can vary based on factors such as race, socioeconomic status, and educational attainment. For instance, research has shown that highly educated women and women in high-paying professions often face a steeper "motherhood penalty" compared to their counterparts in lower-paying occupations. This disparity highlights the need for targeted policies and workplace practices that support and accommodate working mothers across various socioeconomic and professional backgrounds, ensuring that the pursuit of motherhood does not come at the cost of economic security and career advancement.

Occupational segregation remains a significant factor in perpetuating the wage gap. Women are overrepresented in sectors traditionally associated with lower pay, such as education, healthcare, and social services. These fields are vital to society's fabric, yet the remuneration does not mirror their societal value. Conversely, men dominate the higher-paying STEM fields. Initiatives like the European Union's Science: It's a Girl Thing campaign have aimed to steer more girls and young women into these lucrative paths, but their impact has been limited by entrenched gender stereotypes and societal norms.

The issue of occupational segregation is not limited to the traditional divide between "pink-collar" and "blue-collar" jobs but also extends to the underrepresentation of women in leadership and decision-making roles across various sectors and industries. Despite progress in educational attainment and workforce participation, women remain underrepresented in top management and executive positions, reflecting the persistent barriers and biases that hinder their career advancement and progression into higher-paying roles. Addressing this issue requires a multi-pronged approach that includes leadership development programs, mentorship initiatives, and a concerted effort to dismantle the systemic biases and organizational cultures that perpetuate gender-based career obstacles.

The issue of occupational segregation extends beyond the traditional divide between "pink-collar" and "blue-collar" jobs. Within many industries and professions, there exists a vertical segregation, where women are disproportionately concentrated in lower-level positions while men occupy the higher-paying leadership and executive roles. This vertical segregation can be attributed to various factors, including unconscious biases in performance evaluations, limited access to mentorship and sponsorship opportunities, and the persistence of gender-based stereotypes about leadership abilities. Addressing this issue requires a multi-pronged approach that includes leadership development programs, transparent promotion practices, and a commitment to fostering an inclusive organizational culture that values and promotes diverse leadership.

The undervaluation of traditionally female-dominated occupations is a significant contributor to the gender wage gap. Professions like childcare, nursing, and teaching, which are crucial for societal well-being, are often underpaid and underappreciated, reflecting deeply ingrained biases about the value of "women's work."

Addressing this issue requires a fundamental shift in how we value and compensate different types of work, challenging the societal norms and biases that have historically devalued occupations dominated by women.

The undervaluation of female-dominated occupations is not solely an economic issue but also reflects broader societal attitudes and cultural norms surrounding gender roles and the value placed on traditionally "feminine" work. These occupations are often perceived as extensions of unpaid caregiving and domestic labor, leading to the devaluation of the skills, expertise, and emotional labor required for these professions. Challenging this perception requires a concerted effort to reframe the narrative around these occupations, highlighting their essential contributions to societal well-being and advocating for fair compensation that recognizes the true value of this work. This includes initiatives such as public awareness campaigns, educational programs, and policy reforms that promote the recognition and valorization of traditionally undervalued occupations.

The undervaluation of female-dominated occupations is not only an economic issue but also a reflection of deeply rooted gender norms and societal attitudes. These occupations, often associated with caregiving and nurturing roles, are perceived as "natural" extensions of women's societal roles, leading to a devaluation of the skills, effort, and expertise required for these professions. Challenging this perception requires a concerted effort to reframe the narrative around these occupations, highlighting their value and importance to societal well-being, and advocating for fair compensation that reflects the true worth of these professions.

The pursuit of pay equity is multifaceted, involving legislation, corporate governance, and grassroots activism. Laws such as the aforementioned Equal Pay Act laid the foundation, yet enforcement and loopholes leave room for the wage gap to thrive. Pay transparency, where companies are required to disclose salary data and compensation practices, has emerged as a powerful tool in this battle. Countries like the United Kingdom have implemented mandatory gender pay gap reporting for large employers, shining a light on disparities and prompting organizations to take corrective action.

While pay transparency initiatives have been instrumental in raising awareness and driving accountability, their effectiveness is often contingent upon robust enforcement mechanisms and a genuine commitment from employers to address identified disparities. In some cases, the lack of meaningful consequences or penalties for non-compliance has limited the impact of pay transparency measures. To fully realize the potential of these initiatives, a comprehensive approach is needed, combining pay transparency requirements with robust enforcement mechanisms, targeted training and support for employers, and a commitment to fostering a culture of equity and inclusivity within organizations. This requires collaborative efforts between policymakers, employers, labor unions, and civil society organizations to create an enabling environment for pay equity and promote accountability at all levels.

While pay transparency initiatives have been instrumental in raising awareness and holding employers accountable, their implementation and effectiveness have faced challenges. In some cases, employers have found ways to circumvent reporting requirements or present data in a way that obscures significant disparities. Additionally, the voluntary nature of many pay transparency measures has led to uneven adoption and limited impact in some sectors or regions. To fully harness the potential of pay transparency, there is a need for robust enforcement mechanisms, standardized reporting practices, and a commitment to using the data to drive meaningful change in compensation practices and organizational cultures.

Consider the role of negotiation in salary discussions. Conventional wisdom suggests that women are less likely to negotiate their pay. However, research indicates that women do negotiate but are often met with social backlash or perceive the negotiations as futile due to deeply rooted gender biases. Empowerment programs aiming to bolster women's negotiation skills are on the rise, but the question lingers: Should the onus be on women to advocate for fair pay, or should systemic changes pave the way for equity?

The debate around negotiation and pay equity raises deeper questions about the systemic nature of the gender wage gap and the responsibilities of various stakeholders in addressing it. While empowering women with negotiation skills is valuable, some experts argue that this approach places an undue burden on individual women to overcome deeply entrenched societal biases and power dynamics. Instead, they advocate for a more comprehensive approach that focuses on transforming organizational cultures, implementing transparent and objective compensation systems, and addressing the underlying structural barriers that perpetuate the wage gap. This perspective recognizes that pay equity is not solely an individual negotiation issue but a systemic challenge that requires collective action and commitment from employers, policymakers, and society as a whole.

The debate around negotiation and pay equity raises deeper questions about the systemic nature of the gender wage gap and the responsibilities of various stakeholders in addressing it. While empowering women with negotiation skills is valuable, some experts argue that this approach places an undue burden on individual women to overcome deeply entrenched societal biases and power dynamics. Instead, they advocate for a more comprehensive approach that focuses on transforming organizational cultures, implementing transparent and objective compensation systems, and addressing the underlying structural barriers that perpetuate the wage gap. This perspective recognizes that pay equity is not solely an individual negotiation issue but a systemic challenge that requires collective action and commitment from employers, policymakers, and society as a whole.

While negotiation skills are valuable, experts argue that the responsibility for pay equity should not solely fall on women's shoulders. Dr. Linda Babcock, an economist and author of "Women Don't Ask," emphasizes the need for systemic changes in organizational policies and practices to address the underlying biases and barriers that hinder women's advancement and fair compensation. This includes implementing transparent and objective pay structures, conducting regular pay equity audits, and fostering an inclusive culture that values and rewards equitable pay practices.

The effectiveness of systemic changes in organizational policies and practices hinges on a genuine commitment from leadership and a willingness to confront and address unconscious biases and deeply ingrained cultural norms. This requires more than just surface-level initiatives or tokenism; it demands a fundamental shift in mindsets, values, and decision-making processes. Organizations that truly prioritize pay equity must be willing to invest in comprehensive training programs, adopt data-driven decision-making practices, and foster an inclusive culture that empowers and celebrates diversity. By taking a holistic and sustained approach, organizations can create a lasting impact on pay equity and build a more equitable and inclusive workplace for all.

The effectiveness of systemic changes in organizational policies and practices hinges on a genuine commitment from leadership and a willingness to confront and address unconscious biases and deeply ingrained cultural norms. This requires more than just surface-level initiatives or tokenism; it demands a fundamental shift in mindsets, values, and decision-making processes. Organizations that truly prioritize pay equity must be willing to invest in comprehensive training programs, adopt data-driven decision-making practices, and foster an inclusive culture that empowers and celebrates diversity. By taking a holistic and sustained approach, organizations can create a lasting impact on pay equity and build a more equitable and inclusive workplace for all.

True progress lies in dismantling the barriers that inhibit equitable remuneration. In this effort, labor unions and collective bargaining have played a vital role in advocating for fair wages, better working conditions, and addressing gender-based discrimination in the workplace. Unions like the American Federation of Teachers and the Service Employees International Union have been at the forefront of the fight for pay equity, leveraging their collective power to negotiate better contracts and push for policy reforms.

While labor unions have been instrumental in advocating for pay equity, their influence and impact have faced challenges in recent decades. Declining union membership rates, particularly in the private sector, have weakened the collective bargaining power of unions in some industries and regions. Additionally, anti-union legislation and efforts to undermine collective bargaining rights have posed further obstacles. To maintain their effectiveness in the fight for pay equity, labor unions must adapt their strategies, build broader coalitions, and continue to advocate for policies and practices that support fair compensation and protect workers' rights, regardless of gender or other protected characteristics.

While labor unions have been instrumental in advocating for pay equity, their influence and impact have faced challenges in recent decades. Declining union membership rates, particularly in the private sector, have weakened the collective bargaining power of unions in some industries and regions. Additionally, anti-union legislation and efforts to undermine collective bargaining rights have posed further obstacles. To maintain their effectiveness in the fight for pay equity, labor unions must adapt their strategies, build broader coalitions, and continue to advocate for policies and practices that support fair compensation and protect workers' rights, regardless of gender or other protected characteristics.

The collective bargaining power of labor unions has been instrumental in narrowing the gender wage gap within unionized workplaces. According to a report by the Institute for Women's Policy Research (IWPR), the wage gap between unionized women and men is significantly smaller than the overall wage gap. This is due in part to the standardized pay scales and job classifications negotiated by unions, which help mitigate subjective pay decisions that can be influenced by gender biases. Additionally, unions have advocated for policies that support work-life balance, such as paid family leave and flexible work arrangements, which can help reduce the "motherhood penalty" that often contributes to the gender wage gap.

Beyond their direct impact on pay and working conditions, labor unions have also played a crucial role in shaping public discourse and advocacy efforts around pay equity. Through campaigns, lobbying efforts, and grassroots mobilization, unions have raised awareness about the gender wage gap and its intersectional dimensions, advocating for policy changes and legislative reforms at the local, state, and federal levels. Their involvement has helped to elevate the issue of pay equity as a matter of economic and social justice, garnering support from a diverse coalition of stakeholders and amplifying the voices of working women across various sectors and industries.

Beyond their direct impact on pay and working conditions, labor unions have also played a crucial role in shaping public discourse and advocacy efforts around pay equity. Through campaigns, lobbying efforts, and grassroots mobilization, unions have raised awareness about the gender wage gap and its intersectional dimensions, advocating for policy changes and legislative reforms at the local, state, and federal levels. Their involvement has helped to elevate the issue of pay equity as a matter of economic and social justice, garnering support from a diverse coalition of stakeholders and amplifying the voices of working women across various sectors and industries.

In the quest for balance, some countries have taken proactive steps. Iceland, for instance, has implemented mandatory equal pay certification for companies, requiring them to prove that they provide equal pay for work of equal value. This bold move sets a benchmark for other nations to consider, as pay equity audits and certification schemes gain traction as a means of holding employers accountable.

Iceland's equal pay certification scheme has not been without its challenges and critiques. Some employers have raised concerns about the administrative burden and costs associated with the certification process, while others have questioned the methodology used to assess and compare "work of equal value" across different occupations. Additionally, there have been debates around the role of enforcement mechanisms and penalties for non-compliance. Despite these challenges, Iceland's initiative has sparked a broader conversation about the importance of pay transparency and accountability, and has inspired other countries to explore similar approaches to addressing the gender wage gap.

Iceland's equal pay certification scheme has not been without its challenges and critiques. Some employers have raised concerns about the administrative burden and costs associated with the certification process, while others have questioned the methodology used to assess and compare "work of equal value" across different occupations. Additionally, there have been debates around the role of enforcement mechanisms and penalties for non-compliance. Despite these challenges, Iceland's initiative has sparked a broader conversation about the importance of pay transparency and accountability, and has inspired other countries to explore similar approaches to addressing the gender wage gap.

Iceland's equal pay certification scheme has been hailed as a groundbreaking initiative in addressing the gender wage gap. Under this system, companies with 25 or more employees must undergo regular audits to obtain certification that they pay men and women equally for work of equal value. Companies that fail to comply risk facing fines or being barred from participating in public contracts. This proactive approach not only promotes transparency and accountability but also encourages companies to examine and address any pay disparities within their organizations. As a result, Iceland has consistently ranked among the top countries in the World Economic Forum's Global Gender Gap Report, demonstrating the potential impact of such initiatives on achieving pay equity.

Beyond legislation, corporate policies play a pivotal role in addressing the wage gap. Initiatives like gender-neutral parental leave and flexible work arrangements can mitigate the career disruptions that disproportionately affect women's earnings. Companies are also establishing mentorship and sponsorship programs to shepherd women through the ranks, recognizing that leadership diversity can narrow the wage gap. Organizations like Catalyst and the National Association for Female Executives have been instrumental in providing resources, training, and best practices for companies seeking to foster a more equitable and inclusive workplace.

This paragraph highlights the crucial role that corporations can play in addressing the gender wage gap through internal policies and initiatives. Gender-neutral parental leave and flexible work arrangements are identified as key measures to support women's career continuity and prevent the "motherhood penalty" that contributes to lower lifetime earnings. Mentorship, sponsorship, and leadership development programs aimed at advancing more women into higher ranks are also emphasized as important steps companies can take to increase leadership diversity and narrow wage disparities.

The recognition of the business case for pay equity has prompted many companies to take proactive steps in addressing the gender wage gap within their organizations. Research by organizations like Catalyst has shown that companies with more inclusive and equitable practices not only attract and retain top talent but also experience higher levels of innovation, productivity, and profitability. As a result, leading corporations have implemented initiatives such as pay equity audits, unconscious bias training, and leadership development programs specifically tailored for women. These efforts not only promote fairness but also foster a more inclusive and diverse workforce, which can drive long-term business success.

This paragraph notes that an increasing number of companies are taking action on pay equity, driven by research demonstrating the business benefits of diversity and inclusion. It cites studies showing that equitable and inclusive workplaces can enhance talent acquisition, innovation, productivity, and profitability. The paragraph then provides examples of corporate initiatives like pay audits, bias training, and women's leadership programs aimed at fostering a more diverse and equitable workforce, which is positioned as a driver of long-term business success.

"We've seen firsthand the transformative power of equal pay policies," shares a CEO of a leading tech firm. "It's not just about fairness; it's about harnessing the full potential of our workforce and fostering an environment where talent and hard work are rewarded, regardless of gender."

This quote from a tech CEO reinforces the business case for pay equity, framing it not just as a matter of fairness but as a strategy for unlocking the full potential of the workforce by rewarding talent equitably, irrespective of gender. The quote suggests that pay equity policies can create an environment that attracts and motivates top performers, benefiting the company's overall competitiveness.

The technology industry, once known for its gender imbalances and pay disparities, has seen a growing commitment to addressing the gender wage gap in recent years. Companies like Salesforce, Microsoft, and Adobe have conducted extensive pay equity audits and made adjustments to ensure equal pay for equal work. These efforts not only promote fairness but also help attract and retain top talent in a highly competitive industry. As more tech companies recognize the business benefits of pay equity, they are leading the way in implementing best practices and setting industry standards for achieving gender parity in compensation.

This paragraph focuses on the technology industry's efforts to address pay inequities, driven by the need to attract and retain top talent in a highly competitive market. It provides specific examples of major tech firms like Salesforce, Microsoft, and Adobe that have conducted pay equity audits and made compensation adjustments to ensure equal pay for equal work. The paragraph positions pay equity as not only a matter of fairness but also a strategic imperative for tech companies seeking to remain competitive and capitalize on the business benefits of gender parity in compensation practices.

Yet, challenges persist. Societal norms and unconscious biases continue to cast long shadows over the workplace. The mother working a double shift, the woman breaking new ground in a male-dominated industry, the entrepreneur fighting for her worth in the investment world—each faces a labyrinth of subtle and overt barriers rooted in gender stereotypes and discrimination.

This paragraph acknowledges that despite corporate efforts, significant challenges remain in achieving pay equity due to deeply ingrained societal norms and unconscious biases that manifest in the workplace. It uses vivid examples of working mothers juggling professional and domestic responsibilities, women pioneers in male-dominated fields, and female entrepreneurs facing discrimination in the investment world to illustrate the various forms of overt and subtle barriers rooted in gender stereotypes and biases that continue to hinder progress.

One persistent challenge in addressing the gender wage gap is the unconscious biases that influence hiring, performance evaluation, and promotion decisions. Research by organizations like Harvard University's Project Implicit has demonstrated the prevalence of implicit biases, even among well-intentioned individuals. These biases can lead to undervaluing women's contributions, perpetuating gender stereotypes, and creating barriers to advancement. Addressing unconscious biases requires a multipronged approach, including training programs, structured evaluation processes, and fostering an organizational culture that values diversity and inclusion. By acknowledging and actively working to mitigate these biases, organizations can create a more level playing field for women's career advancement and equitable compensation.

This paragraph delves deeper into the issue of unconscious biases as a significant obstacle to achieving pay equity. It cites research demonstrating the pervasiveness of implicit biases, even among those with good intentions, and how these biases can undermine women's career progression and compensation through biased evaluations, stereotyping, and structural barriers. The paragraph advocates for a multi-faceted approach to mitigating unconscious biases, including training programs, structured evaluation processes, and fostering an organizational culture of diversity and inclusion, as a means to create a more equitable playing field for women's advancement and pay.

The impact of unconscious biases on pay equity is not limited to the corporate world but extends to various sectors and institutions, including academia, government agencies, and non-profit organizations. Research has shown that even in fields traditionally associated with progressive values and commitment to equality, unconscious biases can persist, leading to disparities in hiring, promotion, and compensation decisions. Addressing these biases requires a holistic and sustained effort across all sectors, involving not only diversity and inclusion initiatives but also a critical examination of deep-rooted cultural norms, stereotypes, and power dynamics that perpetuate these biases.

The long-term financial impact of the gender wage gap cannot be overstated. Over the course of a lifetime, the cumulative effect of earning less than men can result in a staggering loss of income, hindering women's ability to build wealth, save for retirement, and achieve economic security. This disparity not only affects individual women but also has ripple effects on families and communities, perpetuating cycles of poverty and limiting opportunities for future generations.

The long-term financial consequences of the gender wage gap extend beyond individual earnings and have broader socioeconomic implications. Lower lifetime earnings for women can translate into reduced tax revenues for governments, limiting their ability to fund essential public services and social programs. Additionally, the gender wage gap can exacerbate existing wealth disparities, perpetuating intergenerational cycles of economic inequality and limiting social mobility for families and communities affected by this issue.

The long-term financial consequences of the gender wage gap extend beyond individual women's earnings and can have far-reaching implications for their financial security and well-being. According to a study by the National Institute on Retirement Security, the wage gap leads to significantly lower retirement income and savings for women, with the average woman facing a retirement income deficit of $1.1 million compared to men over their lifetimes. This disparity not only affects women's quality of life in retirement but also places a greater burden on social safety nets and contributes to the feminization of poverty in old age.

The retirement income deficit faced by women due to the gender wage gap is particularly concerning given the longer life expectancy of women compared to men. This means that women not only have lower retirement savings but also need to stretch those limited resources over a longer period, putting them at greater risk of poverty and financial insecurity in their later years. Addressing this issue requires a multifaceted approach that includes closing the wage gap, promoting equal access to retirement savings plans, and ensuring the financial sustainability of social safety nets and public pension systems.

Moreover, the intersectionality of gender with other factors, such as race, ethnicity, and disability, contributes to compounding wage disparities for marginalized groups of women. Women of color, for instance, face a double bind of racial and gender discrimination, resulting in even wider wage gaps compared to their white counterparts. Similarly, women with disabilities often encounter barriers to employment, lower wages, and limited opportunities for advancement, exacerbating their economic vulnerabilities.

The compounding effects of intersectional discrimination on the wage gap highlight the need for targeted and nuanced policy interventions to address the specific challenges faced by diverse groups of women. For example, efforts to promote pay equity for women of color must address not only gender-based discrimination but also the systemic racism and structural barriers that limit their access to educational and employment opportunities. Similarly, addressing the wage gap for women with disabilities requires a comprehensive approach that includes accessible workplaces, accommodations, and inclusive hiring practices.

The intersection of gender, race, and ethnicity creates a compounding effect on the wage gap, with women of color experiencing the most significant disparities. According to data from the National Women's Law Center, Native American women earned just 51 cents for every dollar earned by white, non-Hispanic men in 2021, while Black women earned 64 cents, and Latinas earned 54 cents on the dollar. These stark disparities are rooted in historical and systemic barriers, including racial discrimination, lack of access to education and job opportunities, and the devaluation of work in industries dominated by women of color, such as domestic labor and caregiving.

The staggering wage disparities faced by women of color are not only a matter of economic injustice but also a reflection of deeply entrenched systemic racism and intersectional discrimination. These disparities have far-reaching consequences, including higher rates of poverty, limited access to quality healthcare and education, and diminished opportunities for economic mobility and generational wealth-building. Addressing these disparities requires a multi-pronged approach that tackles both gender-based discrimination and the legacy of racial injustice, including efforts to promote equity in education, workforce development, and access to high-paying industries.

Pay equity legislation plays a vital role in combating wage discrimination and holding employers accountable for fair compensation practices. Laws like the Equal Pay Act and the Lilly Ledbetter Fair Pay Act in the United States have provided avenues for women to challenge discriminatory pay practices and seek legal recourse. However, the effectiveness of these laws depends on robust enforcement, ongoing monitoring, and closing loopholes that allow disparities to persist.

Despite the existence of pay equity legislation, enforcing these laws and ensuring compliance remains a significant challenge. Limited resources for enforcement agencies, complex legal proceedings, and the burden of proof on individuals seeking redress can often discourage or hinder the pursuit of legal action against discriminatory pay practices. Strengthening enforcement mechanisms, increasing funding for oversight and compliance monitoring, and providing legal support and resources to individuals seeking to assert their rights are crucial steps in ensuring that pay equity laws have their intended impact.

While pay equity legislation has been instrumental in addressing the gender wage gap, its impact has been limited by several factors, including insufficient enforcement mechanisms and loopholes that allow employers to justify pay disparities based on factors other than gender. For example, the "factor other than sex" defense in the Equal Pay Act has been criticized for providing employers with a broad justification for pay differences, even when those factors may be influenced by gender biases. Strengthening enforcement mechanisms, increasing transparency in pay data, and narrowing the scope of such loopholes are crucial steps in ensuring that pay equity laws achieve their intended impact.

The debate surrounding the "factor other than sex" defense in the Equal Pay Act highlights the need for ongoing legal and policy reforms to close loopholes and strengthen pay equity protections. Critics argue that this defense can be used to perpetuate discriminatory pay practices by allowing employers to justify wage disparities based on factors that may be influenced by unconscious biases or structural barriers faced by women. Efforts to reform this provision, such as narrowing the scope of acceptable factors or shifting the burden of proof to employers, could help ensure that pay equity laws are more effective in combating wage discrimination.

The concept of "comparable worth" offers another lens through which to examine the gender wage gap. This principle asserts that jobs requiring similar levels of skill, effort, and responsibility should be compensated equally, regardless of whether they are traditionally male or female-dominated. Advocates argue that the undervaluation of female-dominated occupations, such as teaching and nursing, is a form of systemic discrimination that perpetuates the wage gap. Addressing this issue requires a fundamental reevaluation of how we value and compensate different types of work, challenging entrenched societal biases and gender norms.

The concept of comparable worth has sparked considerable debate and controversy, with critics arguing that implementing such a system would be complex, costly, and potentially disruptive to labor markets. Proponents counter that the status quo perpetuates systemic discrimination and devalues the contributions of workers in traditionally female-dominated fields. Finding a balanced and equitable approach to implementing comparable worth principles requires extensive research, stakeholder engagement, and a willingness to confront deep-rooted cultural biases surrounding the value of different types of work.

The comparable worth framework has gained traction as a means of addressing the systemic undervaluation of women's work. By analyzing the skills, effort, responsibility, and working conditions of different occupations, proponents argue that pay disparities between male-dominated and female-dominated jobs with similar job requirements can be identified and rectified. However, implementing comparable worth principles has faced challenges, including resistance from employers due to potential cost implications and the difficulty in determining appropriate compensation levels across diverse occupations. Nonetheless, countries like Canada and several U.S. states have implemented comparable worth policies in the public sector, demonstrating the potential for this approach to combat gender-based pay discrimination.

The implementation of comparable worth policies in the public sector has provided valuable insights and lessons for broader adoption. While challenges remain in terms of developing robust and consistent job evaluation methodologies, and addressing potential cost implications, the experiences of jurisdictions like Canada and various U.S. states have demonstrated that comparable worth initiatives can be successful in reducing gender-based pay disparities. These experiences also highlight the importance of stakeholder engagement, transparent processes, and ongoing monitoring and evaluation to ensure the effectiveness and fairness of comparable worth policies.

Efforts to achieve pay equity are not a solitary march but a collective endeavor, with advocacy groups, researchers, and policymakers playing vital roles. The National Committee on Pay Equity, for instance, mobilizes resources and public support to keep the issue at the forefront of social consciousness, while organizations like the Institute for Women's Policy Research (IWPR) and the American Association of University Women (AAUW) conduct rigorous research and analysis to inform advocacy efforts and policy recommendations.

The collaboration between advocacy groups, research institutions, and policymakers has been instrumental in shaping evidence-based policies and strategies to address the gender wage gap. By leveraging their respective strengths and expertise, these diverse stakeholders have been able to amplify the voices of women, generate actionable data and insights, and influence decision-makers to prioritize pay equity on the policy agenda. This collaborative approach underscores the importance of a multi-stakeholder effort in addressing a complex and multifaceted issue like the gender wage gap.

The involvement of advocacy groups and research organizations has been crucial in advancing the pay equity agenda and keeping the issue at the forefront of public discourse. Organizations like Equal Pay Today, a campaign led by the American Association of University Women (AAUW), have leveraged social media and grassroots activism to raise awareness, promote policy changes, and encourage individuals to take action in their communities. Meanwhile, research institutions like the National Bureau of Economic Research (NBER) and the Economic Policy Institute (EPI) have contributed valuable data and analysis on the drivers and impacts of the gender wage gap, informing evidence-based policymaking and advocacy efforts.

The pursuit of pay equity is not only a matter of economic justice but also a critical step towards realizing the full potential of societies and economies. By unlocking the economic power of women and ensuring their equal participation in the workforce, we can drive innovation, productivity, and sustainable economic growth. Furthermore, promoting pay equity has broader societal benefits, including improved health and educational outcomes for families, reduced poverty rates, and increased social cohesion and stability. As we work towards achieving pay equity, it is essential to recognize the intersectional nature of this issue and tailor solutions that address the unique challenges faced by diverse groups of women, ensuring that no one is left behind on the path to a more just and equitable future.

The success of advocacy campaigns and public awareness efforts has been instrumental in shifting the narrative around pay equity and garnering broader societal support for addressing this issue. By leveraging the power of storytelling, personal testimonies, and powerful data visualization, these efforts have helped to humanize the gender wage gap and highlight its real-world impacts on women's lives. This increased public awareness and support has, in turn, created a more favorable environment for policymakers and decision-makers to take bold action on pay equity initiatives.

In conclusion, the analysis of gender wage gap trends and the pursuit of pay equity are ongoing chapters in the larger narrative of women's rights. The path to parity is laden with obstacles, yet it is trodden with determination by those who envision a world where one's gender does not dictate their financial worth. Each stride towards this goal reverberates through the corridors of power and into the heart of society, reinforcing the belief that economic equality is not just a dream but an attainable reality.

The journey towards pay equity is not a linear path but a multifaceted and complex endeavor that requires sustained commitment, collaboration, and a willingness to challenge deeply ingrained societal norms and power structures. Progress will inevitably be met with resistance and setbacks, as entrenched interests seek to maintain the status quo. However, the resilience and determination of the women's rights movement, bolstered by the support of allies and advocates from all walks of life, will continue to drive this cause forward, one step at a time.

As the pursuit of pay equity continues, it is essential to recognize the intersectional nature of the issue and the diverse experiences of women across different contexts. The wage gap experienced by a single mother in an urban setting may differ from that of a highly educated woman in a male-dominated industry or a woman living in a rural area with limited job opportunities. Addressing these nuances requires a multifaceted approach that considers the unique challenges faced by different groups of women and tailors solutions accordingly. By embracing this intersectional lens, we can ensure that the fight for pay equity is inclusive and addresses the multidimensional barriers that women face in achieving economic parity.

The intersectional approach to pay equity must also consider the unique challenges faced by women in marginalized and underrepresented communities, such as indigenous women, women with disabilities, and LGBTQ+ women. These groups often face compounded forms of discrimination and systemic barriers that exacerbate the wage gap and limit their economic opportunities. Addressing these issues requires a deep understanding of the complex intersections of gender, race, ethnicity, ability, and sexual orientation, and a commitment to centering the voices and experiences of these marginalized groups in the development of policies and initiatives.

As we forge ahead, let us remember the diversity of women's experiences and the need for a tailored approach to address the wage gap. Our collective actions, informed by insight and driven by a shared vision, can and will reshape the economic landscape. The journey toward pay equity is a testament to the unwavering spirit of women and allies alike—each an invaluable thread in the tapestry of a more equitable society, where the value of one's work is measured not by gender but by the content of their character and the strength of their contributions.

The tapestry of pay equity is woven not only by the efforts of women but also by the allyship and solidarity of individuals and organizations committed to the cause of gender equality. Men, too, have a pivotal role to play in this journey, by challenging patriarchal norms, advocating for change within their spheres of influence, and supporting the leadership and empowerment of women in all spheres of life. By working together, across gender lines and in solidarity with marginalized communities, we can create a more equitable and just society that values and celebrates the contributions of all.

The pursuit of pay equity is not only an economic imperative but also a moral and ethical obligation. By addressing the gender wage gap, we challenge deep-rooted biases and systemic inequalities that have perpetuated the devaluation of women's labor and contributions. In doing so, we pave the way for a more just and equitable society, where individuals are valued for their talents, efforts, and merits, regardless of gender. This pursuit is not merely a fight for financial parity but a broader struggle for gender equality, human rights, and social justice. As we continue this journey, let us draw inspiration from the resilience and determination of those who have paved the way, and let us carry forth the torch of progress, guided by the principles of fairness, dignity, and respect for all.

The pursuit of pay equity is not just a matter of economic justice or gender equality, but a fundamental human rights issue that strikes at the core of our shared values of dignity, respect, and equal opportunity for all. By perpetuating the devaluation of women's labor and contributions, we not only perpetuate economic injustice but also undermine the fundamental principles of human rights and the inherent worth and dignity of every individual. As we strive towards pay equity, we are not only fighting for financial parity but also for the realization of a society that truly upholds the principles of human rights, freedom from discrimination, and the equal treatment of all individuals, regardless of gender or any other characteristic.

As we move forward on this journey, it is essential to recognize that progress towards pay equity is not only a matter of economic and social justice but also a critical component of sustainable development and the realization of a more peaceful and prosperous world. Gender equality and women's economic empowerment are inextricably linked to the achievement of the United Nations Sustainable Development Goals, which aim to end poverty, promote inclusive and sustainable economic growth, and foster peaceful and inclusive societies. By addressing the gender wage gap and promoting pay equity, we are not only advancing the rights and opportunities of women but also contributing to the broader global agenda of sustainable development and the creation of a more just, equitable, and prosperous world for all.

Section C: Exploration of workplace policies and initiatives promoting gender diversity and inclusion

As we shift our focus from the stubborn specters of wage inequality to the proactive measures within the workplace, we must ask: What are the tangible steps being taken to foster an environment of gender diversity and inclusion? This chapter endeavors to peel back the layers of corporate policies and initiatives that champion this noble aim, revealing the intricate ecosystem of efforts aimed at creating a more equitable and inclusive work environment for all.

Fostering a diverse and inclusive workplace is not just a moral imperative but also a business imperative. Numerous studies have demonstrated the tangible benefits of gender diversity for organizations, including increased creativity, innovation, and better decision-making. A report by McKinsey & Company found that companies in the top quartile for gender diversity on executive teams were 25% more likely to experience above-average profitability compared to their counterparts in the bottom quartile. This economic case for diversity has prompted many organizations to prioritize gender inclusion as a strategic business objective, recognizing its potential to drive long-term success and competitiveness.

However, the business case for gender diversity and inclusion goes beyond financial performance and extends to a broader range of organizational benefits. A diverse and inclusive workforce can enhance an organization's ability to understand and cater to the needs of diverse customers and stakeholders, fostering better market insights and customer relationships. Additionally, an inclusive culture can contribute to higher employee engagement, reduced turnover, and an improved ability to attract and retain top talent, thereby enhancing organizational resilience and long-term sustainability.

The modern workplace is a mosaic of varying identities, with gender diversity serving as a pivotal piece of the puzzle. Initiatives that promote inclusivity not only support women but also enrich the entire organization. But how deep do these roots grow, and what fruits do they bear?

While gender diversity initiatives have gained traction in many organizations, their effectiveness often depends on the extent to which they are embedded within a broader culture of inclusion and equity. Standalone programs or tokenistic efforts may yield limited results if they are not supported by a genuine commitment to diversity and inclusion at all levels of the organization. Successful organizations in this realm have adopted a holistic approach, integrating diversity and inclusion principles into all aspects of their operations, from recruitment and talent management to performance evaluation and leadership development.

One critical aspect of fostering gender diversity and inclusion is creating an organizational culture that values and celebrates diversity. This goes beyond mere policies and initiatives; it involves embedding a mindset of inclusion into the very fabric of the organization. Leaders play a crucial role in setting the tone and modeling inclusive behaviors, while employees at all levels must actively contribute to creating an environment where diverse perspectives are welcomed and respected. This cultural shift requires ongoing education, open dialogue, and a willingness to challenge deep-rooted biases and assumptions.

Creating an inclusive organizational culture is a continuous journey that requires sustained commitment, self-reflection, and a willingness to confront uncomfortable truths. It involves actively listening to diverse voices, acknowledging and addressing systemic barriers, and fostering a sense of belonging for all employees. Organizations that have successfully cultivated an inclusive culture have often done so by prioritizing open communication, promoting psychological safety, and providing opportunities for employees to engage in courageous conversations about diversity, equity, and inclusion.

Imagine walking into an office where the walls themselves seem to echo a commitment to diversity. Portraits of women leaders adorn the corridors, and policies crafted with an inclusive lens are the bedrock of the company's ethos. This is not a utopian dream; it's a narrative unfurling in businesses worldwide, as organizations increasingly recognize the value of cultivating a diverse and inclusive workforce.

Visual representation and symbolic gestures play a crucial role in fostering an inclusive environment, as they communicate the organization's values and priorities. However, it is important to ensure that these symbols are more than just superficial displays and are backed by substantive policies, initiatives, and a genuine commitment to diversity and inclusion. Organizations that effectively leverage visual representation often do so as part of a broader, multifaceted approach that includes tangible actions, accountability measures, and continuous learning and improvement.

While visual representation and symbolic gestures are important, true gender diversity and inclusion require substantive actions and accountability. Organizations must implement measurable goals, track progress, and hold leaders responsible for creating an inclusive environment. This may involve setting targets for gender representation at various levels, conducting regular pay equity audits, and tying diversity and inclusion metrics to performance evaluations and compensation decisions. By making gender diversity a strategic priority and holding leadership accountable, organizations can drive meaningful and sustainable change.

Accountability and metrics are essential components of any effective diversity and inclusion strategy. By setting clear targets and regularly measuring progress, organizations can identify areas for improvement, allocate resources effectively, and hold leaders responsible for driving change. However, it is crucial to ensure that these metrics are aligned with the organization's broader diversity and inclusion goals and are not solely focused on surface-level indicators. For example, metrics that capture employee sentiment, engagement, and retention rates can provide valuable insights into the organization's inclusive culture and the effectiveness of its initiatives.

One might wonder, what does a robust framework for gender diversity look like? It begins with recruitment, where companies are re-evaluating their hiring practices to mitigate unconscious bias. Blind applications, free of gender identifiers, and the use of AI-powered tools to screen for biased language in job descriptions are emerging as tools to promote more equitable hiring processes. But the journey does not end at the hiring phase. It extends into retention and advancement, where the true test of diversity policies is measured.

A comprehensive approach to gender diversity must address the entire employee lifecycle, from recruitment and onboarding to development, promotion, and retention. Organizations that have been successful in this regard have taken a holistic view, implementing strategies and initiatives at every stage to ensure that diverse talent is attracted, engaged, and empowered to reach their full potential. This may include initiatives such as targeted recruitment efforts, inclusive onboarding programs, career development opportunities, and mentorship and sponsorship programs for women and other underrepresented groups.

To truly foster gender diversity and inclusion, organizations must address the talent pipeline and create pathways for women's advancement. This may involve targeted leadership development programs, mentorship initiatives, and sponsorship opportunities that provide women with access to networks, guidance, and advocacy for career progression. Additionally, organizations can implement succession planning processes that actively identify and groom high-potential women for leadership roles, ensuring a diverse talent pool for future leadership positions.

Addressing the leadership pipeline is a critical component of promoting gender diversity and inclusion, as women continue to be underrepresented in senior leadership roles across many industries. Organizations that have been successful in this area have implemented comprehensive leadership development programs specifically tailored to the unique challenges and experiences of women leaders. These programs often combine formal training with mentorship and sponsorship opportunities, providing women with the skills, networks, and advocacy needed to navigate the complexities of the leadership landscape.

Mentorship programs are sprouting up like seedlings in fertile soil, offering guidance and support to women navigating their career paths. Sponsorship, too, is proving to be a key ingredient in the recipe for success, as senior leaders actively advocate for the advancement of women within the organization. These programs are not mere embellishments; they are catalysts for change, providing women with access to invaluable networks, opportunities for professional growth, and the confidence to pursue leadership roles.

Effective mentorship and sponsorship programs require more than just good intentions; they demand a structured and intentional approach. Organizations that have successfully implemented these initiatives often leverage technology platforms and data analytics to facilitate meaningful matches, track progress, and measure the impact on career advancement and retention rates. Additionally, providing training and resources for both mentors and mentees can enhance the effectiveness of these programs, ensuring that participants are equipped with the necessary skills and knowledge to foster meaningful connections and drive professional growth.

While mentorship and sponsorship programs are often focused on supporting the career growth and advancement of women, organizations that have adopted a truly intersectional approach have also implemented initiatives that address the unique challenges faced by women from diverse backgrounds and identities. For example, programs specifically designed for women of color, LGBTQ+ women, or women with disabilities can provide tailored support and resources to address the compounded barriers and experiences of these groups, fostering a more inclusive and equitable environment for all.

Effective mentorship and sponsorship programs go beyond simply pairing individuals; they require a structured approach, clear goals, and ongoing evaluation. Organizations can leverage technology platforms and data analytics to facilitate meaningful matches, track progress, and measure the impact of these programs on career advancement and retention rates. Additionally, engaging senior leadership as sponsors and providing training on effective mentorship can enhance the success of these initiatives and demonstrate the organization's commitment to developing and retaining diverse talent.

Consider for a moment the transformative power of flexible work arrangements. A mother returns from maternity leave to find that she can adjust her hours to accommodate her new responsibilities. Her value as an employee is not diminished by her role as a parent; instead, it is celebrated and supported through policies that promote work-life balance and challenge traditional gender norms. This is the essence of an inclusive workplace – one that recognizes and embraces the diverse needs and experiences of its employees, creating an environment where everyone can thrive.

Flexible work arrangements are not just a matter of accommodating working parents; they are a critical component of creating an inclusive and equitable workplace for all employees. By offering flexible options such as remote work, compressed workweeks, or job sharing, organizations can tap into a broader pool of talent, including individuals with disabilities, caregiving responsibilities, or those pursuing further education. Additionally, flexible work arrangements can contribute to improved work-life balance, increased productivity, and reduced employee turnover, ultimately enhancing organizational performance and competitiveness.

Flexible work arrangements are not just a perk for working parents; they can benefit employees across various life stages and situations. Organizations that offer flexible options, such as remote work, compressed workweeks, or job sharing, can attract and retain a more diverse workforce, including individuals with disabilities, caregiving responsibilities, or those pursuing further education. By acknowledging the diverse needs of their employees, organizations can create a more inclusive and supportive work environment that fosters engagement, productivity, and overall well-being.

While flexible work arrangements can be a powerful tool for promoting inclusion, their effectiveness often depends on the extent to which they are supported by an organizational culture that values and embraces flexibility. Organizations that have successfully implemented flexible work policies have often done so in conjunction with initiatives that challenge traditional notions of "face time" and productivity, promote trust and autonomy, and provide managers with training and resources to effectively manage remote and flexible teams.

Can you envision a boardroom where women's voices are not only heard but sought after? Inclusion means creating spaces where women can lead and shape the direction of a company. Gender quotas on boards, while a contentious topic, have sparked a dialogue on the importance of representation at the highest levels of decision-making. Countries like Norway, Spain, and France have implemented quotas mandating a certain percentage of board seats be held by women, catalyzing change and challenging the status quo. Such policies have been met with resistance and praise in equal measure, reflecting the complexities of promoting gender diversity in leadership roles.

The debate around gender quotas on corporate boards highlights the tension between the need for immediate action to address the underrepresentation of women in leadership roles and concerns around potential adverse effects or unintended consequences.

Proponents argue that quotas can serve as a powerful catalyst for change, disrupting entrenched biases and promoting greater diversity of thought and perspectives in decision-making processes. Critics, however, contend that quotas may undermine meritocracy, reinforce stereotypes, and lead to tokenism if not accompanied by broader cultural and systemic changes within organizations.

While gender quotas on boards remain a controversial topic, proponents argue that they can serve as a catalyst for change by ensuring that women have a seat at the table and a voice in critical decision-making processes. Opponents, on the other hand, argue that quotas can undermine meritocracy and perpetuate the perception that women are promoted solely based on their gender. Regardless of one's stance on the issue, the debate around board quotas has shed light on the persistent barriers women face in attaining leadership positions and the need for comprehensive strategies to address the root causes of this underrepresentation.

The debate around gender quotas on corporate boards also highlights the need for a multifaceted approach that combines targeted interventions with broader cultural and systemic changes. While quotas can serve as a catalyst for increasing representation, their effectiveness in driving sustainable change often depends on accompanying efforts to address unconscious biases, promote inclusive leadership practices, and create a pipeline of diverse talent through mentorship, sponsorship, and leadership development programs.

What of the companies that have woven these threads into their corporate fabric? Success stories abound, with firms reporting not only a more diverse workforce but also improved performance, innovation, and decision-making. A technology giant boasts that its commitment to diversity has led to a surge in creativity, with women at the helm of groundbreaking projects that have transformed the industry. A global consulting firm credits its inclusive culture for attracting and retaining top talent, fostering a environment where diverse perspectives are valued and leveraged to drive better outcomes for clients.

While success stories of companies embracing gender diversity and inclusion can be inspiring, it is important to recognize that the journey towards creating an inclusive workplace is not a linear path. Even organizations that have made significant strides in this area often face setbacks, challenges, and the need for continuous learning and improvement. Successful companies in this realm have often adopted a growth mindset, acknowledging that diversity and inclusion are ongoing processes that require sustained commitment, self-reflection, and a willingness to adapt and evolve their strategies based on changing needs and circumstances.

The path towards building an inclusive workplace is marked by complexities and nuances that require organizations to remain agile and responsive. As societal norms and cultural landscapes evolve, new challenges may emerge, necessitating a willingness to reassess existing approaches and strategies. Additionally, organizations must be prepared to address setbacks and failures with resilience and a commitment to learning from these experiences. By embracing a growth mindset and fostering a culture of continuous improvement, organizations can navigate the non-linear path of diversity and inclusion more effectively, adapting their efforts to meet the ever-changing needs of their diverse workforce and stakeholders.

One notable example of a company embracing gender diversity and inclusion is Salesforce, a leading technology firm. Salesforce has implemented a range of initiatives, including mandatory unconscious bias training, pay equity audits, and targeted programs to recruit and retain diverse talent. As a result, the company has achieved gender parity in its global workforce, and women hold 35% of leadership positions. Salesforce's Chief Equality Officer, Molly Ford, attributes the company's success to its commitment to creating an inclusive culture and embedding diversity into its core values, stating, "We believe that diverse teams drive better decision-making, innovation, and business performance."

Salesforce's approach to gender diversity and inclusion underscores the importance of a multifaceted strategy that spans the entire employee lifecycle. From recruitment to retention and advancement, the company has implemented targeted initiatives to address potential biases and barriers at every stage. Additionally, Salesforce's commitment to embedding diversity and inclusion into its core values has been instrumental in fostering a culture of accountability and shared responsibility, where every employee is empowered to contribute to creating an inclusive environment.

To add authenticity, a quote from a Chief Diversity Officer: "Our journey towards inclusion is paved with challenges, but each step forward is a stride towards a greater good. By embracing diversity, we not only create a more equitable workplace but also unlock the full potential of our organization."

This quote highlights the transformative power of diversity and inclusion, acknowledging the challenges inherent in the journey while emphasizing the profound benefits that can be achieved when organizations embrace diversity as a source of strength and innovation. By fostering an inclusive environment where diverse perspectives are valued and leveraged, organizations can unlock their full potential, drive innovation, and foster a culture of equity and empowerment for all employees.

Embedding diversity and inclusion into an organization's culture requires a sustained commitment and leadership buy-in at all levels. Companies like Accenture, a global professional services firm, have taken a holistic approach by establishing a comprehensive diversity and inclusion strategy, with clear goals and accountability measures. Accenture's Chief Leadership and Human Resources Officer, Ellyn Shook, emphasizes the importance of leadership ownership, stating, "Our leaders are responsible for driving our diversity and inclusion agenda, and their performance is evaluated based on their progress in creating an inclusive environment where all our people can thrive."

The success of Accenture's diversity and inclusion strategy hinges on the commitment and accountability of its leadership team. By tying diversity and inclusion metrics to performance evaluations and leadership responsibilities, the company has embedded these principles into the very fabric of its organizational culture. This approach not only holds leaders accountable for driving progress but also reinforces the message that diversity and inclusion are strategic imperatives that are central to the company's long-term success and sustainability.

Still, barriers loom large. Women continue to grapple with microaggressions, unconscious biases, and the proverbial glass ceiling. And yet, initiatives such as unconscious bias training, bystander intervention programs, and the establishment of employee resource groups focused on women's issues are chipping away at these impediments, making room for a more equitable landscape.

Despite the progress made in promoting gender diversity and inclusion, significant barriers and challenges persist. Overcoming deeply ingrained societal norms, unconscious biases, and systemic inequalities requires sustained effort, education, and a willingness to confront uncomfortable truths. Initiatives such as unconscious bias training, bystander intervention programs, and employee resource groups are crucial steps in raising awareness, challenging biases, and fostering a culture of allyship and support. However, these initiatives must be accompanied by broader organizational and societal changes that address the root causes of gender inequality and create an enabling environment for women to thrive and reach their full potential.

Addressing unconscious biases is a critical step in creating an inclusive workplace environment. Organizations like Starbucks have implemented comprehensive unconscious bias training programs for all employees, providing them with tools and strategies to recognize and mitigate biases that can impact decision-making and interpersonal interactions. By raising awareness and equipping employees with practical strategies, companies can create a more inclusive culture where diverse perspectives are valued and respected.

While unconscious bias training is an important component of creating an inclusive workplace, it is essential to recognize that it is not a one-time solution but rather part of a broader, ongoing effort. Organizations must complement these training initiatives with other measures, such as regular accountability checks, policy reviews, and fostering a culture of open dialogue and continuous learning. Additionally, unconscious bias training should be tailored to address the specific needs and contexts of different departments, roles, and levels within the organization to ensure its relevance and effectiveness.

It is not enough to simply open the doors to women; the culture within must welcome and embrace them. Employee resource groups provide a sanctum for sharing experiences, fostering solidarity, and advocating for change within the organization. From breastfeeding rooms to robust anti-harassment policies, the minutiae matter in creating an environment where women feel valued, respected, and supported.

Creating a truly inclusive workplace requires a multifaceted approach that addresses not only organizational policies and initiatives but also the lived experiences of diverse employees. Employee resource groups play a vital role in amplifying the voices and perspectives of underrepresented groups, providing a safe space for sharing experiences, and advocating for changes that can enhance inclusivity and support. By actively listening to and engaging with these groups, organizations can gain valuable insights into the unique challenges and barriers faced by their diverse workforce, informing the development of tailored solutions and driving meaningful cultural change.

Employee resource groups (ERGs) play a vital role in fostering a sense of community and support for underrepresented groups within an organization. Companies like Cisco and Procter & Gamble have established thriving ERGs focused on women's issues, providing a platform for networking, mentorship, and advocacy. These groups not only support their members but also serve as a valuable resource for the organization, offering insights and recommendations on policies, programs, and initiatives that can enhance the workplace experience for women and drive greater inclusion.

The success of employee resource groups hinges on their ability to influence organizational decision-making and drive tangible changes. Organizations that have effectively leveraged their ERGs have established clear channels for communication and collaboration, ensuring that the insights and recommendations from these groups are given due consideration and incorporated into the organization's diversity and inclusion strategies. By fostering a culture of mutual respect and partnership between leadership and ERGs, organizations can create a more inclusive environment that reflects the diverse needs and perspectives of their workforce.

But what of the skeptics? Those who view gender initiatives as mere window dressing or a box-ticking exercise? To them, we present the data: organizations with robust diversity and inclusion programs consistently outperform their peers, not just in employee satisfaction and retention, but also in financial returns, innovation, and overall organizational performance. Gender diversity is not charity; it's a strategic advantage that fuels growth, creativity, and long-term sustainability.

The business case for gender diversity and inclusion extends beyond financial performance and encompasses a range of organizational benefits. A diverse and inclusive workforce can enhance an organization's ability to understand and cater to the needs of diverse customers and stakeholders, fostering stronger market insights and customer relationships. Furthermore, an inclusive culture can contribute to higher employee engagement, reduced turnover, and an improved ability to attract and retain top talent, thereby enhancing organizational resilience and long-term sustainability.

Numerous studies have demonstrated the business case for gender diversity and inclusion. A report by the Boston Consulting Group found that companies with above-average diversity scores on factors such as leadership, innovation, and employee engagement reported 19% higher revenue due to increased innovation and better decision-making. Similarly, a study by McKinsey & Company revealed that companies in the top quartile for gender diversity on executive teams were 25% more likely to experience above-average profitability compared to those in the bottom quartile.

While the business case for gender diversity and inclusion is well-documented, it is important to recognize that achieving true inclusivity requires more than just a focus on financial metrics. Sustainable and meaningful change demands a holistic approach that addresses the systemic barriers, biases, and cultural norms that have historically perpetuated gender inequality in the workplace. By prioritizing equity, empowerment, and the creation of a truly inclusive organizational culture, companies can not only reap the business benefits of diversity but also contribute to the broader societal goal of achieving gender equality.

Building a truly inclusive organizational culture requires a deep understanding of the systemic barriers and biases that have perpetuated gender inequality in the workplace. This involves critically examining organizational policies, practices, and structures that may inadvertently perpetuate discrimination or create obstacles for women's advancement. By fostering an environment that values diverse perspectives and experiences, and actively addressing systemic inequities, organizations can create a more equitable and empowering workplace for all employees, regardless of gender.

Creating a culture of allyship and engaging men as partners in promoting gender diversity and inclusion is crucial for sustainable change. Men in leadership positions have a unique opportunity to champion gender equality, challenge biases, and model inclusive behaviors. By actively participating in diversity initiatives, mentoring women colleagues, and advocating for equitable policies, men can be powerful allies in the journey towards a more inclusive workplace. Organizations like the Male Champions of Change and the UN's HeForShe campaign have been instrumental in mobilizing men as advocates for gender equality and fostering a culture of shared responsibility.

Engaging men as allies in the pursuit of gender diversity and inclusion is not only about involving them in initiatives but also about fostering a culture of accountability and shared responsibility. Organizations that have successfully engaged men in this journey have often done so by providing training and education programs that challenge traditional notions of masculinity, promote allyship behaviors, and equip men with the tools to recognize and address gender biases in their daily interactions and decision-making processes. By creating a culture where men are empowered to be active participants in the pursuit of gender equality, organizations can foster a more inclusive and supportive environment for all employees.

Engaging men as allies in the pursuit of gender diversity and inclusion is not just about involving them in initiatives but also about creating a culture where they actively champion and model inclusive behaviors. Organizations like Unilever and Procter & Gamble have implemented programs that encourage men to participate in conversations about gender equality, challenge biases in their teams, and advocate for policies that support work-life balance and career advancement for women. By fostering a culture of allyship, companies can create a more inclusive environment where everyone feels empowered to contribute to the organization's diversity and inclusion goals.

Fostering a culture of allyship and shared responsibility also involves creating safe spaces for open and honest dialogue, where individuals can share their experiences, challenge assumptions, and learn from one another's perspectives. Organizations that have successfully cultivated such an environment have often done so by providing training and resources on effective communication, active listening, and creating inclusive spaces for dialogue. By encouraging open and respectful conversations about gender diversity and inclusion, organizations can build empathy, understanding, and a collective commitment to driving meaningful change.

Leadership accountability is another critical factor in driving organizational change. Setting clear diversity metrics, tying them to performance evaluations, and regularly reporting on progress sends a strong message that gender diversity is a strategic priority. When leaders are held accountable for creating an inclusive culture, it permeates through the ranks and becomes embedded in the organization's DNA.

Holding leaders accountable for diversity and inclusion goals is not just about setting metrics but also about fostering a culture of transparency and continuous improvement. Organizations that have successfully embedded accountability into their culture have often done so by regularly reporting on progress, celebrating successes, and openly acknowledging areas for improvement. By fostering an environment of open communication and shared responsibility, organizations can create a culture where diversity and inclusion are not just top-down initiatives but a collective effort that permeates every level of the organization.

In addition to tying diversity and inclusion metrics to performance evaluations and compensation, organizations can further reinforce accountability by providing comprehensive training and resources for leaders. This can include leadership development programs that focus on inclusive leadership practices, unconscious bias training, and coaching on how to foster a culture of belonging and psychological safety for all employees. By equipping leaders with the necessary knowledge and skills, organizations can empower them to be more effective champions of diversity and inclusion within their teams and across the organization.

Holding leaders accountable for diversity and inclusion goals is crucial for driving meaningful change within an organization. Companies like Sodexo and Deloitte have implemented performance evaluation systems that incorporate diversity and inclusion metrics, ensuring that leaders are evaluated not only on their business results but also on their efforts to foster an inclusive environment. By tying these metrics to compensation and career progression, organizations can reinforce the importance of diversity and inclusion as a core business imperative and incentivize leaders to prioritize these efforts.

Technology and data analytics offer promising avenues for identifying and mitigating bias in hiring, promotion, and compensation decisions. By leveraging tools that analyze job descriptions for gendered language, monitoring pay equity across the organization, and using data to uncover patterns of bias, companies can take a proactive approach to fostering diversity and inclusion. However, it is important to recognize that technology is not a panacea; it must be coupled with human judgment, empathy, and a genuine commitment to change.

While technology and data analytics can be powerful tools in addressing biases and promoting diversity and inclusion, their effectiveness ultimately relies on the organizational culture and the commitment to leveraging these tools responsibly and ethically. Organizations that have successfully integrated technology and data analytics into their diversity and inclusion efforts have often done so by involving diverse stakeholders in the development and implementation of these tools, ensuring transparency and accountability in their use, and fostering a culture of continuous learning and improvement.

Companies like Amazon and IBM are leveraging artificial intelligence (AI) and machine learning technologies to identify and mitigate bias in their hiring and promotion processes. Amazon's AI-powered resume screening tool has been trained to ignore gender-identifying information and focus solely on relevant qualifications, while IBM's AI system analyzes job descriptions and interview questions for potentially biased language. However, experts caution that these technologies must be carefully monitored and calibrated to ensure they do not perpetuate existing biases or create new ones. Additionally, human oversight and ethical considerations remain critical in the deployment and interpretation of these AI-driven solutions.

As organizations increasingly rely on AI and machine learning technologies to support their diversity and inclusion efforts, it is crucial to address the potential risks and ethical concerns associated with these technologies. This includes ensuring that the data used to train these systems is free from biases and that the algorithms are regularly audited and updated to mitigate the potential for perpetuating or amplifying existing biases. Additionally, organizations must prioritize transparency and accountability in the development and deployment of these technologies, involving diverse stakeholders and subject matter experts to ensure that ethical considerations are at the forefront of their implementation.

The exploration of workplace policies and initiatives promoting gender diversity and inclusion would be incomplete without acknowledging the intersection of gender with other dimensions of diversity, such as race, ethnicity, sexual orientation, and disability. An intersectional approach recognizes that women from different backgrounds and identities face compounded barriers and unique challenges in the workplace. Initiatives that address gender diversity alone may fall short in creating an inclusive environment for all women. It is therefore crucial for organizations to adopt a holistic, intersectional lens that considers the multifaceted experiences and needs of their diverse workforce.

Adopting an intersectional approach to diversity and inclusion requires organizations to critically examine the ways in which various forms of discrimination and marginalization intersect and compound the barriers faced by individuals with multiple marginalized identities. This involves actively listening to and amplifying the voices and experiences of individuals from diverse backgrounds, and tailoring policies, programs, and initiatives to address their unique needs and challenges. By embracing intersectionality, organizations can foster a more nuanced understanding of the complexities of diversity and create a more inclusive environment that empowers and supports all individuals, regardless of their intersecting identities.

Many organizations have recognized the importance of an intersectional approach to diversity and inclusion. Companies like Microsoft and Accenture have established employee resource groups and support networks focused on specific intersectional identities, such as women of color, LGBTQ+ women, and women with disabilities. These groups provide a safe space for individuals to share their experiences, offer support and mentorship, and advocate for policies and initiatives that address their unique needs and challenges within the organization. By amplifying these diverse voices and perspectives, companies can better understand and address the compounded barriers faced by women from marginalized communities.

In addition to establishing employee resource groups, organizations that have successfully adopted an intersectional approach have often done so by conducting comprehensive diversity audits and assessments to identify the unique challenges and barriers faced by individuals with intersecting marginalized identities. This data can then inform the development of tailored policies, programs, and initiatives that address these specific needs, as well as provide a baseline for measuring progress and identifying areas for improvement. By taking a data-driven and intersectional approach, organizations can ensure that their diversity and inclusion efforts are truly inclusive and address the multifaceted experiences of their diverse workforce.

As we draw the curtains on this exploration, it is clear that the path to gender diversity and inclusion is multifaceted, requiring a sustained and deliberate effort from all stakeholders – leaders, employees, policymakers, and society at large. The initiatives we have traversed in this chapter are but a constellation in the larger fabric of efforts aimed at creating a more equitable and inclusive workplace.

As organizations navigate the complex journey towards gender diversity and inclusion, it is essential to recognize that progress is not linear, and setbacks and challenges are inevitable. However, by fostering a culture of continuous learning, resilience, and a commitment to ongoing improvement, organizations can weather these challenges and adapt their strategies to meet the ever-evolving needs of their diverse workforce. Additionally, by embracing a growth mindset and viewing setbacks as opportunities for learning and growth, organizations can foster a more agile and responsive approach to diversity and inclusion, ensuring that their efforts remain relevant and impactful.

While organizations play a crucial role in promoting gender diversity and inclusion, the responsibility for driving systemic change extends beyond the workplace. Policymakers and governments must also take action to address the root causes of gender inequality and create an enabling environment for women's economic empowerment. This may involve implementing legislation that promotes pay equity, mandates gender diversity on corporate boards, or provides incentives for companies that prioritize diversity and inclusion. Additionally, educational institutions have a critical role to play in fostering a pipeline of diverse talent and challenging gender stereotypes from an early age.

Addressing the root causes of gender inequality and creating an enabling environment for women's economic empowerment requires a multifaceted and collaborative approach involving various stakeholders, including policymakers, educational institutions, civil society organizations, and the private sector. By working together to implement comprehensive policy frameworks, educational initiatives, and targeted programs, these stakeholders can create a more supportive ecosystem for women's economic participation and advancement. This may include initiatives such as ensuring equal access to quality education, providing financial literacy and entrepreneurship training, and implementing family-friendly policies that support work-life balance for working women.

Each policy, each program, each act of advocacy is a brushstroke in the larger picture of equality, painting a vision of a future where talent and potential are nurtured and rewarded, regardless of gender or any other identity marker. It is a future where the workplace is not merely a reflection of society's diversity but a beacon of progress, fostering innovation, creativity, and sustainable growth through the power of inclusivity.

To realize this vision of a more equitable and inclusive future, it is essential to recognize that the pursuit of gender diversity and inclusion is not a singular endeavor but rather a collective effort that requires sustained commitment and collaboration across sectors and stakeholders. By fostering cross-sector partnerships and leveraging the expertise and resources of diverse organizations, we can amplify our impact and drive more comprehensive and sustainable change. This could involve initiatives such as public-private partnerships to promote gender-responsive policies and programs, multi-stakeholder collaborations to address intersectional barriers to inclusion, and cross-sector knowledge-sharing platforms to disseminate best practices and foster continuous learning.

The benefits of gender diversity and inclusion extend beyond the workplace, contributing to the broader goal of achieving gender equality in society. When women are empowered and given equal opportunities in the workforce, it has a ripple effect on their families, communities, and the overall economy. Women's economic participation and decision-making power can contribute to poverty reduction, improved health and education outcomes, and the overall well-being of societies. As such, promoting gender diversity and inclusion in the workplace is not only a moral imperative but also a strategic investment in the sustainable development of nations.

The ripple effects of gender diversity and inclusion in the workplace extend beyond economic and social development, and can contribute to broader societal progress and sustainability. When women are empowered and have equal opportunities to participate in decision-making processes, it can drive positive changes in areas such as environmental conservation, conflict resolution, and governance. Additionally, by challenging traditional gender roles and stereotypes, a diverse and inclusive workplace can serve as a catalyst for broader cultural shifts, promoting more equitable gender norms and creating role models for future generations, ultimately contributing to the achievement of the United Nations Sustainable Development Goals.

The connection between gender diversity and inclusion in the workplace and the achievement of the United Nations Sustainable Development Goals (SDGs) is multifaceted and profound. By promoting gender equality and women's empowerment in the workplace, organizations can directly contribute to SDG 5 (Gender Equality) and indirectly support the attainment of other goals, such as SDG 1 (No Poverty), SDG 3 (Good Health and Well-Being), and SDG 4 (Quality Education). When women are economically empowered and have equal opportunities to participate in decision-making processes, it can lead to increased investments in education, healthcare, and sustainable development initiatives, ultimately contributing to the overall well-being of societies and the planet.

Let us carry forward the message that diversity is not simply a metric to be achieved but a principle to be embraced. It is the foundation upon which a more just and equitable society is built. As we move ahead, let each of us be an architect of this transformative vision, shaping a world where every individual has the space to thrive, and where the richness of our differences is celebrated as a strength, not a limitation.

Embracing diversity and inclusion as a guiding principle requires a deep commitment to continuous learning, self-reflection, and a willingness to challenge long-held assumptions and biases. It involves actively seeking out perspectives and experiences that differ from our own, and cultivating a genuine curiosity and openness to different ways of thinking and being. By doing so, we not only enrich our own understanding of the world but also create spaces where diverse voices and experiences are valued, respected, and celebrated, ultimately fostering a more inclusive and equitable society for all.

Embracing diversity and inclusion as a guiding principle requires a fundamental shift in mindsets and organizational cultures. It involves challenging deeply ingrained biases, questioning long-held assumptions, and being open to different perspectives and ways of thinking. This shift can be uncomfortable and disruptive, but it is essential for creating truly inclusive environments where every individual can contribute their unique talents and experiences. Organizations that embrace this principle not only foster a more equitable and harmonious workplace but also position themselves as leaders in innovation and driving positive societal change.

Fostering a culture of diversity and inclusion within organizations requires a comprehensive and sustained effort that permeates all aspects of the organization, from leadership and decision-making processes to talent acquisition, employee development, and organizational policies and practices. It involves actively identifying and addressing systemic barriers, biases, and inequities that may hinder the full participation and advancement of diverse talent. By embedding diversity and inclusion into the core values and strategic objectives of the organization, organizations can create a more inclusive and equitable workplace that values and leverages the unique perspectives and experiences of all employees.

The path to gender diversity and inclusion in the workplace is not a straightforward one. It is marked by challenges, resistance, and setbacks. But it is also illuminated by the unwavering commitment of those who believe in the power of equality. Every step forward, no matter how small, is a testament to the resilience and determination of the advocates, allies, and changemakers who refuse to accept the status quo.

One of the significant challenges in the pursuit of gender diversity and inclusion is the persistence of deeply entrenched societal norms and cultural biases. These biases often manifest in subtle ways, such as unconscious assumptions about gender roles, stereotypes about leadership capabilities, or the devaluation of traditionally female-dominated professions. Overcoming these ingrained mindsets requires sustained effort, education, and a willingness to confront uncomfortable truths. It also necessitates the involvement of men as allies, challenging traditional notions of masculinity and creating space for more diverse expressions of identity and leadership.

Engaging men as allies in the pursuit of gender diversity and inclusion is crucial, as they often hold positions of power and influence within organizations and society. By actively involving men in the conversation and empowering them to challenge gender biases and stereotypes, organizations can foster a more inclusive and supportive environment for all employees. Organizations that have successfully engaged men as allies have often done so by providing dedicated training programs that explore the concept of allyship, promote self-awareness and reflection, and equip men with the tools and strategies to actively challenge and dismantle systemic barriers to gender equality.

As we navigate this journey, let us draw strength from the stories of those who have paved the way. From the trailblazing women who shattered glass ceilings to the men who stood alongside them as allies, their experiences serve as a beacon of hope and inspiration. Let us honor their legacy by continuing to push boundaries, challenge norms, and create spaces where every voice is valued.

The stories of trailblazers and pioneers who have fought for gender equality and inclusion serve as a powerful reminder of the resilience, determination, and courage required to challenge the status quo and effect meaningful change. By sharing and amplifying these stories, we not only honor the legacies of those who have paved the way but also inspire and empower current and future generations to continue the fight for a more equitable and inclusive world. These stories can serve as a source of strength and motivation, reminding us that progress is possible, even in the face of formidable obstacles and setbacks.

The journey toward gender diversity and inclusion has been paved by countless pioneers and trailblazers who have challenged societal norms and broken down barriers. Women like Ruth Bader Ginsburg, who fought tirelessly for gender equality in the legal system, and Malala Yousafzai, a champion of girls' education and women's rights, have inspired generations with their courage and resilience. Meanwhile, men like former UN Secretary-General Ban Ki-moon and actor and activist Justin Baldoni have used their platforms to advocate for gender equality and redefine masculinity. Their stories serve as a reminder that progress is possible when individuals from all backgrounds come together to challenge the status quo and create a more inclusive world.

The trailblazers and pioneers who have fought for gender equality and inclusion have not only inspired generations but have also created a lasting legacy that continues to shape and inform the modern-day movement for diversity and inclusion. Their stories serve as powerful case studies, highlighting the strategies, tactics, and approaches that have proven effective in challenging systemic barriers and driving meaningful change. By studying and learning from these stories, organizations and individuals can gain valuable insights and lessons that can inform their own efforts to promote gender diversity and inclusion in the workplace and beyond.

The workplace of the future is one where diversity is not an afterthought but an integral part of its very fabric. It is a place where women and men can bring their whole selves to work, where their unique perspectives and experiences are celebrated as strengths. It is a place where innovation thrives, not despite diversity, but because of it.

Creating the inclusive workplace of the future requires a fundamental shift in organizational culture and mindsets. It involves actively challenging and dismantling systems and structures that have historically perpetuated discrimination and marginalization, and fostering an environment that values and embraces diverse perspectives, experiences, and ways of being. This shift requires a commitment to continuous learning, self-reflection, and a willingness to confront uncomfortable truths about systemic inequities and biases. By embracing a growth mindset and fostering a culture of inclusion, organizations can create a workplace where every individual feels valued, respected, and empowered to contribute their unique talents and perspectives.

Creating the inclusive workplace of the future requires a holistic approach that addresses not only gender diversity but also the intersections of other identities, such as race, ethnicity, age, disability, and sexual orientation. Organizations that embrace a culture of intersectional inclusion foster a sense of belonging for all employees, enabling them to contribute their unique perspectives and experiences without fear of discrimination or marginalization. By valuing and leveraging the richness of diversity across multiple dimensions, organizations can drive innovation, creativity, and better decision-making, ultimately enhancing their competitive advantage in the global marketplace.

Adopting an intersectional approach to diversity and inclusion involves recognizing and addressing the compounded barriers and unique experiences faced by individuals with multiple marginalized identities. This requires a deep understanding of the complex ways in which different forms of discrimination and oppression intersect and manifest in the workplace. By actively engaging with and amplifying the voices of individuals from diverse intersectional backgrounds, organizations can gain valuable insights into the specific challenges and obstacles they face, and tailor their policies, programs, and initiatives to address these unique needs and experiences.

Achieving this vision requires a collective effort. It demands that we confront the biases and barriers that have long held women back, that we have the courage to have difficult conversations, and that we hold ourselves and each other accountable for creating change. It requires that we approach diversity and inclusion not as a destination but as a continuous journey of learning, growth, and transformation.

Fostering a culture of accountability and collective responsibility is crucial in achieving the vision of a truly inclusive and equitable workplace. This involves holding leaders, managers, and all employees accountable for their actions and behaviors, and creating mechanisms for reporting and addressing instances of discrimination, harassment, or exclusion. Organizations that have successfully cultivated a culture of accountability have often done so by implementing robust policies and procedures, providing comprehensive training and education, and creating safe spaces for open and honest dialogue about diversity, inclusion, and equity.

Building an inclusive workplace is a continuous process that requires ongoing commitment, education, and self-reflection. It involves creating safe spaces for open and honest dialogue, where individuals can share their experiences, challenge assumptions, and learn from one another's perspectives. Organizations must be willing to confront uncomfortable truths, acknowledge their shortcomings, and actively work towards creating a more equitable and inclusive environment. This process may be uncomfortable and challenging, but it is essential for fostering a culture of mutual understanding, respect, and acceptance, where every individual can thrive and contribute their best.

Fostering a culture of continuous learning and self-reflection is essential in building an inclusive workplace. This involves creating opportunities for employees to engage in ongoing education and training on topics related to diversity, inclusion, and equity, such as unconscious bias awareness, inclusive leadership practices, and cross-cultural communication. Additionally, organizations can encourage and facilitate employee-led initiatives, such as resource groups, mentorship programs, and community outreach efforts, that promote personal and professional development while fostering a deeper understanding and appreciation of diversity.

As we embark on this journey, let us remember that the benefits of gender diversity and inclusion extend far beyond the workplace. When women thrive in their careers, it has a ripple effect on families, communities, and societies as a whole. It challenges traditional gender roles, breaks down stereotypes, and creates new possibilities for future generations.

The ripple effects of gender diversity and inclusion in the workplace can have a profound impact on societal transformation and cultural change. When women are empowered and have equal opportunities to participate in decision-making processes, it can challenge deeply ingrained gender norms and stereotypes, creating a more inclusive and equitable society for all. Furthermore, by fostering a culture of inclusion and respect in the workplace, organizations can serve as role models and catalysts for broader cultural shifts, inspiring and empowering individuals to embrace and celebrate diversity in all aspects of life.

The benefits of gender diversity and inclusion in the workplace have far-reaching implications for societal progress and sustainable development. When women are economically empowered and have equal opportunities to participate in decision-making processes, it can drive positive changes in areas such as education, healthcare, and poverty reduction. Additionally, by challenging traditional gender roles and stereotypes, a diverse and inclusive workplace can serve as a catalyst for broader cultural shifts, promoting more equitable gender norms and creating role models for future generations of girls and young women.

The connection between gender diversity and inclusion in the workplace and societal progress is multidimensional and reinforcing. When women are empowered economically and have equal representation in decision-making processes, they can better advocate for policies and initiatives that address the specific needs and challenges faced by women and girls in areas such as education, healthcare, and poverty alleviation. This, in turn, can lead to increased investments in these critical areas, ultimately contributing to the overall well-being and development of communities and nations.

The positive impact of gender diversity and inclusion in the workplace extends beyond social and economic development and can contribute to broader environmental sustainability and global well-being. Research has shown that women's participation in decision-making processes, particularly in areas such as natural resource management, environmental conservation, and climate change mitigation, can lead to more sustainable and effective solutions. By promoting gender diversity and inclusion in these critical areas, organizations can leverage the unique perspectives, experiences, and knowledge of women to address some of the world's most pressing environmental challenges.

Women's unique perspectives and experiences often result in a more holistic and inclusive approach to environmental management and conservation efforts. For example, research has shown that women are more likely to prioritize long-term sustainability and the well-being of future generations when making decisions about natural resource management. Additionally, women's traditional knowledge and practices, often passed down through generations, can provide valuable insights into sustainable resource utilization and conservation strategies.

So let us forge ahead with renewed purpose and determination. Let us be bold in our vision, unwavering in our commitment, and steadfast in our belief that a more inclusive world is within our reach. Together, we have the power to create a workplace – and a world – where every individual can flourish, regardless of their gender or any other identity marker.

Forging ahead with renewed purpose and determination in the pursuit of gender diversity and inclusion requires a collective commitment to continuous learning, self-reflection, and a willingness to confront and dismantle systemic barriers. It involves actively seeking out and amplifying the voices and perspectives of those who have been historically marginalized, and creating spaces where diverse experiences and identities are valued, respected, and celebrated. By embracing a spirit of collaboration, empathy, and allyship, we can harness the collective power of our diversity to drive transformative change and create a more just and equitable world for all.

Fostering gender diversity and inclusion in the workplace is not merely a matter of compliance or tokenism; it is a moral and ethical imperative that aligns with the fundamental principles of human rights and dignity. By creating workplaces that value and celebrate diversity, we not only unlock the full potential of our organizations but also contribute to the broader pursuit of a more just and equitable society. It is a journey that requires collective action, courageous leadership, and a commitment to continuous learning and growth. As we forge ahead, let us be guided by a vision of a world where every individual has the opportunity to thrive, where differences are celebrated, and where the richness of our diversity is harnessed as a source of strength and progress.

The moral and ethical imperative of fostering gender diversity and inclusion is rooted in the fundamental principles of human rights and dignity, which affirm that every individual, regardless of gender or any other identity marker, is entitled to equal rights, opportunities, and respect. By creating workplaces that embrace and celebrate diversity, we not only uphold these essential human rights principles but also contribute to the broader societal goal of promoting social justice, equity, and inclusion for all.

The exploration of workplace policies and initiatives promoting gender diversity and inclusion is not just a chapter in a book; it is a call to action. It is an invitation to be part of a movement that has the power to transform not only the workplace but society as a whole. It is a reminder that each of us has a role to play in creating a more just and equitable world.

Responding to the call to action for promoting gender diversity and inclusion requires a collective commitment to challenging the status quo and addressing the root causes of systemic inequalities. This involves actively engaging in difficult conversations, confronting deeply ingrained biases and stereotypes, and advocating for structural and institutional changes that dismantle barriers and create an enabling environment for diverse voices and perspectives to thrive. By embracing this shared responsibility, we can be agents of transformative change, reshaping our workplaces and communities to reflect the values of equity, inclusion, and human dignity.

The journey towards gender diversity and inclusion is not a linear path; it is a multifaceted endeavor that requires sustained effort, collaboration, and a willingness to challenge deeply ingrained systems and structures. It demands that we confront the intersectional barriers faced by marginalized groups, address the root causes of inequality, and embrace a holistic approach that recognizes the interconnectedness of social, economic, and political factors. By joining forces with allies across sectors and disciplines, we can amplify our impact and create a ripple effect that extends beyond the workplace, driving positive change in our communities and shaping a more inclusive and equitable society for all.

Addressing the intersectional barriers faced by marginalized groups is crucial in the journey towards gender diversity and inclusion, as these barriers often reinforce and compound existing inequalities. For example, women of color may face compounded discrimination based on both their gender and race, while LGBTQ+ women may face additional challenges due to their sexual orientation or gender identity. By adopting an intersectional lens and actively engaging with diverse communities and stakeholders, we can better understand and address the unique challenges faced by different groups, and develop tailored strategies and solutions that promote equity and inclusion for all.

As we close this chapter, let us carry forward the lessons learned and the insights gained. Let us continue to challenge the status quo, to push for progress, and to be the change we wish to see in the world. For in the end, the story of gender diversity and inclusion is not just about women; it is about all of us. It is about creating a world where every individual can thrive, where every voice is heard, and where the full potential of humanity can be realized.

As we carry forward the lessons learned and insights gained from this exploration, it is important to recognize that the pursuit of gender diversity and inclusion is not a finite journey with a clear endpoint. Rather, it is an ongoing process that requires sustained commitment, adaptability, and a willingness to continuously learn and evolve. By embracing a growth mindset and fostering a culture of continuous improvement, we can ensure that our efforts remain relevant, responsive, and effective in addressing the ever-changing landscape of diversity, equity, and inclusion challenges.

The journey towards gender diversity and inclusion is a shared responsibility that requires the active participation and commitment of all members of society. It is not a battle to be fought solely by women or marginalized groups; it is a collective endeavor that demands allyship, empathy, and a willingness to confront and dismantle systemic barriers. By embracing this shared responsibility, we can create a more inclusive and equitable world where every individual has the opportunity to contribute their unique talents and perspectives, and where the richness of our diversity is celebrated as a source of strength, innovation, and progress.

Embracing shared responsibility in the pursuit of gender diversity and inclusion requires a shift in mindset, from viewing it as a "women's issue" to recognizing it as a collective responsibility that impacts the well-being and progress of society as a whole. This shift in mindset must be accompanied by concrete actions and a genuine commitment from all members of society, including men, to actively challenge and dismantle systemic barriers, confront biases and discrimination, and create an enabling environment for diverse voices and perspectives to thrive.

So let us step forward with courage, compassion, and conviction. Let us be the architects of a better tomorrow, one where the workplace is a beacon of equality and a catalyst for change. The journey ahead may be long and arduous, but it is a journey worth taking. For in the end, the destination we seek is not just a more diverse and inclusive workplace, but a more just and equitable world for all.

Stepping forward with courage, compassion, and conviction in the pursuit of gender diversity and inclusion requires a deep commitment to personal growth, self-awareness, and a willingness to confront our own biases and blind spots. It involves actively listening to diverse voices and perspectives, embracing humility, and being open to having our assumptions and beliefs challenged. By cultivating a culture of empathy, respect, and mutual understanding, we can create an environment where difficult conversations can take place, where diverse experiences are valued, and where we can work collectively towards a more just and equitable future.

The path to gender diversity and inclusion is not without challenges and setbacks, but it is a journey that holds the promise of a better future for all. As we navigate this path, let us draw inspiration from the resilience and determination of those who have come before us, and let us honor their legacies by continuing to push boundaries, challenge norms, and create spaces where every voice is valued and respected. Together, we can shape a world where diversity is not merely tolerated but celebrated as a source of strength, where inclusion is not just a buzzword but a lived reality, and where every individual has the opportunity to thrive and contribute their unique talents and perspectives to the betterment of society.

As we navigate the path to gender diversity and inclusion, it is crucial to recognize and celebrate the progress that has been made, while also acknowledging the work that remains to be done. By celebrating milestones and achievements, we can draw inspiration and motivation from the resilience and determination of those who have fought for equity and justice. At the same time, we must remain vigilant and continue to challenge systemic barriers, confront biases, and advocate for structural and institutional changes that promote sustainable and lasting progress towards a more just and equitable society.

The journey towards gender diversity and inclusion is a multigenerational endeavor that requires a commitment to fostering an inclusive and equitable environment for future generations. By creating workplaces and communities that celebrate diversity, challenge biases, and promote equal opportunities for all, we can inspire and empower the next generation to carry forward the torch of progress and create a more just and inclusive world. Through education, mentorship, and role modeling, we can instill the values of equity, respect, and appreciation for diversity in the minds and hearts of young people, equipping them with the tools and mindset to continue the legacy of championing inclusion and social justice.

Chapter 5
Education and Access to Opportunities

Section A: Overview of advancements in women's access to education and academic opportunities

The tide of progress in women's rights has swept across various domains, and education stands as a beacon of transformative change. As we delve into this narrative, let's ponder a salient question: How have the doors of learning swung wide open for women, and what has been the impact of their increased access to education?

The pursuit of equal educational opportunities for women is not merely a matter of ensuring access but also fostering an environment that empowers women to thrive and reach their full potential. It involves dismantling systemic barriers, challenging deeply entrenched societal norms and biases, and creating a supportive ecosystem that nurtures women's intellectual growth, leadership abilities, and contributions across various fields of knowledge and endeavor.

The journey towards equal access to education for women has been a long and arduous one, marked by struggles against deeply entrenched societal norms, cultural biases, and systemic barriers. However, the transformative power of education and its ability to empower individuals and drive societal progress has fueled relentless advocacy and policy initiatives aimed at breaking down these barriers and ensuring that the right to education is extended to all, regardless of gender.

According to a report by the UNESCO Global Education Monitoring Report, despite significant progress in recent decades, deep-rooted gender disparities in education persist, particularly in low-income countries and conflict-affected areas. The report highlights that around 129 million girls worldwide are out of school, and women account for nearly two-thirds of the world's illiterate adult population. These staggering figures underscore the need for continued advocacy, targeted interventions, and a comprehensive approach to addressing the systemic barriers that impede girls' and women's access to education.

The struggle for women's access to education has been inextricably linked to the broader quest for gender equality and women's empowerment. Throughout history, denying women access to education has been a powerful tool used to perpetuate patriarchal structures, suppress women's voices, and limit their participation in various spheres of society. By overcoming these barriers, women have not only gained access to knowledge but also the means to challenge oppressive norms, assert their agency, and contribute to societal progress on equal footing with their male counterparts.

A powerful example of the relationship between women's education and empowerment can be found in the work of Malala Yousafzai, the Pakistani activist and Nobel Peace Prize laureate. Yousafzai, who survived an assassination attempt by the Taliban for advocating for girls' education, has become a global symbol of the struggle for gender equality and the transformative power of education. Her story highlights how denying women access to education has been used as a tool to subjugate and oppress, and how education can empower women to challenge oppressive systems and demand their rightful place in society.

Whispers of change began to stir with the recognition of education as a universal human right—one not limited to the male gender. Picture a world where once, not long ago, the majority of girls were denied even the most basic education due to entrenched cultural norms, poverty, and discriminatory policies. Now, envision the present, where girls' enrollment in primary education has reached near parity with boys in many regions, thanks to concerted global efforts and national initiatives.

The recognition of education as a fundamental human right for all, regardless of gender, was a pivotal achievement enshrined in the

Universal Declaration of Human Rights (1948) and reinforced by subsequent international conventions and agreements, such as the Convention on the Elimination of All Forms of Discrimination Against Women (CEDAW) and the Sustainable Development Goals (SDGs). This recognition not only challenged long-standing patriarchal notions but also provided a legal and moral imperative for governments and international organizations to take concrete steps towards ensuring equal access to education for women and girls.

The recognition of education as a universal human right, regardless of gender, has been a pivotal achievement in the struggle for women's empowerment. This acknowledgment not only challenged long-standing patriarchal notions that education was a privilege reserved for men but also laid the foundation for a more equitable and inclusive society, where every individual, irrespective of their gender, has the right to access knowledge and realize their full potential.

According to data from the United Nations Educational, Scientific and Cultural Organization (UNESCO), the global gender parity index for primary education enrollment reached 0.99 in 2019, indicating near parity in access to primary education for girls and boys. However, this progress has not been uniform across regions, with sub-Saharan Africa and some parts of Asia still facing significant gender disparities in primary education enrollment.

Despite the progress made in achieving gender parity in primary education enrollment at the global level, regional disparities persist. According to the UNESCO Institute for Statistics, in sub-Saharan Africa, the gender parity index for primary education was only 0.92 in 2019, indicating that girls in this region remain significantly disadvantaged in accessing primary education compared to boys. Similarly, in some parts of South and West Asia, cultural and socioeconomic factors continue to hinder girls' access to education, with the gender parity index in these regions remaining below the global average.

While the progress towards gender parity in primary education enrollment is commendable, it is crucial to recognize that access alone does not guarantee educational attainment or achievement. In many regions where gender parity has been achieved, girls and women continue to face numerous barriers that hinder their ability to fully engage with and benefit from educational opportunities. These barriers may include gender-based violence, lack of safe and inclusive learning environments, inadequate access to resources and support systems, and persistent societal norms and biases that undervalue women's education.

A report by the United Nations Girls' Education Initiative (UNGEI) highlights the multidimensional challenges that persist in ensuring quality and inclusive education for girls, even in regions where access has improved. The report cites issues such as gender-based violence in and around schools, lack of gender-sensitive curricula and teaching practices, and inadequate sanitation facilities as significant barriers that can undermine girls' ability to fully engage in and benefit from educational opportunities. Addressing these challenges requires a comprehensive approach that goes beyond merely increasing enrollment rates and focuses on creating safe, inclusive, and empowering learning environments for girls.

This seismic shift did not occur overnight but through relentless advocacy, policy reforms, and grassroots movements. Governments and institutions implemented policies aimed at eradicating the gender gap in education, such as India's Right to Education Act and the World Bank's initiatives to promote girls' education in developing countries. Scholarships and grants tailored for women and girls emerged, breaking down the financial barriers that once stood like sentinels, guarding the gates of knowledge.

One notable example of a policy initiative aimed at promoting girls' education is the Camfed (Campaign for Female Education) program, which has been operating in several African countries since 1993. Camfed's approach combines financial support through scholarships and bursaries with a comprehensive support system that includes mentoring, life skills training, and community engagement. This holistic approach has not only increased enrollment and retention rates for girls but also fostered a more enabling environment for their personal and academic development.

The implementation of targeted policies and initiatives to promote girls' education has been a crucial catalyst for change, but their success has often been contingent on a multifaceted approach that addresses the underlying social, cultural, and economic factors that perpetuate gender disparities in education. For example, in addition to providing financial support through scholarships and grants, effective initiatives have also focused on community engagement, awareness-raising campaigns, and addressing issues such as child marriage, gender-based violence, and harmful cultural practices that impede girls' access to education.

The impact of targeted policies and initiatives aimed at promoting girls' education has been significant. For instance, the World Bank's Adolescent Girls Initiative, implemented in over 20 countries, has improved access to education, life skills training, and employment opportunities for underserved adolescent girls. In Bangladesh, the Female Secondary School Assistance Project, which provided stipends and tuition assistance to girls in secondary schools, contributed to a remarkable increase in female enrollment and retention rates.

According to a report by the World Bank, the Adolescent Girls Initiative has directly benefited over 20,000 adolescent girls across various countries, providing them with access to education, life skills training, and employment opportunities. The initiative's impact extends beyond the immediate beneficiaries, as it also aims to challenge social norms and create a more enabling environment for girls' empowerment. For example, in Rwanda, the initiative has worked with local communities to address issues such as child marriage and gender-based violence, which can impede girls' access to education.

The success stories of initiatives like the World Bank's Adolescent Girls Initiative and Bangladesh's Female Secondary School Assistance Project highlight the transformative impact that targeted interventions can have on girls' education and empowerment. By addressing financial barriers, providing life skills training, and creating an enabling environment for girls to pursue their educational aspirations, these initiatives have not only improved enrollment and retention rates but also laid the foundation for greater economic and social opportunities for young women.

The impact of initiatives like these extends beyond the immediate beneficiaries and has broader implications for societal development and progress. According to a study by the United Nations Population Fund (UNFPA), educating girls is a powerful catalyst for achieving various Sustainable Development Goals, including reducing poverty (SDG 1), promoting good health and well-being (SDG 3), and fostering gender equality (SDG 5). The study highlights that educating girls not only empowers them as individuals but also contributes to breaking the intergenerational cycle of poverty and inequality, ultimately benefiting entire communities and societies.

In the not-so-distant past, higher education was a citadel largely reserved for men, with women's attendance seen as an anomaly or a privilege. Today, women are not only attending universities but, in many countries, they are now the majority. The corridors of academia that once echoed with predominantly deep voices now resound with the vibrant tones of women eager to learn, research, and innovate. Countries like Sri Lanka and Cuba have led the way in promoting gender parity in higher education through targeted policies and support programs.

The increasing representation of women in higher education is not merely a matter of statistical parity but a reflection of the profound societal and cultural shifts that have taken place. According to a report by the United Nations Educational, Scientific and Cultural Organization (UNESCO), the global participation rate of women in tertiary education nearly doubled between 1970 and 2019, from 24% to 41%. This remarkable progress can be attributed to a combination of factors, including targeted policies, increased access to primary and secondary education for girls, and the growing recognition of the economic and societal benefits of investing in women's education.

The increasing representation of women in higher education institutions is a testament to the progress made in dismantling long-standing barriers and challenging societal perceptions about women's intellectual capabilities and their role in academia. However, it is important to recognize that this progress has not been uniform across disciplines and fields of study. In certain domains, such as STEM (Science, Technology, Engineering, and Mathematics), women remain underrepresented, highlighting the need for targeted interventions to address the persistent gender gaps and biases within these fields.

According to the United Nations Statistics Division, as of 2019, women accounted for over 50% of tertiary education enrollment in nearly half of the countries worldwide. This remarkable achievement has been driven by a combination of factors, including increased access to primary and secondary education for girls, targeted financial aid and scholarship programs, and a growing recognition of the societal and economic benefits of empowering women through higher education.

The growing recognition of the societal and economic benefits of empowering women through higher education has been a driving force behind the increase in women's enrollment in tertiary institutions. Numerous studies have demonstrated the positive impact of women's education on various development indicators, including improved health outcomes, reduced poverty, and increased economic growth. As a result, governments, international organizations, and private sector entities have increasingly recognized the value of investing in women's education as a catalyst for sustainable development and societal progress.

A report by the World Bank highlights the significant economic returns of investing in women's higher education. The report estimates that closing the gender gap in tertiary education could boost productivity and increase economic growth by as much as 0.3 percentage points per year in some countries. Furthermore, educated women are more likely to participate in the labor force, earn higher incomes, and contribute to the overall well-being of their families and communities, creating a virtuous cycle of development and empowerment.

Consider the impact of role models and mentorship programs. Can you feel the power of a young girl seeing a woman in a position of academic authority, realizing that her own potential is limitless? Female professors, researchers, and administrators are no longer rarities; they are the norm in many educational institutions, guiding the next generation and serving as beacons of inspiration.

The importance of female role models and mentors in academic settings cannot be overstated. According to a study by the American Psychological Association, the presence of female faculty and administrators in higher education institutions can have a profound impact on the academic and personal development of female students. By seeing women in positions of authority and leadership, young women are empowered to envision themselves in similar roles, challenge gender stereotypes, and pursue their academic and professional aspirations with greater confidence and determination.

The presence of female role models and mentors in academic settings is crucial for fostering a sense of belonging and self-efficacy among young girls and women pursuing education. By seeing women in positions of authority and leadership within educational institutions, girls and young women can envision their own potential and aspire to achieve similar success. Moreover, female mentors can provide guidance, support, and share their experiences navigating the challenges and biases that women often face in academic and professional environments.

The presence of female role models and mentors in academic settings has been shown to have a profound impact on girls' educational aspirations and achievement. According to a study by the American Psychological Association, having a female mentor can help young women develop greater self-confidence, resilience, and a stronger sense of belonging in academic environments. Additionally, female faculty members can serve as powerful role models, inspiring girls to pursue fields and careers that were once considered predominantly male domains.

The impact of female role models and mentors extends beyond the academic realm and can influence societal perceptions and norms. According to a report by the United Nations Entity for Gender Equality and the Empowerment of Women (UN Women), the presence of women in leadership positions across various sectors, including academia, can challenge gender stereotypes and promote a more inclusive and equitable society. By occupying positions of authority and influence, women in academic leadership roles can serve as catalysts for broader societal change, inspiring and empowering girls and women to pursue their ambitions and contribute to the advancement of their communities.

The impact of female role models and mentors extends beyond fostering self-confidence and belonging; it can also inspire young women to challenge gender stereotypes and pursue fields and careers that have traditionally been male-dominated. By seeing women succeeding in STEM fields, for example, girls may be more inclined to explore these disciplines, ultimately contributing to a more diverse and inclusive workforce in these crucial areas of innovation and technological advancement.

But what of the fields where women remain underrepresented? In the realms of science, technology, engineering, and mathematics (STEM), the journey towards gender balance is ongoing. Yet, even here, we witness progress as initiatives like the L'Oréal-UNESCO For Women in Science program and outreach programs by organizations such as the Association for Women in Science encourage girls to explore these disciplines. Girls Who Code, for example, has become a battle cry for empowerment in the digital age.

The underrepresentation of women in STEM fields is a complex issue rooted in various sociocultural and systemic factors, including gender stereotypes, lack of role models and mentors, and biases in educational and professional environments. However, initiatives like the L'Oréal-UNESCO For Women in Science program, Girls Who Code, and others are working to address these challenges through a multifaceted approach that includes promoting female role models, providing mentorship and networking opportunities, and fostering inclusive learning environments that encourage girls' participation and interest in STEM subjects from an early age.

The persistent underrepresentation of women in STEM fields is a complex issue that stems from a confluence of factors, including deeply ingrained societal biases, lack of role models and mentors, and systemic barriers within educational systems and institutional cultures. To address this challenge, a multifaceted approach is required, involving interventions at various levels, from early childhood education to higher education and professional development opportunities. By fostering an inclusive and supportive environment, promoting female role models and mentors, and challenging gender stereotypes from an early age, initiatives like L'Oréal-UNESCO For Women in Science and Girls Who Code aim to inspire and empower young women to pursue their passions and contribute to the advancement of STEM fields.

Despite the progress made in promoting women's participation in STEM fields, significant gender disparities persist. According to the United Nations Educational, Scientific and Cultural Organization (UNESCO), only 35% of STEM students in higher education globally are women. To address this gap, initiatives like the European Union's Horizon 2020 program have allocated funding and resources to support women's participation and leadership in STEM research and innovation.

The underrepresentation of women in STEM fields is not merely a matter of gender equality but also has far-reaching implications for scientific progress, innovation, and economic development. According to a report by the Organization for Economic Co-operation and Development (OECD), increasing the participation of women in STEM fields could significantly boost economic growth and productivity. The report highlights that gender diversity in STEM can foster innovation by bringing diverse perspectives, experiences, and approaches to problem-solving, ultimately leading to more creative and effective solutions.

The underrepresentation of women in STEM fields not only perpetuates gender inequalities but also has far-reaching implications for scientific and technological progress, innovation, and economic development. By failing to tap into the full potential of women's talents and perspectives, we risk stifling the advancement of knowledge and missing out on diverse approaches and solutions to complex challenges. Initiatives like the European Union's Horizon

2020 program aim to address this issue by providing targeted funding and resources to support women's participation and leadership in STEM research and innovation, ultimately fostering a more diverse and inclusive scientific community.

According to a report by the United Nations Educational, Scientific and Cultural Organization (UNESCO), the underrepresentation of women in STEM fields is a global phenomenon, with significant disparities across regions and disciplines. The report highlights that while women account for nearly 53% of the world's bachelor's and master's graduates, they represent only around 28% of researchers in the fields of science, technology, engineering, and mathematics. This gender gap not only represents a loss of talent and potential but also limits the diversity of perspectives and approaches that drive innovation and scientific breakthroughs.

Dive deeper into the narrative, and you'll find that education has become more than just attending school. It's about creating environments where women can thrive academically. Universities are adapting curricula, ensuring that they reflect a diverse array of perspectives and experiences. Course offerings now frequently include women's studies and other subjects that were once invisible in the academic landscape, fostering a more inclusive and representative learning experience.

The integration of women's studies and gender-focused curricula in higher education has been driven by a growing recognition of the importance of diverse perspectives and experiences in shaping knowledge and understanding. According to a report by the Association of American Colleges and Universities, courses that explore gender, race, and other social identities can enhance students' critical thinking skills, cultural competence, and ability to engage with complex societal issues. By incorporating these perspectives into the curriculum, universities are not only fostering a more inclusive learning environment but also equipping students with the knowledge and skills needed to navigate and contribute to an increasingly diverse and interconnected world.

The integration of diverse perspectives and experiences into academic curricula is essential for creating an inclusive and representative learning environment that empowers and validates the voices of women and other underrepresented groups. By incorporating women's studies and other interdisciplinary fields that explore issues of gender, power, and identity, educational institutions can challenge traditional narratives, foster critical thinking, and promote a more nuanced understanding of the intersections between gender and other social, cultural, and political factors.

The integration of women's studies and gender-focused curricula in higher education has been a significant step towards creating inclusive learning environments that validate and acknowledge the experiences and perspectives of women. These academic programs not only provide a platform for exploring issues related to gender, power, and identity but also challenge traditional narratives and foster critical thinking about the intersections of gender with other social, cultural, and political factors.

The emergence of women's studies and gender-focused curricula in higher education institutions has been driven by a combination of factors, including the Women's Liberation Movement of the 1960s and 1970s, as well as a growing body of interdisciplinary scholarship that explored issues of gender, power, and identity. According to a historical analysis by the National Women's Studies Association, the first women's studies program was established at San Diego State University in 1970, marking a significant milestone in the academic recognition and legitimization of this field of study.

The integration of women's studies and gender-focused curricula in higher education institutions has been instrumental in fostering a more inclusive and empowering academic environment for women. By providing a dedicated space for exploring gender-related issues, these programs not only validate and acknowledge women's experiences and perspectives but also equip students with the critical thinking skills and theoretical frameworks necessary to analyze and challenge systemic gender inequalities and power dynamics. Furthermore, these programs often serve as platforms for interdisciplinary collaboration and research, contributing to the advancement of knowledge and scholarship in the field of gender studies and related disciplines.

The impact of women's studies and gender-focused curricula extends beyond the classroom and into the broader academic community. According to a study by the American Association of University Professors, the presence of these programs has contributed to increased diversity and representation among faculty, staff, and administrators in higher education institutions. By fostering a more inclusive and supportive environment for women and underrepresented groups, these programs have helped to cultivate a more diverse and representative academic workforce, which in turn can serve as role models and mentors for future generations of scholars and students.

The integration of women's studies and gender-focused curricula in academic institutions has played a pivotal role in shaping the discourse around gender equality and women's empowerment. By fostering critical inquiry and scholarly research into the complexities of gender dynamics, these programs have contributed to a deeper understanding of the systemic barriers, biases, and power structures that perpetuate gender inequalities across various domains, including education, employment, healthcare, and political representation. This knowledge has informed policy discussions, advocacy efforts, and the development of strategies aimed at addressing gender-based discrimination and promoting women's rights and advancement.

The growth of women's studies and gender-focused curricula in academic institutions has been accompanied by a proliferation of interdisciplinary research and scholarship examining the intersections of gender with other social identities and systems of oppression. According to a review by the Journal of Women's History, this interdisciplinary approach has been instrumental in understanding the complex and multifaceted nature of gender inequalities, as well as the ways in which gender intersects with race, class, sexuality, and other forms of marginalization. This scholarly work has informed critical analysis and advocacy efforts aimed at addressing intersectional forms of discrimination and promoting social justice for all marginalized groups.

The ripple effects of this educational renaissance are far-reaching. Educated women are changing the socio-economic fabric of their communities, nations, and indeed, the world. They are taking on leadership roles, starting businesses, advocating for social change, and contributing to sustainable development. The empowerment gained through education is a catalyst for broader societal transformation, as evidenced by the link between higher levels of female education and improved health outcomes, reduced poverty, and economic growth.

The transformative impact of women's education on societal development is exemplified by the rise of women-led businesses and entrepreneurship. According to a report by the Global Entrepreneurship Monitor, countries with higher levels of female education tend to have higher rates of women's entrepreneurial activity. This is because education not only equips women with the necessary skills and knowledge but also fosters confidence, leadership abilities, and access to networks and resources that support entrepreneurial endeavors. By empowering women to start and grow their own businesses, education contributes to economic growth, job creation, and the development of innovative products and services that can address societal needs.

The transformative impact of women's education is multidimensional, transcending individual empowerment and contributing to broader societal progress across various spheres. Educated women are not only more likely to participate in the formal labor market and contribute to economic growth but also play a pivotal role in shaping the future of their communities and nations. By gaining access to knowledge and critical thinking skills, women are better equipped to challenge harmful cultural practices, advocate for policy changes, and contribute to the development of sustainable solutions to complex social and environmental challenges.

The positive impact of women's education on societal development extends beyond economic indicators and into the realm of political participation and decision-making. According to a study by the Inter-Parliamentary Union, countries with higher levels of girls' education tend to have greater representation of women in national parliaments and decision-making bodies. This increased political representation can lead to the prioritization of issues that affect women and families, such as healthcare, education, and gender equality, ultimately contributing to the development of more inclusive and equitable policies and social programs.

The transformative impact of women's education extends beyond individual empowerment and has far-reaching implications for societal development. According to a report by the United Nations Population Fund (UNFPA), every additional year of education for a girl can increase her future income by up to 20%, contributing to overall economic growth and poverty reduction. Additionally, educated women are more likely to participate in decision-making processes, advocate for their rights, and promote sustainable practices, ultimately contributing to the achievement of the United Nations Sustainable Development Goals.

The impact of women's education on societal development is particularly evident in the area of health and well-being. According to a report by the World Health Organization (WHO), educated women are more likely to have better knowledge and understanding of health issues, seek preventive care, and adopt healthy behaviors. This not only benefits their own health but also that of their families and communities. Educated mothers are more likely to seek prenatal care, have fewer children, and invest in their children's education and health, contributing to a virtuous cycle of improved health outcomes and human development.

The positive impact of women's education extends beyond economic indicators and has profound implications for human development and societal well-being. Educated women are more likely to delay marriage and childbirth, have smaller and healthier families, and invest in the education and health of their children, contributing to a virtuous cycle of development and progress. Furthermore, women's participation in decision-making processes at various levels, from households to communities and national governments, can lead to more inclusive and equitable policies, ultimately fostering a more just and sustainable society.

The positive impact of women's education on societal well-being is particularly evident in the area of environmental sustainability. According to a report by the United Nations Environment Programme (UNEP), educated women are more likely to adopt sustainable practices and advocate for environmental protection. This is because education fosters a deeper understanding of the interconnectedness between human activities and the environment, as well as the potential consequences of unsustainable practices. By empowering women through education, societies can benefit from their unique perspectives, knowledge, and leadership in addressing environmental challenges, such as climate change, biodiversity loss, and resource depletion.

However, the COVID-19 pandemic has exposed the fragility of these gains and the persistent inequalities in access to education. The shift to remote learning has widened the digital divide, disproportionately affecting women and girls from underserved communities, particularly in developing nations. The pandemic has also exacerbated the burden of unpaid care work, forcing many women to prioritize family responsibilities over their own education and professional development.

The impact of the COVID-19 pandemic on women's education has been compounded by the existing gender disparities in access to digital technologies and resources. According to a report by the International Telecommunication Union (ITU), women globally are 17% less likely than men to have access to the internet, and this gap widens in developing countries. As educational institutions shifted to remote learning during the pandemic, this digital divide put many women and girls at a significant disadvantage, further exacerbating the already existing barriers to their educational attainment.

The COVID-19 pandemic has not only disrupted educational systems but has also exacerbated existing gender inequalities and exposed the vulnerabilities faced by women and girls in accessing and benefiting from educational opportunities. In many contexts, the shift to remote learning has highlighted the digital divide, with women and girls from marginalized communities facing significant barriers in accessing the necessary technological infrastructure and resources.

Additionally, the increased burden of unpaid care work during the pandemic has disproportionately fallen on women, further limiting their ability to engage in educational pursuits and jeopardizing their academic and professional advancement.

The disproportionate burden of unpaid care work on women during the COVID-19 pandemic has been a significant obstacle to their educational and professional development. According to a report by UN Women, the closure of schools and childcare facilities, combined with the increased care needs of family members due to illness or lockdown measures, have resulted in a significant increase in women's unpaid care work. This added responsibility has forced many women to juggle caregiving duties with their educational pursuits or professional responsibilities, leading to increased stress, burnout, and potential setbacks in their academic or career trajectories.

The impact of the COVID-19 pandemic on women's education has been particularly severe in low-income and conflict-affected regions. According to a report by the United Nations Educational, Scientific and Cultural Organization (UNESCO), around 11 million girls from pre-primary to secondary education levels are at risk of not returning to school due to the pandemic's economic and social consequences. This setback could potentially reverse decades of progress in promoting gender parity in education and exacerbate existing inequalities.

In addition to the direct impact on educational access and attainment, the COVID-19 pandemic has also exacerbated other challenges that disproportionately affect girls' and women's education in low-income and conflict-affected regions. According to a report by Plan International, the pandemic has led to an increase in child marriages, gender-based violence, and exploitation, all of which can further hinder girls' ability to continue their education. Additionally, the economic hardships caused by the pandemic have forced many families to prioritize the education of boys over girls, perpetuating existing gender biases and social norms.

The disproportionate impact of the COVID-19 pandemic on women's education in low-income and conflict-affected regions underscores the need for targeted interventions and support systems to mitigate the long-term consequences of this disruption. Without concerted efforts to address the economic, social, and psychological barriers exacerbated by the pandemic, millions of girls and young women may face significant setbacks in their educational journeys, perpetuating the cycle of marginalization and limiting their future prospects. Addressing this challenge will require a coordinated response from governments, international organizations, and civil society, focusing on bridging the digital divide, providing financial support, and implementing strategies to reengage and retain girls in educational programs.

To address the disproportionate impact of the COVID-19 pandemic on women's education, particularly in low-income and conflict-affected regions, a multifaceted approach is necessary. According to recommendations by UNESCO, this should include targeted financial assistance and scholarships to mitigate the economic hardships faced by families, as well as investing in community-based initiatives to raise awareness about the importance of girls' education and combat harmful social norms and practices. Additionally, leveraging technology and distance learning platforms, while addressing the digital divide, can help ensure continuity of education and support for girls during periods of disruption.

Moreover, the pursuit of educational equity must be intersectional, recognizing the unique barriers faced by women from marginalized groups. Women of color, indigenous women, women with disabilities, and LGBTQ+ women often encounter compounded challenges in accessing and thriving in educational spaces. Initiatives like the United Nations Girls' Education Initiative (UNGEI) have focused on addressing these intersecting forms of discrimination and ensuring that no girl is left behind.

The importance of an intersectional approach to promoting educational equity is highlighted by the experiences of indigenous women and girls, who often face multiple and intersecting forms of marginalization. According to a report by the United Nations

Permanent Forum on Indigenous Issues, indigenous girls and women face significant barriers to education due to factors such as poverty, geographic isolation, language barriers, and cultural biases. These challenges are compounded by the ongoing impacts of colonialism, discrimination, and lack of representation in educational systems and curricula. Initiatives like UNGEI play a crucial role in addressing these intersectional barriers and ensuring that the unique needs and experiences of indigenous girls and women are taken into account in educational policies and programs.

Adopting an intersectional approach to promoting educational equity is crucial because the barriers faced by women and girls are often compounded by other forms of marginalization based on race, ethnicity, disability, sexual orientation, and other intersecting identities. For example, a woman with a disability from an indigenous community may face multidimensional challenges, including physical accessibility barriers, cultural biases, and limited access to resources, which can significantly impede her educational attainment and success. By acknowledging and addressing these intersecting forms of oppression, initiatives like UNGEI can develop more comprehensive and tailored strategies that address the unique needs and experiences of diverse groups of women and girls.

The importance of an intersectional approach to promoting educational equity is further underscored by the experiences of women and girls with disabilities. According to a report by the United Nations Children's Fund (UNICEF), children with disabilities are among the most marginalized groups in education systems, facing numerous barriers such as physical inaccessibility, lack of assistive technologies, and discriminatory attitudes. For girls with disabilities, these challenges are compounded by gender-based discrimination and social norms that often prioritize the education of boys. Initiatives that recognize and address these intersecting forms of marginalization are essential to create truly inclusive and equitable educational opportunities for all.

Adopting an intersectional approach to promoting educational equity is crucial to ensure that the diverse experiences and challenges faced by women from marginalized communities are addressed. For instance, indigenous women often face barriers related to language, cultural differences, and geographic remoteness, while women with disabilities may encounter physical and attitudinal barriers that hinder their access to educational opportunities. By acknowledging and addressing these intersecting forms of marginalization, initiatives like UNGEI can develop tailored strategies and solutions to promote inclusive and equitable access to education for all girls and women.

One example of an initiative that adopts an intersectional approach is the Malala Fund, founded by Nobel Prize laureate Malala Yousafzai. The Malala Fund recognizes that girls face multiple and intersecting barriers to education, including poverty, conflict, child marriage, and gender-based violence. To address these challenges, the organization partners with local organizations and communities to implement context-specific strategies, such as providing financial assistance, advocating for policy changes, and raising awareness about the importance of girls' education. By acknowledging and addressing the intersectional nature of the barriers faced by girls, the Malala Fund aims to create a more inclusive and equitable educational landscape.

Alternative education models, such as online learning, vocational training, and adult literacy programs, have emerged as potential avenues for expanding women's access to education and skill development. These flexible and accessible options can provide opportunities for women who may face constraints in attending traditional educational institutions due to poverty, geographical barriers, or cultural norms. However, it is essential to ensure that these alternative pathways are of high quality, culturally relevant, and aligned with the needs of the labor market.

While alternative education models offer promising avenues for expanding access to education, it is crucial to recognize that they are not a one-size-fits-all solution. The effectiveness of these models depends on their ability to address the specific needs and contexts of diverse groups of women and girls. For instance, online learning programs may be more accessible for women in urban areas with reliable internet connectivity but may not be suitable for those in remote or rural regions with limited digital infrastructure. Similarly, vocational training programs must be tailored to the local economic and cultural contexts to ensure relevance and employability.

The rise of alternative education models has opened up new avenues for women to access educational opportunities, particularly in regions where traditional schooling may not be feasible or accessible. For example, mobile learning initiatives like the UN Women's Buy From Women platform have leveraged technology to provide women entrepreneurs with access to business skills training and mentorship opportunities. Similarly, community-based adult literacy programs have been instrumental in empowering women in rural areas and promoting their participation in local decision-making processes.

While alternative education models have the potential to expand access to education for women, it is essential to ensure that these initiatives are designed and implemented in a gender-responsive manner. This involves addressing the unique needs, challenges, and experiences of women and girls, such as safety concerns, mobility constraints, and sociocultural barriers that may limit their ability to fully engage with and benefit from these educational opportunities. By adopting a gender-sensitive approach and involving women in the design and implementation of these initiatives, alternative education models can better address the intersectional barriers faced by diverse groups of women and contribute to their empowerment and advancement.

But let's not be complacent. Challenges remain, as girls in some regions still face formidable barriers to education, including poverty, armed conflicts, child marriage, and harmful cultural practices. Each hurdle requires a tailored response that addresses the specific socio-cultural and economic factors contributing to educational inequalities. The quest for universal access to education is not yet complete, and the struggle continues with a fierce determination to leave no girl behind, championed by international organizations like UNESCO and grassroots movements alike.

The challenges facing girls' education in regions affected by armed conflicts, humanitarian crises, and entrenched cultural practices are multifaceted and require a holistic approach that addresses the root causes of these barriers. In conflict-affected areas, for instance, ensuring access to education may involve efforts to protect schools and education facilities, provide psychosocial support for students and teachers, and implement conflict-sensitive curricula that promote peace and reconciliation. In regions where harmful cultural practices like child marriage are prevalent, initiatives must work closely with local communities to challenge these practices, raise awareness about the importance of girls' education, and provide support systems for girls at risk of dropping out.

Despite the progress made in promoting access to education for girls and women, significant challenges persist, particularly in regions affected by armed conflicts, humanitarian crises, and entrenched cultural practices that discriminate against girls' education. According to UNICEF, over 130 million girls worldwide are out of school, with conflict-affected countries accounting for a significant portion of this figure. Addressing these challenges requires a multifaceted approach that combines educational interventions with broader efforts to combat poverty, promote gender equality, and address the root causes of armed conflicts and cultural barriers.

The barriers to girls' education in conflict-affected regions are multifaceted and deeply rooted. In addition to the disruption caused by armed conflicts, which often result in the destruction of educational infrastructure and displacement of communities, these regions also grapple with entrenched cultural norms and practices that devalue girls' education. For instance, in some societies, girls are expected to assume domestic responsibilities or are married off at a young age, effectively curtailing their educational opportunities. Furthermore, poverty and economic instability, exacerbated by conflicts, can force families to prioritize the education of boys over girls, perpetuating the cycle of gender inequality.

Addressing the persistent challenges facing girls' education in regions affected by armed conflicts, humanitarian crises, and entrenched cultural practices requires a collaborative and coordinated effort among various stakeholders, including governments, international organizations, civil society, and local communities. By leveraging the expertise and resources of diverse actors, initiatives can be developed that address the multidimensional nature of these challenges, combining educational interventions with broader efforts to promote peace, security, economic development, and cultural transformation. Successful initiatives in these contexts often involve a comprehensive approach that includes community engagement, capacity building, policy advocacy, and the provision of support services to address the specific needs and vulnerabilities of girls and their families.

A prime example of such a collaborative effort is the Safe Schools Initiative, launched by the United Nations and several non-governmental organizations in response to the abduction of schoolgirls in Chibok, Nigeria, by Boko Haram in 2014. This initiative aims to protect students, teachers, and educational facilities during armed conflicts, while also promoting access to quality education in regions affected by violence and insecurity. Through a combination of advocacy, policy reform, and targeted interventions, the Safe Schools Initiative has made significant strides in raising awareness about the importance of safeguarding education in conflict zones and mobilizing resources to support affected communities.

In the words of a renowned education activist, "One child, one teacher, one book, and one pen can change the world." The truth of this statement is witnessed in the lives of countless women who, armed with education, are dismantling the bastions of inequality and shaping a more just and prosperous future for themselves, their families, and their communities.

One such inspiring example is Mukhtar Mai, a Pakistani woman who, after being subjected to a horrific act of violence, used her education to establish schools and a women's shelter in her village. Despite facing immense societal pressure and threats, Mai's unwavering determination and the power of education have transformed her community, empowering countless women and girls to pursue their dreams and break free from the shackles of oppression. Her story serves as a powerful reminder that education is not merely a means of acquiring knowledge but a liberating force that can catalyze positive change and challenge deeply entrenched systems of inequality.

The transformative power of education is not merely a rhetorical sentiment but a lived reality for countless women who have defied overwhelming odds to access educational opportunities and harness the knowledge and skills gained to challenge injustice, advocate for change, and shape a more equitable future. Their stories serve as powerful testimonies to the enduring resilience of the human spirit and the profound impact that education can have in breaking the intergenerational cycle of marginalization and oppression. By amplifying these narratives and celebrating the achievements of these remarkable women, we not only honor their struggles but also inspire and empower future generations to continue the pursuit of educational equity and social justice.

The power of education to transform lives and drive societal progress is exemplified by the stories of women who have overcome immense obstacles to access educational opportunities. From Malala Yousafzai, the Pakistani activist who survived an assassination attempt by Taliban gunmen for advocating for girls' education, to Waris Dirie, the Somali model and activist who underwent female genital mutilation as a child and later became a vocal advocate for ending this harmful practice, these women have used their education as a powerful tool to challenge injustice, promote human rights, and inspire generations of girls and women around the world.

Beyond individual stories of resilience and determination, the impact of girls' education on societal development cannot be overstated. According to a report by the World Bank, increasing the proportion of women with secondary education by just 1% could raise a country's annual per capita income growth by 0.3 percentage points. Furthermore, educated women are more likely to participate in the labor force, contribute to household income, and invest in the health and education of their children, creating a virtuous cycle of development and empowerment.

As we reflect on the journey thus far, let us not lose sight of the destination—a world where every woman has the opportunity to learn, grow, and contribute to her fullest potential, regardless of her background or circumstances. The advancements in women's access to education and academic opportunities are not just milestones; they are the foundations upon which a more equitable and enlightened society is being built, stone by stone.

To reach this destination, however, it is crucial to address the intersectional challenges faced by women and girls from marginalized communities. For instance, girls with disabilities, those belonging to ethnic or religious minorities, or those living in remote or rural areas often face compounded barriers to accessing quality education. Targeted interventions, such as providing accessible educational resources, promoting inclusive learning environments, and addressing cultural biases and discrimination, are essential to ensuring that no girl is left behind on the path to educational equity.

While the advancements in women's access to education are significant and worthy of celebration, it is crucial to acknowledge that much work remains to be done to achieve true educational equity. Systemic barriers, such as poverty, gender discrimination, and societal norms that devalue women's education, continue to impede progress in many parts of the world. Achieving the goal of providing every woman with the opportunity to learn and contribute to her fullest potential will require sustained commitment, collaboration among diverse stakeholders, and a willingness to challenge and dismantle deeply entrenched systems of oppression and marginalization.

One promising approach to addressing these systemic barriers is the adoption of a human rights-based approach to education. This framework recognizes education as a fundamental human right and emphasizes the principles of non-discrimination, participation, and accountability. By adopting this approach, governments and other stakeholders can be held accountable for ensuring equal access to quality education for all, regardless of gender, socioeconomic status, or any other factor. Moreover, this approach empowers communities to actively participate in shaping educational policies and programs, ensuring that they are responsive to local needs and cultural contexts.

In closing, the story of women's education is a constellation woven with tenacity, courage, and hope. It is a narrative that continues to evolve, with each generation adding its own vibrant threads. The advancements we celebrate today are the legacy of those who dared to dream of a more just and educated world. And as the torch is passed to new hands, the flame of knowledge burns ever brighter, illuminating the path to a future where barriers are broken and possibilities are boundless.

As we look to the future, it is essential to invest in innovative and scalable solutions that can accelerate progress towards educational equity for girls and women. One promising avenue is the use of technology and digital learning platforms, which can help overcome barriers related to access, infrastructure, and resource constraints. For instance, online courses and educational apps can provide girls in remote or conflict-affected areas with access to quality educational content, while also fostering a safe and inclusive learning environment. However, it is crucial to address the digital divide and ensure that these technological solutions are accessible and tailored to the specific needs and contexts of marginalized communities.

The story of women's education is not just a narrative of progress and achievement; it is also a testament to the power of collective action, resilience, and the unwavering belief in the transformative potential of education. As we move forward, it is essential to honor the legacies of those who have fought tirelessly for educational equity, while also recognizing that the journey is far from over. By fostering intergenerational solidarity, amplifying the voices of those on the frontlines, and leveraging the power of education as a catalyst for social change, we can continue to forge a path towards a more just and equitable world, where every individual, regardless of gender or background, has the opportunity to learn, grow, and thrive.

In addition to technological solutions, it is imperative to strengthen the capacity of educational systems and institutions to provide quality, gender-responsive education. This includes investing in teacher training programs that equip educators with the skills and knowledge to create inclusive and empowering learning environments, as well as developing curricula and teaching materials that challenge gender stereotypes and promote positive representations of women and girls. Furthermore, ensuring adequate funding and resource allocation for girls' education programs, particularly in resource-constrained settings, is crucial for sustaining long-term progress.

Let this be our collective resolve: to forge ahead with the knowledge that education is the most potent tool for emancipation and progress. May we all be champions of this noble cause, ensuring that the doors of learning remain open for all who seek to pass through them, irrespective of their gender, race, or any other identity marker.

Ultimately, the fight for girls' education is not merely an educational issue; it is a battle for human rights, gender equality, and sustainable development. By investing in girls' education, we are investing in the future of our communities, nations, and the world at large. When girls and women have access to quality education, they gain the knowledge, skills, and confidence to break free from cycles of poverty, challenge gender-based discrimination, and contribute to the social, economic, and political fabric of their societies. It is a virtuous cycle that benefits us all, and one that we must continue to nurture and support with unwavering commitment and resolve.

Section B: Analysis of efforts to address gender disparities in STEM fields and higher education

In the quest to dismantle the fortifications of gender inequality, STEM fields stand as a formidable frontier. The landscape of science, technology, engineering, and mathematics is not merely an academic challenge; it is a cultural battleground where stereotypes are confronted, and new norms are forged. But what are the strategies that have proven efficacious in this endeavor, and how do they reshape the terrain of higher education?

The persistent underrepresentation of women in STEM fields has far-reaching implications, not only for gender equality but also for scientific progress, innovation, and economic development. By failing to tap into the full potential of women's talent and perspectives, we risk stifling the advancement of knowledge and missing out on the diverse perspectives and approaches that can drive breakthroughs and novel solutions to complex challenges. Addressing gender disparities in STEM is therefore not just a matter of social justice but also a strategic imperative for fostering a more innovative, competitive, and sustainable future.

According to a report by the UNESCO Institute for Statistics, only around 30% of the world's researchers are women, and this gender gap is even more pronounced in STEM fields. This underrepresentation not only limits the talent pool and diversity of perspectives in these fields but also has economic consequences. A study by the European Commission estimates that the European Union's GDP could increase by up to €820 billion by 2050 if women were fully integrated into the labor market, including in STEM professions.

Initiatives dedicated to bridging the gender divide in STEM are as diverse as the disciplines themselves. One such effort is the establishment of programs focused on early engagement. It's crucial to ask, why wait until higher education to spark a girl's interest in science or engineering? Programs like FIRST Robotics, Science Olympiad, and the European Union's Science: It's a Girl Thing campaign captivate young minds, fostering a passion that can lead to lifelong curiosity. By providing hands-on experiences and exposure to STEM role models, these initiatives allow girls to see themselves as future scientists and engineers, challenging traditional gender stereotypes.

Early engagement programs play a pivotal role in countering the socialization processes and gender norms that often discourage girls from pursuing interests in STEM fields. By exposing girls to engaging and accessible STEM activities at a young age, these programs can challenge the perception that these disciplines are inherently "masculine" or "too difficult" for girls. This early exposure can foster a sense of self-efficacy and confidence in girls' abilities to succeed in STEM, potentially mitigating the impact of negative stereotypes and biases that may emerge later in their educational journey.

One notable example of an early engagement program is the Girls Who Code initiative, which aims to close the gender gap in technology by providing computer science education and exposure to female role models in tech. According to the organization's impact report, participants in their programs are 15 times more likely to pursue a career in computer science than their non-participant peers.

Mentorship has emerged as a linchpin in the architecture of support for women in STEM. Through connections with seasoned professionals, young women gain insights into the realities of careers in these fields. Mentorship serves as a bridge, spanning the gap between aspiration and achievement. Consider the impact of a young woman receiving guidance from a female astronaut, a leading tech entrepreneur, or a pioneering researcher; it's an invaluable affirmation that her dreams are not only valid but achievable. Organizations like MentorNet and Million Women Mentors have been instrumental in facilitating these vital mentoring relationships.

Research by the National Center for Women & Information Technology (NCWIT) highlights the significant impact of mentorship on women's persistence and success in STEM fields. According to their findings, women who participate in mentoring programs are more likely to report higher levels of confidence, career satisfaction, and a sense of belonging in their field. Furthermore, having a mentor has been shown to increase the likelihood of women pursuing advanced degrees and leadership positions in STEM.

Mentorship programs for women in STEM not only provide access to role models and guidance but also foster a sense of community and belonging within these male-dominated fields. Mentors can share their personal experiences navigating the challenges and biases that women often face in STEM, offering strategies for overcoming obstacles and developing resilience. Additionally, mentors can serve as advocates and sponsors, actively supporting their mentees' career advancement and creating opportunities for professional growth and visibility.

Scholarships and fellowships specifically for women in STEM fields act as catalysts for change. Organizations and institutions realize that financial support can turn the tide for many potential female scholars. By alleviating the burden of tuition, these financial aids empower women to pursue studies that were once deemed beyond their reach. Imagine the relief and determination felt by a recipient of the Schlumberger Faculty for the Future Fellowship or the L'Oréal-UNESCO For Women in Science Fellowship, as she sets her sights on a future in computer science, astrophysics, or biomedical engineering.

The impact of targeted scholarships and fellowships for women in STEM extends beyond financial support. These opportunities serve as powerful symbols of institutional commitment to promoting gender diversity and inclusion within these fields. By dedicating resources and funding specifically for women, organizations and institutions send a clear message that they value and actively seek to cultivate female talent and leadership in STEM. This recognition and support can foster a greater sense of belonging and validation for women pursuing these disciplines, ultimately contributing to their retention and success.

According to the National Science Foundation, targeted funding initiatives for women in STEM have played a significant role in increasing their representation in these fields. For example, the NSF's ADVANCE program, which aims to promote the recruitment, retention, and advancement of women in academic STEM careers, has helped to increase the percentage of women in tenured and tenure-track positions at participating institutions by an average of 6.9% over a decade.

Higher education itself is undergoing a metamorphosis, as universities strive to create more inclusive environments. One strategy has been to revise curricula that have historically been male-centric and Eurocentric. By incorporating the achievements and perspectives of women and underrepresented minorities in STEM, educational materials now offer a more balanced and representative view of these fields. The narrative of science and technology is being rewritten to include those who have been overlooked for far too long, fostering a sense of belonging and inspiration for a diverse student body.

Curriculum reform efforts in STEM education have also extended to pedagogical approaches and learning environments. Recognizing that traditional lecture-based instruction and competitive learning environments may disadvantage or alienate women and underrepresented groups, many institutions have adopted more inclusive teaching methodologies, such as active learning, problem-based learning, and collaborative group work. By creating learning environments that value diverse perspectives, foster a growth mindset, and promote supportive peer relationships, these pedagogical approaches can help counter stereotypes, build confidence, and foster a greater sense of belonging for women in STEM.

A study by the American Society for Engineering Education found that incorporating active learning strategies, such as project-based learning and collaborative group work, can significantly improve the retention and performance of women and underrepresented minorities in engineering programs. The study also highlighted the importance of creating an inclusive classroom climate, where diverse perspectives and experiences are valued and respected.

But let's consider the role of policy in this equation. Governments and educational institutions have implemented policies designed to promote gender equity in STEM. Title IX in the United States, for example, is a powerful legislative tool that prohibits gender discrimination in any federally funded education program or activity. Such policies send a clear message: gender bias has no place in the pursuit of knowledge and innovation. They also provide legal recourse for addressing discriminatory practices and holding institutions accountable.

While policies like Title IX have been instrumental in promoting gender equity in STEM education, their effectiveness often hinges on robust implementation, enforcement, and accountability mechanisms. Institutions must be proactive in identifying and addressing potential areas of discrimination, from admissions and recruitment processes to campus climate and support services. Additionally, robust data collection and monitoring systems are crucial for assessing progress, identifying areas for improvement, and ensuring compliance with these policies.

According to a report by the American Association of University Women (AAUW), many institutions struggle with effectively implementing and enforcing Title IX due to a lack of resources, training, and institutional commitment. The report highlights the need for dedicated Title IX coordinators, comprehensive training for faculty and staff, and transparent reporting and accountability mechanisms to ensure compliance and address instances of gender discrimination effectively.

Outreach programs are another critical element in the constellation of efforts to address gender disparities in STEM. Organizations like the Association for Women in Science, the Society of Women Engineers, and the National Girls Collaborative Project extend their reach to women and girls at various stages of their STEM journeys, offering resources, networking opportunities, and advocacy. The support rendered by these organizations is not just a lifeline; it's a springboard that propels women into realms they might not have otherwise dared to enter.

Outreach programs play a vital role in fostering a sense of community and support for women in STEM, particularly in educational and professional settings where they may feel isolated or underrepresented. By providing access to role models, mentors, and networking opportunities, these programs can help combat feelings of isolation and imposter syndrome, which are often cited as significant barriers to women's persistence and advancement in STEM fields. Additionally, outreach programs can serve as advocacy platforms, amplifying the voices and experiences of women in STEM and driving institutional and policy changes that promote greater inclusion and equity.

One notable example of an outreach program is the Society of Women Engineers (SWE), which has been a leading advocate for the advancement of women in engineering and technology since its founding in 1950. SWE's initiatives include professional development opportunities, networking events, and advocacy efforts to address issues such as pay equity, workplace discrimination, and the retention of women in engineering careers.

Industry partnerships with educational institutions are also instrumental in fostering a more inclusive and diverse STEM pipeline. Companies in the tech and engineering sectors are increasingly recognizing the value of a diverse workforce and the competitive advantage it brings. They collaborate with universities to offer internships, job placements, and real-world projects. These partnerships provide a glimpse into the professional world, equipping women with the experience and confidence needed to navigate the STEM landscape while also exposing them to potential career paths and mentors within the industry.

Industry-academia partnerships offer a unique opportunity to bridge the gap between theory and practice, providing students with valuable hands-on experience and exposure to real-world challenges and applications. For women in STEM, these partnerships can be particularly beneficial, as they offer opportunities to engage with diverse role models, mentors, and professional networks within the industry. Additionally, these collaborations can inform curriculum development and help align educational programs with the evolving needs and trends of the STEM workforce, ensuring that graduates are well-prepared and competitive in the job market.

One successful example of an industry-academia partnership is the collaboration between the Massachusetts Institute of Technology (MIT) and IBM, which has led to the development of the MIT-IBM Watson AI Lab. This joint research initiative focuses on advancing artificial intelligence technologies and provides opportunities for students, including women, to work alongside industry experts and gain valuable experience in cutting-edge AI research and development.

Let us pause and contemplate the transformative power of visibility and representation. Role models play a crucial role in shattering the glass ceiling and inspiring the next generation. When a young woman sees someone like herself leading a tech company, publishing groundbreaking research, or receiving a Nobel Prize in Physics, it alters her perception of what's possible. These trailblazers do more than achieve personal success; they illuminate the path for others to follow, challenging the notion that STEM fields are inherently masculine domains.

The impact of visible role models and representation in STEM cannot be overstated. According to research by the American Association of University Women (AAUW), exposure to successful female role models in STEM can increase girls' interest and self-efficacy in these fields, ultimately influencing their academic and career choices. Furthermore, diverse representation in STEM can challenge negative stereotypes and biases, fostering a more inclusive environment that values and celebrates the contributions of women and underrepresented groups.

A study by the Geena Davis Institute on Gender in Media found that exposure to STEM role models in media and popular culture can significantly influence young girls' perceptions and aspirations. The study highlighted the impact of characters like Dana Scully from "The X-Files," who inspired many young women to pursue careers in fields like forensic science and medicine.

However, the journey of women in STEM is not without its internal struggles. Imposter syndrome, the persistent feeling of self-doubt and inadequacy despite evident success, plagues many women in these fields. Overcoming this psychological barrier requires a robust support system, both within educational institutions and professional networks. Mentorship, peer support groups, and resilience-building programs can help women navigate these challenges and maintain confidence in their abilities, fostering a sense of belonging and empowerment.

Addressing the issue of imposter syndrome among women in STEM requires a multifaceted approach that targets both individual and systemic factors. At the individual level, interventions such as mindfulness training, cognitive-behavioral techniques, and resilience-building workshops can help women develop coping strategies and reframe negative self-perceptions. However, it is equally important to address the systemic biases, discrimination, and stereotypes that often contribute to feelings of self-doubt and inadequacy among women in STEM environments. By fostering inclusive cultures, promoting diverse representation, and challenging biases, institutions and organizations can create environments where women's contributions are valued and celebrated, ultimately mitigating the impact of imposter syndrome.

A study by the University of Texas at Austin found that participating in a structured intervention program focused on building resilience and self-affirmation can significantly reduce the impact of imposter syndrome among women in STEM graduate programs. The program included exercises aimed at reframing negative self-talk, cultivating a growth mindset, and fostering a sense of belonging within the academic community.

Moreover, addressing systemic biases and discrimination in STEM academia and workplaces is crucial for creating truly inclusive environments. From hiring practices to promotion opportunities and workplace culture, every aspect of the STEM ecosystem must be scrutinized for hidden biases. Initiatives like blind resume reviews, diversity and inclusion training, and transparent performance evaluation systems are just a few strategies that can help level the playing field and mitigate the impact of unconscious biases and stereotypical assumptions.

Addressing systemic biases and discrimination in STEM requires a comprehensive and sustained effort that goes beyond isolated initiatives or one-time training sessions. Organizations and institutions must be committed to conducting regular audits and assessments to identify potential areas of bias or discrimination, and implement evidence-based strategies to mitigate these issues. This may involve revising and updating policies, procedures, and evaluation criteria to ensure they are fair, objective, and free from bias. Additionally, promoting accountability and transparency in decision-making processes, such as hiring, promotion, and resource allocation, can help build trust and ensure that these processes are equitable and merit-based.

One example of an initiative aimed at promoting transparency and accountability in STEM workplaces is the STEM Equity Achievement (SEA) Change initiative, launched by the American Association for the Advancement of Science (AAAS). This program provides a framework and tools for organizations to conduct self-assessments, identify areas of bias or inequity, and develop action plans to address these issues. Participating organizations are required to publicly report on their progress and commitments, fostering accountability and encouraging industry-wide adoption of best practices.

Interdisciplinary approaches and collaboration between STEM and non-STEM fields also hold promise for fostering innovation, broadening perspectives, and creating more inclusive learning environments. By bridging the gaps between disciplines, we can harness the power of diverse viewpoints and encourage creative problem-solving. Women in STEM can benefit from the insights and skills of their colleagues in the arts, humanities, and social sciences, and vice versa, cultivating a cross-pollination of ideas and fostering a more holistic and well-rounded educational experience.

Interdisciplinary collaboration and the integration of diverse perspectives can play a crucial role in fostering innovation and addressing complex global challenges that often require multidimensional approaches. By bringing together different ways of thinking, methodologies, and perspectives from various disciplines, interdisciplinary teams can develop more holistic and innovative solutions that may not have been possible within the confines of a single discipline. For women in STEM, engaging in interdisciplinary collaborations can provide opportunities to challenge traditional boundaries, explore new avenues for research and problem-solving, and contribute their unique perspectives and experiences to the broader discourse.

One example of a successful interdisciplinary collaboration is the FemTech initiative at the University of Michigan, which brings together researchers from engineering, computer science, medicine, and social sciences to develop innovative technologies and solutions aimed at addressing women's health issues. This collaborative approach has led to the development of cutting-edge medical devices, wearable technologies, and data-driven solutions that address the unique needs and experiences of women.

It is also crucial to recognize the intersectional nature of the barriers faced by women in STEM. Women of color, women from low-income backgrounds, and those with disabilities often face compounded challenges, including discrimination based on multiple aspects of their identity. Initiatives that address gender disparities alone may fall short in creating an inclusive environment for all women. An intersectional approach that considers the diverse experiences and needs of women from various backgrounds is essential to ensuring that the benefits of STEM education and career opportunities are truly accessible and equitable.

While the efforts to address gender disparities in STEM have yielded significant progress, it is important to acknowledge that the journey towards true equity and inclusion is a long-term endeavor that requires sustained commitment and vigilance. Deeply rooted societal norms, cultural biases, and systemic barriers can be resistant to change, and setbacks or challenges may arise along the way. However, by maintaining a steadfast dedication to this cause, continuously evaluating and adapting strategies, and fostering a culture of continuous learning and improvement, we can navigate these obstacles and stay the course towards a more equitable and inclusive future for women in STEM

Adopting an intersectional approach to promoting gender diversity and inclusion in STEM requires a deep understanding of the complex ways in which various forms of marginalization and oppression intersect and compound the barriers faced by different groups of women. This involves actively engaging with and amplifying the voices of women from diverse backgrounds, and tailoring strategies and initiatives to address their specific needs and experiences. For example, initiatives aimed at increasing access to STEM education for women from low-income backgrounds may need to address financial barriers, as well as provide academic support and mentorship to help navigate systemic challenges and biases.

While these efforts have made significant inroads, the journey is far from over. Women in STEM continue to face challenges, from implicit biases and microaggressions to the pressures of balancing professional careers with personal responsibilities. The road to equality is a marathon, not a sprint, and every step forward is both an achievement and a reminder of the distance yet to travel.

According to a survey by the Pew Research Center, a significant proportion of women in STEM fields report experiencing gender-based discrimination, harassment, and unfair treatment in their workplaces. These experiences not only create hostile environments but can also deter women from pursuing or remaining in STEM careers. Addressing these systemic issues requires a concerted effort from institutions, organizations, and individuals to implement comprehensive policies, provide training, and foster a culture of respect and inclusivity.

The Pew Research Center survey found that around 50% of women in STEM jobs reported experiencing gender discrimination at work, ranging from being treated as incompetent, denied opportunities for advancement, or receiving less support from supervisors and colleagues than their male counterparts. Furthermore, a study by the National Academies of Sciences, Engineering, and Medicine revealed that sexual harassment in STEM academic settings is prevalent, with up to 58% of women faculty and staff experiencing harassment from colleagues or students.

The challenges faced by women in STEM fields extend beyond the confines of academic and professional settings and often intersect with broader societal issues. For example, the persistent gender gap in unpaid care work and domestic responsibilities can create significant barriers for women in STEM, limiting their ability to dedicate time and energy to their careers or pursue advanced degrees and research opportunities. Additionally, the lack of affordable and accessible childcare options can disproportionately impact women's career trajectories, forcing them to make difficult choices between professional advancement and family responsibilities.

According to data from the Organization for Economic Co-operation and Development (OECD), women spend an average of 4.5 hours per day on unpaid care work, compared to just 2.5 hours for men. This disproportionate burden can create significant challenges for women in STEM, who often face long hours and demanding schedules. A study by the American Institutes for Research found that women in STEM fields who have children are more likely to leave their careers or shift to part-time work, citing the difficulties in balancing work and family responsibilities.

Reflecting on the strides made thus far, we see a narrative punctuated by courage, innovation, and a collective will to reshape the future. The advancements in addressing gender disparities within STEM and higher education are not mere footnotes in history; they are bold statements of progress, etched into the annals of academia and beyond.

One notable example of these advancements is the rise of women in leadership positions within STEM academia and research institutions. According to data from the National Science Foundation, the percentage of women serving as presidents or chancellors of major research universities in the United States has increased from just 5% in the early 1990s to over 20% in recent years. These women leaders are not only breaking glass ceilings but also serving as role models and advocates for the next generation of women in STEM.

The advancements in addressing gender disparities in STEM and higher education are not only significant in their own right but also serve as powerful catalysts for broader societal change. By empowering women in these fields, we are challenging long-held stereotypes and biases, reshaping cultural narratives, and fostering a more equitable and inclusive environment for future generations. The ripple effects of these advancements extend beyond academia and STEM professions, influencing societal attitudes, norms, and perceptions about gender roles and women's capabilities.

The impact of these advancements can be seen in the growing representation of women in fields traditionally dominated by men, such as engineering and computer science. According to the National Center for Education Statistics, the percentage of bachelor's degrees awarded to women in engineering has increased from 16.9% in the 1990s to 22.6% in recent years, while the percentage of women earning degrees in computer and information sciences has nearly doubled over the same period.

As we turn the pages of this ongoing story, we must maintain our resolve to mentor, inspire, and empower the next generation of women in STEM. For in their hands lies the potential not only to break barriers but to build bridges to a world where gender disparity in any field becomes a relic of the past. Let us continue to champion the cause of equality with conviction and purpose, knowing that the arc of history bends towards justice, and with concerted effort, we can accelerate its curve.

Mentoring and empowering the next generation of women in STEM requires a multi-faceted approach that addresses not only academic and professional development but also personal growth and resilience. Initiatives such as the National Girls Collaborative Project, which brings together organizations and individuals dedicated to encouraging girls' interest and participation in STEM, provide a range of resources and opportunities, from hands-on STEM experiences and role model engagement to leadership development and career exploration.

Mentoring, inspiring, and empowering the next generation of women in STEM is not just a responsibility but a profound investment in the future. By nurturing and supporting young women's interests and aspirations in these fields, we are cultivating a pipeline of talented and innovative leaders who will drive scientific and technological advancements, tackle complex global challenges, and shape the course of human progress. Furthermore, by fostering a more diverse and inclusive STEM workforce, we can harness the power of diverse perspectives, experiences, and approaches, ultimately leading to more innovative and impactful solutions.

According to a report by the U.S. Department of Commerce, increasing the participation of women and underrepresented minorities in STEM fields could help address critical workforce shortages and boost economic growth. The report estimates that closing the gender gap in STEM employment could add over $700 billion to the U.S. economy by 2050, highlighting the immense potential and economic imperative of fostering a diverse and inclusive STEM workforce.

The momentum and progress achieved thus far in addressing gender disparities in STEM and higher education serve as a testament to the power of collective action, unwavering determination, and a shared commitment to creating a more equitable and inclusive society. As we look towards the future, it is imperative that we sustain and build upon this momentum, fostering intergenerational solidarity and amplifying the voices and perspectives of those at the forefront of this movement. By embracing a spirit of collaboration, innovation, and resilience, we can continue to push boundaries, challenge norms, and forge new pathways towards a world where gender is no longer a barrier to success, achievement, or self-actualization in any field.

One way to sustain and build upon the momentum is through the creation of robust networks and coalitions that bring together stakeholders from various sectors, including academia, industry, government, and advocacy organizations. These networks can facilitate the sharing of best practices, collaborative research and initiatives, and the development of comprehensive strategies to address the multifaceted challenges faced by women in STEM. An example of such a network is the STEM Equity Brain Trust, a coalition of over 80 organizations dedicated to promoting equity and inclusion in STEM fields.

The path towards achieving true gender equity in STEM and higher education is not without its challenges and obstacles, but it is a journey worth undertaking. By embracing a growth mindset, fostering a culture of continuous learning and improvement, and remaining steadfast in our commitment to this cause, we can navigate these challenges and continue to make meaningful progress. The rewards of this journey extend far beyond the boundaries of academia and scientific fields; they encompass the broader pursuit of social justice, human rights, and the realization of a world where every individual, regardless of gender or background, has the opportunity to contribute their unique talents and perspectives to the betterment of society.

One of the critical challenges in achieving true gender equity in STEM and higher education is the need for systemic and cultural change. This requires a sustained commitment to addressing deeply rooted biases, stereotypes, and structural barriers that have historically hindered women's participation and success in these fields. Institutions and organizations must be willing to engage in critical self-reflection, conduct comprehensive audits and assessments, and implement evidence-based strategies to foster inclusive and equitable environments.

The journey towards gender equity in STEM and higher education is not merely an academic pursuit or a matter of institutional policy; it is a movement that embodies the fundamental principles of human rights, dignity, and the pursuit of a more just and equitable society. By addressing the systemic barriers and biases that have historically limited women's participation and achievement in these fields, we are not only unlocking the full potential of human knowledge and innovation but also challenging the very structures and systems that have perpetuated marginalization and oppression. It is a journey that demands courage, perseverance, and a unwavering commitment to social transformation, and one that holds the promise of a future where every individual, regardless of gender or background, can contribute their unique talents and perspectives to the advancement of humanity.

The journey towards gender equity in STEM and higher education is inextricably linked to broader global efforts to achieve gender equality and empower women and girls. It aligns with the United Nations Sustainable Development Goals (SDGs), particularly Goal 5: Achieve gender equality and empower all women and girls, and Goal 4: Ensure inclusive and equitable quality education and promote lifelong learning opportunities for all. By addressing the barriers and biases that limit women's participation and achievement in STEM, we are not only contributing to scientific and technological progress but also advancing the fundamental human rights and societal well-being embodied in these global goals.

A report by the International Telecommunication Union (ITU) emphasizes the critical role of promoting gender equality and empowerment in STEM fields in achieving the Sustainable Development Goals (SDGs). The report highlights that increasing women's participation and leadership in STEM fields can drive innovation and progress across various sectors, including healthcare, environmental sustainability, and economic development. By addressing gender disparities in STEM education and careers, initiatives can contribute to the realization of multiple SDGs, such as good health and well-being (SDG 3), quality education (SDG 4), decent work and economic growth (SDG 8), and industry, innovation, and infrastructure (SDG 9).

Section C: Examination of initiatives promoting girls' education and empowerment globally

In the ever-evolving narrative of human progress, the empowerment of girls through education stands as a beacon of hope and transformation. The global landscape is dotted with initiatives that not only champion the cause of girls' education but also weave the very fabric of their empowerment into the societal tapestry. These efforts, though varied in approach, are united in their pursuit to dismantle the bastions of patriarchy and open up a world of opportunities for women and girls.

The empowerment of girls through education is not merely an aspirational goal but a catalyst for broader social, economic, and political transformation. By ensuring that girls have access to quality education and the necessary support systems, we are not only upholding their fundamental human rights but also investing in the future prosperity and well-being of entire communities and nations. Educated and empowered girls are more likely to become active participants in decision-making processes, agents of positive change, and drivers of sustainable development, ultimately contributing to the realization of a more just, equitable, and inclusive society.

How do these programs navigate the complex labyrinth of cultural, economic, and political barriers to effect change? It is through a constellation of strategies, each thread strengthening the overall design, that these initiatives begin to rewrite the story of gender equality.

Navigating the complex web of barriers to girls' education and empowerment requires a multifaceted approach that addresses the root causes of gender inequality and marginalization. These initiatives must tackle deeply entrenched societal norms, cultural biases, and systemic inequalities that have historically limited opportunities for girls and women. By employing a combination of strategies that engage communities, challenge harmful practices, promote policy reforms, and provide comprehensive support systems, these initiatives can effectively dismantle the barriers that impede girls' access to education and their ability to reach their full potential.

According to UNESCO, cultural and social norms that perpetuate gender discrimination and promote the idea that girls are less deserving of education remain significant barriers to achieving gender parity in education globally. Initiatives that promote girls' education must address these deeply rooted societal norms through community engagement, awareness campaigns, and collaboration with local leaders and influencers. By fostering dialogue and promoting the value of girls' education, these initiatives can challenge harmful gender stereotypes and create an enabling environment for girls to pursue their educational aspirations.

Take, for example, the international campaign "Let Girls Learn," launched by the Obama administration in 2015, which was based on the powerful premise that educating girls is a key to global prosperity, peace, and sustainable development. The initiative emphasizes not only access to education but also the quality and relevance of that education. It recognizes the multifaceted challenges girls face, from early marriage and gender-based violence to societal norms that discourage female education, and addresses these through community engagement, policy reforms, and support for local leaders who advocate for girls' education.

The "Let Girls Learn" initiative exemplifies the need for a comprehensive and contextualized approach to promoting girls' education and empowerment. By acknowledging the multidimensional challenges faced by girls, such as early marriage, gender-based violence, and harmful societal norms, the initiative addresses these issues through a combination of strategies, including community engagement, policy advocacy, and support for local leaders. This holistic approach recognizes that access to education alone is not sufficient; it must be accompanied by efforts to address the underlying social, cultural, and economic factors that perpetuate gender inequalities and impede girls' educational attainment.

A report by the United Nations Population Fund (UNFPA) highlights the detrimental impact of child marriage on girls' education and empowerment. The report estimates that globally, one in five girls is married before the age of 18, significantly increasing the likelihood of dropping out of school and experiencing adverse health and economic consequences. Initiatives like "Let Girls Learn" that address this issue through policy advocacy, community engagement, and support for local leaders play a crucial role in mitigating the negative impacts of child marriage and promoting girls' educational attainment.

But what does it truly mean to empower girls through education? It is to instill in them the confidence to question, to challenge, and to aspire. Organizations such as Camfed (Campaign for Female Education) take this to heart, focusing on the poorest regions in Africa where the barriers to girls' education are highest. Camfed's model is unique; it employs a community-driven approach, ensuring that the benefits of educating girls are felt throughout the society. They provide not only financial support but also mentorship, life skills training, and access to technology, preparing girls to be agents of change in their communities while addressing intersectional challenges like poverty, child marriage, and gender-based violence.

Camfed's approach highlights the importance of adopting an intersectional lens in promoting girls' education and empowerment. By recognizing the intersecting forms of marginalization and oppression faced by girls, such as poverty, child marriage, and gender-based violence, Camfed's initiatives address these intersectional challenges through a comprehensive model that combines financial support, mentorship, life skills training, and access to technology. This holistic approach not only facilitates access to education but also equips girls with the tools, resources, and support systems necessary to overcome the multidimensional barriers they face and become agents of positive change in their communities.

According to a study by the Brookings Institution, adopting an intersectional approach to girls' education and empowerment is crucial for addressing the compounding effects of multiple forms of marginalization. The study found that girls from low-income households, rural areas, or marginalized ethnic or religious groups often face intersecting barriers that exacerbate their disadvantages in accessing education and realizing their full potential. Initiatives like Camfed that recognize and address these intersectional challenges are more effective in promoting sustainable and equitable outcomes for girls from diverse backgrounds.

The ripple effect of such an empowering education is profound. Picture a girl in rural Tanzania, stepping into a classroom for the first time, her eyes wide with the promise of learning. Fast forward several years and see her now, a young woman leading a local health initiative, starting her own business, or advocating for girls' rights. This is the power of education—it transforms lives, families, and entire communities, breaking the intergenerational cycle of poverty and marginalization.

The transformative power of girls' education extends beyond individual empowerment and has far-reaching implications for societal development and progress. Educated and empowered girls are more likely to delay marriage and childbirth, participate in the formal labor market, and contribute to their communities' economic growth. Additionally, they are more likely to invest in the health and education of their own children, creating a virtuous cycle that can break the intergenerational transmission of poverty and marginalization. By investing in girls' education, we are not only upholding their fundamental rights but also laying the foundation for sustainable development, gender equality, and the overall well-being of societies.

A report by the World Bank highlights the substantial economic benefits of investing in girls' education. The report estimates that for every year of secondary education completed by girls, their future wages increase by 15-25%. Additionally, if all girls received 12 years of quality education, global wealth could increase by $30 trillion over their lifetimes. These findings underscore the significant role that girls' education plays in promoting economic growth, poverty reduction, and overall societal well-being.

The Global Partnership for Education (GPE) expands on this vision by mobilizing international resources to close the education gap for girls, particularly in conflict-affected and fragile states. With a pledge to support education in the most vulnerable countries, GPE brings together governments, private sector partners, NGOs, and civil society organizations to fund and implement holistic programs that can reach even the most isolated girls. Their approach includes improving infrastructure, training teachers, promoting gender-responsive curricula, and providing comprehensive support services to address the unique challenges faced by girls in these contexts.

The Global Partnership for Education (GPE) exemplifies the power of collaboration and collective action in addressing the complex challenges of promoting girls' education in conflict-affected and fragile states. By leveraging the resources and expertise of diverse stakeholders, including governments, private sector partners, NGOs, and civil society organizations, GPE is able to implement holistic programs that address the multidimensional barriers faced by girls in these contexts. This comprehensive approach, which includes improving infrastructure, teacher training, gender-responsive curricula, and support services, recognizes that ensuring access to quality education for girls in these challenging environments requires a multifaceted and coordinated effort.

According to the GPE's 2021 Results Report, the partnership has made significant strides in increasing access to education for girls in conflict-affected and fragile states. The report highlights that in partner countries where GPE has invested, the number of girls enrolled in primary school has increased by 22.6 million since 2002. Additionally, the gender parity index in primary education has improved from 0.84 in 2002 to 0.91 in 2019, demonstrating the positive impact of GPE's holistic and collaborative approach.

Yet, is financial investment enough? The answer lies in the innovative ways these funds are utilized and the engagement of local communities and stakeholders. For instance, some initiatives focus on safe transportation for girls to and from school, recognizing that a journey through unsafe areas can be a significant barrier to education. Others provide sanitary products, facilities, and education to address the challenges of menstruation that often result in girls missing school or dropping out altogether.

The effective utilization of financial resources and the engagement of local communities are critical components of successful initiatives promoting girls' education and empowerment. By addressing context-specific challenges, such as ensuring safe transportation for girls or providing access to sanitary products and menstrual health education, these initiatives demonstrate a deep understanding of the unique barriers faced by girls in different contexts. Moreover, the involvement of local communities and stakeholders not only ensures that initiatives are culturally relevant and responsive but also fosters a sense of ownership and sustainability, crucial for long-term impact and success.

A study by the United Nations Educational, Scientific and Cultural Organization (UNESCO) highlights the importance of community engagement and ownership in promoting girls' education. The study found that initiatives that actively involved local communities and stakeholders in the design, implementation, and monitoring of programs were more effective in addressing context-specific barriers and achieving sustainable outcomes. By fostering a sense of ownership and accountability among community members, these initiatives ensured that the interventions were culturally relevant and responsive to the unique needs and challenges faced by girls in their local contexts.

Imagine the scene: a brightly colored bus, adorned with inspirational messages, winds through the countryside, collecting girls from distant villages and bringing them safely to school. It is not just a vehicle but a symbol of the journey towards an educated and empowered future, a tangible representation of the community's commitment to its daughters' education.

The image of the brightly colored bus adorned with inspirational messages serves as a powerful metaphor for the transformative potential of girls' education and the collective efforts required to realize this vision. It represents the journey towards empowerment, a journey that requires breaking down physical barriers, such as lack of safe transportation, as well as societal barriers, such as harmful cultural norms and biases. The bus's symbolic nature also highlights the importance of community engagement and ownership, as it serves as a tangible representation of the community's commitment to investing in the education and future of its daughters.

Engagement with technology is another pivotal element in these initiatives. With the digital age upon us, access to technology in education has become a gateway to empowerment. Initiatives like the Technovation Challenge invite girls from around the world to develop mobile apps that address community issues. Through this program, girls learn coding, entrepreneurship, and business skills, but more importantly, they learn that their ideas have value and that they can be creators of technology, not just consumers. Organizations like Girls Who Code and the UNICEF Giga initiative work to bridge the digital divide and equip girls with the necessary skills to thrive in an increasingly tech-driven world.

The integration of technology in girls' education initiatives not only equips them with essential digital skills but also challenges traditional gender norms and stereotypes surrounding women's participation in technology-related fields. By providing opportunities for girls to engage in coding, app development, and entrepreneurship, these initiatives empower them to become active creators and innovators in the digital realm, traditionally perceived as a male-dominated domain. This exposure and skill development can foster a greater sense of self-efficacy and confidence among girls, inspiring them to pursue careers in science, technology, engineering, and mathematics (STEM) fields, ultimately contributing to a more diverse and inclusive workforce in these crucial sectors.

According to a report by the World Economic Forum, addressing the gender gap in STEM fields is critical for driving innovation, economic growth, and addressing global challenges. The report estimates that if women were to participate in the STEM workforce at the same rate as men, the global economy could benefit from an additional $12 trillion to $28 trillion in GDP by 2025. Initiatives that empower girls with digital and STEM skills not only contribute to their personal empowerment but also have far-reaching implications for societal progress and sustainable development.

Yet, the question lingers: How do we sustain the momentum? The answer lies in the continuous nurturing of these initiatives and their adaptation to changing needs and contexts. They must grow as living entities, responsive to the evolving challenges faced by girls and the shifting global landscape.

Sustaining the momentum and ensuring the long-term impact of initiatives promoting girls' education and empowerment requires a commitment to continuous learning, evaluation, and adaptation. As societal contexts and challenges evolve, these initiatives must remain agile and responsive, adapting their strategies and approaches to address emerging needs and barriers. This involves regularly evaluating program effectiveness, collecting data and feedback from beneficiaries and stakeholders, and incorporating lessons learned into program design and implementation. By fostering a culture of continuous improvement and adaptation, these initiatives can remain relevant and effective, ensuring that they continue to meet the diverse and dynamic needs of girls and their communities.

A report by the Overseas Development Institute (ODI) emphasizes the importance of monitoring, evaluation, and learning (MEL) in ensuring the sustainability and impact of girls' education initiatives. The report highlights that effective MEL systems not only enable organizations to track progress and measure outcomes but also provide valuable insights into what works, what doesn't, and why. By incorporating these insights into program design and implementation, initiatives can continuously improve and adapt their approaches, ensuring that they remain responsive to the evolving needs and contexts of the communities they serve.

To breathe life into these programs, partnerships are essential, fostering collaboration between international organizations, governments, civil society, and local communities. The role of men and boys cannot be overlooked; they are integral to the conversation, serving as allies in reshaping societal norms and supporting the education and empowerment of their sisters, daughters, and mothers.

Programs like the HeForShe campaign and initiatives by organizations like Promundo engage men and boys in dialogue and education about gender equality, fostering a culture of mutual respect and shared responsibility.

Engaging men and boys as allies in the pursuit of girls' education and empowerment is crucial for creating lasting and sustainable change. By challenging traditional gender norms and promoting a culture of mutual respect and shared responsibility, these initiatives have the potential to transform societal attitudes and behaviors that perpetuate gender inequalities and hinder girls' access to education. Moreover, the involvement of men and boys as active participants and advocates can help dismantle deeply entrenched patriarchal structures and power dynamics that have historically marginalized and oppressed women and girls.

A study by Promundo, an organization that promotes gender equality and positive masculinities, highlights the importance of engaging men and boys in efforts to promote girls' education and empowerment. The study found that when men and boys are involved as allies and advocates, they can play a significant role in challenging harmful gender norms, promoting positive role models, and creating an enabling environment for girls' education and empowerment. However, the study also emphasizes the need for comprehensive and gender-transformative approaches that address underlying power dynamics and promote a culture of shared responsibility and mutual respect.

Moreover, the power of local grassroots organizations and women-led initiatives cannot be underestimated. These groups have a deep understanding of the specific challenges faced by girls in their communities and can tailor their approaches accordingly. Supporting and amplifying the efforts of these local champions is crucial to creating sustainable change and ensuring that initiatives are culturally relevant and responsive to the diverse needs of different communities.

The success and sustainability of initiatives promoting girls' education and empowerment are deeply rooted in the involvement and leadership of local grassroots organizations and women-led initiatives. These groups possess invaluable knowledge and insights into the unique challenges, cultural contexts, and lived experiences of girls and women within their communities. By supporting and amplifying the efforts of these local champions, international organizations and initiatives can ensure that their strategies and approaches are culturally relevant, responsive, and tailored to the specific needs and realities of diverse communities, enhancing the effectiveness and long-term impact of their interventions.

A report by the Association for Women's Rights in Development (AWID) highlights the critical role of women's rights organizations and grassroots initiatives in advancing gender equality and promoting girls' education and empowerment. The report emphasizes that these organizations often have a deep understanding of the local context, enabling them to develop contextualized strategies that address the specific barriers and challenges faced by girls and women in their communities. By supporting and amplifying the voices and efforts of these local champions, international initiatives can ensure that their interventions are responsive, sustainable, and aligned with the lived experiences and aspirations of the communities they serve.

As we look to the future, we must also consider the impact of climate change and environmental degradation on girls' education and empowerment. In many rural and marginalized communities, girls are often the first to be pulled out of school to help with household chores or to walk long distances to fetch water when resources become scarce. Sustainable and resilient solutions, such as rainwater harvesting systems, renewable energy sources, and climate-resilient infrastructure, can help mitigate these challenges and ensure that girls can continue their education uninterrupted, even in the face of environmental stresses.

The impact of climate change and environmental degradation on girls' education and empowerment cannot be overlooked. In many communities, particularly in rural and marginalized areas, girls bear a disproportionate burden of the consequences of environmental stresses, such as water scarcity and resource depletion. By addressing these environmental challenges through sustainable and resilient solutions, initiatives can help mitigate the barriers that hinder girls' access to education and create an enabling environment for their empowerment. Initiatives that integrate environmental sustainability and resilience into their strategies can not only ensure the continuity of girls' education but also equip them with the knowledge and skills necessary to tackle environmental issues and contribute to the development of sustainable solutions for their communities.

A report by the United Nations Children's Fund (UNICEF) highlights the disproportionate impact of climate change and environmental degradation on girls' education and empowerment. The report cites examples from various regions where girls are forced to drop out of school to collect water or firewood due to resource scarcity, or where natural disasters and extreme weather events disrupt their access to education. The report emphasizes the need for initiatives that address environmental challenges through sustainable solutions, such as renewable energy, water conservation, and climate-resilient infrastructure, to ensure that girls' education and empowerment are not hindered by environmental stresses.

The arts, sports, and creative expression also have a vital role to play in empowering girls and fostering holistic development. These activities provide a platform for girls to explore their talents, build confidence, develop leadership skills, and express themselves in meaningful ways. Initiatives that incorporate the arts, music, dance, and sports into girls' education programs can help create a more engaging and enriching learning experience, fostering self-esteem, creativity, and overall well-being.

Incorporating the arts, sports, and creative expression into initiatives promoting girls' education and empowerment can have a transformative impact on their overall development and well-being. These activities not only provide girls with opportunities to explore their talents and interests but also serve as powerful tools for building self-confidence, fostering creativity, and developing essential life skills such as teamwork, communication, and leadership. By creating a more holistic and engaging learning environment, these initiatives can help cultivate a sense of belonging, self-expression, and empowerment among girls, ultimately contributing to their overall personal growth and academic success.

A study by the United Nations Educational, Scientific and Cultural Organization (UNESCO) highlights the benefits of incorporating arts, sports, and creative expression into girls' education initiatives. The study found that these activities not only contribute to girls' overall well-being and personal development but also improve their academic performance, attendance, and retention in school. Furthermore, the study emphasizes that these activities can serve as powerful tools for breaking down gender stereotypes, fostering self-expression, and promoting social and emotional learning, all of which are essential for girls' empowerment and overall development.

Furthermore, the empowerment of girls through education cannot be viewed in isolation; it must be part of a broader agenda for gender equality and women's rights. Initiatives that address harmful gender norms, promote women's economic empowerment, and advocate for legal and policy reforms are essential in creating an enabling environment for girls' education and empowerment to thrive. Organizations like UN Women, the Association for Women's Rights in Development (AWID), and the African Women's Development Fund (AWDF) play crucial roles in advancing this holistic agenda.

The empowerment of girls through education is inextricably linked to the broader struggle for gender equality and the realization of women's rights. By addressing harmful gender norms, advocating for women's economic empowerment, and promoting legal and policy reforms that protect and advance the rights of women and girls, these initiatives contribute to creating an enabling environment that supports and sustains the gains made in girls' education and empowerment. This holistic approach recognizes that the barriers to girls' education and empowerment are multidimensional and deeply rooted in systemic gender inequalities, necessitating a comprehensive and multifaceted response that addresses the underlying structures and systems that perpetuate discrimination and marginalization.

A report by UN Women highlights the crucial links between girls' education, women's economic empowerment, and the realization of gender equality. The report emphasizes that investing in girls' education is not only a matter of individual empowerment but also a critical component of broader efforts to promote women's economic participation, leadership, and decision-making power. By addressing systemic barriers and promoting an enabling environment for women's economic and political empowerment, initiatives can create a virtuous cycle that reinforces the gains made in girls' education and contributes to the realization of gender equality and women's rights.

In conclusion, the global examination of initiatives promoting girls' education and empowerment is a testament to the power of collective action and the unwavering commitment of countless individuals, communities, and organizations. It shows that when we invest in girls, we invest in a brighter, more equitable, and sustainable future for all. As we turn our gaze to the horizon, we see glimmers of a world where every girl has the chance to learn, to grow, and to thrive, unleashing her full potential and contributing to the development of her community and the world at large.

The power of collective action and collaboration is at the heart of these global initiatives promoting girls' education and empowerment. By bringing together diverse stakeholders, including international organizations, governments, civil society, and local communities, these initiatives harness the collective wisdom, resources, and expertise necessary to address the multidimensional barriers faced by girls. This collaborative approach not only enhances the effectiveness and impact of these initiatives but also fosters a shared sense of responsibility and ownership, critical for creating sustainable and lasting change.

The vision of an educated and empowered girl as a force for positive change is not merely an aspirational ideal but a tangible reality that we can collectively shape. By supporting and amplifying initiatives that promote girls' education and empowerment, we are not only investing in individual futures but also contributing to the broader pursuit of a more just, equitable, and sustainable world for all. It is a call to action that demands a shared commitment to dismantling systemic barriers, challenging harmful norms, and creating an enabling environment where every girl can reach her full potential, unhindered by the shackles of discrimination and marginalization.

A statement by Malala Yousafzai, the renowned activist for girls' education and Nobel Peace Prize laureate, underscores the transformative power of educated and empowered girls. Yousafzai states, "One child, one teacher, one book, and one pen can change the world. Education is the only solution. Education first." These powerful words remind us that by investing in girls' education and empowerment, we are not only upholding their fundamental rights but also unlocking their potential to drive positive change and contribute to the creation of a more just and equitable world.

A report by the United Nations Development Programme (UNDP) highlights the transformative power of educated and empowered girls and women in achieving the Sustainable Development Goals (SDGs). The report emphasizes that investing in girls' education and empowerment is not only a matter of upholding their fundamental rights but also a critical pathway to achieving sustainable development, promoting peace and security, and addressing global challenges such as poverty, inequality, and climate change. By supporting initiatives that promote girls' education and empowerment, we are contributing to the broader pursuit of a more just, equitable, and sustainable world for all.

The UNDP report, titled "Unleashing the Potential of Girls and Women," cites numerous examples of how investing in girls' education and empowerment can drive progress across multiple SDGs. For instance, educating girls has been shown to reduce child mortality rates (SDG 3), increase economic productivity (SDG 8), and promote sustainable consumption patterns (SDG 12). Additionally, the report emphasizes that empowering women and girls is crucial for achieving gender equality (SDG 5) and fostering inclusive and peaceful societies (SDG 16).

It is a vision that compels us to act with urgency and hope, for the potential of an educated and empowered girl is a force that can change the world. Let us continue to support and amplify these initiatives, recognizing that they are not merely investments in individual futures but in the very future of humanity itself – a future where gender equality is not just an aspiration but a lived reality, and where every girl can soar to new heights, unencumbered by the shackles of discrimination and marginalization.

According to Phumzile Mlambo-Ngcuka, the former Executive Director of UN Women, "Investing in girls' education is the closest thing we have to a silver bullet for sustainable development." This sentiment underscores the far-reaching and transformative impact that empowering girls through education can have on societies and communities. By fostering an environment where every girl can reach her full potential, we are not only upholding their fundamental rights but also cultivating a generation of leaders, innovators, and changemakers who will drive progress and contribute to the creation of a more just and equitable world.

As we strive to realize this vision, it is imperative that we remain steadfast in our commitment, resilient in the face of challenges, and unwavering in our belief in the transformative power of education and empowerment. The journey ahead will be marked by obstacles and setbacks, but it is a journey worth undertaking, for it holds the promise of a more just, equitable, and prosperous future for all. By continuing to support and amplify initiatives that promote girls' education and empowerment, we are not only upholding the fundamental rights and dignity of girls and women but also investing in the collective well-being and progress of humanity as a whole.

A report by the World Bank highlights the significant economic benefits of investing in girls' education and empowerment. The report estimates that if all girls had access to secondary education, global wealth could increase by $30 trillion over their lifetimes. This staggering figure underscores the immense potential for economic growth and development that can be unlocked by removing barriers to girls' education and fostering an environment that enables their empowerment.

The realization of this vision requires a collective commitment to ongoing learning, adaptation, and innovation. As societal contexts and challenges evolve, we must remain agile and responsive, constantly evaluating and refining our approaches to ensure that they remain relevant and effective. This involves fostering a culture of continuous improvement, embracing new technologies and methodologies, and actively engaging with diverse stakeholders, including the girls and women we seek to empower, to ensure that our efforts are truly responsive to their needs and aspirations.

A study by the Brookings Institution emphasizes the importance of adopting a localized and context-specific approach to promoting girls' education and empowerment. The study found that initiatives that actively engaged with local communities, incorporated cultural perspectives, and tailored their strategies to address specific socio-economic and environmental challenges were more effective in achieving sustainable outcomes. By fostering a culture of continuous learning and adaptation, initiatives can remain responsive to the evolving needs and contexts of the communities they serve.

As we embark on this journey, it is crucial to recognize that the empowerment of girls through education is not merely a matter of individual transformation but a collective endeavor that has the power to shape the course of entire societies and nations. By investing in girls' education and empowerment, we are cultivating a generation of leaders, innovators, and change agents who will drive positive change, challenge systemic inequalities, and contribute to the realization of a more just, equitable, and sustainable world for all.

A report by the United Nations Educational, Scientific and Cultural Organization (UNESCO) highlights the multiplier effect of investing in girls' education and empowerment. The report emphasizes that educated and empowered girls and women are more likely to participate in decision-making processes, advocate for their rights, and contribute to the development of their communities. This, in turn, can have a ripple effect, fostering more inclusive and equitable societies, promoting sustainable development, and driving progress across various sectors.

As we continue to support and amplify initiatives that promote girls' education and empowerment, let us be guided by a spirit of solidarity, respect, and a deep commitment to human rights and dignity. Let us celebrate the diversity of voices, experiences, and perspectives that enrich these efforts, and let us remain steadfast in our pursuit of a future where every individual, regardless of gender or background, has the opportunity to reach their full potential and contribute to the betterment of humanity.

A statement by Audrey Azoulay, the Director-General of UNESCO, emphasizes the importance of embracing diversity and fostering inclusive approaches in promoting girls' education and empowerment. Azoulay states, "Education is a fundamental human right and a driver of progress, but it can only truly empower when it embraces diversity and fosters an environment of respect, understanding, and inclusion." By celebrating the diverse voices and experiences that enrich these efforts, we can ensure that initiatives are responsive, culturally sensitive, and aligned with the aspirations and realities of diverse communities.

A statement by Amartya Sen, the Nobel Laureate in Economics, highlights the importance of embracing diversity and fostering inclusive approaches in promoting girls' education and empowerment. Sen states, "Education is not only about acquiring knowledge and skills, but also about cultivating a sense of agency, self-worth, and the ability to participate fully in society. By celebrating the diversity of voices and experiences, and fostering an environment of respect and inclusion, we can truly empower girls and women to reach their full potential and contribute to the betterment of humanity."

Chapter 6
Social and Cultural Transformations

Section A: Exploration of changing societal attitudes towards gender roles and stereotypes in women

In the constellation of human history, the threads of gender roles and stereotypes have been deeply interwoven, shaping the experiences and opportunities of women across generations. However, as society evolves, so too do the attitudes and perceptions surrounding these entrenched norms, weaving a tapestry of progress and resistance, of challenge and change.

Judith Butler, a prominent philosopher and gender theorist, has been influential in challenging the traditional notions of gender as a fixed, biologically determined construct. In her groundbreaking work, "Gender Trouble," Butler argues that gender is a performance, shaped by societal norms and expectations, rather than an innate or essential characteristic. This perspective has been instrumental in challenging the rigid gender roles and stereotypes that have historically constrained and oppressed women, opening up new avenues for questioning and deconstructing the very foundations of gender norms.

The persistence of gender roles and stereotypes throughout human history can be attributed to a complex interplay of sociocultural, religious, and socioeconomic factors. According to a report by the United Nations Development Programme (UNDP), these deeply rooted beliefs and norms have been perpetuated through socialization processes, cultural traditions, and patriarchal power structures that have historically relegated women to subordinate roles and limited their access to education, employment, and decision-making opportunities.

The impact of religious beliefs and cultural traditions on perpetuating gender roles and stereotypes has been well-documented by scholars and researchers. For instance, in many traditional religious teachings and cultural narratives, women are often portrayed as subordinate to men, with their primary roles defined as caregivers, homemakers, and child-bearers. These narratives have been internalized and reinforced through socialization processes, effectively limiting women's aspirations and opportunities for self-actualization beyond the confines of traditional gender roles.

Picture a world where the very notion of a woman's place was confined to the domestic sphere, her worth measured by her ability to fulfill the roles of wife, mother, and homemaker. This was the reality for countless generations of women, their aspirations and potential often suffocated by the weight of societal expectations rooted in patriarchal norms and traditions. But as the tides of change began to sweep across nations, so too did the questioning and dismantling of these long-held beliefs.

The confinement of women to domestic roles and the devaluation of their worth beyond these traditional gender roles had far-reaching consequences, not only for individual women but also for societies as a whole. According to a report by the United Nations Entity for Gender Equality and the Empowerment of Women (UN Women), gender discrimination and the marginalization of women in various spheres, including education, employment, and decision-making processes, have hindered economic growth and perpetuated cycles of poverty and inequality.

The impact of gender socialization on perpetuating harmful gender roles and stereotypes has been well-documented. A study by the Geena Davis Institute on Gender in Media found that children's media often reinforces gender stereotypes, with female characters being underrepresented and portrayed in limited roles, such as princesses or caregivers. This lack of diverse and empowering representations can shape children's perceptions of gender roles and limit their aspirations from an early age.

The confinement of women to domestic roles and the devaluation of their worth beyond these traditional gender roles were perpetuated through various societal mechanisms. According to a study by the American Psychological Association, women were often socialized from a young age to prioritize caregiving and domestic responsibilities, while men were encouraged to pursue careers and leadership roles. This gender socialization process was reinforced through media representations, educational curricula, and religious teachings, effectively limiting women's aspirations and opportunities.

The rise of feminist movements in the 20th century marked a pivotal shift in the way society perceived gender roles. Women began to challenge the status quo, demanding equal rights and opportunities in the workplace, in education, and in the political arena. They refused to be defined by the narrow confines of traditional gender stereotypes, asserting their right to pursue their dreams and define their own identities. Pioneering voices like Simone de Beauvoir, Betty Friedan, and Gloria Steinem played a pivotal role in shaping these movements and inspiring generations of women to reclaim their agency and autonomy.

The feminist movements of the 20th century were not monolithic; they encompassed diverse perspectives, approaches, and priorities. While some focused on achieving legal and political equality, others sought to challenge the underlying patriarchal structures and belief systems that perpetuated gender oppression. Intersectional feminists, such as bell hooks and Audre Lorde, brought attention to the unique experiences and challenges faced by women of color, LGBTQ+ women, and other marginalized groups, highlighting the importance of addressing the intersections of gender with other forms of oppression.

The feminist movements of the 20th century, such as the Women's Suffrage Movement and the Second Wave Feminism of the 1960s and 1970s, were instrumental in challenging the prevailing gender norms and stereotypes of their time. According to a historical analysis by the National Women's Studies Association, these movements not only advocated for women's rights and equality but also sought to dismantle the patriarchal structures and belief systems that perpetuated gender oppression and marginalization.

The impact of feminist movements on changing societal attitudes towards gender roles and stereotypes has been significant, but the path to progress has been marked by challenges and setbacks. Backlash and resistance to feminist ideals have emerged in various forms, from political and religious opposition to the perpetuation of harmful gender stereotypes in media and popular culture. Addressing these challenges requires sustained effort, intersectional approaches, and a commitment to challenging deeply entrenched beliefs and power structures.

One of the most significant changes in societal attitudes has been the increasing acceptance of women in the workforce. For decades, women were relegated to lower-paying, less prestigious jobs, their contributions often undervalued and overlooked due to pervasive gender stereotypes. However, as more women entered the workforce and proved their competence, attitudes began to shift, albeit gradually. Today, while challenges persist, women are breaking barriers in every field, from science and technology to business and politics, challenging the notion that certain careers are unsuitable for women.

Despite the increasing acceptance of women in the workforce, significant barriers and challenges persist. According to a report by the International Labour Organization (ILO), women continue to face the "glass ceiling" phenomenon, where they are underrepresented in leadership and decision-making roles, even in fields where they are well-represented. This barrier is often attributed to deeply entrenched gender stereotypes, unconscious biases, and the persistent double burden of balancing work and domestic responsibilities.

According to a report by the International Labour Organization (ILO), the global labor force participation rate for women has increased from 50.2% in 1990 to 51.8% in 2021. However, significant disparities persist across regions and sectors, with women often concentrated in lower-paying, less secure jobs and facing significant wage gaps compared to their male counterparts. Despite these challenges, the increasing presence of women in traditionally male-dominated fields has contributed to a gradual shift in societal attitudes, challenging long-held stereotypes about women's capabilities and suitability for certain professions.

The gender pay gap, which refers to the difference in average earnings between men and women, is a persistent challenge that reflects deeply rooted gender stereotypes and discrimination in the workforce. According to a report by the International Labour Organization (ILO), the global gender pay gap stands at around 20%, with women earning approximately 80% of what men earn for work of equal value. This disparity not only perpetuates economic inequality but also reinforces harmful gender stereotypes about the value of women's labor and contributions.

The media has also played a crucial role in shaping societal attitudes towards gender roles and stereotypes, both perpetuating and challenging traditional norms. In the past, women were often portrayed in limited and stereotypical ways, reinforcing the idea that their primary value lay in their appearance and domestic abilities. However, as the demand for diverse and realistic representations grew, the media landscape began to change, reflecting and shaping societal attitudes in turn. Today, we see a growing number of strong, complex female characters in film, television, and literature, challenging traditional gender stereotypes and providing young girls with positive role models.

The impact of media representations on societal attitudes towards gender roles and stereotypes is not limited to traditional media outlets like television and film. Social media platforms and online content have also played a significant role in shaping narratives and perceptions around gender. While these platforms have provided a space for diverse voices and perspectives, they have also been breeding grounds for the perpetuation of harmful stereotypes, online harassment, and the spread of misinformation and hate speech targeting women and marginalized groups.

The impact of media representations on societal attitudes towards gender roles and stereotypes has been well-documented by various studies. According to research by the Geena Davis Institute on Gender in Media, exposure to gender-balanced and diverse media representations can positively influence children's attitudes and perceptions about gender roles and the potential of women and girls. Conversely, media that perpetuates harmful gender stereotypes and underrepresents women in leadership and non-traditional roles can reinforce negative societal attitudes and limit young girls' aspirations.

The impact of media representations on societal attitudes towards gender roles and stereotypes extends beyond childhood and adolescence. A study by the United Nations Entity for Gender Equality and the Empowerment of Women (UN Women) found that exposure to sexist or stereotypical media content can negatively influence adults' attitudes towards women's rights, leadership abilities, and career aspirations. This highlights the need for concerted efforts to promote diverse, empowering, and non-stereotypical representations of women across all forms of media.

Education has been another key driver of change, empowering women and girls with the knowledge and skills to challenge gender norms and stereotypes. As more women have gained access to higher education, they have challenged the notion that certain fields of study are off-limits to them. Women are now earning degrees in traditionally male-dominated areas such as engineering, computer science, and mathematics, proving that gender is no barrier to intellectual achievement. This shift in educational opportunities has not only empowered individual women but has also contributed to a broader societal shift in attitudes towards gender roles.

Despite the progress made in increasing women's access to education, significant challenges persist in many regions of the world. According to a report by UNESCO, over 130 million girls globally are out of school, with poverty, cultural norms, and gender-based violence being major barriers to their education. Addressing these challenges requires a multifaceted approach that combines policy reforms, community engagement, and the promotion of gender-responsive educational environments that challenge harmful gender stereotypes and empower girls and young women.

The impact of education on challenging gender roles and stereotypes extends beyond individual empowerment. According to a report by UNESCO, countries with higher levels of girls' education tend to have lower levels of gender discrimination and more progressive attitudes towards women's rights and opportunities. Education not only equips women with the knowledge and skills to challenge gender norms but also contributes to broader societal shifts by shaping the attitudes and perceptions of future generations.

However, it is important to recognize that progress has not been uniform across all societies and cultures. In many parts of the world, deeply entrenched gender stereotypes and traditional gender roles continue to limit women's opportunities and freedoms. Women continue to face discrimination, violence, and unequal access to resources and decision-making power. Changing these deeply rooted attitudes requires sustained effort and commitment from all members of society, addressing the intersectional challenges faced by women from diverse backgrounds, including those marginalized due to race, class, sexuality, disability, or other identities.

The persistence of harmful gender stereotypes and traditional gender roles in certain regions and cultures can have devastating consequences for women's well-being, autonomy, and overall human rights. For instance, in some parts of the world, women and girls are subjected to harmful practices such as female genital mutilation (FGM), child marriage, and honor killings, often justified by deeply entrenched cultural traditions and gender norms. According to the United Nations Population Fund (UNFPA), an estimated 200 million girls and women alive today have undergone FGM, a practice that has no medical benefits and can cause severe physical and psychological harm.

Religious and cultural beliefs can play a significant role in perpetuating harmful gender stereotypes and traditional gender roles. In some contexts, religious teachings and interpretations have been used to justify the subordination of women, limit their rights and opportunities, and reinforce patriarchal power structures. However, it is important to recognize that these interpretations are not monolithic, and many religious and cultural traditions also contain teachings that promote gender equality and respect for women's rights.

The persistence of gender stereotypes and traditional gender roles in certain societies and cultures can be attributed to a complex interplay of factors, including religious beliefs, cultural traditions, and deeply rooted patriarchal power structures. According to a report by the United Nations Population Fund (UNFPA), addressing these challenges requires a multifaceted approach that combines legal and policy reforms, community engagement, and the promotion of women's empowerment and leadership in all spheres of society.

One of the most promising developments in recent years has been the growing recognition of the importance of engaging men and boys in the fight for gender equality. Historically, the burden of challenging gender stereotypes has fallen primarily on women. However, there is a growing understanding that true equality can only be achieved when men also challenge the norms and expectations that perpetuate gender inequalities. Programs like the HeForShe campaign and initiatives by organizations such as Promundo engage men and boys in dialogue and education about gender equality, fostering a culture of mutual respect and shared responsibility.

The engagement of men and boys in the fight for gender equality is not only a matter of shifting societal attitudes and norms but also a crucial step towards addressing issues such as gender-based violence. According to a report by the World Health Organization, one of the key risk factors for perpetrating violence against women is having witnessed or experienced violence in childhood, highlighting the importance of challenging harmful masculinity norms and promoting positive, non-violent models of manhood from an early age.

The engagement of men and boys in the fight for gender equality has been recognized as a critical component of sustainable and transformative change. According to a report by the United Nations Entity for Gender Equality and the Empowerment of Women (UN Women), involving men and boys in challenging gender norms and promoting positive masculinities can contribute to a more comprehensive and effective approach to achieving gender equality.

By addressing the socialization processes and cultural narratives that reinforce harmful gender stereotypes and expectations, these initiatives can foster a more inclusive and supportive environment for women's empowerment.

Initiatives like the MenEngage Alliance, a global network of organizations and individuals working to engage men and boys in promoting gender equality, have been instrumental in developing and implementing programs that challenge toxic masculinity, promote healthy relationships, and encourage men to become allies and advocates for women's rights. These programs recognize that gender equality is not a zero-sum game, but rather a shared journey towards creating more just and equitable societies that benefit everyone.

Dialogue and storytelling have also emerged as powerful tools for changing societal attitudes towards gender roles and stereotypes. By sharing their experiences and perspectives, women are challenging the dominant narratives and creating space for new understandings of gender. Social media has amplified these voices, allowing women from all walks of life to connect, support each other, and advocate for change. The #MeToo movement, for example, sparked a global conversation about sexual harassment and assault, challenging long-held attitudes about what constitutes acceptable behavior and empowering women to speak out against gender-based violence and discrimination.

The power of storytelling and personal narratives in challenging gender roles and stereotypes lies in their ability to humanize experiences, evoke empathy, and create a sense of shared struggle and solidarity. As Roxane Gay, the acclaimed author and feminist, notes, "We need to share our stories, not just for ourselves but for the generations that come after us. Our stories are powerful, and they have the potential to change the world around us."

The power of dialogue and storytelling in challenging gender roles and stereotypes lies in their ability to humanize experiences, evoke empathy, and foster a deeper understanding of the complexities of gender-based discrimination and oppression. According to a study by the Harvard Business Review, exposure to personal narratives and first-hand accounts of discrimination can be more effective in changing attitudes and behaviors than statistics or abstract information alone. By sharing their stories, women are not only raising awareness but also creating a sense of shared experience and solidarity that can inspire collective action towards change.

The power of storytelling and personal narratives in challenging gender roles and stereotypes extends beyond individual experiences. These stories also shed light on the systemic and structural barriers that perpetuate gender inequality, such as discriminatory laws, policies, and institutional practices. By amplifying these narratives, women's rights advocates and activists can build a stronger case for policy reforms, legislative changes, and institutional accountability measures that address the root causes of gender-based discrimination and oppression.

In recent years, the power of social media and online activism has become increasingly apparent in challenging gender roles and stereotypes. Platforms like Twitter, Facebook, and Instagram have given women a global stage to share their experiences, raise awareness about gender-based issues, and mobilize support for change. Online campaigns such as #EverydaySexism and #YesAllWomen have highlighted the pervasive nature of gender discrimination and harassment, while also creating a sense of solidarity among women across the world, fostering a collective movement for change.

While social media and online activism have provided powerful platforms for amplifying women's voices and challenging gender stereotypes, they have also exposed women to new forms of online harassment and abuse. According to a report by Amnesty International, women who speak out on social media platforms are often subjected to targeted harassment, threats, and cyberbullying, which can have severe psychological and emotional consequences. Addressing these challenges requires a multi-stakeholder approach involving social media companies, policymakers, and civil society organizations to create safer online spaces and support systems for women activists and advocates.

The rise of social media and online activism has not only amplified women's voices but has also created new spaces for dialogue, knowledge-sharing, and collective action. According to a report by Amnesty International, online platforms have enabled women's rights activists and advocates to connect, coordinate efforts, and mobilize support on a global scale, transcending geographical boundaries and traditional power structures. However, the report also acknowledges the potential risks associated with online activism, such as online harassment, censorship, and privacy concerns, underscoring the need for digital security measures and support systems for women activists.

The power of digital activism and online platforms in challenging gender roles and stereotypes extends beyond raising awareness and fostering solidarity. These platforms have also been instrumental in driving concrete policy changes and legal reforms. For instance, the #MeToo movement, which gained momentum through social media, has led to legislative changes and institutional policies aimed at addressing sexual harassment and holding perpetrators accountable in various sectors, including entertainment, media, and politics.

Moreover, legislative and policy changes have played a crucial role in promoting gender equality and challenging discriminatory practices. Laws such as the Equal Pay Act, Title VII of the Civil Rights Act, and the Violence Against Women Act in the United States, as well as similar legislation enacted in countries around the world, have provided legal protections and recourse for women facing discrimination and abuse. These legislative milestones reflect a growing recognition of the need for systemic change to address gender inequalities and challenge harmful gender stereotypes and norms.

While legislative and policy changes have been crucial in advancing gender equality and challenging discriminatory practices, their impact is often dependent on effective implementation, enforcement, and societal buy-in. In many countries, despite progressive laws on paper, deeply entrenched societal attitudes, lack of institutional capacity, and resistance from powerful groups can hinder the practical realization of these legal protections and reforms. Addressing these challenges requires a multifaceted approach that combines legal reforms with public awareness campaigns, capacity-building initiatives, and the promotion of gender-responsive governance and accountability mechanisms.

The impact of legislative and policy changes on challenging gender roles and stereotypes has been significant, but implementation and enforcement remain crucial challenges. According to a report by the World Bank, while many countries have enacted laws prohibiting gender discrimination and promoting equal rights, the effectiveness of these laws often depends on factors such as institutional capacity, political will, and societal attitudes. Addressing these challenges requires a multi-faceted approach that combines legal reforms with awareness-raising campaigns, capacity-building initiatives, and the promotion of gender-responsive governance and accountability mechanisms.

The importance of effective implementation and enforcement of gender equality laws and policies is underscored by the persistent gender pay gap, which remains a significant challenge in many parts of the world. Despite the existence of equal pay laws, women continue to earn less than men for work of equal value, a disparity that reflects deeply entrenched societal attitudes and stereotypes about the value of women's labor and contributions.

Another critical aspect of challenging gender roles and stereotypes is the importance of intersectional approaches. Women are not a monolithic group, and their experiences are shaped by a complex interplay of factors such as race, class, sexuality, and disability status. Women from marginalized communities often face unique challenges and barriers that are not adequately addressed by mainstream feminist movements or gender equality initiatives. Intersectional feminism recognizes that gender oppression is inextricably linked to other forms of oppression, and that true equality can only be achieved by addressing these intersecting forms of discrimination and amplifying the voices and perspectives of women from diverse backgrounds.

The importance of intersectional approaches in challenging gender roles and stereotypes is exemplified by the experiences of indigenous women, who often face compounded forms of discrimination and marginalization based on their gender, race, and cultural identities. According to a report by the United Nations Permanent Forum on Indigenous Issues, indigenous women are disproportionately affected by poverty, lack of access to education and healthcare, and gender-based violence, exacerbated by the legacies of colonialism, land dispossession, and cultural erosion.

The importance of intersectional approaches in challenging gender roles and stereotypes has been highlighted by various scholars and activists. According to Kimberlé Crenshaw, a pioneering scholar in intersectional theory, the experiences of women of color and other marginalized groups are often overlooked or marginalized within mainstream feminist discourse, perpetuating their oppression and invisibility. By adopting an intersectional lens, initiatives aimed at challenging gender stereotypes and promoting equality can better address the unique experiences and challenges faced by women from diverse backgrounds, ensuring that no woman is left behind in the pursuit of gender justice.

As we look to the future, it is clear that the work of challenging gender roles and stereotypes is far from over. While progress has been made, there is still a long way to go before true gender equality is achieved. Persistent gender-based violence, discrimination in the workplace and education, and the backlash against feminist ideals in some regions or communities serve as stark reminders that complacency is not an option. It will require ongoing efforts from individuals, communities, and institutions to dismantle the deeply entrenched beliefs and practices that limit women's potential and perpetuate harmful gender stereotypes.

However, there is reason for hope. As younger generations grow up in a world where gender roles are increasingly fluid and where women are breaking barriers in every field, there is the potential for even greater change. By continuing to challenge stereotypes, advocate for equality, and create inclusive environments, we can build a future where every individual, regardless of gender, has the opportunity to thrive and define their own path, unencumbered by the constraints of outdated gender norms and expectations.

The potential for change lies not only with younger generations but also with the collective efforts of individuals, communities, and institutions across all sectors of society. By fostering intergenerational dialogue, promoting inclusive education and media representation, advocating for gender-responsive policies and practices, and challenging harmful gender norms and stereotypes in our daily lives, we can create a ripple effect that drives sustainable and transformative change towards a more equitable and inclusive society for all.

The exploration of changing societal attitudes towards gender roles and stereotypes in women is a testament to the resilience, courage, and determination of those who have fought for equality. It is a reminder that change is possible, even in the face of deeply entrenched beliefs and practices. As we move forward, let us draw strength from the progress that has been made and continue to work towards a world where every woman has the freedom to define her own path and reach her full potential, unshackled by the limitations of gender stereotypes and oppressive societal norms.

As we continue on this journey towards gender equality and the dismantling of harmful gender roles and stereotypes, it is essential to embrace a spirit of empathy, compassion, and intersectional solidarity. By recognizing and amplifying the voices and experiences of marginalized women, we can create a more inclusive and representative movement that addresses the diverse challenges and forms of oppression faced by women across different contexts and identities. Through collective action, sustained advocacy, and a commitment to challenging oppressive systems and structures, we can forge a path towards a more just and equitable world for all.

Section B: Analysis of media representations of women and their impact on social perceptions

In the vast expanse of the modern media landscape, the portrayal of women is a constellation of influence and impact. From the glossy pages of fashion magazines to the captivating screens of cinema, the images and narratives that are presented to the world shape and mold our perceptions of women and their roles in society. In this exploration, we will embark on a journey to analyze the profound effects of these representations and the ways in which they influence social perceptions.

The media, like a gentle breeze, whispers its messages into the collective consciousness of society. It paints vivid portraits of femininity, often adorned with the hues of glamour and unattainable beauty standards. The airwaves carry the melodies of advertisements that beckon women to conform to narrow ideals of physical perfection. The glossy pages of magazines display images of flawlessness, creating an illusion that true beauty is narrowly defined and unattainable for the majority. These representations, like delicate petals in a garden, seep into the psyche, shaping the way we perceive and judge women based on their appearance.

The impact of these media representations extends beyond the surface, delving deep into the psyche of society. The seeds of objectification are sown, nurturing a culture that reduces women to mere objects of desire, disregarding their inherent complexities and strengths. The stories told on our screens often pigeonhole women into narrow roles, perpetuating harmful stereotypes and limiting the scope of their capabilities. These narratives, like a soft melody, echo through the corridors of our minds, influencing the way we view and interact with women in our daily lives.

However, amidst the tumultuous waves of media influence, there are moments of hope and resilience. Like delicate blossoms in a storm, there exist representations of women that break free from the confines of stereotypes and limitations. These are the stories of strength, resilience, and empowerment that gently nudge us to reimagine the roles and potential of women. These representations, like a soothing lullaby, inspire us to challenge the status quo and strive for a more inclusive and equitable society.

As we navigate the web of media representations, it becomes clear that the impact on social perceptions goes beyond mere observation. The images and narratives we encounter in the media shape the way we perceive and treat women in our communities. They influence the opportunities available to women, the expectations placed upon them, and the barriers they face in their pursuit of equality. The media holds the power to uplift and empower women, but it also has the potential to perpetuate harmful stereotypes and biases.

In the realm of media representations, we are called to be discerning observers, to question the narratives presented to us, and to seek out representations that celebrate the diversity and strength of women. As we engage with media, we must strive to uplift and amplify the voices of women from all walks of life, ensuring that their stories are told with authenticity and depth. By doing so, we can cultivate a media landscape that nurtures understanding, empathy, and progress.

The importance of critically analyzing media representations of women and actively seeking out diverse and authentic narratives cannot be overstated. According to a study by the Geena Davis Institute on Gender in Media, exposure to stereotypical and narrow representations of women in media can have a profound impact on children's attitudes and behaviors towards gender roles and expectations. Conversely, exposure to positive and diverse representations of women can foster greater empathy, self-esteem, and aspirations among girls and young women.

One area where media representations have a significant impact is in specific industries, such as video games, sports media, and news media. In the gaming industry, for example, women have long been underrepresented and often portrayed in overly sexualized or stereotypical roles. This lack of diverse and empowering representations can shape perceptions of women in gaming culture and discourage young girls from pursuing careers in the field.

The underrepresentation and stereotypical portrayal of women in the gaming industry have been well-documented by various studies and reports. According to a report by the International Game Developers Association (IGDA), only 24% of game developers identify as women, and many of them report experiencing discrimination, harassment, and bias in the industry. Furthermore, research by the University of Southern California's Annenberg Inclusion Initiative found that in top-selling video games, less than

25% of the protagonists were female, and female characters were often depicted in a highly sexualized or stereotypical manner.

Similarly, in sports media, the coverage of women's sports is often overshadowed by their male counterparts, with female athletes receiving less airtime, fewer sponsorships, and lower pay. This disparity in representation can perpetuate the notion that women's sports are less valuable or exciting than men's, affecting both the perceptions of fans and the opportunities available to female athletes.

The disparity in media coverage and representation of women's sports has been a longstanding issue. According to a study by the University of Minnesota's Tucker Center for Research on Girls & Women in Sport, only 4% of all sports media coverage is dedicated to women's sports. This lack of visibility not only affects public perception but also has tangible consequences for female athletes in terms of sponsorship opportunities, pay equity, and overall investment in women's sports programs.

In the arena of news media, the way women are portrayed and the roles they are given can also have a significant impact on social perceptions. Women are often underrepresented in leadership positions in news organizations, and their voices and perspectives are sometimes marginalized in coverage of important issues. This lack of diversity in the newsroom can lead to biased or incomplete reporting that fails to capture the full range of women's experiences and concerns.

A report by the Women's Media Center found that in the United States, only 41% of newsroom employees are women, and women make up only 28% of leadership roles in news organizations. This gender imbalance in newsrooms has been linked to biased or incomplete coverage of issues that disproportionately affect women, such as reproductive rights, gender-based violence, and workplace discrimination. According to the report, news stories that lack diverse perspectives and fail to represent the full range of women's experiences can perpetuate harmful stereotypes and limit public understanding of important social and political issues.

The rise of social media has also added a new dimension to the impact of media representations on social perceptions. Social media influencers and celebrities have become powerful cultural forces, with the ability to shape trends, opinions, and behaviors. When these influencers perpetuate gender stereotypes or promote narrow standards of beauty and success, it can have a profound impact on the self-esteem and aspirations of their followers, particularly young women.

The influence of social media on body image and self-esteem, particularly among young women, has been well-documented by researchers. A study by the University of Missouri-Columbia found that exposure to idealized body images on social media was associated with higher levels of body dissatisfaction and disordered eating behaviors among college-aged women. Furthermore, a report by the American Psychological Association highlighted the potential negative impact of social media influencers promoting unrealistic beauty standards and perpetuating gender stereotypes, which can contribute to issues such as low self-esteem, anxiety, and depression among young women.

However, social media influencers also have the potential to challenge gender norms and promote positive representations of women. By using their platforms to showcase diverse voices, advocate for social justice, and celebrate women's achievements, influencers can help to shift social perceptions and create a more inclusive and empowering media landscape.

The potential of social media influencers to challenge gender norms and promote positive representations of women has been recognized by various organizations and advocates. For example, the United Nations' Global Initiative for Gender Equality in the Media has partnered with social media influencers to raise awareness about gender equality issues and amplify the voices of women and girls. Similarly, organizations like Girl Up and the Malala Fund have leveraged the power of social media to promote education and empowerment for girls, using influencers to reach and inspire younger audiences.

To navigate this complex media landscape, it is essential to promote media literacy education that equips individuals with the skills to critically analyze and question media representations. This education should start at a young age, helping children to develop a critical eye for the messages they encounter in media and to understand the impact these messages can have on their perceptions and beliefs.

The importance of media literacy education has been emphasized by various experts and organizations, including UNESCO, which has developed a comprehensive Media and Information Literacy (MIL) curriculum for educators. According to UNESCO, media literacy skills are essential for empowering individuals to critically engage with media content, recognize biases and stereotypes, and make informed decisions about the media they consume. By fostering media literacy from an early age, individuals can develop the ability to critically analyze media representations and challenge harmful or limiting narratives about gender, race, or other social identities.

Media literacy education can also help individuals to recognize and challenge gender stereotypes, to seek out diverse perspectives and voices, and to demand more authentic and empowering representations of women in media. By fostering a culture of critical engagement with media, we can work towards a media landscape that truly reflects the diversity and complexity of women's experiences.

The importance of media literacy education in challenging gender stereotypes and promoting diverse representations has been highlighted by various organizations and initiatives. For example, the Geena Davis Institute on Gender in Media has developed a comprehensive media literacy program aimed at empowering students to recognize and challenge gender biases in media. Similarly, the National Association for Media Literacy Education (NAMLE) offers resources and professional development opportunities for educators to integrate media literacy into their curricula, with a focus on promoting diverse and inclusive representations.

In conclusion, the analysis of media representations of women and their impact on social perceptions reveals a complex and multifaceted relationship. The media, like a gentle breeze, has the power to sway the perceptions and attitudes of society. It is a force that shapes the way we view and interact with women, influencing the opportunities and challenges they encounter.

As we navigate the complex landscape of media representations and their impact on social perceptions, it is essential to recognize the power of individual agency and collective action. While the media industry plays a significant role in shaping narratives and representations, individuals and communities also have the ability to demand change, challenge harmful stereotypes, and amplify diverse and empowering narratives. By engaging in critical media literacy education, supporting initiatives that promote diverse representations, and holding media organizations accountable, we can collectively work towards a media landscape that celebrates and uplifts the diversity and strength of women in all their wondrous forms.

Yet, amidst the complexities and challenges, there exists the potential for change and transformation. As we navigate the constellation of media representations, let us embrace a spirit of discernment and seek out portrayals that honor the diversity and strength of women. Together, we can foster a society that celebrates and uplifts the contributions and potential of women in all their wondrous forms, unencumbered by the constraints of harmful stereotypes and biases.

The potential for change and transformation in media representations lies not only in the hands of media organizations and content creators but also in the collective power of consumers and audiences. By consciously choosing to support and amplify media that celebrates diversity, challenges stereotypes, and uplifts the voices and experiences of women from all walks of life, we can create a cultural shift towards more inclusive and empowering narratives. Furthermore, by actively engaging in dialogue, advocacy, and accountability efforts, we can hold media organizations accountable for their representations and demand more diverse, authentic, and empowering narratives that reflect the true complexity and richness of women's experiences.

Section C: Examination of cultural movements and grassroots activism driving social change

In the fertile soil of society, cultural movements and grassroots activism take root, growing into powerful forces that shape our world in ways both subtle and profound. As we delve into the examination of these movements, we witness the unstoppable momentum that drives social change, particularly in the realm of women's rights and gender equality.

The power of cultural movements and grassroots activism to drive social change lies in their ability to challenge dominant narratives, disrupt oppressive systems, and amplify marginalized voices. According to a report by the United Nations Development Programme (UNDP), these movements have been instrumental in advancing human rights, promoting democratic governance, and fostering sustainable development across the globe. By engaging communities, mobilizing collective action, and advocating for structural and systemic change, cultural movements and grassroots activism have the potential to transform societal norms, policies, and power dynamics.

The emergence of cultural movements and grassroots activism as catalysts for social change can be traced back to various historical periods and contexts. According to a report by the United Nations Research Institute for Social Development (UNRISD), these movements have played a critical role in challenging oppressive systems, amplifying marginalized voices, and driving transformative change in areas such as civil rights, labor rights, and women's empowerment. Their ability to mobilize collective action and disrupt the status quo has often been driven by a shared sense of injustice, a commitment to solidarity, and a vision for a more equitable and inclusive society.

Have you ever stood witness to a moment in history when the voices of the unheard become a resounding chorus, impossible to ignore? Such is the essence of grassroots activism. It begins as a whisper, a murmur of dissent, until it crescendos into a roar that shakes the foundations of the status quo. Women across the globe have been at the forefront of these movements, dismantling long-standing barriers and forging new paths of opportunity and equality.

The power of grassroots activism lies in its ability to amplify the voices of those who have been historically marginalized and excluded from traditional power structures. According to a study by the Institute for Women's Policy Research, women have played a pivotal role in driving grassroots movements for social change, often drawing upon their lived experiences of marginalization and oppression to fuel their activism. By organizing at the community level, sharing personal narratives, and building coalitions, women activists have challenged systemic inequalities and fought for greater representation, rights, and opportunities.<

The power of grassroots activism lies in its ability to amplify the voices of those who have been historically marginalized and excluded from traditional power structures. According to a study by the Institute for Women's Policy Research, women have played a pivotal role in driving grassroots movements for social change, often drawing upon their lived experiences of marginalization and oppression to fuel their activism. By organizing at the community level, sharing personal narratives, and building coalitions, women activists have challenged systemic inequalities and fought for greater representation, rights, and opportunities.

Consider the Women's March, a sprawling constellation of pink hats and determined faces that stretched across cities worldwide. What began as a response to a singular political event quickly transcended its origins, becoming a symbol of resistance and solidarity. Millions of women, and men, gathered to raise their voices for gender equality, reproductive rights, and social justice. The imagery was striking—waves of protesters like a sea of change, each individual a drop that contributed to the overwhelming tide.

The Women's March of 2017, which drew millions of participants across the United States and around the world, exemplified the power of grassroots mobilization and the importance of intersectional solidarity. According to a report by the Woodrow Wilson

International Center for Scholars, the march not only served as a powerful statement of resistance against policies and rhetoric perceived as threatening to women's rights but also created a platform for diverse voices and experiences to be represented and amplified. By bringing together women from various backgrounds, ethnicities, and identities, the march highlighted the intersectional nature of the struggle for gender equality and the need for inclusive and intersectional approaches to activism.

The Women's March of 2017, which drew millions of participants across the United States and around the world, exemplified the power of grassroots mobilization and the importance of intersectional solidarity. According to a report by the Woodrow Wilson International Center for Scholars, the march not only served as a powerful statement of resistance against policies and rhetoric perceived as threatening to women's rights but also created a platform for diverse voices and experiences to be represented and amplified. By bringing together women from various backgrounds, ethnicities, and identities, the march highlighted the intersectional nature of the struggle for gender equality and the need for inclusive and intersectional approaches to activism.

But movements are not just made of marches and protests; they are also crafted through the quiet, relentless work of community organizers and activists. Picture a small room filled with passionate individuals, strategizing over cups of lukewarm coffee, their resources limited but their resolve unwavering. They are the architects of change, drawing blueprints that will alter the landscape of society. Their efforts often go unnoticed by the broader public, yet their impact is undeniable.

The role of community organizers and grassroots activists in driving social change cannot be overstated. According to a study by the Centre for Applied Studies in International Negotiations (CASIN), effective community organizing is a critical component of successful social movements, as it helps to build trust, mobilize resources, and develop collective strategies for action. These organizers and activists serve as the backbone of movements, working tirelessly to engage communities, raise awareness, and coordinate collective action, often with limited resources but unwavering determination.

The role of community organizers and grassroots activists in driving social change cannot be overstated. According to a study by the Centre for Applied Studies in International Negotiations (CASIN), effective community organizing is a critical component of successful social movements, as it helps to build trust, mobilize resources, and develop collective strategies for action. These organizers and activists serve as the backbone of movements, working tirelessly to engage communities, raise awareness, and coordinate collective action, often with limited resources but unwavering determination.

Grassroots activism is an ecosystem of countless campaigns and initiatives. Each piece, no matter how small, adds color and depth to the larger picture. Campaigns like #HeForShe invite men to join the fight for gender equality, acknowledging that the burden of change should not rest solely on women's shoulders. Education drives like the Malala Fund work tirelessly to ensure that every girl has the opportunity to learn and lead. These efforts underscore a powerful truth: when we lift barriers for women, we elevate society as a whole.

The diversity of campaigns and initiatives within grassroots activism reflects the multifaceted nature of the challenges faced by women and the various approaches needed to address them. According to a report by the Association for Women's Rights in Development (AWID), successful grassroots movements for women's rights often combine multiple strategies, including advocacy, education, community mobilization, and strategic litigation, to create a comprehensive and holistic approach to social change.

The diversity of campaigns and initiatives within grassroots activism reflects the multifaceted nature of the challenges faced by women and the various approaches needed to address them. According to a report by the Association for Women's Rights in Development (AWID), successful grassroots movements for women's rights often combine multiple strategies, including advocacy, education, community mobilization, and strategic litigation, to create a comprehensive and holistic approach to social change.

Are you aware of the local heroes who make a difference in their communities every day? The women who challenge discriminatory laws, who start mentorship programs for at-risk youth, who advocate for safer workplaces—these champions of change operate at the grassroots level, often out of the limelight, but their contributions are the bedrock of societal transformation.

The role of local heroes and community-based activists in driving social change is often overlooked, yet their impact cannot be overstated. According to a study by the United Nations Development Programme (UNDP), grassroots women's organizations and community-based initiatives play a crucial role in addressing specific local challenges, advocating for policy changes, and fostering community resilience. These local activists have a deep understanding of the cultural, social, and economic contexts in which they operate, enabling them to develop contextualized strategies and solutions that resonate with their communities and address their unique needs.

The role of local heroes and community-based activists in driving social change is often overlooked, yet their impact cannot be overstated. According to a study by the United Nations Development Programme (UNDP), grassroots women's organizations and community-based initiatives play a crucial role in addressing specific local challenges, advocating for policy changes, and fostering community resilience. These local activists have a deep understanding of the cultural, social, and economic contexts in which they operate, enabling them to develop contextualized strategies and solutions that resonate with their communities and address their unique needs.

It is crucial to recognize the diversity within these movements. Women from different backgrounds, ethnicities, and orientations bring unique perspectives and experiences to the table. The intersectionality of these movements ensures that no one is left behind. The LGBTQ+ community, women of color, indigenous women, and those with disabilities—all have vital roles to play in the quest for equality.

The recognition of intersectionality within cultural movements and grassroots activism has been a critical development in recent years. According to a report by the United Nations Entity for Gender Equality and the Empowerment of Women (UN Women), intersectional approaches to women's rights and gender equality are essential for addressing the compounded forms of marginalization and discrimination faced by women from diverse backgrounds. By acknowledging the intersections of gender with factors such as race, ethnicity, class, disability, and sexual orientation, these movements can better address the unique challenges and experiences of different groups of women and ensure that their voices and perspectives are represented and amplified.

The recognition of intersectionality within cultural movements and grassroots activism has been a critical development in recent years. According to a report by the United Nations Entity for Gender Equality and the Empowerment of Women (UN Women), intersectional approaches to women's rights and gender equality are essential for addressing the compounded forms of marginalization and discrimination faced by women from diverse backgrounds. By acknowledging the intersections of gender with factors such as race, ethnicity, class, disability, and sexual orientation, these movements can better address the unique challenges and experiences of different groups of women and ensure that their voices and perspectives are represented and amplified.

One cannot ignore the digital universe, a modern-day agora where activism thrives. Social media campaigns can ignite within hours, mobilizing thousands to stand up for causes they believe in. Hashtags become banners under which people rally. #TimesUp, #SayHerName, and #MeToo are just a few examples of how digital platforms have amplified voices that might otherwise go unheard, catalyzing global movements and sparking conversations that challenge gender norms and expose systemic inequalities.

The rise of digital activism and the use of social media platforms have revolutionized the landscape of cultural movements and grassroots activism. According to a report by the United Nations Broadband Commission, digital technologies have enabled marginalized groups, including women and LGBTQ+ communities, to connect, organize, and amplify their voices on a global scale.

Hashtag campaigns like #MeToo and #BlackLivesMatter have demonstrated the power of digital activism to raise awareness, mobilize support, and catalyze collective action around critical issues of gender-based violence, racial injustice, and systemic discrimination.

The rise of digital activism and the use of social media platforms have revolutionized the landscape of cultural movements and grassroots activism. According to a report by the United Nations Broadband Commission, digital technologies have enabled marginalized groups, including women and LGBTQ+ communities, to connect, organize, and amplify their voices on a global scale. Hashtag campaigns like #MeToo and #BlackLivesMatter have demonstrated the power of digital activism to raise awareness, mobilize support, and catalyze collective action around critical issues of gender-based violence, racial injustice, and systemic discrimination.

But, let us not don rose-colored glasses; the path of activism is fraught with challenges. Backlash, burnout, and the struggle for resources are constant companions to those who dare to push against the inertia of tradition. Yet, it is the very act of overcoming these obstacles that strengthens the resolve of activists and deepens the impact of their work.

The challenges faced by cultural movements and grassroots activists are multifaceted and often daunting. According to a report by the International Center for Not-for-Profit Law (ICNL), activists worldwide face a range of threats, including restrictive laws, harassment, violence, and limited access to funding and resources. Additionally, activists often face burnout and emotional strain due to the demanding nature of their work and the constant exposure to trauma and injustice. Despite these challenges, the resilience and determination of activists remain unwavering, as they continue to find innovative ways to overcome obstacles and drive positive change.

Activism is not a sprint; it is a marathon—a relentless pursuit that demands endurance and passion. It's the kind of race where each baton passed is a story of struggle and triumph, and the finish line is a world where equality is not an ideal but a reality.

The enduring nature of activism and the pursuit of social change is a testament to the unwavering commitment of those involved. According to a study by the Carnegie Endowment for International Peace, successful social movements often span decades, requiring sustained effort, strategic planning, and intergenerational solidarity. The metaphor of a marathon captures the essence of this long-term struggle, where activists must maintain their stamina, adapt to changing circumstances, and pass the baton of leadership and knowledge to future generations, ensuring the continuation of the movement and the eventual realization of its goals.

Let us also acknowledge the transformative power of art, music, and literature in driving social change and challenging gender norms. Throughout history, creative expressions have served as potent vehicles for activism, giving voice to the marginalized and inspiring collective action. From the subversive poetry of Audre Lorde to the provocative art of Frida Kahlo, women have harnessed the power of their creativity to challenge the status quo and envision a more just and equitable world.

The role of art, music, and literature in cultural movements and grassroots activism cannot be underestimated. According to a report by the United Nations Educational, Scientific and Cultural Organization (UNESCO), artistic expressions have played a crucial role in raising awareness, fostering empathy, and inspiring collective action for social change throughout history. By providing powerful visual and emotional representations of marginalized experiences and perspectives, art has the ability to challenge dominant narratives, disrupt oppressive ideologies, and spark critical dialogue and reflection.

In the world of music, artists like Beyoncé, Janelle Monáe, and Lizzo have used their platforms to celebrate female empowerment, challenge gender stereotypes, and advocate for body positivity and social justice. Their songs become anthems of resistance, uniting people across boundaries and inspiring a new generation of activists.

Similarly, authors like Chimamanda Ngozi Adichie, Roxane Gay, and Jesmyn Ward have used the power of storytelling to explore the complexities of gender, race, and identity, inviting readers to confront their own biases and imagine a more inclusive society.

The impact of influential artists and writers in shaping cultural narratives and driving social change cannot be overstated. According to a study by the American Psychological Association, exposure to diverse and empowering representations of marginalized groups in art and media can positively influence attitudes, foster empathy, and inspire collective action for social justice. By using their platforms and creative voices to challenge stereotypes, celebrate diversity, and amplify marginalized perspectives, these artists and writers have played a crucial role in shifting cultural paradigms and inspiring movements for gender equality, racial justice, and LGBTQ+ rights.

The impact of these creative works extends beyond the realm of art and culture, influencing social and political discourse and inspiring concrete action. They serve as catalysts for change, sparking conversations and mobilizing communities to demand justice and equality. The power of art and activism converge, creating a potent force that has the potential to shift cultural narratives and transform societal attitudes.

The convergence of art and activism has been a powerful force in driving social change throughout history. According to a report by the International Center for Nonviolent Conflict, artistic expressions have often played a crucial role in nonviolent resistance movements, serving as a means of challenging oppressive systems, fostering solidarity, and inspiring collective action. From the civil rights anthems of the 1960s to the protest songs of the Arab Spring, music and art have the ability to transcend boundaries, unite communities, and amplify the voices of those fighting for justice and equality.

Moreover, the power of cultural movements and grassroots activism is amplified by international solidarity and global connectivity. In an increasingly interconnected world, the struggles and triumphs of women in one corner of the globe can resonate with and inspire those in another. The #MeToo movement, for example, started as a local campaign in the United States but quickly spread to countries around the world, sparking a global reckoning with sexual harassment and assault, and fostering a sense of shared purpose among women from diverse backgrounds.

The ability of cultural movements and grassroots activism to transcend borders and foster global solidarity has been facilitated by the rise of digital technologies and social media platforms. According to a report by the United Nations Development Programme (UNDP), these technologies have enabled activists and organizers to connect, share resources, and coordinate collective action across geographic boundaries. This global connectivity has not only amplified the voices of marginalized communities but has also facilitated the exchange of knowledge, strategies, and best practices among activists worldwide, strengthening the overall impact of these movements.

This international solidarity is crucial in the face of transnational challenges like human trafficking, forced migration, and climate change, which disproportionately affect women and girls. By building alliances across borders and learning from each other's experiences, activists can develop more effective strategies and advocate for policies that protect the rights and dignity of women everywhere. Organizations like the Association for Women's Rights in Development (AWID) and the African Women's Development Fund (AWDF) play vital roles in fostering these global connections and amplifying the voices of grassroots women's rights movements.

The importance of international solidarity and collaboration in addressing transnational challenges that disproportionately affect women and girls has been highlighted by various international organizations and experts. According to a report by the United Nations Office on Drugs and Crime (UNODC), combating human trafficking and other forms of gender-based violence requires a coordinated global response, involving collaboration between governments, civil society organizations, and grassroots movements. By sharing knowledge, resources, and best practices across borders, these collaborative efforts can develop more effective strategies and advocate for stronger international policies and frameworks to protect the rights and dignity of women and girls worldwide.

However, it is important to recognize that the fight for gender equality cannot be won by women alone. Men have a crucial role to play as allies and advocates, challenging the patriarchal norms and structures that perpetuate inequality. This requires a fundamental shift in the way we socialize boys and men, encouraging them to embrace empathy, vulnerability, and respect for women. Programs like Promundo and the White Ribbon Campaign engage men and boys in the fight against gender-based violence, promoting healthy masculinity and challenging harmful stereotypes. By creating a culture of allyship and accountability, these initiatives help to create a more supportive environment for women's rights and gender equality.

The importance of engaging men and boys as allies in the fight for gender equality has been emphasized by various experts and organizations. Michael Kaufman, a co-founder of the White Ribbon Campaign, argues that men have a responsibility to challenge the societal norms and power structures that perpetuate gender inequality and violence against women. By actively promoting positive masculinities and challenging toxic masculinity, men can play a crucial role in dismantling the patriarchal systems that oppress and marginalize women.

The engagement of men and boys as allies in the fight for gender equality has been recognized as a critical component of sustainable and transformative change. According to a report by UN Women, involving men and boys in challenging gender norms and promoting positive masculinities can contribute to a more comprehensive and effective approach to achieving gender equality. By addressing the socialization processes and cultural narratives that reinforce harmful gender stereotypes and expectations, these initiatives can foster a more inclusive and supportive environment for women's empowerment and create a culture of shared responsibility for advancing gender justice.

The impact of engaging men and boys in promoting gender equality has been demonstrated by various initiatives and programs. For example, the Promundo organization has worked with men and boys in over 40 countries to challenge harmful gender norms and promote positive masculinities. According to their impact report, their programs have led to significant changes in attitudes and behaviors, with participants reporting increased support for gender equality, reduced acceptance of violence against women, and greater involvement in caregiving and domestic responsibilities.

As we reflect on the power of cultural movements and grassroots activism in driving social change, we are reminded that the fight for women's rights is not a solitary endeavor. It is a collective struggle, woven from the threads of countless individual stories and experiences. Each voice, each action, each act of resistance contributes to the larger fabric of change, strengthening the tapestry of progress and inspiring others to join the movement.

The collective nature of cultural movements and grassroots activism is a testament to the power of solidarity and the recognition that individual struggles are interconnected. According to a study by the International Center for Research on Women (ICRW), women's rights movements that have embraced intersectionality and built coalitions across various identities and causes have been more effective in achieving sustainable change. By acknowledging the intersections of gender with other forms of oppression, these movements have amplified the voices of diverse groups of women and fostered a more inclusive and representative approach to advocacy and activism.

So, dear reader, as we reflect upon these cultural movements and grassroots activism, let us ask ourselves: How can we contribute to this ongoing narrative of change? How can we support the tireless work of these unsung heroes? The answers may vary, but the underlying truth remains constant—every action, no matter how small, is a step towards breaking barriers and sculpting a fairer, more just society.

The power of individual action in supporting cultural movements and grassroots activism cannot be underestimated. According to a report by Oxfam International, small acts of solidarity and support, such as amplifying the voices of activists, donating to grassroots organizations, and participating in collective actions, can contribute to the momentum and impact of these movements. By recognizing our individual agency and taking action, no matter how small, we can collectively drive social change and support the tireless work of activists and organizers on the frontlines.

In conclusion, the advancements in women's rights owe much to the cultural movements and grassroots activism that drive social change. These efforts are the heartbeat of progress, pumping vitality and vigor into the cause of equality. As we turn the page, we must acknowledge the immense power of collective action and the unyielding spirit of those who champion it. Let us carry forward with the knowledge that each of us plays a role in this story, a story that continues to unfold with every barrier we break and every right we secure for women in modern society.

The impact of cultural movements and grassroots activism on advancing women's rights is not only measured by tangible policy changes or legal victories but also by the transformative power they hold in shifting societal attitudes and norms. According to a report by the Wellesley Centers for Women, these movements have played a crucial role in challenging deeply entrenched patriarchal systems, redefining gender roles and expectations, and creating space for diverse voices and perspectives to be heard and valued.

The examination of cultural movements and grassroots activism reveals a constellation of resilience, courage, and hope. It is a testament to the indomitable spirit of those who refuse to accept the status quo, who dare to imagine a world where every woman can live with dignity, freedom, and equality. As we navigate the path forward, let us draw strength from their example and commit ourselves to the ongoing work of building a more just and equitable society for all.

The resilience and courage displayed by cultural movements and grassroots activists in the face of adversity is a testament to the power of collective resistance and the unwavering pursuit of justice. According to a study by the Institute for Women's Policy Research, women's rights activists and organizers around the world often face significant risks, including threats, harassment, and violence, yet they continue to persevere in their fight for gender equality and social change. Their resilience serves as an inspiration and a reminder that true progress requires unwavering determination and a commitment to creating a more just and equitable world for all.

Chapter 7
Intersectionality and Inclusivity

Section A: Discussion of the intersectional nature of women's rights and the importance of inclusivity

In the intricate web of human rights, the threads of gender, race, class, sexuality, and disability interweave to form the multifaceted pattern of intersectionality. This concept, first coined by the pioneering legal scholar and critical race theorist Kimberlé Crenshaw, illuminates the multiple and intersecting facets of identity that shape the diverse experiences of women around the globe. It posits a crucial question: How do we navigate the labyrinth of layered oppressions that women face in their pursuit of equality and empowerment?

The introduction of intersectionality theory by Kimberlé Crenshaw has had a profound impact on various fields of study, social movements, and human rights discourse. According to a report by the United Nations Research Institute for Social Development (UNRISD), intersectionality has emerged as a powerful analytical framework for understanding the complex and multidimensional nature of oppression and marginalization, challenging the idea of a singular or universal experience of discrimination. By providing a nuanced lens through which to examine the intersections of various forms of oppression, intersectionality has contributed to a deeper understanding of the diverse experiences of marginalized groups and has informed the development of more inclusive and effective strategies for addressing systemic inequalities.

The concept of intersectionality, as introduced by Kimberlé Crenshaw, has had a profound impact on various fields of study and social movements. According to a report by the United Nations Research Institute for Social Development (UNRISD), intersectionality has emerged as a powerful analytical framework for understanding the complex and multidimensional nature of oppression and marginalization, challenging the idea of a singular or universal experience of discrimination. By acknowledging the intersections of different forms of oppression, intersectionality provides a more nuanced and comprehensive approach to addressing social inequalities and promoting human rights.

The importance of intersectionality in understanding and addressing the complex experiences of marginalized groups has been widely recognized by scholars and activists across various fields. According to a report by the United Nations Entity for Gender Equality and the Empowerment of Women (UN Women), adopting an intersectional approach is essential for creating inclusive and effective policies and programs that address the unique challenges faced by women at the intersections of multiple forms of oppression, such as gender, race, class, and disability.

Envision a world that recognizes the myriad ways in which women's lived realities diverge and converge, a world that acknowledges that the struggles of a woman of color, a queer woman, a woman with disabilities, or an indigenous woman are not mere variants of a universal female experience. They are shaped by the interlocking and compounding systems of privilege and oppression that permeate our societies. It's a realization that the fight for women's rights is not a monolithic endeavor; it is as multifaceted and diverse as the women it aims to empower.

The recognition of the diverse and intersecting experiences of women is not merely a theoretical concept but a lived reality that shapes the lives of millions of individuals worldwide. According to a report by the United Nations Department of Economic and Social Affairs, women and girls with disabilities face compounded barriers to education, employment, and healthcare due to the intersections of gender-based discrimination and ableism. Similarly, a report by the United Nations Permanent Forum on Indigenous Issues highlights the ongoing marginalization and discrimination faced by indigenous women, who often grapple with intersecting forms of oppression based on their gender, race, and cultural identity.

The recognition of the diverse and intersecting experiences of women has been a central tenet of intersectional feminism, which emerged from the work of Black feminist scholars and activists such as the Combahee River Collective. According to their influential statement, "The Combahee River Collective Statement," intersectional feminism acknowledges that "the synthesis of these oppressions creates the conditions of our lives." This perspective challenges the notion of a universal "women's experience" and highlights the need to address the unique challenges faced by women at the intersections of multiple forms of marginalization.

The importance of intersectional inclusivity in the women's rights movement cannot be overstated. To exclude is to diminish the potential for real, transformative change. When we neglect the specific needs and perspectives of transgender women, when we overlook the voices of those living in poverty, when we ignore the barriers faced by immigrant women, or when we fail to recognize the historical trauma and ongoing marginalization experienced by indigenous women, we fail to address the full spectrum of discrimination and oppression that women confront.

The consequences of failing to adopt an intersectional approach in the women's rights movement have been well-documented by various scholars and activists. According to a report by the United Nations Population Fund (UNFPA), a lack of intersectional perspectives in policy and program development can lead to ineffective or even harmful outcomes for marginalized women and girls. For example, reproductive health initiatives that fail to consider the unique experiences and barriers faced by women with disabilities, LGBTQ+ individuals, or those living in poverty may inadvertently perpetuate existing inequalities and further marginalize these groups.

The consequences of failing to adopt an intersectional approach in the women's rights movement have been well-documented by various scholars and activists. According to a report by the African American Policy Forum, the exclusion of Black women's experiences and perspectives from mainstream feminist discourse has led to a lack of attention and resources dedicated to addressing issues such as police brutality, reproductive injustice, and the criminalization of Black women and girls.

Consider the story of a young girl from a marginalized community who dreams of becoming a leader in her field. The obstacles she faces are not solely because she is a woman. Her path is strewn with additional hurdles—perhaps poverty, racial discrimination, ableism, or the legacy of colonialism. When we fight for her right to education, to equal pay, to healthcare, and bodily autonomy, we must do so with an understanding of these intersecting challenges. Only then can we dismantle the complex web of barriers that stand in her way.

The importance of addressing intersecting forms of oppression is exemplified by the experiences of immigrant women and girls, who often face compounded barriers due to the intersections of gender, race, class, and immigration status. According to a report by the Migration Policy Institute, immigrant women and girls are disproportionately affected by issues such as poverty, language barriers, lack of access to healthcare and social services, and vulnerability to exploitation and violence. By adopting an intersectional approach that considers these intersecting challenges, initiatives and policies can be better tailored to address the unique needs and experiences of immigrant women and girls.

The intersectional challenges faced by marginalized women in their pursuit of education, economic opportunities, and personal autonomy have been highlighted by various studies and reports. According to a report by the United Nations Development Programme (UNDP), girls and women from low-income, rural, or minority communities often face compounded barriers to accessing quality education due to factors such as poverty, cultural norms, and lack of resources. Similarly, a report by the International Labour Organization (ILO) highlights the significant wage gaps and discrimination faced by women with disabilities in the workplace.

Why, then, does intersectional inclusivity matter? It matters because the victories of women's rights are incomplete if they do not lift all women. It matters because solidarity across differences is the bedrock of a robust and truly transformative movement. Inclusivity is not a mere buzzword; it is a commitment to justice that leaves no one behind, recognizing that the liberation of all women is inextricably linked.

The importance of intersectional inclusivity in the women's rights movement is not merely a moral imperative but a strategic necessity for achieving sustainable and transformative change. According to a report by the United Nations Development Programme (UNDP), adopting an intersectional approach can enhance the effectiveness, relevance, and impact of initiatives aimed at promoting gender equality and women's empowerment. By acknowledging and addressing the diverse and intersecting experiences of women, these initiatives can better address the root causes of inequality and create an enabling environment for the full participation and empowerment of all women.

The importance of intersectional inclusivity in the women's rights movement has been emphasized by various feminist scholars and activists. According to bell hooks, a renowned feminist theorist and social activist, "Feminism is a movement to end sexist oppression. Therefore, it is necessarily a movement to eradicate the ideology of domination that permeates Western culture on various levels, and a commitment to reorganizing society so that the self-development of people can take precedence over imperialism, economic expansion, and material desires." This perspective highlights the need for a comprehensive and inclusive approach that addresses the intersections of gender with other forms of oppression, such as racism, classism, and heteronormativity.

The journey toward intersectional inclusivity requires us to listen—to truly hear and amplify the stories of those whose experiences differ from our own. Can you imagine the strength of a movement that harnesses the collective power of all women, in all their diversity? Such a movement has the potential to reshape the world, challenging and dismantling the interlocking systems of oppression that have historically marginalized and disempowered women from various backgrounds.

The power of collective action and solidarity across diverse identities and experiences has been a driving force behind many successful social movements throughout history. According to a report by the United Nations Research Institute for Social Development (UNRISD), movements that have embraced intersectionality and built coalitions across various marginalized groups have been more effective in achieving sustainable change and addressing systemic inequalities. By harnessing the collective power of all women, in all their diversity, the women's rights movement can challenge and dismantle the intersecting systems of oppression that have historically marginalized and disempowered women from various backgrounds.

The power of an intersectional and inclusive women's rights movement lies in its ability to foster solidarity, collective action, and a comprehensive understanding of the diverse experiences and challenges faced by women from various backgrounds. According to a report by the Association for Women's Rights in Development (AWID), movements that embrace intersectionality and build coalitions across different identities and causes have been more effective in achieving sustainable change and addressing the root causes of systemic oppression.

The concept of "intersectional feminism," building upon Crenshaw's groundbreaking work, has become a guiding principle for many contemporary feminist movements and activism. Pioneered by Black feminist scholars and activists like bell hooks, the Combahee River Collective, and Patricia Hill Collins, intersectional feminism recognizes that women's experiences are not homogeneous and that the fight for gender equality must be inclusive of all women, particularly those who face multiple and intersecting forms of oppression based on their race, class, sexuality, disability status, and other identities.

The impact of intersectional feminism on contemporary social movements and activism has been profound. According to a report by the Association for Women's Rights in Development (AWID), intersectional feminist approaches have been instrumental in challenging dominant narratives, amplifying marginalized voices, and fostering solidarity across diverse identities and experiences. By centering the perspectives and experiences of women from various backgrounds, intersectional feminism has contributed to a more nuanced and inclusive understanding of the complexities of gender-based oppression and the strategies needed to achieve true liberation and empowerment for all women.

The impact of intersectional feminism on contemporary feminist activism and discourse has been significant. According to a report by the United Nations Entity for Gender Equality and the Empowerment of Women (UN Women), intersectional approaches have been adopted by various women's rights organizations and movements to address the diverse and intersecting experiences of marginalized women. For example, the #MeToo movement has highlighted the unique challenges faced by women of color, LGBTQ+ individuals, and disabled women in addressing sexual harassment and assault.

Intersectional feminism has been applied in various feminist movements and campaigns, from the Women's March to the #MeToo movement, as well as in the development of policies, programs, and initiatives aimed at advancing women's rights. These efforts have sought to amplify the voices of marginalized women, create spaces for solidarity and collective action, and address the unique challenges faced by women at the intersections of various forms of oppression.

The application of intersectional approaches in feminist activism has not been without challenges and critiques. According to a report by the Feminist Review Trust, while intersectionality has been widely embraced in theory, its practical implementation within social movements and advocacy efforts has often fallen short, with marginalized voices and perspectives still being overlooked or tokenized. These critiques underscore the need for ongoing self-reflection, accountability, and a genuine commitment to inclusive and representative practices within the women's rights movement.

The application of intersectional approaches in feminist activism has been instrumental in ensuring that the diverse experiences and perspectives of marginalized women are represented and addressed. For example, the Women's March on Washington in 2017 was organized with a specific focus on intersectionality, with organizers and speakers representing a wide range of identities, including women of color, transgender women, and women with disabilities. This approach aimed to create an inclusive and representative platform that acknowledged the interconnected struggles faced by women from various backgrounds.

It is crucial to recognize and address the unique experiences of women who face multiple forms of oppression. For example, trans women of color often encounter discrimination based on their gender identity, race, and class, which can lead to higher rates of violence, poverty, and social exclusion. Similarly, women with disabilities from low-income backgrounds may face compounded barriers to education, employment, and healthcare due to the intersections of ableism, sexism, and classism.

The unique experiences and challenges faced by women at the intersections of multiple forms of oppression have been the focus of various research and advocacy efforts. For example, the Movement Advancement Project (MAP) has conducted extensive research on the experiences of LGBTQ+ people of color, highlighting the compounded forms of discrimination and marginalization they face due to the intersections of their racial, gender, and sexual identities. Similarly, organizations like the Disabled Women's Network (DAWN) have been at the forefront of advocating for the rights and empowerment of women with disabilities, addressing the intersections of gender, disability, and other forms of marginalization.

The intersectional challenges faced by marginalized women have been well-documented by various research studies and reports. According to a report by the National Center for Transgender Equality, trans women of color face disproportionately high rates of poverty, homelessness, and discrimination in employment and healthcare due to the compounding effects of transphobia, racism, and misogyny. Similarly, a report by the United Nations Department of Economic and Social Affairs highlights the significant barriers faced by women with disabilities in accessing education, employment, and healthcare services, which are further exacerbated by socioeconomic status and other intersecting factors.

By acknowledging and addressing these intersecting forms of oppression, we can work towards a more equitable and just society for all women, one that celebrates and uplifts the diverse experiences, perspectives, and contributions of women from various backgrounds.

The pursuit of a more equitable and just society for all women requires a holistic and comprehensive approach that addresses the root causes of intersecting forms of oppression. According to a report by the United Nations Entity for Gender Equality and the Empowerment of Women (UN Women), this involves adopting a multidimensional approach that combines legal and policy reforms, targeted interventions, and community-based initiatives to address the unique challenges faced by women at the intersections of various forms of marginalization. By embracing such a holistic and intersectional approach, we can work towards a society that truly celebrates and uplifts the diverse experiences, perspectives, and contributions of all women.

The importance of adopting a multidimensional and intersectional approach to addressing the challenges faced by marginalized women has been highlighted by various experts and organizations. According to a report by the Association for Women's Rights in Development (AWID), effective strategies must combine top-down policy reforms with bottom-up community-based initiatives that empower women and address the specific contextual factors that contribute to their marginalization. This approach recognizes that sustainable change requires addressing both systemic barriers and local realities, and that the voices and experiences of marginalized women must be central to the development and implementation of these strategies.

The importance of addressing intersecting forms of oppression has been emphasized by various feminist scholars and activists. According to bell hooks, "No one is free until we are all free." This sentiment underscores the interconnected nature of struggles for social justice and the need for a comprehensive approach that addresses the intersections of gender with other forms of marginalization, such as race, class, and disability. By acknowledging and uplifting the diverse experiences and perspectives of all women, we can work towards a more inclusive and equitable society that celebrates and empowers women in all their diversity.

The interconnected nature of struggles for social justice and the importance of addressing intersecting forms of oppression have been highlighted by various social justice movements and initiatives. For example, the Black Lives Matter movement has been at the forefront of advocating for an intersectional approach to addressing systemic racism, police brutality, and the intersections of race with gender, class, and other forms of marginalization. By centering the experiences of Black women and LGBTQ+ individuals within the broader movement, Black Lives Matter has challenged the notion of single-issue activism and emphasized the need for a comprehensive and intersectional approach to achieving true liberation and justice for all.

Moreover, the empowerment of women cannot be viewed in isolation; it must be part of a broader agenda for intersectional social justice that challenges all forms of oppression, including racism, classism, ableism, and heteronormativity. Organizations like INCITE! Women of Color Against Violence and the Audre Lorde Project have played pivotal roles in advancing intersectional approaches to women's rights and advocating for the rights of LGBTQ+ people, people of color, and other marginalized communities.

The work of organizations like INCITE! Women of Color Against Violence and the Audre Lorde Project has been instrumental in highlighting the intersections of gender-based violence with other forms of oppression, such as racism, homophobia, and transphobia. By adopting an intersectional approach, these organizations have challenged the traditional narratives that often focus on gender-based violence as a singular issue, and have advocated for comprehensive solutions that address the root causes of violence and oppression within marginalized communities.

The importance of adopting an intersectional approach to social justice and human rights has been recognized by various international organizations and human rights bodies. According to the United Nations Office of the High Commissioner for Human Rights

(OHCHR), addressing the intersections of gender with other forms of discrimination is crucial for realizing the fundamental principles of human rights, such as equality, non-discrimination, and the right to dignity and self-determination for all individuals.

The recognition of intersectionality as a crucial framework for addressing human rights and social justice has been reflected in various international initiatives and efforts. For example, the 2030 Agenda for Sustainable Development, adopted by the United Nations in 2015, emphasizes the importance of addressing intersecting forms of discrimination and marginalization in order to achieve the Sustainable Development Goals (SDGs). The SDGs, which include targets related to gender equality, reducing inequalities, and promoting inclusive societies, explicitly acknowledge the need for intersectional approaches that address the diverse and intersecting experiences of marginalized groups.

As we move forward, it is essential to prioritize the use of inclusive language and representation within the women's rights movement. This means actively centering and amplifying the voices, narratives, and leadership of women from diverse backgrounds, using gender-inclusive terminology, and challenging the dominance of white, cisgender, able-bodied, and middle-class perspectives within mainstream feminist discourse.

The importance of inclusive language and representation within the women's rights movement has been emphasized by various feminist scholars and activists. According to Audre Lorde, a pioneering Black feminist writer and activist, "If you are not part of the solution, then you are part of the problem." This sentiment underscores the need for the women's rights movement to actively challenge and dismantle the dominance of certain perspectives and narratives, and to create space for the voices and leadership of marginalized women to be heard and valued.

The importance of inclusive language and representation in the women's rights movement has been highlighted by various organizations and initiatives. For example, the LGBTQ+ advocacy organization GLAAD has developed a comprehensive media reference guide that provides recommendations for using inclusive and respectful language when discussing gender identity, sexual orientation, and other related topics. By adopting inclusive language and challenging the dominance of certain perspectives, the women's rights movement can create a more welcoming and representative environment that empowers and uplifts the diverse voices and experiences of all women.

The impact of inclusive language and representation goes beyond creating a welcoming environment; it also plays a crucial role in shaping societal attitudes and perceptions. According to a report by the United Nations Educational, Scientific and Cultural Organization (UNESCO), media representations and narratives can perpetuate harmful stereotypes and biases or challenge them, depending on the language and perspectives employed. By embracing inclusive language and diverse representations within the women's rights movement, activists and advocates can contribute to broader societal shifts towards greater understanding, acceptance, and celebration of diversity.

The importance of inclusive language and representation in shaping societal attitudes and perceptions has been further emphasized by various experts and organizations. According to a report by the United Nations Development Programme (UNDP), inclusive and diverse media representations can contribute to the empowerment of marginalized groups by challenging negative stereotypes, fostering a sense of belonging, and inspiring individuals to pursue their aspirations and dreams. By embracing inclusive language and representation within the women's rights movement, activists and advocates can play a crucial role in creating a more empowering and inclusive environment for all women, regardless of their backgrounds or intersecting identities.

Initiatives like the Say Her Name campaign, led by the African American Policy Forum, have been instrumental in highlighting the intersections of race and gender in cases of police brutality against Black women and girls, while organizations like DISPOSABLE FILM and Women With Disabilities Arts & Culture have created platforms for disabled women to share their stories and advocate for their rights.

The impact of initiatives like the Say Her Name campaign and organizations like DISPOSABLE FILM and Women With Disabilities Arts & Culture extends beyond raising awareness and advocacy; they also serve as powerful platforms for amplifying marginalized voices and fostering community empowerment. According to a report by the United Nations Development Programme (UNDP), creating spaces for marginalized groups to share their narratives and experiences can contribute to collective healing, resilience, and the development of community-driven solutions to address systemic oppression and marginalization.

The impact of initiatives like the Say Her Name campaign and organizations like DISPOSABLE FILM and Women With Disabilities Arts & Culture extends beyond raising awareness and advocacy. According to a report by the United Nations Development Programme (UNDP), creating platforms for marginalized women to share their stories and experiences can have a transformative impact on their sense of empowerment, self-worth, and collective agency. By amplifying these diverse voices and narratives, these initiatives challenge dominant narratives, disrupt systems of oppression, and contribute to the broader struggle for intersectional social justice.

The transformative impact of amplifying marginalized voices and narratives has been further highlighted by various feminist scholars and activists. According to bell hooks, "Storytelling is a powerful tool for resisting oppression and marginalization." By sharing their stories and experiences, marginalized women not only challenge dominant narratives but also reclaim their agency, affirm their humanity, and contribute to the collective struggle for intersectional social justice. Through initiatives like the Say Her Name campaign and organizations like DISPOSABLE FILM and Women With Disabilities Arts & Culture, marginalized women are not only raising awareness but also fostering a sense of solidarity, collective empowerment, and resilience in the face of systemic oppression.

In closing, let us envision a future where the advancements in women's rights reflect the full complexity and diversity of women's lived experiences. A future where intersectional inclusivity is not a lofty ideal but a lived reality. A future where every woman, in all her uniqueness, is valued, heard, and empowered to reach her full potential. This is the future we must strive for—a future where barriers are not only broken but are rendered obsolete by the unyielding force of intersectional solidarity and collective liberation.

The vision of a future where intersectional inclusivity is a lived reality is not merely an aspirational ideal but a moral and ethical imperative. According to the United Nations Guiding Principles on Business and Human Rights, businesses and institutions have a responsibility to respect and promote human rights, including the rights of marginalized and vulnerable groups. By embracing intersectional inclusivity and ensuring that the advancements in women's rights reflect the diverse experiences and needs of all women, we can contribute to the realization of a more just and equitable society that upholds the fundamental principles of human rights and dignity for all.

The pursuit of intersectional inclusivity and the realization of a just and equitable society for all women is not only a moral and ethical imperative but also a strategic imperative for achieving sustainable development and addressing global challenges. According to a report by the United Nations Development Programme (UNDP), addressing intersecting forms of oppression and marginalization is crucial for achieving the Sustainable Development Goals (SDGs), which aim to eradicate poverty, promote gender equality, and foster inclusive and peaceful societies. By embracing intersectional approaches and ensuring that no one is left behind, we can unlock the full potential of women and girls as agents of positive change and contributors to sustainable development.

Let us carry this torch of intersectional inclusivity as we forge ahead. Let us illuminate the path for those who follow, ensuring that the advancements in women's rights we celebrate today pave the way for an even brighter, more equitable, and inclusive tomorrow for all women, across all intersections of identity and experience.

The pursuit of intersectional inclusivity and the advancement of women's rights require a collective commitment to ongoing learning, reflection, and action. According to a report by the Association for Women's Rights in Development (AWID), effective social movements and advocacy efforts must embrace a culture of continuous learning, acknowledging that the journey towards intersectional justice is an ongoing process that requires humility, self-reflection, and a willingness to adapt and evolve in response to emerging challenges and changing contexts.

The importance of intergenerational solidarity and knowledge-sharing in the pursuit of intersectional inclusivity cannot be overstated. According to a report by the Association for Women's Rights in Development (AWID), the transfer of knowledge, experiences, and strategies across generations has been a critical factor in sustaining and strengthening social movements and advocacy efforts for women's rights and intersectional justice. By embracing intergenerational collaboration and mentorship, we can ensure that the hard-won advancements of today serve as a foundation for even greater progress and inclusion tomorrow.

The importance of intergenerational solidarity and knowledge-sharing has been further emphasized by various feminist scholars and activists. According to Audre Lorde, "It is not our differences that divide us. It is our inability to recognize, accept, and celebrate those differences." By fostering intergenerational dialogue and collaborative spaces, we can learn from the experiences and wisdom of those who have been at the forefront of the struggle for intersectional justice, while also cultivating the leadership and perspectives of younger generations who bring fresh insights and innovative approaches to advancing intersectional inclusivity.

Section B: Analysis of challenges faced by marginalized communities within the women's rights movement

Within the fervent struggles for women's rights, the voices of the most marginalized communities often struggle to be heard above the din of mainstream narratives. These communities face an intricate web of socio-economic, cultural, and systemic challenges that require our undivided attention and unwavering commitment. To truly break barriers, we must delve into the depths of these challenges, shining a light on the injustices that thwart the progress of women's rights in modern society.

According to a report by the United Nations Entity for Gender Equality and the Empowerment of Women (UN Women), marginalized communities of women often face compounded forms of discrimination and oppression due to the intersections of gender with other factors such as race, ethnicity, disability, sexual orientation, and socioeconomic status. Addressing the specific challenges faced by these communities is crucial for advancing women's rights in a truly inclusive and equitable manner.

At the heart of this discourse lies the question: What specific obstacles do women from marginalized communities confront in their quest for equality? Their stories are not just footnotes in the larger narrative of women's rights; they are critical chapters that demand our focus and understanding, for their liberation is inextricably linked to the liberation of all women.

The recognition of the diverse and intersecting challenges faced by marginalized women has been a central tenet of intersectional feminism. According to the Combahee River Collective, a pioneering Black feminist organization, "We struggle together with Black men against racism, while we also struggle with Black men about sexism." This statement highlights the importance of acknowledging the multiple and intersecting forms of oppression faced by marginalized women and the need for a comprehensive approach that addresses these intersections.

Consider the plight of indigenous women, whose experiences often remain invisible within the broader women's movement. Their struggle is multifaceted: they combat the systemic discrimination that affects indigenous peoples, the gender-based violence and inequality that affect women, and the ongoing impacts of colonialism, land dispossession, and cultural suppression. Indigenous women's rights are frequently trampled under the weight of exploitation and the extraction of natural resources from their ancestral lands. Their voices are stifled by a history of colonial oppression and ongoing marginalization. How can we amplify their voices and ensure their rights are not just recognized but actively protected and upheld?

The challenges faced by indigenous women are deeply rooted in the legacy of colonialism and its ongoing consequences. According to a report by the United Nations Permanent Forum on Indigenous Issues, indigenous women are disproportionately affected by poverty, lack of access to education and healthcare, and high rates of violence, including human trafficking and sexual exploitation. These issues are exacerbated by the dispossession of indigenous lands, the destruction of traditional livelihoods, and the suppression of indigenous cultures and languages.

The impact of colonialism and historical trauma on indigenous women cannot be overstated. The legacy of forced assimilation, cultural genocide, and land dispossession has created a complex web of challenges that indigenous women must navigate. From the epidemic of missing and murdered indigenous women and girls in Canada and the United States to the fight for land rights, self-determination, and environmental justice by indigenous women in Latin America, these struggles are rooted in a long history of colonial violence and oppression. Addressing these challenges requires a decolonial approach that centers indigenous women's voices, knowledge, and leadership, and that upholds their rights to self-determination and sovereignty over their lands and bodies.

The issue of missing and murdered indigenous women and girls (MMIWG) has been a longstanding crisis in both Canada and the United States. According to the National Crime Information Center, there were over 5,700 cases of missing or murdered Native American and Alaskan Native women and girls reported in 2021 alone. This crisis is rooted in systemic racism, poverty, and the ongoing impacts of colonialism, which have left indigenous communities vulnerable to violence and exploitation. Addressing the MMIWG crisis requires a multifaceted approach that involves improving data collection, providing adequate resources for investigations, and addressing the underlying social and economic factors that contribute to this violence.

Women with disabilities face additional barriers to accessing their rights and participating fully in the women's rights movement. Society frequently overlooks their unique challenges, rendering them doubly invisible. These women grapple with inaccessible environments, healthcare systems ill-equipped to address their needs, and prejudiced attitudes that question their agency and autonomy. They confront not only the glass ceiling but a myriad of structural walls that impede their journey toward equality. What steps must we take to dismantle these walls and foster an environment of true inclusivity and accessibility for women with disabilities?

The challenges faced by women with disabilities in accessing their rights and participating in social movements are multifaceted and deeply rooted in systemic ableism. According to a report by the United Nations Department of Economic and Social Affairs, women with disabilities are often denied the right to make decisions about their lives, subjected to forced sterilization and institutionalization, and face higher rates of gender-based violence compared to women without disabilities. These challenges are compounded by limited access to education, employment opportunities, and healthcare services that cater to their specific needs.

Ableism intersects with sexism and other forms of oppression in insidious ways, creating compounded challenges for women with disabilities. They often face limited access to reproductive healthcare, as medical professionals may dismiss their desires for motherhood or subject them to forced sterilization. Women with disabilities also experience higher rates of gender-based violence, as perpetrators may view them as easy targets or doubt their credibility when they report abuse. Dismantling these barriers requires a concerted effort to challenge ableist attitudes, ensure accessibility in all spheres of life, amplify the voices and leadership of women with disabilities within the feminist movement, and provide adequate support and resources to address their specific needs and experiences.

The issue of violence against women with disabilities has been a significant concern, with research indicating that women with disabilities are more likely to experience various forms of abuse, including physical, sexual, emotional, and financial abuse. According to a report by the United Nations Population Fund (UNFPA), women with disabilities are at a higher risk of experiencing violence due to their increased vulnerability, social isolation, and dependence on caregivers. Addressing this issue requires a multifaceted approach that includes improving access to support services, providing education and training to caregivers and service providers, and fostering a culture of respect and inclusion for women with disabilities.

In the urban sprawls and rural corners of our world, women from lower socio-economic backgrounds battle against the tide of economic injustice. Their labor is undervalued, their access to education limited, and their potential stifled by the chains of poverty and lack of economic opportunities. They are often the first to feel the harsh sting of economic downturns and the last to recover. Their fight for equal rights is entwined with the struggle for economic empowerment and access to resources. How can we reshape economic policies and structures to be equitable and just, ensuring these women are no longer relegated to the margins?

Women from lower socio-economic backgrounds face intersecting forms of oppression, as poverty and economic marginalization exacerbate the challenges posed by gender-based discrimination and inequality. According to a report by the International Labour Organization (ILO), women are more likely than men to be employed in precarious, low-wage jobs, with limited access to social protection and opportunities for advancement. This economic vulnerability is further compounded by the disproportionate burden of unpaid care work that women bear, limiting their ability to participate in the formal labor market and contributing to the perpetuation of the cycle of poverty.

The LGBTQ+ community, particularly queer women and transgender individuals, faces a unique set of challenges within the women's rights movement. They navigate a minefield of discrimination, often exacerbated by a lack of legal protections, social acceptance, and access to affirming healthcare. The fight for women's rights must be inclusive of all gender identities and expressions, recognizing that the right to live authentically, free from violence and discrimination, is a fundamental human right. How do we create a movement that not only accepts but celebrates this diversity and upholds the rights and dignity of LGBTQ+ women?

The challenges faced by LGBTQ+ women and transgender individuals within the women's rights movement are rooted in the intersections of gender-based discrimination, homophobia, and transphobia. According to a report by the United Nations Development Programme (UNDP), LGBTQ+ individuals, particularly transgender women, face disproportionately high rates of violence, harassment, and discrimination in various spheres of life, including employment, housing, and healthcare. This discrimination is often exacerbated by a lack of legal protections, societal stigma, and limited access to resources and support services.

Women from immigrant and refugee communities often face intersecting barriers to accessing their rights and participating in the women's rights movement. Language barriers, cultural stigma, precarious legal status, and the trauma of displacement can compound the challenges they face in navigating new societies. Many immigrant women work in low-wage, exploitative industries, such as domestic work or garment factories, where they are vulnerable to abuse, trafficking, and discrimination. Undocumented women may fear reporting violence or seeking help due to the risk of deportation. Creating safe, inclusive, and culturally responsive spaces for immigrant and refugee women requires language accessibility, legal protections, and advocacy for humane immigration policies that uphold their rights and dignity.

The experiences of immigrant and refugee women are shaped by the intersections of gender, race, ethnicity, and immigration status. According to a report by the United Nations High Commissioner for Refugees (UNHCR), refugee women and girls are particularly vulnerable to gender-based violence, exploitation, and human trafficking during the displacement process and in refugee camps. Furthermore, immigrant women often face language barriers, cultural stigma, and precarious legal status in their host countries, which can limit their access to essential services, such as healthcare, education, and legal support.

As we explore these challenges, a singular truth emerges: the path to equality is not a one-size-fits-all journey. Each community requires tailored strategies that address their specific needs, experiences, and barriers. Our actions must be as diverse and intersectional as the women we seek to support and empower.

The recognition that a one-size-fits-all approach is inadequate in addressing the diverse challenges faced by marginalized women has been a central tenet of intersectional feminism. According to Kimberlé Crenshaw, the pioneering legal scholar who coined the term "intersectionality," traditional feminist theory and activism have often failed to address the specific needs and experiences of women who face multiple and intersecting forms of oppression, such as women of color, LGBTQ+ individuals, and women with disabilities. Crenshaw emphasizes the importance of developing strategies that are tailored to the unique circumstances and lived experiences of these communities.

Let us now turn to the resilience of these communities, for within their stories of struggle are also tales of profound strength, resistance, and determination. The indigenous woman who fights for the sovereignty of her people and the protection of her ancestral lands, the woman with a disability who advocates for accessible spaces and inclusive healthcare, the single mother who toils day and night to provide for her family, and the transgender woman who reclaims her place in society—each of them is a testament to the indomitable spirit of women and the power of collective resistance.

The resilience and strength of marginalized women in the face of systemic oppression and intersecting forms of discrimination have been a source of inspiration for many social movements and advocates. According to a report by the Association for Women's Rights in Development (AWID), the leadership and activism of marginalized women have been instrumental in challenging oppressive systems, amplifying diverse voices, and driving transformative change. By drawing upon their lived experiences and collective resistance, these women have not only fought for their own liberation but have also contributed to broader struggles for social justice and human rights.

We must listen to their voices, learn from their experiences, and join hands with them in solidarity. In doing so, we forge a movement that is not fragmented but whole, a constellation of diverse voices singing a shared song of freedom, justice, and intersectional liberation.

The importance of listening to and amplifying the voices of marginalized women has been emphasized by various feminist scholars and activists. According to bell hooks, a pioneering Black feminist theorist, "No woman is free until all women are free." This sentiment underscores the interconnected nature of the struggles faced by marginalized women and the need for solidarity and collective action across diverse communities. By centering the voices and experiences of those who face multiple and intersecting forms of oppression, the women's rights movement can better address the specific challenges and barriers faced by these communities and work towards a truly intersectional and inclusive vision of liberation.

To conclude, the challenges faced by marginalized communities within the women's rights movement are multifaceted and interlocking, but they are not insurmountable. With a commitment to intersectional inclusivity, empathy, and action, we can overcome these barriers. We can build a world where every woman, regardless of her background or identity, has the opportunity to lead a life of dignity, respect, and equality. This is the foundation upon which a truly progressive, intersectional feminist movement is built—a movement that recognizes that the liberation of all women is inextricably linked, and that our struggles are interconnected.

The pursuit of a truly intersectional and inclusive women's rights movement is not merely a matter of theoretical discourse but a practical imperative for achieving sustainable and transformative change. According to a report by the United Nations Development Programme (UNDP), addressing intersecting forms of discrimination and marginalization is crucial for achieving the Sustainable Development Goals (SDGs), which aim to promote gender equality, reduce inequalities, and foster inclusive and peaceful societies. By embracing intersectional approaches and centering the voices and experiences of marginalized women, the women's rights movement can contribute to the realization of these global goals and work towards a more just and equitable world for all.

Let this be our pledge: to recognize the multitude of challenges faced by marginalized women, to elevate the voices that are often silenced, and to work tirelessly until the advancements in women's rights are shared by every woman, everywhere. It is a task of monumental importance, but together, united in our diversity and strengthened by our intersectional solidarity, we can—and we will—forge a future that is fair, just, and inclusive for all.

The pursuit of intersectional inclusivity and the advancement of women's rights is not merely a matter of theoretical discourse or abstract ideals; it is a call to action that demands sustained commitment, collective action, and a willingness to challenge and transform oppressive systems and structures. According to a report by the Association for Women's Rights in Development (AWID), effective social movements and advocacy efforts must embrace a culture of continuous learning, intersectional collaboration, and adaptive strategies that are responsive to the dynamic and evolving challenges faced by marginalized communities. By embracing this approach, we can forge a future where the advancements in women's rights are truly inclusive and transformative, leaving no one behind.

Section C: Examination of efforts to prioritize diversity, equity, and inclusion in feminist activism

In an ever-evolving world, the feminist movement has been a beacon of change, tirelessly striving to dismantle the archaic structures that have long oppressed women. Yet, as we forge ahead, it is crucial that our march towards equality is marked by the footsteps of every woman, from every walk of life. The path to liberation is woven with the threads of diversity, equity, and inclusion, and our commitment to these principles is what will define the future of feminist activism.

The importance of prioritizing diversity, equity, and inclusion within the feminist movement has been recognized as a crucial imperative for achieving sustainable and transformative change. According to a report by the Association for Women's Rights in Development (AWID), feminist activism that embraces intersectionality and centers the voices and experiences of marginalized women has been more effective in challenging systemic oppression, promoting gender equality, and fostering solidarity across diverse communities.

The importance of prioritizing diversity, equity, and inclusion within the feminist movement has been recognized as a crucial imperative for achieving sustainable and transformative change. According to a report by the Association for Women's Rights in Development (AWID), feminist activism that embraces intersectionality and centers the voices and experiences of marginalized women has been more effective in challenging systemic oppression, promoting gender equality, and fostering solidarity across diverse communities.

Delving into the heart of feminist activism reveals a mosaic woven with the threads of diversity. It is a vibrant constellation where the hues of race, ethnicity, socio-economic background, sexual orientation, gender identity, ability, and age are interlaced. The recognition of this diversity is not merely a nod to variety but a profound acknowledgment that the intersectionality of these identities shapes the lived experiences of women in distinct and significant ways.

The recognition of the intersectionality of women's experiences has been a central tenet of contemporary feminist thought and activism. According to the Combahee River Collective, a pioneering Black feminist organization, "The synthesis of these oppressions creates the conditions of our lives." This perspective highlights the importance of acknowledging and addressing the multiple and intersecting forms of oppression faced by marginalized women, such as women of color, LGBTQ+ individuals, women with disabilities, and those from lower socioeconomic backgrounds.

The recognition of the intersectionality of women's experiences has been a central tenet of contemporary feminist thought and activism. According to the Combahee River Collective, a pioneering Black feminist organization, "The synthesis of these oppressions creates the conditions of our lives." This perspective highlights the importance of acknowledging and addressing the multiple and intersecting forms of oppression faced by marginalized women, such as women of color, LGBTQ+ individuals, women with disabilities, and those from lower socioeconomic backgrounds.

But what does it mean to truly prioritize diversity within the realm of feminist activism? It means actively seeking out the voices that have been marginalized, creating platforms for these voices to resonate with authority and power. It is the Black woman who speaks of racial injustice intertwined with gender bias, the immigrant woman whose narrative is laced with the struggle of assimilation and acceptance, and the elderly woman whose wisdom is often dismissed in a culture obsessed with youth. Each story is a thread, and without these threads, the fabric of our movement is incomplete.

The importance of amplifying marginalized voices within feminist activism has been emphasized by various scholars and activists. According to bell hooks, a renowned Black feminist theorist, "Feminist movement that does not embrace diversity and work to eradicate racism, classism, and heterosexism will never be able to eradicate sexist oppression." This perspective highlights the need for feminist activism to actively create spaces for marginalized women to share their stories and experiences, and to challenge dominant narratives that often reflect the perspectives of privileged groups.

Equity, the fair treatment of all individuals, is the backbone of a just movement. It recognizes that while equality gives everyone the same resources, equity tailors support based on individual circumstances. In the context of feminist activism, this means acknowledging that some women start their journey from further back due to systemic inequalities and historical injustices. It's about dismantling the institutional barriers that hold women back and creating pathways for success that are accessible to all, regardless of their identities or backgrounds. But how can we ensure that our actions are equitable? By crafting policies, programs, and initiatives that account for the varying needs, experiences, and challenges faced by diverse groups of women, we build the scaffolding that supports every woman's ascent to her highest potential.

The importance of equity in feminist activism is rooted in the recognition that different groups of women face varying degrees of oppression and marginalization due to intersecting systems of privilege and disadvantage. According to a report by the United Nations Entity for Gender Equality and the Empowerment of Women (UN Women), addressing gender-based discrimination alone is insufficient; efforts must also address the compounded effects of other forms of oppression, such as racism, classism, and ableism, to ensure that all women can access and benefit from initiatives aimed at promoting gender equality and women's empowerment.

Inclusion goes hand-in-hand with diversity and equity, forming the trinity of a truly progressive feminist movement. It is the warm embrace that welcomes every woman into the fold, assuring her that her voice is not only heard but is also integral to the symphony of change. But inclusion is not a passive act; it is a dynamic process that involves constant self-reflection, learning, and growth. It requires us to challenge our preconceptions, to stretch the boundaries of our comfort zones, and to engage with perspectives that are foreign to our own.

The importance of fostering inclusive spaces within feminist activism has been highlighted by various organizations and experts. According to a report by the European Institute for Gender Equality, creating inclusive environments that celebrate diversity and actively involve marginalized groups in decision-making processes is crucial for promoting a sense of belonging, empowerment, and collective ownership of the feminist movement. This approach not only amplifies the voices and experiences of marginalized women but also contributes to the development of more effective and sustainable strategies for addressing intersectional forms of oppression.

Let us then paint a picture of what feminist activism looks like when it prioritizes diversity, equity, and inclusion. Imagine a conference, brimming with the energy of impassioned women from diverse backgrounds. The panelists reflect the intersectional nature of the movement, with women of color, LGBTQ+ women, women with disabilities, and indigenous women taking center stage. Sign language interpreters stand alongside, their hands weaving the words into a visual dance for those who communicate differently. Childcare services bustle with activity, ensuring that mothers can participate fully without worry. Scholarships and grants ensure that economic status is not a barrier to involvement. Gender-neutral restrooms and accessible facilities cater to the needs of transgender and disabled attendees. This is not a utopian fantasy; it is a blueprint for a movement that truly represents and uplifts the voices and experiences of all women.

The vision of an inclusive and intersectional feminist conference or event is not merely an aspirational ideal but a tangible reality that various organizations and movements have strived to create. For example, the Women's Convention, organized by the Women's March in 2017, made concerted efforts to prioritize diversity, equity, and inclusion by ensuring that the speakers, panelists, and attendees reflected a wide range of identities and experiences, and by providing accommodations such as gender-neutral restrooms, childcare services, and accessibility features for people with disabilities.

But challenges abound. Institutional biases, resistance to change, and the sheer inertia of established systems stand in our way. How can we, as a collective force, confront these challenges? How do we ensure that every effort to advance women's rights is steeped in the principles of diversity, equity, and inclusion?

The challenges in prioritizing diversity, equity, and inclusion within feminist activism are multifaceted and deeply rooted in systemic forms of oppression and marginalization. According to a report by the Association for Women's Rights in Development (AWID), these challenges include the persistence of institutional biases, lack of resources and funding for marginalized groups, and resistance to change within mainstream feminist organizations and movements. Addressing these challenges requires a comprehensive and sustained effort that involves ongoing education, capacity-building, and the dismantling of oppressive systems and structures that perpetuate exclusion and marginalization.

First, we must practice active listening and create spaces for marginalized voices to be heard and centered. We must listen—to the transgender woman fighting for her right to exist, to the woman of color demanding an end to systemic racism, to the working-class woman seeking fair wages and economic justice, and to every woman whose story has been overshadowed by a narrative that does not reflect her reality. We must listen, not to respond but to understand and to act.

The importance of active listening and centering marginalized voices has been emphasized by various feminist scholars and activists. According to Audre Lorde, a pioneering Black feminist writer and activist, "The master's tools will never dismantle the master's house. They may allow us temporarily to beat him at his own game, but they will never enable us to bring about genuine change." This sentiment underscores the need for feminist activism to actively challenge dominant narratives and create spaces where marginalized women can share their stories, perspectives, and lived experiences, enabling the movement to develop more effective and inclusive strategies for achieving transformative change.

Second, education must be our tool and our weapon. We must educate ourselves about the different forms of oppression and how they intersect, educate others to foster empathy and solidarity, and educate the next generation to continue the fight for intersectional feminism. This education must go beyond theoretical discussions and translate into tangible actions, policies, and programs that dismantle the systemic barriers faced by marginalized women.

The role of education in promoting intersectional feminism and addressing systemic barriers has been recognized by various organizations and initiatives. For example, the African Feminist Forum, a pan-African network of feminist activists and organizations, has prioritized feminist education and capacity-building as a key strategy for fostering solidarity, amplifying marginalized voices, and developing effective strategies for addressing intersectional forms of oppression across the African continent.

Third, our actions must be intersectional. Our advocacy must be informed by an understanding of how different forms of discrimination overlap and compound. Our campaigns must not only call out sexism but also confront racism, classism, ableism, homophobia, transphobia, and all other forms of prejudice that inhibit a woman's right to thrive. By centering intersectionality, we can build a movement that truly represents and uplifts the diverse experiences and needs of all women.

The importance of adopting an intersectional approach in feminist activism has been highlighted by various scholars and organizations. According to the United Nations Entity for Gender Equality and the Empowerment of Women (UN Women), intersectional approaches are essential for addressing the compounded forms of discrimination and marginalization faced by women from diverse backgrounds, such as women of color, indigenous women, women with disabilities, and LGBTQ+ individuals. By centering intersectionality, feminist activism can develop more holistic and effective strategies for promoting women's rights and empowerment while also challenging intersecting systems of oppression.

Intersectional data collection and analysis play a crucial role in identifying and addressing disparities within the women's rights movement. By disaggregating data based on various identity markers, such as race, ethnicity, disability status, sexual orientation, and socioeconomic background, we can uncover the unique challenges and barriers faced by different groups of women. This information can then be used to develop targeted strategies, allocate resources more effectively, and ensure that no one is left behind.

The importance of intersectional data collection and analysis has been emphasized by various organizations and researchers. According to a report by the European Institute for Gender Equality, the lack of disaggregated data on the intersecting forms of discrimination faced by marginalized women has been a significant barrier to developing effective policies and programs that address their specific needs and experiences. By collecting and analyzing data that captures the intersections of gender with other identity markers, feminist organizations and movements can better understand the diverse experiences and challenges faced by different groups of women, enabling them to develop more targeted and inclusive strategies.<

Feminist organizations and movements are also working to create more inclusive and accessible spaces. This includes providing childcare at events to enable mothers to participate fully, using inclusive language that acknowledges diverse gender identities and expressions, ensuring that physical spaces are accessible to people with disabilities, and offering language interpretation and translation services to accommodate non-English speakers. By creating environments that are welcoming and inclusive, we can foster a sense of belonging and empowerment for all women, regardless of their backgrounds or identities.

The efforts to create inclusive and accessible spaces within feminist activism have been driven by the recognition that physical, linguistic, and cultural barriers can often exclude or marginalize certain groups of women from fully participating in and benefiting from these movements. According to a report by the United Nations Development Programme (UNDP), addressing these barriers is crucial for promoting meaningful participation, fostering a sense of belonging, and ensuring that the diverse perspectives and experiences of all women are represented and valued within feminist spaces and initiatives.

Building coalitions and solidarity across different marginalized communities is another key aspect of prioritizing diversity, equity, and inclusion in feminist activism. Recognizing that the struggles for women's rights, racial justice, LGBTQ+ equality, disability rights, and other social justice movements are interconnected, feminist activists are working to build bridges and forge alliances. By standing together and supporting each other's struggles, we can create a more powerful and unified movement that can effect real, transformative change.

The importance of building intersectional coalitions and solidarity across diverse social justice movements has been emphasized by various feminist scholars and activists. According to Kimberlé Crenshaw, "The struggle for gender justice must be anti-racist and intersectional, and the struggle for racial justice must be gendered and intersectional." This perspective highlights the interconnected nature of struggles against various forms of oppression and the need for feminist activism to actively collaborate with and support other movements that are working to dismantle intersecting systems of marginalization and discrimination.<

Organizations like the National Black Women's Reproductive Justice Agenda, the Transgender Law Center, and the Disability Rights Education & Defense Fund (DREDF) have been at the forefront of this intersectional work, advocating for the rights and dignity of Black women, transgender individuals, and people with disabilities, respectively, while also promoting collaboration and solidarity across movements.

The intersectional work of organizations like the National Black Women's Reproductive Justice Agenda, the Transgender Law Center, and the Disability Rights Education & Defense Fund (DREDF) has been instrumental in highlighting the compounded forms of oppression and marginalization faced by individuals at the intersections of various identities and experiences. By advocating for the rights and dignity of specific marginalized groups while also promoting collaboration and solidarity across movements, these organizations have contributed to the development of more comprehensive and inclusive strategies for addressing intersectional forms of discrimination and promoting social justice for all.

Moreover, the power of cultural movements and grassroots activism is amplified by international solidarity and global connectivity. In an increasingly interconnected world, the struggles and triumphs of women in one corner of the globe can resonate with and inspire those in another. The #MeToo movement, for example, started as a local campaign in the United States but quickly spread to countries around the world, sparking a global reckoning with sexual harassment and assault.

The power of international solidarity and global connectivity in amplifying cultural movements and grassroots activism has been facilitated by the rise of digital technologies and social media platforms. According to a report by the United Nations Broadband Commission, digital technologies have enabled marginalized groups, including women and LGBTQ+ communities, to connect, organize, and amplify their voices on a global scale. Initiatives like the #MeToo movement have demonstrated the potential of digital activism to transcend geographical boundaries, foster global solidarity, and catalyze collective action around critical issues of gender-based violence and oppression.

This international solidarity is crucial in the face of transnational challenges like human trafficking, forced migration, and climate change, which disproportionately affect women and girls from marginalized communities. By building alliances across borders and learning from each other's experiences, activists can develop more effective strategies and advocate for policies that protect the rights and dignity of women everywhere.

The importance of international solidarity and collaboration in addressing transnational challenges that disproportionately affect marginalized women has been recognized by various international organizations and experts. According to a report by the United Nations Office on Drugs and Crime (UNODC), combating human trafficking and other forms of gender-based violence requires a coordinated global response, involving collaboration between governments, civil society organizations, and grassroots movements across borders. By sharing knowledge, resources, and best practices, these collaborative efforts can develop more effective strategies and advocate for stronger international policies and frameworks to protect the rights and dignity of marginalized women and girls worldwide.

However, it is important to recognize that the fight for gender equality cannot be won by women alone. Men have a crucial role to play as allies and advocates, challenging the patriarchal norms and structures that perpetuate inequality. This requires a fundamental shift in the way we socialize boys and men, encouraging them to embrace empathy, vulnerability, and respect for women.

The importance of engaging men and boys as allies in the fight for gender equality has been recognized by various international organizations and initiatives. According to a report by the United Nations Entity for Gender Equality and the Empowerment of Women (UN Women), involving men and boys in challenging harmful gender norms and promoting positive masculinities can contribute to a more comprehensive and effective approach to achieving gender equality. By addressing the socialization processes and cultural narratives that reinforce harmful gender stereotypes and expectations, these initiatives can foster a more inclusive and supportive environment for women's empowerment.

Programs like Promundo and the White Ribbon Campaign engage men and boys in the fight against gender-based violence, promoting healthy masculinity and challenging harmful stereotypes. By creating a culture of allyship and accountability, these initiatives help to create a more supportive environment for women's rights and gender equality.

The impact of engaging men and boys as allies in promoting gender equality has been demonstrated by various initiatives and programs. For example, the Promundo organization has worked with men and boys in over 40 countries to challenge harmful gender norms and promote positive masculinities. According to their impact report, their programs have led to significant changes in attitudes and behaviors, with participants reporting increased support for gender equality, reduced acceptance of violence against women, and greater involvement in caregiving and domestic responsibilities.

As we reflect on the power of prioritizing diversity, equity, and inclusion in feminist activism, we are reminded that the fight for women's rights is not a solitary endeavor. It is a collective struggle, woven from the threads of countless individual stories and experiences. Each voice, each action, each act of resistance contributes to the larger fabric of change, strengthening the tapestry of progress and inspiring others to join the movement.

The collective nature of feminist activism and the importance of amplifying diverse voices and experiences have been emphasized by various scholars and organizations. According to a report by the Association for Women's Rights in Development (AWID), movements that have embraced intersectionality and built coalitions across various marginalized groups have been more effective in achieving sustainable change and addressing systemic inequalities. By harnessing the collective power of diverse voices and experiences, feminist activism can challenge and dismantle intersecting systems of oppression and marginalization, ultimately contributing to a more just and equitable society for all.

So, dear reader, as we reflect upon these efforts, let us ask ourselves: How can we contribute to this ongoing narrative of intersectional change? How can we support the tireless work of these unsung heroes? The answers may vary, but the underlying truth remains constant—every action, no matter how small, is a step towards breaking barriers and sculpting a fairer, more just society for all women, across all intersections of identity and experience.

The power of individual action and collective engagement in supporting efforts to prioritize diversity, equity, and inclusion in feminist activism has been recognized by various organizations and initiatives. According to a report by Oxfam International, small acts of solidarity and support, such as amplifying the voices of marginalized women, donating to grassroots organizations, and participating in collective actions, can contribute to the momentum and impact of these efforts. By recognizing our individual agency and taking action, no matter how small, we can collectively drive intersectional change and support the tireless work of activists and organizers on the frontlines.

In conclusion, the advancements in women's rights owe much to the efforts to prioritize diversity, equity, and inclusion within feminist activism. These efforts are the heartbeat of progress, pumping vitality and vigor into the cause of intersectional equality. As we turn the page, we must acknowledge the immense power of collective action and the unyielding spirit of those who champion intersectionality. Let us carry forward with the knowledge that each of us plays a role in this story, a story that continues to unfold with every barrier we break and every right we secure for women in modern society.

The impact of efforts to prioritize diversity, equity, and inclusion within feminist activism extends beyond tangible policy changes or legal victories; it also holds transformative power in shifting societal attitudes, narratives, and cultural norms. According to a report by the Wellesley Centers for Women, these efforts have played a crucial role in challenging deeply entrenched patriarchal systems, redefining gender roles and expectations, and creating space for diverse voices and perspectives to be heard and valued within mainstream discourse and narratives.

The examination of efforts to prioritize diversity, equity, and inclusion in feminist activism reveals a constellation of resilience, courage, and hope. It is a testament to the indomitable spirit of those who refuse to accept the status quo, who dare to imagine a world where every woman can live with dignity, freedom, and equality, regardless of her intersecting identities and experiences. As we navigate the path forward, let us draw strength from their example and commit ourselves to the ongoing work of building a more just, equitable, and inclusive society for all.

The resilience and courage displayed by feminist activists and organizers in their efforts to prioritize diversity, equity, and inclusion are a testament to the power of collective resistance and the unwavering pursuit of justice. According to a study by the Institute for Women's Policy Research, women's rights activists and organizers around the world often face significant risks, including threats, harassment, and violence, yet they continue to persevere in their fight for gender equality and social change. Their resilience serves as an inspiration and a reminder that true progress requires unwavering determination and a commitment to creating a more just and equitable world for all.

Chapter 8
Global Perspectives on Women's Rights

Section A: Overview of women's rights movements and challenges worldwide

Women's rights movements have etched their narratives across the annals of history, interweaving stories of resilience that transcend borders and time. These movements, global in scope yet rooted in local contexts, have been catalysts for change, challenging the status quo and breaking through the ceilings that have long confined women to the margins of society. But what are the contours of this struggle on a worldwide canvas? What shapes the challenges that women face from one country to the next, and how have these movements adapted to the multifaceted and intersectional nature of gender inequality?

The global landscape of women's rights movements reflects the diversity of cultural, socio-economic, and political contexts in which these struggles unfold. According to a report by the United Nations Development Programme (UNDP), the challenges faced by women vary significantly across regions, with factors such as poverty, conflict, religious fundamentalism, and deeply entrenched patriarchal norms contributing to the specific forms of discrimination and oppression experienced by women in different parts of the world.

Across the globe, women have raised their voices, often in the face of stark opposition and repressive regimes. In the bustling streets of India, we find women's rights activists fighting against the weight of a deeply entrenched patriarchal culture that often blames victims rather than perpetrators of gender-based violence. The brutal gang rape and murder of Jyoti Singh in 2012 sparked nationwide protests and a collective reckoning with the endemic problem of sexual violence, leading to legal reforms and a reinvigorated dialogue on women's safety and bodily autonomy. How can women navigate a world where their very existence becomes a battleground?

The struggle for women's rights in India has been shaped by the intersection of gender-based violence and deeply rooted cultural norms that perpetuate victim-blaming and patriarchal attitudes. According to a report by the United Nations Population Fund (UNFPA), one in three women in India has experienced physical or sexual violence perpetrated by their intimate partners. The case of Jyoti Singh, whose brutal gang rape and murder sparked nationwide protests, exposed the pervasiveness of sexual violence and the need for systemic changes to address this issue.

Venture to the Middle East, and you'll encounter women's movements pushing against the boundaries imposed by conservative societies and religious fundamentalism. Iranian women, for example, have taken to the streets in defiant protest against mandatory hijab laws, their hijabs becoming symbols of resistance as they demand the right to choose. Their struggle is not just against a piece of cloth but against a system that seeks to control women's bodies and choices, rooted in the intersections of gender and religious oppression. Can you imagine the courage it takes to stand against such deeply entrenched norms?

The women's rights movement in Iran has been at the forefront of challenging the country's strict dress codes and mandatory hijab laws, which are seen as a form of state-sanctioned oppression and control over women's bodies. According to a report by Amnesty International, Iranian women have faced arrest, imprisonment, and other forms of punishment for peacefully protesting against these laws. The courage and resilience of these activists in the face of state repression have drawn global attention to the intersections of gender and religious oppression faced by women in Iran.

In the corporate high-rises of the Western world, women grapple with glass ceilings and persistent gender pay gaps. The pinstripe suit of the boardroom, once the exclusive domain of men, now sees women striding with purpose. They are CEOs, innovators, and leaders, yet they still fight for equal recognition, remuneration, and representation at the highest levels of decision-making. Why must a woman prove her worth time and again when her male counterpart's capabilities are seldom questioned? The #MeToo movement, which erupted in 2017, exposed the pervasiveness of sexual harassment and misconduct in the workplace, galvanizing women to demand accountability and systemic change.

Despite significant progress in women's participation in the workforce and leadership roles, persistent gender gaps and barriers remain in the corporate world. According to a report by the International Labour Organization (ILO), women earn on average 20% less than men globally, and only a small percentage of CEOs and board members in large corporations are women. The #MeToo movement shed light on the pervasiveness of sexual harassment and gender-based discrimination in workplaces, highlighting the need for systemic changes and accountability measures to ensure a safe and equitable environment for women.

The challenges are indeed varied, but women's rights movements worldwide share a common goal: equality and empowerment. In Latin America, feminist collectives like Ni Una Menos (Not One Less) combat femicide, domestic violence, and the cultural normalization of gender-based violence, their cries resonating through the streets as a haunting reminder that for some women, home is not a sanctuary but a site of oppression.

The Ni Una Menos movement in Latin America has been a powerful force in addressing the epidemic of gender-based violence and femicide in the region. According to data from the United Nations Economic Commission for Latin America and the Caribbean (ECLAC), at least 4,640 women were victims of femicide in 2020, with rates of violence against women increasing during the COVID-19 pandemic. The Ni Una Menos movement has mobilized massive protests and advocacy efforts to demand government action, legal reforms, and societal change to address the root causes of this violence.

In Africa, women's rights activists confront practices like female genital mutilation (FGM) and child marriage, striving to protect the innocence of childhood and the autonomy of women's bodies. Their mission is to rewrite cultural narratives and transform them into stories of empowerment rather than subjugation. But how do you change traditions that have been woven into the fabric of society for generations? The work of organizations like the Solidarity for African Women's Rights (SOAWR) and the African Women's Development and Communication Network (FEMNET) has been instrumental in amplifying the voices and leadership of African women in shaping regional and global policies.

The struggle against harmful traditional practices like female genital mutilation (FGM) and child marriage in Africa has been a longstanding priority for women's rights activists on the continent. According to the United Nations Population Fund (UNFPA), at least 200 million girls and women alive today have undergone FGM, with the practice concentrated in 30 countries across Africa, the Middle East, and Asia. Organizations like SOAWR and FEMNET have been at the forefront of advocating for legal and policy reforms, community education, and the empowerment of women and girls to challenge these harmful practices.

Education emerges as a beacon of hope, a tool with the power to illuminate minds and alter destinies. Girls who once had their futures dictated by circumstance are now authors of their own stories, learning to read and write, to calculate and question. What happens when a girl is given a book instead of a broom, a pen instead of a pan? She becomes a force that can challenge the very foundations of oppression. Initiatives like the United Nations Girls' Education Initiative (UNGEI) and the Malala Fund have been at the forefront of promoting girls' access to quality education, particularly in conflict-affected and marginalized communities.

The importance of education as a catalyst for women's empowerment and the advancement of gender equality has been widely recognized by international organizations and advocacy groups. According to a report by the United Nations Educational, Scientific and Cultural Organization (UNESCO), every additional year of schooling for girls can increase their future earnings by up to 20%. Initiatives like UNGEI and the Malala Fund have played a crucial role in promoting access to education for girls, particularly in regions affected by conflict, poverty, and cultural barriers.

Yet, for all the progress, the journey is far from over. Women's rights movements continue to face backlash, resistance, and outright violence. In some parts of the world, activists are met with threats, imprisonment, and even assassination for their advocacy work. The rise of populist, authoritarian, and conservative regimes poses a new threat, with some leaders openly hostile to women's rights and gender equality. In these turbulent waters, how do feminist movements maintain their course and momentum?

The challenges faced by women's rights activists and movements in the face of backlash, repression, and violence have been well-documented by various human rights organizations. According to a report by Amnesty International, women human rights defenders and activists face a range of threats, including physical attacks, arbitrary arrests, judicial harassment, and targeted online abuse, often perpetrated by state and non-state actors. In some countries, the rise of authoritarian and populist regimes has led to a further crackdown on civil society, making it increasingly difficult for women's rights movements to operate and mobilize.

The digital age has opened new frontiers for activism, presenting both opportunities and challenges. Social media has become a battleground where hashtags serve as rallying cries, connecting local struggles to global movements. Campaigns like #MeToo, #NiUnaMenos, and #BringBackOurGirls have shown the power of collective storytelling and shared experiences that resonate across borders. Online platforms have given women a voice where they might otherwise be silenced, but they have also exposed activists to online harassment, surveillance, and censorship.

The rise of digital activism and the use of social media platforms have revolutionized the landscape of women's rights movements, enabling activists to connect, mobilize, and amplify their voices on a global scale. However, this digital frontier has also brought new challenges, including online harassment, censorship, and surveillance of activists. According to a report by the United Nations Broadband Commission, women are disproportionately targeted for online abuse and harassment, which can have a chilling effect on their ability to participate freely in digital spaces and advocacy efforts.

The COVID-19 pandemic has further exposed the deep-rooted inequalities that women face worldwide. From the disproportionate impact on women's livelihoods and the surge in domestic violence cases to the increased burden of unpaid care work, the pandemic has highlighted the urgent need for gender-responsive policies and robust social protection systems. Women's rights movements have had to adapt to these new challenges, finding innovative ways to organize, advocate, and provide support to those most affected, while also grappling with the digital divide and limited resources.

The COVID-19 pandemic has had a devastating impact on women's rights and gender equality, exacerbating existing inequalities and exposing the vulnerability of women in various spheres of life. According to a report by UN Women, the pandemic has led to significant setbacks in women's economic participation, with women being overrepresented in sectors most affected by job losses and economic downturns. The report also highlights the increased burden of unpaid care work shouldered by women during the pandemic, as well as a surge in cases of domestic violence and other forms of gender-based violence.

Moreover, the fight for women's rights cannot be divorced from the broader struggle for social justice and intersectional equality. Intersectional feminism recognizes that women's experiences are shaped by multiple and overlapping forms of oppression, including race, class, sexuality, disability, and indigeneity. Indigenous women, for example, face the dual burden of gender discrimination and the ongoing legacy of colonialism, displacement, and environmental injustice. LGBTQ+ women confront not only sexism but also homophobia, transphobia, and marginalization within their own communities. Addressing these intersecting inequalities requires a holistic and inclusive approach that centers the voices, experiences, and leadership of marginalized women.

The recognition of the intersectional nature of women's experiences and the need for a holistic approach to addressing intersecting forms of oppression has been a central tenet of contemporary feminist thought and activism. According to the Association for Women's Rights in Development (AWID), intersectional feminism has been instrumental in amplifying the voices and experiences of marginalized women, challenging dominant narratives, and shaping more inclusive and effective strategies for achieving gender equality and social justice.

Men and boys also have a crucial role to play as allies in the fight for gender equality. Challenging toxic masculinity, patriarchal norms, and the socialization that perpetuates violence and discrimination against women is not solely the responsibility of women. Engaging men and boys in the conversation, educating them about the benefits of gender equality, and encouraging them to be active partners in creating change is essential for sustained progress. Initiatives like the UN Women's HeForShe campaign and the White Ribbon Movement have been instrumental in mobilizing men and boys as allies and advocates for gender equality.

The importance of engaging men and boys as allies in the fight for gender equality has been recognized by various international organizations and initiatives. According to a report by the United Nations Entity for Gender Equality and the Empowerment of Women (UN Women), involving men and boys in challenging harmful gender norms and promoting positive masculinities can contribute to a more comprehensive and effective approach to achieving gender equality. By addressing the socialization processes and cultural narratives that reinforce harmful gender stereotypes and expectations, these initiatives can foster a more inclusive and supportive environment for women's empowerment.

The narrative of women's rights is still being written, its pages filled with both victories and ongoing battles. Each chapter tells a story of barriers broken and new ones erected, of laws reformed and minds that remain unchanged. It tells of a world where a woman's rights are recognized in the legislature but not always in the living room or the workplace.

The ongoing struggle for women's rights is a testament to the resilience and determination of activists and movements worldwide. Despite significant progress in legal and policy reforms, the implementation and realization of gender equality and women's rights remain a challenge in many societies. According to a report by the United Nations Development Programme (UNDP), deeply entrenched cultural norms, discriminatory practices, and a lack of political will and resources continue to hinder the full realization of women's rights, even in countries with progressive laws and policies.

As we turn the pages of this global chronicle, let us remember the faces behind the facts—the women whose lives are the essence of this narrative. They are the ones who march in the streets, who stand up in boardrooms, who run for office, who teach the next generation, and who rebuild their communities in the aftermath of conflict and crisis. They are the ones who laugh in the face of adversity and who cry when the weight of the world seems too heavy to bear. They are the ones who break barriers and forge new paths, often at great personal risk and sacrifice.

The stories of individual women activists and their struggles for equality are a powerful reminder of the human face behind the global movement for women's rights. From Malala Yousafzai, the Pakistani education activist who survived an assassination attempt by the Taliban, to Greta Thunberg, the Swedish environmental activist who has inspired a global youth movement against climate change, these women have risked their safety and well-being to champion causes that affect women and marginalized communities around the world.

In conclusion, the constellation of women's rights movements worldwide is rich, complex, and deeply interconnected. It is a mosaic of progress and setbacks, a narrative of courage in the face of adversity. Women's rights challenges are as diverse as the cultures and contexts they spring from, but the spirit that drives these movements is universal—a longing for a world where every woman is free to live her truth, to realize her full potential, and to participate equally in all spheres of life. How will this story evolve, and what role will each of us play in shaping its outcome? The answer lies not in the stars but in our collective will to act, to push forward, to keep breaking barriers until the day when gender equality is not just an aspiration but a lived reality for all women, everywhere.

The global movement for women's rights is a testament to the power of collective action, resilience, and the unwavering pursuit of justice and equality. While the challenges faced by women around the world are diverse and deeply rooted in cultural, socio-economic, and political contexts, the shared spirit of these movements is one of hope, determination, and a commitment to creating a more just and equitable world for all. As we continue to shape this narrative, it is our collective responsibility to amplify the voices of marginalized women, challenge systemic forms of oppression, and work towards a future where gender equality is not just an aspiration but a lived reality for every woman, everywhere.

Section B: Analysis of cultural and legal barriers to gender equality in different regions

In the intricate web of cultural norms and legal frameworks, gender equality often finds itself ensnared, struggling to break free and assert its rightful place in societies worldwide. The journey toward this end is fraught with obstacles that are as diverse and complex as the regions that fabricate them. What are these barriers that persistently hinder the progress of women's rights in various parts of our globe? How do they manifest, and what impact do they wield on the lives of women seeking to claim their equality?

The barriers to gender equality are deeply rooted in patriarchal systems and societal structures that have historically marginalized and oppressed women. According to a report by the United Nations Development Programme (UNDP), these barriers are multidimensional and intersectional, encompassing socio-cultural norms, legal frameworks, economic inequalities, and political marginalization. Overcoming these barriers requires a comprehensive and sustained effort to challenge and transform the underlying power structures and ideologies that perpetuate gender-based discrimination.

Consider Sub-Saharan Africa, where cultural barriers are often deeply rooted in traditional practices and belief systems. Here, the echoes of patriarchy are loud, influencing social norms and expectations that confine women to subordinate roles within the family and community. In some communities, the practice of female genital mutilation (FGM) persists, a harrowing rite of passage that serves to diminish a woman's bodily integrity and autonomy. How do we reconcile respect for cultural heritage with the imperative need to protect women's fundamental human rights?

The persistence of harmful traditional practices like female genital mutilation (FGM) in parts of Sub-Saharan Africa highlights the complex interplay between cultural norms and women's rights. According to a report by the United Nations Population Fund (UNFPA), at least 200 million women and girls alive today have undergone FGM, with the practice concentrated in 30 countries across Africa, the Middle East, and Asia. These practices, often deeply rooted in cultural traditions, pose a significant threat to women's bodily autonomy, physical and psychological well-being, and human rights.

Legal barriers can be equally challenging to dismantle. In countries where laws are ostensibly gender-neutral, the application and enforcement of such laws can be marred by bias, discrimination, and a lack of institutional capacity. For instance, property rights may exist on paper, but in reality, women may find themselves disenfranchised, their claims to land and inheritance summarily dismissed by customary laws and patriarchal systems that favor male relatives. What does it mean for a woman to navigate a legal maze that acknowledges her rights in theory but denies them in practice?

The discrepancy between legal provisions and their implementation on the ground is a significant barrier to achieving gender equality in many countries. According to a report by the World Bank, while many countries have adopted laws to promote gender equality in areas such as property rights and inheritance, discriminatory customary laws and practices often take precedence, leaving women without legal recourse or protection. This gap between de jure and de facto equality undermines women's economic empowerment, access to resources, and overall participation in society.

Travel further north, to the Middle East, where women encounter a constellation of cultural and legal constraints rooted in religious fundamentalism and conservative ideologies. In some nations, guardianship laws place women's mobility, decision-making, and access to basic rights under the purview of male relatives. The simple act of traveling, working, or accessing healthcare can become a negotiation, with autonomy hanging in the balance. When a woman's life choices are contingent on another's permission, how does she carve out a space for her own voice, her own identity, and her own empowerment?

The issue of guardianship laws in some Middle Eastern countries highlights the intersection of cultural and legal barriers that restrict women's autonomy and decision-making power. According to a report by Human Rights Watch, these laws, which require women to obtain permission from a male guardian for various aspects of their lives, effectively render women as legal minors, subject to the control and authority of their husbands, fathers, or other male relatives. This system perpetuates gender-based discrimination and reinforces patriarchal power structures, undermining women's fundamental human rights and freedoms.

Yet, amidst the thorns of these barriers, there are blossoms of resistance and reform. Saudi Arabia, for example, has recently lifted some restrictions under its guardianship system, allowing women to obtain passports and travel abroad without a male guardian's approval. These changes, though incremental, are significant. They demonstrate that the walls of cultural and legal confinement can indeed be scaled, albeit with effort, perseverance, and sustained advocacy from women's rights movements and civil society organizations.

The recent reforms to the guardianship system in Saudi Arabia are a testament to the impact of sustained advocacy and international pressure on advancing women's rights. However, experts caution that these reforms, while significant, are limited in scope and do not address the underlying structural inequalities and discrimination faced by women in the country. According to a report by the United Nations Working Group on Discrimination against Women and Girls, further reforms are needed to dismantle the male guardianship system entirely and ensure equal rights and opportunities for women in all aspects of life.

Asia presents its own myriad of challenges. In countries like Japan and South Korea, women grapple with workplaces steeped in gender bias and discrimination. Despite high levels of education and competence, women struggle to climb the corporate ladder, often hitting the 'bamboo ceiling' that seems impervious to their skills and qualifications. Maternity leave and childcare support, or the lack thereof, further complicate women's professional advancement and economic empowerment. How do we recalibrate a corporate culture that all too often forces women to choose between career and family?

The issue of the "bamboo ceiling" and the persistent gender gap in leadership positions in Asian corporations highlights the deeply entrenched cultural and institutional barriers that women face in the workplace. According to a report by the International Labour Organization (ILO), women in Asia are significantly underrepresented in managerial and executive roles, with cultural biases, lack of family-friendly policies, and limited access to mentorship and sponsorship contributing to this imbalance. Addressing this challenge requires a multifaceted approach that includes challenging gender stereotypes, promoting workplace policies that support work-life balance, and fostering a more inclusive and supportive corporate culture for women's advancement.

In many parts of Asia, societal expectations about marriage and motherhood further entrench rigid gender roles and stereotypes. The stigmatization of single women and childless couples remains a silent barrier, exerting pressure on women to conform to traditional family models. How do we shift societal attitudes to embrace a broader spectrum of womanhood, one that includes diverse lifestyles, choices, and expressions of gender identity?

The societal pressures and stigma surrounding marriage and motherhood in many Asian societies reflect deeply rooted cultural norms and expectations about gender roles and family structures. According to a report by the United Nations Population Fund (UNFPA), these societal pressures can have a significant impact on women's reproductive choices, mental health, and overall well-being. Challenging these norms requires a multi-faceted approach that includes public awareness campaigns, education initiatives, and the promotion of diverse representations of womanhood in media and popular culture.

Across the Pacific, in Latin America, the struggle for gender equality is marked by a visceral fight against gender-based violence. The scourge of femicide looms large, with the region possessing some of the highest rates of violence against women in the world. Legal systems often fail to protect women adequately, with impunity for perpetrators being a grim and persistent issue. When the very institutions meant to safeguard citizens turn a blind eye, where does a woman turn for justice and redress?

The epidemic of gender-based violence and femicide in Latin America is a severe human rights crisis that underscores the urgent need for systemic legal and institutional reforms. According to data from the United Nations Economic Commission for Latin America and the Caribbean (ECLAC), at least 4,640 women were victims of femicide in the region in 2020. Impunity for perpetrators remains a significant issue, with many cases going unreported or inadequately investigated due to institutional biases, lack of resources, and a culture of victim-blaming.

Activism in Latin America, however, is vibrant and unyielding. Campaigns like "Ni Una Menos" have galvanized society, demanding action, accountability, and a fundamental shift in the cultural narratives that normalize and perpetuate violence against women. These movements not only seek justice but also work to challenge the deeply entrenched patriarchal attitudes and machismo culture that underpin gender-based violence.

The "Ni Una Menos" (Not One Less) movement, which originated in Argentina and has spread across Latin America, has been a powerful force in raising awareness about gender-based violence and demanding government action to address this issue. According to a report by the United Nations Development Programme (UNDP), the movement has played a crucial role in advocating for legal reforms, improved data collection, and increased funding for prevention and support services for survivors of violence.

In Western societies, legal frameworks are typically more progressive regarding gender equality on paper. However, cultural barriers persist in subtle, insidious ways. Gender stereotypes continue to influence the division of labor within households, the portrayal of women in media, and the expectations placed upon them in professional settings. Women who assert themselves are often labeled as aggressive or unfeminine, while their male counterparts are praised for the same attributes. How do we dismantle these pervasive cultural norms that continue to pigeonhole women and limit their potential?

Despite the existence of legal protections and policies aimed at promoting gender equality in Western societies, deeply ingrained cultural biases and stereotypes continue to perpetuate gender-based discrimination and inequality. According to a report by the European Institute for Gender Equality, gender stereotypes and societal expectations about women's roles and capabilities are a significant barrier to their participation and advancement in various spheres of life, including the workplace, politics, and leadership positions.

The legal landscape is not without its faults, either. Legislation may address overt discrimination, but less tangible forms of inequality—such as unconscious bias in hiring and promotions, sexual harassment in the workplace, or the gender wage gap—prove more resistant to legal remedies. The challenge here is to craft laws and policies that can effectively target these elusive forms of discrimination and dismantle the systemic barriers that perpetuate gender inequality in the labor market and beyond.

The persistence of less overt forms of gender-based discrimination, such as unconscious bias and the gender wage gap, highlights the limitations of legal remedies alone in achieving substantive equality. According to a report by the International Labour Organization (ILO), despite efforts to promote gender equality in the workplace, women continue to face significant wage gaps and barriers to career advancement due to factors such as gender stereotypes, lack of family-friendly policies, and discrimination in hiring and promotion processes. Addressing these issues requires a multi-pronged approach that combines legal protections with institutional reforms, awareness-raising campaigns, and efforts to challenge deeply rooted cultural biases and stereotypes.

Religious fundamentalism and extremism pose significant threats to women's rights in various regions. The rise of religious extremist groups and the increasing influence of conservative religious ideologies in politics and society have led to the erosion of hard-won gains in gender equality. Women are often the primary targets of religious extremism, facing restrictions on their freedoms, dress codes, access to education and employment, and even physical violence and subjugation. Reconciling religious freedom with gender equality is a complex challenge that requires dialogue, education, and the promotion of moderate and progressive interpretations of religious texts and traditions.

The impact of religious fundamentalism and extremism on women's rights has been well-documented by various human rights organizations. According to a report by Amnesty International, women and girls in regions affected by the rise of extremist groups such as Boko Haram and the Islamic State have faced systematic violations of their fundamental rights, including abductions, sexual violence, and restrictions on their freedom of movement, education, and participation in public life. Addressing this issue requires a multi-faceted approach that combines security measures, legal reforms, and efforts to promote gender equality and human rights education within affected communities.

Moreover, customary and traditional legal systems often exist alongside formal legal frameworks, creating a complex web of laws that can perpetuate gender inequality. In many countries, customary laws and practices, such as male-only inheritance rights or the payment of bride prices, continue to discriminate against women and reinforce patriarchal power structures. Efforts to harmonize these parallel legal systems with international human rights standards and principles of gender equality have been met with resistance, as they are often seen as an imposition of Western values on local cultures. Navigating this delicate balance requires sensitivity, community engagement, and the empowerment of local women's rights advocates and leaders.

The persistence of discriminatory customary laws and practices highlights the complex interplay between legal frameworks, cultural norms, and traditional power structures that perpetuate gender inequality. According to a report by the United Nations Office of the High Commissioner for Human Rights (OHCHR), the harmonization of customary and formal legal systems with international human rights standards is a critical step in ensuring the full realization of women's rights and gender equality. This process requires a nuanced and context-specific approach that involves collaboration with local communities, respect for cultural diversity, and the empowerment of women as agents of change within their own communities.

Gender inequality also intersects with other forms of discrimination, such as racism, classism, ableism, and homophobia/transphobia, creating unique challenges for women who face multiple and overlapping forms of oppression. For example, women from ethnic minority communities may face discrimination based on both their gender and their race, limiting their access to education, employment, and justice. Women with disabilities encounter barriers to accessibility and are often excluded from decision-making processes that affect their lives. LGBTQ+ women face compounded marginalization and violence due to the intersections of gender-based discrimination and homophobia/transphobia. Addressing these intersecting inequalities requires an approach that recognizes the complex and multifaceted nature of oppression and seeks to dismantle all forms of discrimination simultaneously.

The intersectional nature of discrimination and oppression faced by marginalized women has been a central focus of feminist scholarship and activism in recent years. According to the Association for Women's Rights in Development (AWID), addressing these intersecting forms of oppression requires a holistic and inclusive approach that centers the voices and experiences of marginalized women, challenges dominant narratives and power structures, and builds coalitions across diverse movements and communities. By recognizing and addressing the complex intersections of gender with other identity markers and systems of oppression, the women's rights movement can develop more comprehensive and effective strategies for achieving substantive equality and justice for all women.

In summary, the constellation of cultural and legal barriers to gender equality is vast and multifaceted, spanning regions and contexts. From Africa to Asia, from the Middle East to Latin America, and within Western societies, these obstacles take different forms but ultimately serve the same function: to maintain the status quo of gender disparity and uphold patriarchal systems of power and privilege. Challenging these barriers requires a multifaceted approach that addresses both the legal frameworks and the cultural narratives that sustain inequality, while also centering the voices, experiences, and leadership of women from diverse backgrounds and marginalized communities.

Section C: Examination of international collaborations and initiatives advancing women's rights globally

In an ever-shrinking world, where the ripple of one nation's actions can create waves across oceans, international collaborations and initiatives play a pivotal role in the advancement of women's rights globally. As we cast our gaze across the varied landscape of progress and struggle, we must now turn our attention to the collective efforts that transcend borders and cultures. How are nations, international organizations, civil society, and diverse stakeholders coming together to champion the cause of gender equality, and what shape do these global endeavors take?

The United Nations has long stood as a bastion for universal human rights, and within its hallowed chambers, the plight and power of women have found a formidable ally. The Commission on the Status of Women (CSW) is a prime example, dedicated to promoting women's rights, documenting the reality of women's lives throughout the world, and shaping global policies and norms. How significant is the role of such an entity in shaping a more equitable future for women from all walks of life?

The CSW has played a crucial role in advancing women's rights globally through its annual sessions, where member states gather to review progress, identify challenges, and set global norms and standards. For instance, in 2023, the CSW's 67th session focused on the theme of "Innovation and technological change, and education in the digital age for achieving gender equality and the empowerment of all women and girls." This session highlighted the importance of bridging the digital divide and ensuring that women and girls have equal access to education and opportunities in the digital era. The CSW's agreed conclusions and recommendations from this session will guide global efforts in these areas, demonstrating its influential role in shaping policies and priorities related to women's rights.

Another luminary initiative is the Convention on the Elimination of All Forms of Discrimination Against Women (CEDAW), often described as the international bill of rights for women. With its comprehensive framework aimed at ending discrimination and affirming principles of gender equality, CEDAW has been instrumental in pushing nations to enact legal reforms, adopt gender-responsive policies, and uphold their commitments to women's rights. But beyond the ink on treaties and the grandeur of declarations, what tangible changes have stemmed from this convention, and where does the gap between promise and practice still yawn wide?

CEDAW has been ratified by 189 countries, making it one of the most widely adopted international human rights treaties. Its impact can be seen in various legal reforms undertaken by signatory countries, such as criminalizing domestic violence, improving access to education and employment for women, and granting equal rights in marriage and family life. However, challenges remain in the full implementation of CEDAW's provisions, particularly in regions where deeply entrenched patriarchal norms and practices persist. According to UN Women, as of 2020, only 10 countries had enacted legal reforms to give women and men equal rights to transfer citizenship to their children, and 39 countries maintained discriminatory laws preventing women from passing their nationality to their foreign spouses on an equal basis with men.

Let us not overlook the influence of international non-governmental organizations (NGOs) and women's rights groups that work tirelessly to bridge this gap. Organizations like Women for Women International, the Association for Women's Rights in Development (AWID), and the Global Fund for Women provide not only advocacy but also material support, education, training, and capacity-building to empower women in some of the most challenging environments. The web they weave is one of grassroots connections coupled with global solidarity. In the hands of these organizations, small victories are celebrated with the same fervor as larger legislative triumphs. But what are the stories behind these victories? Can we grasp the depth of transformation that occurs when a woman, once mired in disenfranchisement, stands up to claim her space in the community?

One powerful example of the impact of women's rights NGOs comes from the work of Madre, an international women's human rights organization. Madre has partnered with grassroots organizations in regions affected by conflict and natural disasters to provide essential support and resources to women and families. In the aftermath of the 2010 Haiti earthquake, Madre worked with local partners to establish a community center that provided vital services, including medical care, counseling, and job training, to women and their families. This center became a safe haven and a hub for empowerment, enabling women to rebuild their lives and livelihoods while also advocating for their rights and addressing issues like gender-based violence. Such initiatives demonstrate the transformative potential of NGOs in creating real, tangible change in the lives of women, even in the most challenging circumstances.

Partnerships between nations and regional bodies also play a crucial role in advancing women's rights. The African Union's Protocol on the Rights of Women in Africa, also known as the Maputo Protocol, showcases the power of regional commitment. This groundbreaking document, which covers a wide array of rights, from bodily autonomy to economic empowerment, is a testament to what can be achieved when nations unite under a common cause. What lessons can be learned from the African continent's collaborative pursuit of gender equality?

The Maputo Protocol has been hailed as a significant achievement in advancing women's rights in Africa, with provisions addressing issues such as harmful traditional practices, reproductive rights, and political participation. However, its full implementation has been uneven across the continent. As of 2022, only 42 out of 55 African Union member states had ratified the protocol, and even among those that had, several countries maintained reservations or failed to align their domestic laws with the protocol's provisions. Nevertheless, the protocol has served as a powerful advocacy tool for civil society organizations and a framework for regional collaboration on issues like ending child marriage, ensuring access to safe abortion, and promoting women's land rights. The African Union's efforts to monitor implementation and support member states in harmonizing their laws with the protocol's standards remain crucial for translating its promises into reality.

In the Americas, the Inter-American Commission of Women (CIM) works to promote women's rights and gender equity through the Organization of American States (OAS). This commission serves as a reminder that international collaboration is not solely about lofty ideals; it is about concrete actions and measurable outcomes. How has the CIM's dedication to integrating a gender perspective into all policies and programs of the OAS reshaped the landscape for women in the region?

The CIM has played a pivotal role in advancing gender mainstreaming across the OAS, ensuring that a gender perspective is incorporated into all policies, programs, and activities of the organization. One notable achievement is the adoption of the Inter-American Program on the Promotion of Women's Human Rights and Gender Equity and Equality (PIA) in 2000, which established a comprehensive framework for action on issues ranging from women's political participation to gender-based violence. Through the PIA, the CIM has supported member states in developing national action plans, implementing legislative reforms, and strengthening institutional mechanisms for gender equality. Additionally, the CIM has been instrumental in promoting the ratification and implementation of the Inter-American Convention on the Prevention, Punishment, and Eradication of Violence against Women (Belém do Pará Convention), a groundbreaking regional treaty addressing violence against women.

Europe, with its diversity of cultures and political structures, offers its own brand of collaboration through the Council of Europe's Gender Equality Strategy and the European Union's commitments to gender mainstreaming. These initiatives aim to combat gender stereotypes, ensure equal access to justice, promote women's leadership, and protect women against violence. Amid these ambitious goals, what strides have been made, and how are European nations holding one another accountable?

The European Union's efforts towards gender mainstreaming have yielded notable progress, such as the adoption of the Istanbul Convention on preventing and combating violence against women and domestic violence, which has been ratified by 21 EU member states as of 2022. Additionally, the EU's Strategic Engagement for Gender Equality 2016-2019 led to the introduction of legislative proposals to improve work-life balance for parents and carers, and the adoption of measures to address the gender pay gap. However, challenges persist, with women in the EU still facing significant disparities in employment, pay, and decision-making roles. The European Institute for Gender Equality's 2022 Gender Equality Index found that progress towards gender equality in the EU has been stagnating in recent years, highlighting the need for continued efforts and accountability mechanisms to ensure that member states uphold their commitments to gender equality.

Perhaps most importantly, we must consider the power of transnational advocacy networks that operate beyond the confines of individual nation-states. These networks, often composed of activists, academics, policy-makers, and civil society organizations, are instrumental in shaping global norms and influencing policy through their relentless advocacy. They are the unseen threads that connect local struggles to global movements. But who are the individuals behind these networks? What drives them to dedicate their lives to the cause of women's rights across the globe?

One such influential transnational advocacy network is the Association for Women's Rights in Development (AWID), which brings together over 6,000 women's rights organizations and activists from around the world. AWID has played a crucial role in amplifying the voices of grassroots movements and shaping global discourse on issues such as bodily autonomy, economic justice, and the rights of marginalized communities. Through its biennial forums, research initiatives, and advocacy campaigns, AWID has fostered cross-border solidarity and mobilized collective action toward achieving gender equality and women's empowerment. Individuals like Lydia Alpízar Durán, AWID's former Executive Director, have dedicated their careers to building this global movement, driven by a deep commitment to intersectional feminism and a belief in the transformative power of women's leadership.

The United Nations' Sustainable Development Goals (SDGs) have also become a powerful framework for global action and collaboration on women's rights. Goal 5, which specifically focuses on achieving gender equality and empowering all women and girls, has galvanized efforts across nations, sectors, and stakeholders. The SDGs recognize that gender equality is not only a fundamental human right but also a necessary foundation for a peaceful, prosperous, and sustainable world. By setting specific targets and indicators, the SDGs provide a roadmap for progress and a mechanism for holding governments and international actors accountable.

However, progress towards achieving SDG 5 has been uneven, with significant gaps remaining in areas such as women's economic empowerment, political representation, and access to sexual and reproductive health services. According to UN Women's 2022 report on the SDGs, only 28% of women aged 25-54 are employed, compared to 71% of men in the same age group. Additionally, only 21% of national parliamentarians worldwide are women, and an estimated 290,000 women died from complications related to pregnancy and childbirth in 2020. These stark realities underscore the need for increased investments, targeted policies, and concerted efforts to address the root causes of gender inequality and accelerate progress towards achieving SDG 5 and its related targets.

However, the path to achieving the SDGs is not without obstacles. Financing remains a significant challenge, as does the need for more robust data collection, monitoring systems, and accountability mechanisms. Moreover, the COVID-19 pandemic has threatened to derail progress on many of the SDGs, including those related to gender equality. The pandemic has exacerbated existing inequalities and exposed the vulnerabilities of women and girls in times of crisis. As we look to the future, it is clear that achieving the SDGs will require renewed commitment, innovation, collaboration, and a recognition of the interconnected nature of sustainable development and women's empowerment.

The COVID-19 pandemic has had a disproportionate impact on women and girls, exacerbating existing gender inequalities and threatening to undo decades of progress. According to UN Women, the pandemic has led to increased rates of gender-based violence, disruptions in access to reproductive health services, and a disproportionate burden of unpaid care work for women. Additionally, women have been disproportionately affected by job losses and economic insecurity, with the International Labour Organization estimating that 5% of women globally lost their jobs in 2020, compared to 3.9% of men. Addressing the gendered impacts of the pandemic and ensuring a gender-responsive recovery will be crucial for achieving the SDGs and advancing women's rights globally.

Another area where international collaboration is vital is in the realm of economic policy and trade agreements. Too often, these agreements have been negotiated without considering their impact on women's rights and gender equality. Trade liberalization, for example, can lead to the exploitation of women workers in global supply chains, while austerity measures can disproportionately affect women's access to healthcare, education, and social services. There is a growing recognition of the need for gender-responsive economic governance, which takes into account the different needs and experiences of women and men in the design and implementation of economic policies.

The World Trade Organization (WTO) has taken steps to address gender considerations in trade policy, establishing the Trade and Gender Working Group in 2017 to explore the links between trade and gender equality. However, progress has been slow, and critics argue that the WTO's current framework fails to adequately address the unique challenges faced by women in global trade, such as their overrepresentation in precarious and low-wage employment in export-oriented industries. Experts have called for a more comprehensive approach that integrates gender analysis into all aspects of trade policy-making, including impact assessments, capacity-building initiatives, and mechanisms for monitoring and enforcing gender-related commitments.

In this regard, the work of international financial institutions like the World Bank and the International Monetary Fund is crucial. These institutions have the power to shape the economic policies of nations around the world, and they have increasingly recognized the importance of promoting gender equality as a means of achieving sustainable development. However, critics argue that these institutions have not gone far enough in integrating gender considerations into their operations and that more needs to be done to ensure that their policies and programs benefit women and girls, particularly those from marginalized communities.

In recent years, both the World Bank and the International Monetary Fund (IMF) have taken steps to mainstream gender considerations into their operations and lending policies. The World Bank has introduced gender-responsive strategies and targets, such as the Gender Strategy 2016-2023, which aims to increase women's economic empowerment, remove barriers to women's ownership of assets, and improve women's access to social services. The IMF, meanwhile, has introduced gender-budgeting initiatives and incorporated gender analysis into its surveillance and policy advice. However, civil society organizations and gender experts have critiqued these efforts as insufficient, arguing that deeper structural changes are needed to ensure that these institutions prioritize gender equality and do not perpetuate harmful gender biases through their economic policy prescriptions.

Beyond the scope of international institutions and agreements, there is also a growing recognition of the potential of South-South cooperation and knowledge-sharing in advancing women's rights. Countries in the Global South face many similar challenges when it comes to gender equality, from high rates of maternal mortality to limited access to education and employment opportunities. By sharing experiences, best practices, and resources, these countries can learn from each other and develop innovative solutions to common problems.

One notable example of South-South cooperation in advancing women's rights is the Forum for East Asia-Latin America Cooperation (FEALAC), which brings together countries from these two regions to promote sustainable development and cultural exchange. Through its Working Group on Gender, FEALAC has facilitated the sharing of best practices and experiences related to women's political participation, economic empowerment, and access to education. This collaboration has led to initiatives such as the establishment of a virtual platform for women entrepreneurs, as well as joint research and capacity-building programs focused on addressing gender-based violence and promoting women's leadership in decision-making processes.

One example of this is the work of the African Women's Development and Communication Network (FEMNET), which brings together women's rights organizations from across the African continent to advocate for gender equality and women's empowerment. Through its various programs and initiatives, FEMNET facilitates knowledge-sharing, capacity-building, and joint advocacy efforts, amplifying the voices of African women and pushing for change at the national, regional, and international levels.

Furthermore, the rise of digital activism and online advocacy has created new opportunities for international collaboration and solidarity. Social media platforms and digital tools have enabled women's rights activists from around the world to connect, share information, and coordinate campaigns and initiatives. Movements like #NiUnaMenos in Latin America and #BringBackOurGirls in Nigeria have leveraged the power of digital media to raise awareness, mobilize support, and demand action on issues ranging from gender-based violence to the rights of girls and women in conflict zones.

The power of digital activism was evident in the global response to the Taliban's crackdown on women's rights in Afghanistan following their takeover in 2021. Campaigns like #NoGoingBack and #AfghanWomenVoices amplified the voices of Afghan women, raising awareness about the violations of their fundamental rights and mobilizing international pressure on the Taliban regime. Social media platforms served as virtual spaces for Afghan women to share their stories, connect with supporters worldwide, and coordinate advocacy efforts. This digital solidarity movement not only kept the plight of Afghan women on the global agenda but also demonstrated the potential of online activism to transcend borders and amplify marginalized voices.

Through all these endeavors, a common thread emerges: the recognition that women's rights are human rights, and their advancement is not merely a moral imperative but a prerequisite for sustainable development, peace, and prosperity. Yet, this is not merely a slogan to be chanted; it is a principle to be actualized through sustained effort, collective action, and unwavering commitment.

This recognition has been reinforced by a growing body of research and data highlighting the substantial economic and societal benefits of gender equality. According to a report by the McKinsey Global Institute, achieving gender parity could add $12 trillion to global GDP by 2025. Similarly, a study by the International Monetary Fund found that closing the gender gap in labor force participation could increase GDP by up to 35% in some countries. Beyond economic gains, research has also linked gender equality to improved health outcomes, lower rates of violent conflict, and greater environmental sustainability. These findings underscore the urgency of prioritizing women's rights and empowerment as a catalyst for sustainable and equitable development worldwide.

The path is strewn with challenges—political upheavals, cultural resistance, economic constraints, and the ever-present threat of backlash and regression. Yet, the march towards gender equality continues unabated, fueled by the resilience and determination of women's rights advocates and the growing recognition that the empowerment of women is not only a matter of justice but also a driver of positive change for societies as a whole.

Despite the challenges, the global women's rights movement has demonstrated remarkable resilience and perseverance in the face of adversity. From the suffragettes who fought for women's right to vote in the early 20th century to the activists at the forefront of the #MeToo movement, women have continuously pushed boundaries and challenged systemic oppression. This resilience is exemplified by individuals like Malala Yousafzai, the Pakistani education activist who survived an assassination attempt by the Taliban and went on to become the youngest Nobel Prize laureate, or Greta Thunberg, the Swedish environmental activist who has inspired a global youth movement for climate action while confronting misogynistic attacks and dismissals due to her age and gender.

In this constellation of international collaborations and initiatives, we have glimpsed the vast and interconnected web of efforts aimed at advancing women's rights globally. But what of the future? As we stand at the crossroads of progress and inertia, we must ask ourselves: are we ready to take the necessary steps to ensure that the advancements in women's rights are not just ephemeral victories but enduring legacies?

One critical step in ensuring the enduring legacy of women's rights is the prioritization of intergenerational leadership and knowledge transfer. By empowering and mentoring the next generation of women leaders, activists, and changemakers, we can ensure the continuity and evolution of the global women's rights movement. This involves not only providing education and capacity-building opportunities but also creating inclusive spaces where young women's voices are amplified and their perspectives are valued. Organizations like the Global Fund for Women and the Association for Women's Rights in Development (AWID) have recognized the importance of this intergenerational approach, investing in programs that foster mentorship, leadership development, and the exchange of knowledge between experienced advocates and emerging leaders.

The answer lies not just in the hands of those in power, not only within the pages of international treaties, but also in the voices of women and men, activists and allies, who dare to imagine a world where equality is not an exception but the rule. This is the challenge we must accept, the mantle we must bear, and the journey we must continue with unwavering resolve. For in breaking barriers and building bridges, we do more than change laws and policies—we change lives, empower communities, and ultimately, we change the course of history.

Achieving lasting gender equality will also require a concerted effort to address the intersecting forms of oppression and marginalization that many women face. Women from diverse backgrounds, including those with disabilities, indigenous women, LGBTQI+ women, and women from racial and ethnic minorities, often confront multiple layers of discrimination and barriers to their rights and empowerment. Intersectional feminism, which recognizes and addresses these overlapping systems of oppression, must be at the core of the global women's rights movement. By centering the voices and experiences of those at the margins, we can ensure that no woman is left behind and that the fight for gender equality is truly inclusive and transformative.

The global struggle for women's rights is a testament to the resilience, courage, and determination of countless individuals, organizations, and movements around the world. It is a struggle that has been fought on many fronts, from the halls of power to the grassroots of local communities. And while much has been achieved, much more remains to be done.

One of the enduring challenges in the global struggle for women's rights is the persistence of harmful gender norms and patriarchal attitudes that perpetuate discrimination and violence against women. Despite legal and policy reforms, deeply entrenched social and cultural beliefs about gender roles and hierarchies continue to undermine women's rights and agency in many societies. Addressing these root causes of gender inequality will require sustained efforts in education, media, and public awareness campaigns to challenge and transform these harmful norms. This work must engage men and boys as allies and partners, recognizing that gender equality benefits everyone and that dismantling patriarchy is a collective responsibility.

Engaging men and boys as allies in the fight for gender equality is a critical strategy that has gained increasing attention in recent years. Organizations like Promundo, a global leader in promoting gender justice, have developed innovative programs that work with men and boys to challenge harmful gender norms and promote positive masculinities. These programs have shown promising results in shifting attitudes and behaviors, particularly among younger generations. For instance, Promundo's Program H initiative, implemented in over 35 countries, has been found to reduce men's use of violence against women and increase their involvement in household tasks and childcare. Such initiatives demonstrate the potential for transformative change when men and boys are actively engaged as partners in dismantling patriarchal systems.

As we look to the future, we must reaffirm our commitment to the principles of equality, justice, and human rights that underpin the fight for women's rights. We must continue to build on the progress that has been made, while also acknowledging and addressing the persistent barriers and challenges that remain, including the intersecting forms of oppression and marginalization faced by women from diverse backgrounds and identities.

One of the key barriers to achieving substantive gender equality is the persistent wage gap and economic disparities faced by women globally. According to a report by the International Labour Organization, the global gender wage gap stands at 20%, with women earning on average 80% of what men earn for doing work of equal value. This gap is even wider for women from marginalized groups, such as women of color, indigenous women, and women with disabilities. Closing this gap will require comprehensive measures, including pay transparency legislation, policies to address occupational segregation, and support for women's entrepreneurship and access to productive resources.

This will require a multifaceted approach that encompasses legal and policy reforms, cultural and attitudinal shifts, economic empowerment, and the meaningful participation and leadership of women in all spheres of decision-making. It will require the engagement and support of men and boys, who have a crucial role to play as allies and partners in dismantling patriarchal systems and creating an enabling environment for gender equality.

The meaningful participation and leadership of women in decision-making processes is a critical component of achieving gender equality. According to UN Women, as of January 2023, women hold only 26.1% of parliamentary seats globally, and only 22 countries have a woman as Head of State or Head of Government. Increasing women's political representation and leadership in all spheres, from government to corporate boardrooms to civil society organizations, is essential for ensuring that policies and decisions reflect the diverse perspectives and priorities of women. Initiatives such as gender quotas, leadership training programs, and efforts to address barriers to women's political participation, including violence and harassment, can help accelerate progress in this area.

Moreover, it will require sustained international collaboration, solidarity, and collective action, recognizing that the advancement of women's rights is a shared global imperative that transcends borders and cultures. By strengthening partnerships, sharing knowledge and resources, and amplifying the voices of women's rights advocates and grassroots movements, we can build a more powerful and inclusive global movement for change.

One example of sustained international collaboration and collective action is the Generation Equality Forum, convened by UN Women and co-hosted by Mexico and France in 2021. This global gathering brought together governments, civil society, the private sector, and international organizations to make concrete commitments and launch a five-year action plan to accelerate progress on gender equality. The forum's Action Coalitions focused on critical issues such as gender-based violence, economic justice and rights, feminist movements and leadership, and technology and innovation for gender equality. This coordinated, multi-stakeholder approach demonstrates the potential for collective action to drive transformative change at a global scale.

Ultimately, the advancement of women's rights is not just a matter of justice and fairness, but also a prerequisite for the achievement of sustainable development, peace, and prosperity for all. When women are empowered to fully participate in all aspects of society, from the political to the economic to the social, everyone benefits. This is the vision that drives the global movement for women's rights, and it is a vision that we must continue to strive towards with unwavering commitment and resolve.

The COVID-19 pandemic has further underscored the inextricable link between gender equality and sustainable development, as well as the disproportionate impact of crises on women and girls. According to the United Nations Development Programme (UNDP), the pandemic has reversed decades of progress on gender equality, with women facing increased economic insecurity, higher rates of gender-based violence, and greater burdens of unpaid care work. Addressing these setbacks and building back better will require a gender-responsive approach to recovery efforts, including targeted investments in women's economic empowerment, access to essential services, and leadership in decision-making processes related to pandemic response and recovery.

The pandemic has also highlighted the essential role of women in various sectors, particularly in healthcare and frontline services. Women make up 70% of the global healthcare workforce, and their contributions have been crucial in responding to the COVID-19 crisis. However, this has also exposed the gender inequalities within the healthcare sector, with women often occupying lower-paid roles and facing greater risks of infection and burnout. Addressing these disparities and ensuring decent working conditions, fair remuneration, and leadership opportunities for women in healthcare and other essential services must be a priority in the post-pandemic recovery efforts.

As we conclude this examination of global perspectives on women's rights, let us draw inspiration from the countless women and men who have fought tirelessly for gender equality throughout history and around the world. Let us honor their legacy by continuing to push forward, breaking down barriers and building bridges, until the day when every woman and girl can live freely, safely, and with dignity. This is the promise of the global women's rights movement, and it is a promise that we must all work to fulfill.

One source of inspiration can be found in the life and work of Wangari Maathai, the Kenyan environmental and political activist who founded the Green Belt Movement and became the first African woman to receive the Nobel Peace Prize in 2004. Maathai's work empowered rural women to plant and nurture millions of trees, not only combating deforestation and environmental degradation but also creating economic opportunities and fostering women's leadership in their communities. Her legacy serves as a powerful reminder that the struggles for gender equality, environmental sustainability, and human rights are deeply interconnected, and that grassroots movements led by women can drive transformative change.

The fight for women's rights is not an easy one, nor is it one that will be won overnight. But it is a fight that we cannot afford to lose. The stakes are too high, the consequences too grave. We owe it to ourselves, to each other, and to future generations to create a world in which gender equality is not just an aspiration, but a reality.

The consequences of failing to achieve gender equality are indeed grave, impacting not only the lives and well-being of women and girls but also the overall progress and prosperity of societies. According to the World Bank, gender inequality costs the global economy an estimated $160 trillion in lost human capital wealth. Moreover, countries with higher levels of gender inequality tend to experience higher rates of poverty, malnutrition, and poor health outcomes, as well as increased vulnerability to conflicts and environmental degradation. These staggering costs underscore the urgency of prioritizing gender equality as a fundamental human right and a critical driver of sustainable development.

So let us go forth with courage, with determination, and with hope. Let us continue to raise our voices, to stand up for what is right, and to work tirelessly for a world in which every woman and girl can thrive. Together, we can forge a path towards a more just, equitable, and inclusive future for all, where the rights and dignity of women are upheld and celebrated, and where our shared dreams of equality and empowerment become a lived reality.

In this journey towards gender equality, we must also recognize the power of art, culture, and storytelling as catalysts for change. Throughout history, women artists, writers, musicians, and filmmakers have used their creative voices to challenge gender norms, raise awareness about women's struggles, and inspire social transformation. From the groundbreaking works of authors like Toni Morrison and Chimamanda Ngozi Adichie to the powerful performances of artists like Beyoncé and Malala Yousafzai, the arts have served as a potent medium for amplifying women's voices, celebrating their resilience, and envisioning a more just and equitable world.

Ultimately, the fight for gender equality is not just a struggle for women's rights; it is a struggle for the realization of fundamental human rights and the creation of a more just, inclusive, and sustainable world for all. As we forge ahead, we must remain steadfast in our commitment, drawing strength from the countless individuals and movements that have paved the way, and embracing the transformative power of collective action, intersectional solidarity, and unwavering hope. For in this shared struggle, we are not merely fighting for ourselves, but for the generations to come – a legacy of equality, empowerment, and the fulfillment of our shared dreams of a better world.

Chapter 9
Remaining Challenges and Future Directions

Section A: Identification of Persistent Barriers to Gender Equality and Women's Rights

In the fervent quest for gender equality, it is imperative that we pause and take stock of the barriers that persistently hinder the realization of women's rights. Despite significant strides made over the past few decades, a constellation of obstacles continues to cast long shadows over the landscape of progress. What are these barriers, and why do they stubbornly refuse to crumble under the weight of advocacy and policy reform?

One such barrier is the enduring grip of gender stereotypes. These are the insidious beliefs that dictate 'appropriate' behavior and roles for women and men, often relegating women to a secondary status in society. Gender stereotypes are deeply entrenched, seeping into the fabric of our daily lives through social norms, media representations, and popular culture—so much so that they often go unnoticed, like the air we breathe. How frequently do we encounter the assumption that women are better suited for caregiving roles, or that leadership and assertiveness are inherently masculine traits? These stereotypes shape the opportunities available to women and, more importantly, how women perceive their own potential and worth.

According to the United Nations Educational, Scientific and Cultural Organization (UNESCO), gender stereotypes are reinforced from an early age, with children as young as six years old exhibiting gender-biased attitudes and behaviors. These learned biases have profound implications, influencing everything from self-perception and career aspirations to interpersonal relationships and decision-making.

Dr. Shelly Grabe, a professor of psychology and expert on the impact of media on gender stereotypes, explains: "Children are exposed to a barrage of gender-stereotypical messages through television, books, toys, and even the language used by adults around them. These messages shape their understanding of gender roles and expectations from a very young age, often leading them to internalize limitations on their potential and aspirations." For instance, a study by the Geena Davis Institute on Gender in Media found that in family films, male characters outnumbered female characters three to one, perpetuating the notion that men are more important and capable.

Dr. Ximena Regueiro, a renowned gender studies scholar, notes that "Gender stereotypes are often unconsciously internalized, shaping our beliefs about what is 'normal' or 'acceptable' for men and women. They become self-perpetuating cycles that limit individual potential and perpetuate systemic inequalities."

One striking example of the impact of gender stereotypes can be found in the field of science, technology, engineering, and mathematics (STEM). Despite decades of efforts to promote gender equality in these areas, women remain underrepresented, accounting for only 35% of STEM students in higher education globally, according to UNESCO data. This disparity is often attributed to the persistent stereotype that portrays STEM fields as inherently masculine and incompatible with traditional gender roles for women. As a result, many young girls may unconsciously steer away from pursuing interests and careers in these fields, self-limiting their potential due to internalized biases.

The prevalence and impact of gender stereotypes are staggering. According to a study by the United Nations, over 90% of people hold at least one bias against women, reflecting the pervasiveness of these harmful beliefs across cultures and societies. These stereotypes not only limit women's educational and career prospects but also contribute to the normalization of gender-based violence, as women who defy traditional gender norms are often viewed as transgressive and deserving of punishment.

Mónica Ramírez, a prominent civil rights attorney and advocate for gender justice, explains: "Gender stereotypes create a climate of permissibility for violence against women. When women are perceived as inferior or as violating prescribed gender roles, it becomes easier to justify and perpetrate acts of violence against them." This normalization of violence can manifest in various forms, from domestic abuse and intimate partner violence to sexual harassment and assault in the workplace, on college campuses, or in public spaces.

Dr. Lilia Cortina, a leading expert on workplace harassment, explains, "Stereotypes that portray women as weak, emotional, or inferior to men can create hostile environments where harassment and discrimination are more likely to occur. When women challenge these stereotypes by exhibiting strength, assertiveness, or leadership, they may face backlash and be perceived as violating societal expectations." This backlash can manifest in various forms, from subtle microaggressions to overt acts of violence, further perpetuating the cycle of oppression.

A study by the Equal Employment Opportunity Commission (EEOC) found that approximately 25% of women in the United States have experienced workplace harassment, including unwanted sexual attention, verbal or physical harassment, and even sexual assault. The impact of such harassment can be devastating, leading to decreased job satisfaction, higher rates of absenteeism and turnover, and long-lasting psychological and emotional trauma for the victims.

Economic inequality is another formidable barrier that hinders women's empowerment and autonomy. The gender pay gap persists as a stark reality, with women globally earning only 77 cents for every dollar earned by men, according to the World Economic Forum's Global Gender Gap Report 2022. This economic disparity extends beyond wages into the realms of property ownership, inheritance rights, and access to credit. Imagine a world where a woman's work is undervalued, her financial independence stifled; it is a reality for many women, particularly those from marginalized communities.

According to the International Labour Organization (ILO), women's labor force participation rate stands at just over 47%, compared to 72% for men. Furthermore, women are overrepresented in informal and precarious employment, often lacking access to social protection and basic labor rights.

In many developing countries, the gender pay gap is even more pronounced, with women earning as little as 60% of what their male counterparts earn for similar work, according to the United Nations Development Programme (UNDP). This economic disparity is further exacerbated by the disproportionate burden of unpaid care work that falls on women, limiting their ability to participate in the formal labor market and advance their careers.

Esther Duflo, a Nobel Laureate in Economics, emphasizes the significance of economic empowerment for women: "When women have control over their own income and assets, they invest more in the well-being of their families and communities, creating a virtuous cycle of development and gender equality."

A study by the World Bank found that increasing women's labor force participation and closing the gender gap in employment could boost global GDP by up to $28 trillion by 2025. Furthermore, research by the International Monetary Fund (IMF) suggests that countries with greater gender equality tend to have higher levels of economic growth and development, underscoring the far-reaching benefits of addressing this barrier.

Economic dependence on male counterparts can leave women vulnerable and hinder their ability to make autonomous decisions about their lives, perpetuating cycles of poverty and disempowerment. The impact of this barrier is profound, as economic empowerment is a crucial pathway to achieving gender equality and realizing other fundamental rights.

Violence against women is another pervasive barrier, casting a long and ominous shadow across all cultures and societies. From domestic abuse and intimate partner violence to sexual harassment, assault, and femicide, the threat of violence looms large in the lives of countless women. It acts as a powerful tool of control, instilling fear and limiting freedom. Can we fathom the toll this takes on the physical, emotional, and psychological well-being of victims? Such violence not only scars individuals but also reinforces societal norms that devalue and subjugate women.

The World Health Organization estimates that globally, one in three women has experienced physical or sexual violence by an intimate partner, or sexual violence from a non-partner. In conflict zones and humanitarian crises, the risk of gender-based violence escalates, with women and girls facing heightened vulnerability to sexual exploitation, trafficking, and abuse.

Zainab Bangura, former Special Representative of the UN Secretary-General on Sexual Violence in Conflict, notes: "Sexual violence in conflict is not merely a consequence of war; it is used as a tactic of war, a means of achieving military and political objectives." In regions like the Democratic Republic of Congo, Syria, and Myanmar, reports of systematic sexual violence against women and girls have been widespread, with perpetrators often acting with impunity and survivors facing stigma and lack of access to support services.

Dr. Rashida Manjoo, a former UN Special Rapporteur on Violence against Women, notes, "Violence against women is not only a violation of human rights but also a barrier to the achievement of gender equality, development, and peace. It reinforces gender stereotypes, perpetuates cycles of poverty, and undermines the potential of women and girls to contribute fully to their communities and societies."

The economic costs of violence against women are staggering, with estimates suggesting that the global cost of intimate partner violence alone amounts to approximately $1.5 trillion per year, according to a report by the Copenhagen Consensus Center. This figure includes direct costs related to healthcare, legal services, and social services, as well as indirect costs associated with lost productivity, decreased economic output, and the intergenerational impact on children exposed to violence.

Globally, an estimated one in three women has experienced physical or sexual violence in their lifetime, according to the World Health Organization. This staggering statistic underscores the pervasiveness of this barrier and its impact on women's ability to fully participate in all aspects of life.

Phumzile Mlambo-Ngcuka, former Executive Director of UN Women, emphasizes the urgency of addressing violence against women: "Violence against women and girls is a human rights violation, a public health pandemic, and a moral indictment on our societies. It robs women and girls of their fundamental rights and freedoms, undermines their dignity, and prevents them from contributing fully to the development of their communities and societies."

The political sphere presents another labyrinth of obstacles for women's rights and gender equality. Women's representation in political leadership and decision-making roles remains woefully inadequate, with only 25.9% of national parliamentary seats held by women as of 2022, according to the Inter-Parliamentary Union. When the halls of power echo with a predominantly male voice, policies and legislation often fail to prioritize or adequately address women's issues and concerns.

This underrepresentation has far-reaching consequences, as policies and legislation often fail to adequately address the unique needs and perspectives of women. Madeleine Albright, the first woman to become the U.S. Secretary of State, famously stated, "There is a special place in hell for women who do not help other women." Her words underscore the importance of women's political participation in shaping a more equitable and inclusive society. When women are excluded from decision-making processes, their voices and experiences are marginalized, perpetuating systemic inequalities.

Why is the political arena so resistant to gender parity, and what can be done to ensure women's perspectives are not merely included but are influential in shaping the governance of societies? The barriers to women's political participation are multifaceted, ranging from structural and institutional biases to cultural norms that discourage women's leadership, as well as the persistent threat of violence and harassment against women in politics.

According to the Inter-Parliamentary Union, women in politics face numerous challenges, including gender-based violence, online harassment, and lack of access to financial resources and support networks. Additionally, cultural and social norms that portray leadership as a masculine trait can create an inhospitable environment for women seeking political office.

A study by the National Democratic Institute (NDI) found that 82% of women parliamentarians across 39 countries had experienced psychological violence, such as intimidation, threats, and online harassment, while in office. This hostile environment can deter women from entering or remaining in politics, further exacerbating the issue of underrepresentation and hindering efforts to promote gender-responsive policies and legislation.

Dr. Amanda Gouws, a political scientist, notes, "Breaking down these barriers requires a multifaceted approach that addresses the systemic and structural impediments, while also challenging the deeply rooted cultural and societal biases that perpetuate gender inequalities in political representation."

One promising approach to increasing women's political representation is the implementation of gender quotas, which have been adopted by several countries around the world. According to the Inter-Parliamentary Union, countries with legislated gender quotas for parliamentary seats have an average of 27.5% women in parliament, compared to 19.8% in countries without such quotas. While quotas alone are not a panacea, they can serve as a powerful tool to accelerate progress and challenge deeply entrenched biases.

Soraya Chemaly, a renowned feminist writer and activist, emphasizes the importance of quotas: "Gender quotas are not a favor to women; they are a necessary corrective to centuries of systemic exclusion and discrimination. By ensuring a critical mass of women in decision-making roles, we challenge the notion that leadership is inherently masculine and create more inclusive and representative governance."

Education inequality must also be addressed as a critical barrier to gender equality. Although more girls are attending school than ever before, disparities in access to quality education persist, particularly in developing countries and marginalized communities. Moreover, the hidden curriculum—what is taught implicitly through cultural norms and institutional practices—can reinforce gender disparities and limit girls' aspirations.

A study by the World Bank found that in low-income countries, only 49% of girls complete upper secondary education, compared to 59% of boys. This educational gap not only limits girls' future economic opportunities but also perpetuates intergenerational cycles of poverty and disempowerment. Furthermore, according to UNESCO, textbooks and curricula in many countries continue to promote gender stereotypes, with women and girls often depicted in subservient roles or underrepresented in fields like science and technology.

According to UNESCO estimates, around 130 million girls worldwide are still out of school, with poverty, child marriage, and gender-based violence being major contributors to this educational exclusion. Even when girls do access education, they often face biased curricula, lack of female role models in STEM fields, and societal pressures to prioritize domestic responsibilities over academic pursuits.

Malala Yousafzai, the renowned Pakistani activist for female education and the youngest Nobel Prize laureate, has consistently advocated for girls' right to education. In her book "I Am Malala," she writes: "One child, one teacher, one book, and one pen can change the world. Education is the only solution. Education first." Her personal story of resilience and advocacy serves as a powerful reminder of the transformative impact of education on breaking down barriers and empowering girls and women.

Cultural and religious practices can also pose significant barriers to gender equality, particularly when they are used to justify the subjugation of women and the violation of their fundamental rights. The practice of female genital mutilation (FGM), for instance, persists in some communities despite its recognition as a form of violence against women and a violation of human rights.

According to the United Nations Population Fund (UNFPA), at least 200 million girls and women alive today have undergone FGM, with the practice most prevalent in parts of Africa, the Middle East, and Asia. FGM is not only a violation of women's bodily autonomy and a form of gender-based violence but also carries severe health risks, including complications during childbirth, psychological trauma, and even death.

Similarly, certain interpretations of religious doctrines are wielded to deny women's autonomy over their bodies, restrict their freedom of movement, and exclude them from positions of leadership and decision-making. How do we navigate the delicate balance between respecting cultural diversity and challenging practices that infringe upon women's rights and human dignity?

Karima Bennoune, a professor of international law and author of "Your Fatwa Docs Not Apply Here," argues that cultural relativism should not be used as an excuse to justify human rights violations against women. She notes, "We must engage with the diversity of views within cultures and religions, and support those voices that are promoting equality, dignity, and human rights for all." By amplifying the voices of progressive religious and cultural leaders who advocate for women's rights, we can challenge harmful practices from within while respecting the diversity of beliefs and traditions.

The lack of comprehensive legal frameworks and the ineffective enforcement of existing laws remain major hurdles in the quest for gender equality. While many countries have laws on the books aimed at promoting women's rights, the gap between legislation and implementation is vast. What use are laws that are not upheld by the judicial system, or when those tasked with enforcement turn a blind eye to violations?

A report by the World Bank and the International Development Law Organization (IDLO) found that in many countries, discriminatory laws and inadequate legal protections continue to hinder women's economic empowerment, access to property rights, and participation in the workforce. Furthermore, even when progressive laws are in place, weak rule of law, corruption, and lack of accountability can undermine their effectiveness, leaving women vulnerable to exploitation and abuse.

Moreover, the intersection of gender with other forms of discrimination, such as racism, ableism, and homophobia/transphobia, further compounds the barriers faced by marginalized women. For example, a woman of color may face the double burden of gender and racial discrimination, limiting her access to education, employment, and healthcare. A transgender woman may confront both sexism and transphobia, facing unique challenges in asserting her rights and living authentically.

Kimberlé Crenshaw, a pioneering scholar on intersectionality, explains: "The intersectional experience is greater than the sum of racism and sexism. There is a complex interplay that creates a distinct form of discrimination and oppression." This intersection of multiple marginalized identities often results in compounded barriers, increased vulnerability to violence, and the lack of access to support systems tailored to their unique experiences and needs.

Recognizing and addressing these intersecting identities and forms of oppression is crucial in the fight for gender equality, as marginalized women often face heightened barriers and increased vulnerability to violence, exploitation, and discrimination.

Tarana Burke, the founder of the 'Me Too' movement, emphasizes the importance of centering the voices and experiences of marginalized women: "The work to dismantle the systems that allow sexual violence to persist must include a commitment to addressing the intersections of race, class, and gender identity. We cannot achieve lasting change if we leave anyone behind."

The impact of globalization, economic policies, and armed conflicts on women's rights cannot be overlooked, particularly in developing countries and marginalized communities. The pursuit of economic growth and development has often come at the cost of women's well-being, with the feminization of poverty, the exploitation of women in low-wage jobs, and the displacement of indigenous women from their lands.

Naomi Klein, author of "The Shock Doctrine," argues that neoliberal economic policies have disproportionately impacted women, particularly in the Global South. She writes, "In country after country, women have been the shock troops of the shock doctrine, overrepresented among the workers displaced by privatization, the households torn apart by utility privatization, and the students turned away from public schools by user fees." This exploitation of women's labor and resources has perpetuated cycles of poverty and disempowerment.

Armed conflicts and humanitarian crises also exacerbate existing gender inequalities and expose women and girls to heightened risks of gender-based violence, human trafficking, and limited access to essential services and resources. Ensuring that economic policies, conflict resolution efforts, and humanitarian interventions are gender-responsive and prioritize the needs and rights of women and girls is a critical step towards breaking down these persistent barriers.

During the Syrian refugee crisis, reports emerged of widespread sexual exploitation and abuse of women and girls in refugee camps, as well as the prevalence of child marriages and human trafficking. Angelina Jolie, in her role as Special Envoy for the United Nations High Commissioner for Refugees (UNHCR), highlighted the need for greater protection and assistance for displaced women and girls, stating: "We have to meet this crisis with support for the millions of displaced people, and with a firm commitment to address the root causes of this war and violence against women and girls."

In confronting these barriers, it is not enough to simply acknowledge their existence. We must delve into the root causes and understand the complex interplay of social, economic, political, and cultural factors that give them life. By doing so, we can begin to dismantle them piece by piece, not with blunt force but with the precision of those who know the labyrinth from within.

Dr. Raewyn Connell, a renowned sociologist and gender studies scholar, emphasizes the need for a holistic approach: "Gender inequality is deeply embedded in our social structures, institutions, and cultural norms. To dismantle these barriers, we must adopt an intersectional lens and address the root causes – the patriarchal power structures, the economic systems that exploit and marginalize women, and the cultural narratives that perpetuate harmful stereotypes and practices."

Grassroots movements, community-led initiatives, and local activism play a vital role in challenging persistent barriers and advocating for change at the grassroots level. These movements, often led by women who have experienced discrimination and marginalization firsthand, bring a unique perspective and a deep understanding of the specific challenges faced by their communities. By amplifying their voices and supporting their efforts, we can create more targeted and effective strategies for breaking down barriers and driving sustainable change.

One such grassroots movement is the Self-Employed Women's Association (SEWA) in India, which has been empowering and advocating for the rights of poor, self-employed women workers since 1972. SEWA's founder, Ela Bhatt, recognized that these women faced multiple barriers, including lack of access to credit, markets, and social security. Through collective action and community-based initiatives, SEWA has helped millions of women gain economic independence, access to healthcare, and a voice in shaping policies that affect their lives.

The path forward demands resilience, creativity, and an unwavering belief in the possibility of change. It is a challenge that calls for the collective efforts of all sectors of society—governments, businesses, civil society organizations, and individuals. How do we foster a culture that values and promotes the rights of women? How do we empower women to become agents of change in their own lives and in the broader society?

Michelle Bachelet, the former Executive Director of UN Women and the first female President of Chile, emphasizes the importance of transformative leadership: "We need leaders who are willing to challenge the status quo, to question deeply entrenched norms and biases, and to create an enabling environment for women's empowerment. This requires not only political will but also the commitment of resources and the involvement of all stakeholders, including men and boys, in dismantling the structures that perpetuate gender inequality."

As we continue to chronicle the journey toward gender equality, let us not forget the barriers that women face every day. In recognizing and addressing these persistent obstacles, we forge a path to a future where women's rights are not an aspirational goal but a lived reality. It is through the relentless pursuit of this vision that we can hope to break the barriers once and for all, ensuring that the advancements in women's rights are not transient but enduring achievements that reshape the world for generations to come.

Chimamanda Ngozi Adichie, the renowned Nigerian author and feminist, reminds us: "The problem with gender is that it prescribes how we should be rather than recognizing how we are. Imagine how much happier we would be, how much freer to be our true individual selves, if we didn't have the weight of gender expectations." By dismantling the barriers that perpetuate gender inequality, we not only liberate women but also create a more just and equitable society for all.

The role of men and boys in breaking down barriers to gender equality is crucial. While women have been at the forefront of advocating for their rights, true progress requires the active engagement and allyship of men and boys in challenging patriarchal norms and structures. Michael Kaufman, co-founder of the White Ribbon Campaign, emphasizes the need for men to take responsibility: "We must challenge the notion that gender inequality is solely a women's issue. Men must be willing to reflect on their privilege, confront toxic masculinity, and actively work towards creating a more equitable society."

Education is not only a barrier in itself but also a powerful tool for breaking down other barriers. By providing girls and women with access to quality education, we equip them with the knowledge and skills to navigate and challenge systemic inequalities. According to a report by the United Nations Children's Fund (UNICEF), each additional year of education for girls can increase their future earnings by 20%, while also delaying early marriage and reducing maternal mortality rates. Investing in girls' education is an investment in their empowerment and the overall development of communities and nations.

The COVID-19 pandemic has exacerbated existing gender inequalities and exposed the fragility of progress made in women's rights. According to UN Women, the pandemic has increased the risk of gender-based violence, disrupted access to essential health services for women, and disproportionately impacted women's economic security and participation in the workforce. As we navigate the aftermath of this global crisis, it is crucial to adopt a gender-responsive approach to recovery efforts and prioritize the needs and rights of women and girls.

In the age of digital technology and social media, online harassment and cyber violence have emerged as new barriers to women's rights and participation in public spaces. According to a report by Amnesty International, women are disproportionately targeted with online abuse, including threats of sexual violence, misogynistic language, and the non-consensual sharing of intimate images. This form of harassment not only infringes on women's freedom of expression but also perpetuates a culture of fear and exclusion, deterring them from fully engaging in the digital sphere.

The representation of women in science, technology, engineering, and mathematics (STEM) fields remains a persistent challenge, with deeply entrenched gender stereotypes and biases contributing to the underrepresentation of women in these disciplines. According to the United Nations Educational, Scientific and Cultural Organization (UNESCO), only 35% of students pursuing STEM-related fields in higher education globally are women. Breaking down these barriers requires a multifaceted approach, including challenging gender stereotypes from an early age, providing mentorship and role models, and creating inclusive and supportive environments for women in STEM.

Climate change and environmental degradation disproportionately impact women, particularly in developing countries and marginalized communities. Women often bear the brunt of resource scarcity, natural disasters, and the displacement caused by climate-related events, exacerbating existing gender inequalities. Addressing this barrier requires a comprehensive approach that integrates gender perspectives into climate change mitigation and adaptation strategies, while also empowering women as agents of change in environmental conservation and sustainable development.

The COVID-19 pandemic has highlighted the critical role of care work, traditionally performed by women, in sustaining societies and economies. However, this essential labor remains undervalued, underpaid, and often invisible in economic policies and decision-making processes. Recognizing and valuing care work as a vital contribution to societal well-being is crucial for addressing the persistent barriers faced by women in the workforce and achieving true gender equality.

The media plays a significant role in shaping societal attitudes and perceptions about gender roles and women's rights. Stereotypical portrayals of women in media and advertising perpetuate harmful gender norms and can contribute to the normalization of gender-based violence and discrimination. Challenging these narratives and promoting diverse, empowering representations of women is essential in breaking down the barriers that stem from ingrained cultural biases and stereotypes.

Access to comprehensive and inclusive healthcare services remains a significant barrier for many women, particularly those from marginalized communities. Reproductive rights, mental health support, and specialized care for gender-specific health issues are often neglected or stigmatized, hindering women's overall well-being and autonomy. Addressing this barrier requires a human rights-based approach to healthcare that prioritizes women's needs and empowers them to make informed decisions about their bodies and health.

The persistent gender data gap, where data on women's experiences, needs, and contributions are often incomplete or lacking, poses a significant challenge in identifying and addressing barriers to gender equality. Investing in gender-responsive data collection and analysis is crucial for informing evidence-based policymaking, targeted interventions, and the effective allocation of resources to address the specific challenges faced by women and girls in various contexts.

Section B: Analysis of Emerging Issues and Challenges Facing Women in the Modern Era

In the ever-shifting landscape of modern society, the challenges and issues facing women continue to evolve. Women today are navigating a complex web of new societal norms, technological advancements, and global phenomena that shape their experiences and rights in unprecedented ways. It is within this context that we must delve into the emerging issues that underscore the struggle for gender equality and the empowerment of women.

Digital Divide and Cyber Violence: In the digital age, the internet has become a double-edged sword for women. On one hand, it offers opportunities for learning, entrepreneurship, and global connections. On the other, a persistent digital divide persists, with women less likely to have access to technology and the internet, especially in developing nations and marginalized communities.

Anita Gurumurthy, executive director of IT for Change, a non-profit organization working on gender and digital justice, highlights the intersectional nature of the digital divide: "The digital divide is not just about access to technology, but it's also about the ability to effectively use and shape these technologies. Women from marginalized communities face multiple barriers, including lack of digital skills, language barriers, and limited access to resources, which compound the challenges they face in engaging with digital platforms and spaces."

According to the International Telecommunication Union, the global internet user gender gap stands at 62.9% for men and 57.1% for women, with the gap being more pronounced in least developed countries. Can we truly harness the benefits of technology for women's advancement if a significant portion of the world's women remains offline and excluded from the digital revolution?

The consequences of the digital divide are far-reaching, extending beyond access to information and knowledge. According to the World Bank, increasing women's digital inclusion could unlock significant economic opportunities, with estimates suggesting that bringing an additional 600 million women and girls online could boost global GDP by up to $18 billion. Furthermore, digital technologies have the potential to empower women by providing access to online education, financial services, and remote work opportunities, enabling greater economic independence and autonomy.

Moreover, the online world has opened up new avenues for harassment, exploitation, and violence against women. Cyberbullying, revenge porn, online stalking, and doxxing (the malicious publication of private information) have emerged as serious threats, often leaving deep psychological scars and limiting women's freedom of expression and online participation.

The impacts of cyber violence on women are far-reaching and can have severe consequences for their mental health, career prospects, and overall well-being. According to a study by the European Institute for Gender Equality, women who experience cyber violence are more likely to self-censor, withdraw from online spaces, and even change their career paths or educational goals to avoid further harassment. This not only infringes on their fundamental rights but also perpetuates the exclusion of women from digital spaces and opportunities.

A study by the Economist Intelligence Unit found that 85% of women worldwide have experienced online violence, with severe consequences for their mental health, professional lives, and overall well-being. How do we enforce boundaries in a cyberspace that is inherently boundless? When a woman's safety can be compromised with a few keystrokes, society must grapple with the challenge of protecting her in virtual environments just as we do in physical ones.

Addressing cyber violence against women requires a multi-pronged approach that involves legal and policy reforms, improved reporting and support mechanisms, and efforts to challenge the underlying cultural attitudes and norms that enable and perpetuate such behaviors. According to the United Nations Special Rapporteur on Violence Against Women, Reem Alsalem, "Cyber violence is a form of gender-based violence that must be addressed through a comprehensive and coordinated approach, involving all stakeholders, including governments, technology companies, civil society organizations, and educational institutions."

Workplace Inequality in the Gig Economy: The rise of the gig economy and non-traditional forms of employment has reshaped the labor market, offering flexibility and autonomy for some, but posing risks and challenges for women workers. The lack of job security, benefits, and protections that are often part and parcel of gig work can disproportionately affect women, who may already be juggling multiple roles and responsibilities as caregivers and breadwinners.

According to a report by the International Labour Organization (ILO), women are overrepresented in the gig economy, particularly in low-skilled and low-paid sectors such as domestic work, care work, and online task work. This precarious and often informal nature of gig work leaves women vulnerable to exploitation, poor working conditions, and a lack of social protection. Furthermore, the gender pay gap persists in the gig economy, with women earning an estimated 34% less than men for similar work, according to a study by the Stanford Graduate School of Business.

Moreover, women in the gig economy often face lower pay rates, limited opportunities for advancement, and a lack of representation and bargaining power compared to their male counterparts. With the erosion of traditional labor unions and collective bargaining mechanisms, advocating for fair treatment and equality in this fragmented labor landscape becomes more difficult. What mechanisms can be put in place to amplify the voices of women in the gig economy and ensure their rights are protected?

Sarah Jaffe, a labor journalist and author of "Work Won't Love You Back," emphasizes the need for collective action and worker organizing in the gig economy: "Women gig workers face unique challenges, from the gender pay gap to the lack of protections for caregiving responsibilities. By coming together and forming worker-led organizations, they can amplify their voices, advocate for better policies and working conditions, and challenge the exploitative practices that disproportionately affect women in the gig economy."

Climate Change and Environmental Impact: As the planet faces the escalating crisis of climate change, women often bear the brunt of environmental degradation and its consequences. In many parts of the world, women are the primary managers of household resources and are deeply dependent on local natural resources for their livelihoods and subsistence. When these resources are threatened by drought, desertification, or natural disasters, it is women who must walk farther for water, work harder for less yield, and find new ways to sustain their families.

According to the United Nations Environment Programme (UNEP), women in developing countries are particularly vulnerable to the impacts of climate change due to their disproportionate representation in agriculture, their reliance on natural resources for subsistence, and their limited access to land ownership and decision-making power. Furthermore, climate-related disasters such as floods and hurricanes can increase the risk of gender-based violence, as women and girls may be forced to seek shelter in insecure environments or face displacement and disruption of support networks.

Additionally, women are disproportionately affected by climate-related displacement and migration, as well as the increased risk of gender-based violence and exploitation that often accompanies humanitarian crises. How do we address the gendered impact of climate change and ensure that women are at the forefront of environmental resilience, decision-making, and climate action?

Empowering women as leaders and decision-makers in climate action is crucial to addressing the disproportionate impacts they face and ensuring that solutions are gender-responsive. According to the International Union for Conservation of Nature (IUCN), involving women in natural resource management and climate change adaptation efforts can lead to better outcomes and more sustainable solutions. However, women remain underrepresented in environmental decision-making at all levels, with only a handful of national climate change policies explicitly addressing gender considerations.

Moreover, women are underrepresented in the fields of science, technology, engineering, and mathematics (STEM) that are crucial to combating climate change and developing sustainable solutions. Ensuring that women have a seat at the table in these discussions and can contribute their knowledge, perspectives, and expertise is not just about equity—it is about harnessing all available talent and resources to address one of the greatest challenges of our time.

According to UNESCO data, less than 30% of the world's researchers are women, and this gender gap is particularly pronounced in fields like computer science, physics, and engineering. This underrepresentation not only limits the diversity of perspectives and approaches to addressing climate change but also perpetuates the systemic biases and barriers that discourage women from pursuing STEM careers. Increasing women's participation and leadership in these fields is crucial for developing innovative, inclusive, and effective solutions to the climate crisis.

Healthcare Disparities and Bodily Autonomy: Women's health and bodily autonomy remain contentious issues in the modern era. Women's health is often marginalized in medical research and healthcare policies, resulting in disparities that affect their well-being. Diseases and conditions that predominantly affect women, such as autoimmune disorders, endometriosis, and maternal health complications, are frequently underdiagnosed, undertreated, and underfunded in research efforts.

Dr. Carolyn Mazure, director of the Women's Health Research at Yale, emphasizes the urgent need for a gender-specific approach to medical research and healthcare: "For far too long, women's health has been understudied and underrepresented in clinical trials and medical research. This 'one-size-fits-all' approach to healthcare has led to misdiagnoses, ineffective treatments, and a lack of understanding of how diseases and conditions uniquely affect women. By prioritizing sex-specific research and tailoring healthcare to the unique needs of women, we can bridge this gap and improve health outcomes for half of the world's population."

The issue of reproductive rights and bodily autonomy remains a battleground in many societies, with attacks on access to safe and legal abortion services, comprehensive sexual and reproductive health education, and contraceptive options. With these challenges to women's fundamental rights over their own bodies, their autonomy and ability to make informed decisions about their reproductive health and lives are under siege.

Alaa Murabit, a global advocate for women's rights and founder of the Voice of Libyan Women, highlights the far-reaching consequences of restricting reproductive rights: "When women are denied the right to make decisions about their own bodies and reproductive health, it not only infringes on their fundamental human rights but also perpetuates cycles of poverty, limits their educational and economic opportunities, and puts their lives at risk. Ensuring bodily autonomy and access to comprehensive reproductive healthcare is essential for the empowerment and well-being of women and girls, and for the sustainable development of societies as a whole."

The COVID-19 pandemic has further exposed and exacerbated the inequalities faced by women globally. From the surge in domestic violence cases due to lockdowns and increased economic stress, to the disproportionate job losses in female-dominated sectors like healthcare and service industries, the pandemic has highlighted the precarious position of women in times of crisis.

According to a report by UN Women, the COVID-19 pandemic has had a disproportionate impact on women's economic security, with an estimated 54 million women globally at risk of losing their jobs. Furthermore, the report highlights the increased burden of unpaid care work shouldered by women during the pandemic, as well as the rise in gender-based violence, with many women trapped at home with their abusers due to lockdown measures. These findings underscore the need for gender-responsive policies and targeted interventions to address the unique challenges faced by women during public health crises and to build more resilient and equitable societies.

Moreover, women have borne the brunt of increased care work during the pandemic, often juggling paid employment, childcare responsibilities, and the care of sick or elderly family members. This added burden has taken a toll on women's mental health, economic security, and overall well-being, underscoring the need to prioritize gender-responsive policies and support systems in crisis response and recovery efforts.

The pandemic has also highlighted the essential role of care workers, a field dominated by women, in sustaining societies and economies. Yet, these workers often face precarious employment conditions, low wages, and limited access to social protections. According to the International Labour Organization (ILO), the COVID-19 crisis has underscored the need to recognize and value care work as a critical component of sustainable development, and to ensure that care workers have decent working conditions, fair compensation, and access to social protections.

The rise of artificial intelligence (AI) and automation also presents both challenges and opportunities for women's empowerment and gender equality. While these technologies have the potential to create new job opportunities, increase efficiency, and support women's entrepreneurship, they also risk perpetuating existing biases and disparities if not developed and deployed with fairness, transparency, and accountability in mind.

According to a report by the World Economic Forum, women are disproportionately at risk of job displacement due to automation, with an estimated 57% of women's jobs at risk of being automated, compared to 47% of men's jobs. This disparity is particularly pronounced in certain sectors, such as clerical and administrative work, where women are overrepresented. Ensuring that the development and deployment of AI and automation technologies are guided by principles of gender equality and non-discrimination is crucial to preventing the widening of existing gender gaps in the workforce.

For example, if AI algorithms used in hiring, promotion, and performance evaluation decisions are trained on historical data that reflects gender biases, they may inadvertently discriminate against women or reinforce harmful stereotypes. Ensuring that the development and deployment of these technologies are guided by principles of equity and inclusion is essential to prevent the widening of gender gaps and ensure that the benefits of technological progress are shared equally.

Timnit Gebru, a leading expert on AI ethics and co-founder of the AI research institute Black in AI, warns about the potential risks of biased AI systems: "If we don't take proactive steps to ensure that AI systems are developed and deployed with fairness and accountability in mind, we risk perpetuating and amplifying existing societal biases and discrimination. This could lead to further marginalization of already disadvantaged groups, including women, and undermine efforts towards achieving gender equality and social justice."

Furthermore, the intersection of women's rights with other social justice issues, such as racial justice, disability rights, and LGBTQ+ rights, cannot be overlooked. Queer and transgender women, in particular, face unique challenges and discrimination based on both their gender identity and sexual orientation. They are often at higher risk of violence, harassment, exclusion from mainstream women's movements, and barriers to accessing affirming healthcare, employment, and legal protections.

According to a report by the National Center for Transgender Equality, transgender women, particularly those of color, face alarmingly high rates of violence, discrimination, and economic insecurity. The report highlights that 53% of transgender women have experienced intimate partner violence, and 30% have experienced homelessness due to discrimination and lack of familial support. Addressing the specific needs and challenges faced by transgender women requires a concerted effort to challenge transphobia, promote inclusivity, and ensure access to affirming healthcare, legal protections, and support services.

Recognizing and addressing the specific needs and experiences of LGBTQ+ women is crucial in the fight for gender equality and requires an intersectional approach that acknowledges and challenges the multiple and interconnected forms of oppression they face.

Kimberlé Crenshaw, a pioneering scholar on intersectionality, emphasizes the importance of centering the voices and experiences of those at the intersection of multiple marginalized identities: "When we fail to acknowledge the intersections of gender, race, sexuality, and other forms of oppression, we risk leaving behind those who face the most acute and compounded forms of discrimination and violence. An inclusive feminist movement must embrace intersectionality and amplify the voices of queer women, transgender women, and women of color, who have historically been sidelined and erased from mainstream narratives."

Engaging men and boys as allies in the fight for gender equality is also crucial. While women have been at the forefront of advocating for their rights, true progress requires challenging the deeply ingrained societal norms and power structures that perpetuate gender inequality. Michael Kaufman, co-founder of the White Ribbon Campaign, emphasizes the importance of men taking responsibility: "Men must be willing to reflect on their privilege, confront toxic masculinity, and actively work towards creating a more equitable society. By engaging men and boys as partners in this struggle, we can dismantle the patriarchal systems and attitudes that continue to oppress women."

In conclusion, as society progresses, new hurdles emerge to challenge the advancement of women's rights. The modern era presents a complex constellation of issues that require nuanced understanding and strategic action. Throughout history, women have demonstrated resilience and ingenuity in the face of adversity. The current era is no different.

The COVID-19 pandemic has served as a stark reminder of the fragility of progress made in women's rights and the disproportionate impact that global crises can have on women and girls. As the world grapples with the long-term consequences of the pandemic, it is crucial to prioritize gender-responsive policies and interventions that address the unique challenges faced by women, from economic insecurity and increased care burdens to the rise in gender-based violence and barriers to essential services.

With concerted effort, collaborative resolve, and a commitment to addressing these emerging challenges through intersectional and gender-responsive approaches, we can ensure that women not only survive but thrive in the modern world. By harnessing the power of technology, addressing the disproportionate impact of climate change, and challenging persistent barriers in the realms of healthcare, the workplace, and online spaces, we can forge a path towards a more equitable and inclusive future for all women.

Phumzile Mlambo-Ngcuka, former Executive Director of UN Women, emphasizes the urgency of addressing emerging challenges to women's rights: "The world cannot afford to ignore or deprioritize gender equality. It is not only a fundamental human right but also a prerequisite for sustainable development, peace, and prosperity. By tackling the new and persistent barriers facing women and girls, we are investing in the future of our societies and unlocking the full potential of half the world's population."

As we continue to write this narrative, let us remember that every challenge presents an opportunity—an opportunity to innovate, to dismantle outdated norms, and to build a more just and equitable society. It is through our collective endeavors that we will forge a path forward, not only breaking barriers but also constructing bridges to a world where women's rights are realized and celebrated, in all their intersectional complexity.

Chimamanda Ngozi Adichie, the renowned Nigerian author and feminist, reminds us: "Culture does not make people; people make culture. If it is true that the full humanity of women is not our culture, then we can and must make it our culture." By challenging the status quo and embracing a culture of equality, inclusion, and respect for human rights, we can create a world where women's rights are not just aspirations but lived realities.

The COVID-19 pandemic has also highlighted the importance of gender data and gender-responsive budgeting in addressing the unique needs and challenges faced by women and girls during crises. According to a report by UN Women, the lack of gender-disaggregated data and gender-responsive budgeting in many countries' COVID-19 response efforts has hampered the ability to effectively address the disproportionate impacts on women and girls. Investing in robust data collection and gender-responsive resource allocation is crucial for ensuring that future crisis response and recovery efforts are inclusive and equitable.

The rise of populism and authoritarian regimes around the world poses a serious threat to women's rights and gender equality. In many countries, we have witnessed a resurgence of oppressive policies and rhetoric that seek to curtail women's autonomy, restrict their access to reproductive healthcare, and reinforce traditional gender roles. Safeguarding hard-won gains in women's rights and pushing back against these regressive forces requires a concerted global effort and solidarity among women's rights advocates, civil society organizations, and international bodies.

The ongoing refugee and displacement crises resulting from armed conflicts, persecution, and climate-related disasters also present unique challenges for women and girls. In addition to facing heightened risks of gender-based violence and exploitation, displaced women and girls often lack access to essential services, education, and livelihood opportunities. Ensuring that humanitarian aid and refugee support systems are gender-responsive and prioritize the safety, empowerment, and well-being of women and girls is crucial in addressing this emerging challenge.

The COVID-19 pandemic has also exposed the precarious situation of millions of women in the informal economy, who often lack access to social protections, healthcare, and stable incomes. As the world grapples with the economic fallout of the pandemic, it is crucial to prioritize the formalization and protection of informal workers, many of whom are women, to ensure their economic security, access to basic rights, and overall well-being.

The mental health impacts of the COVID-19 pandemic on women and girls cannot be overlooked. With increased caregiving responsibilities, economic insecurity, and the added stress of navigating the challenges posed by the pandemic, many women have experienced heightened levels of anxiety, depression, and burnout. Addressing the mental health needs of women and ensuring access to adequate support services and resources is crucial for their overall well-being and resilience in the face of ongoing and future crises.

The rise of nationalism and populist rhetoric in some parts of the world has also posed challenges to women's rights and gender equality. In several countries, we have witnessed a backlash against progressive policies and a resurgence of conservative ideologies that seek to reinforce traditional gender roles and curtail women's autonomy. Countering these regressive forces requires a concerted effort by civil society organizations, human rights advocates, and international bodies to protect and advance women's rights.

The impact of armed conflicts and humanitarian crises on women and girls cannot be overstated. In addition to facing heightened risks of gender-based violence, displacement, and exploitation, women and girls in conflict zones often lack access to essential services, education, and livelihood opportunities. Ensuring that conflict resolution efforts, peace-building processes, and humanitarian interventions prioritize the needs and perspectives of women and girls is crucial for addressing this ongoing challenge and promoting sustainable peace and development.

As the world grapples with the existential threat of climate change, it is crucial to recognize and address the disproportionate impact it has on women, particularly in developing countries and marginalized communities. From the increased burden of collecting water and firewood due to droughts and deforestation, to the heightened risks of gender-based violence in the aftermath of natural disasters, the effects of climate change exacerbate existing gender inequalities and pose unique challenges for women. Ensuring that climate change mitigation and adaptation strategies are gender-responsive and inclusive of women's perspectives and leadership is essential for building resilient and equitable communities.

The COVID-19 pandemic has also highlighted the essential role of care work, traditionally performed by women, in sustaining societies and economies. However, this vital labor often remains undervalued, underpaid, and largely invisible in economic policies and decision-making processes. Recognizing and valuing care work as a critical contribution to societal well-being is crucial for addressing the persistent barriers faced by women in the workforce and achieving true gender equality.

The ongoing struggle for gender equality in the political sphere remains a significant challenge, as women continue to be underrepresented in decision-making roles and leadership positions across the globe. Addressing this barrier requires a multi-faceted approach that includes implementing gender quotas, challenging cultural and societal norms that discourage women's political participation, and creating an enabling environment that supports and empowers women in politics.

Section C: Discussion of Future Directions and Strategies for Achieving Full Gender Equality

In the quest for a world where gender equality is the norm rather than the aspiration, we must cast our gaze forward. What strategies and directions should we pursue to dismantle the lingering inequities that tarnish the fabric of modern society? It is a question that beckons not just reflection but also decisive action, grounded in an intersectional understanding of the multifaceted challenges women face across diverse contexts and identities.

Where might we begin? Education, undoubtedly, serves as the cornerstone of empowerment. Yet, our task extends beyond simply opening the doors to classrooms. We need to cultivate learning environments where girls and young women can pursue knowledge free from stereotypes, discrimination, and limitations. Could we imagine a future where curricula celebrate female scientists, leaders, and thought leaders with the same fervor as their male counterparts? Where gender-responsive pedagogies and inclusive learning materials challenge harmful gender norms and promote positive representations of women and girls?

Dr. Sakena Yacoobi, the founder of the Afghan Institute of Learning, emphasizes the transformative power of education in fostering gender equality: "Education is the key to breaking the cycle of poverty and oppression that has trapped generations of women and girls. By providing access to quality education and creating learning environments that empower and celebrate the potential of girls, we not only equip them with knowledge and skills but also instill a sense of self-worth and resilience that can challenge deeply entrenched gender norms and stereotypes."

Such a shift would require a renaissance in education, one that champions a more inclusive and empowering narrative of history, achievement, and human potential. It would involve revising textbooks, training educators to address unconscious biases, and creating safe and supportive spaces for girls to explore their interests, talents, and aspirations without the constraints of gender stereotypes.

A study by UNESCO found that in many countries, textbooks and learning materials perpetuate gender stereotypes by portraying women in limited roles, underrepresenting their contributions, and reinforcing harmful gender norms. By revising curricula and educational materials to reflect diverse and empowering narratives of women's achievements, we can challenge these stereotypes and inspire future generations of girls to pursue their dreams without limitations.<

The workplace, too, demands our attention. Corporate cultures steeped in gender bias and discriminatory practices must be transformed through comprehensive policies, training, and accountability measures. How do we foster an environment where women's contributions are valued equally, their leadership potential is nurtured, and their career progression is not impeded by the proverbial glass ceiling, maternal wall, or unconscious biases?

According to a report by the International Labour Organization (ILO), despite progress in closing gender gaps in education and employment, persistent discrimination and gender biases in the workplace continue to hinder women's economic empowerment and career advancement. The report highlights the need for comprehensive policies and initiatives, such as pay transparency, gender-neutral recruitment and promotion practices, and robust mechanisms for addressing sexual harassment and discrimination, to create a level playing field for women in the workforce.

Policies promoting equal pay, parental leave, flexible working arrangements, and robust mechanisms for addressing sexual harassment and discrimination must be advocated for and rigorously implemented. The goal is not merely to open doors for women but to ensure that once inside, they are met with a level playing field, free from systemic barriers and biases that hinder their advancement and equal participation.

Inimai Chettiar, the director of the Women's Rights Project at the American Civil Liberties Union (ACLU), emphasizes the importance of legal protections and enforcement: "While progress has been made in advancing women's rights in the workplace, the persistence of the gender pay gap, discrimination, and harassment underscores the need for strong legal safeguards and robust enforcement mechanisms. By holding employers accountable and ensuring that women have access to legal recourse when their rights are violated, we can create a more equitable and inclusive work environment for all."

Moreover, gender diversity and inclusive leadership must become priorities at the highest levels of decision-making. Initiatives to promote women's representation on corporate boards, in executive roles, and across all levels of management can help shift organizational cultures and challenge entrenched gender norms that have historically favored men's leadership and authority.

A study by the Harvard Business Review found that companies with more gender-diverse leadership teams outperformed their counterparts in terms of profitability, innovation, and employee satisfaction. Additionally, research by McKinsey & Company suggests that companies in the top quartile for gender diversity on executive teams are 25% more likely to achieve above-average profitability. These findings underscore the business case for promoting gender diversity in leadership and decision-making roles, as well as the broader societal benefits of challenging traditional gender norms and fostering inclusive workplace cultures.

Technology offers an expansive horizon of possibilities for advancing gender equality, but only if we intentionally harness its potential to empower women and address persistent inequalities. Could we envision a future where artificial intelligence and machine learning are leveraged to create tools that support women's economic empowerment, entrepreneurship, and access to vital information and services?

Marieme Jamme, a Senegalese technology entrepreneur and founder of iamtheCODE, an organization that promotes STEM education for girls, envisions a future where technology is a powerful tool for women's empowerment: "By leveraging the power of technology and equipping women and girls with digital skills, we can unlock new opportunities for economic independence, entrepreneurship, and access to vital information and services. Imagine a world where AI-powered platforms provide tailored support for women entrepreneurs, connecting them to mentors, financing, and markets, or where mobile apps provide real-time information on healthcare, legal rights, and support services for women in remote or marginalized communities."

Imagine a suite of apps tailored to support women entrepreneurs in remote areas, providing access to financial services, market information, and digital training opportunities. Envision platforms designed to connect women professionals across industries for mentorship, networking, and skill-sharing. The key lies in ensuring that technological advancements are accessible, inclusive, and beneficial to all women, not just a privileged few.

According to the World Bank, closing the digital gender divide and increasing women's access to technology and digital skills could potentially unlock $170 billion in revenue for the digital economy by 2025. However, achieving this potential requires concerted efforts to address the barriers that prevent women from fully benefiting from technological advancements, such as lack of access, affordability, digital literacy, and gender-biased algorithms and products.

In a world where the climate crisis looms large, the future of gender equality is intertwined with environmental sustainability and climate action. Women, often the stewards of natural resources and disproportionately affected by the impacts of climate change, must be at the forefront of decision-making, policymaking, and implementation of climate solutions.

Christiana Figueres, the former Executive Secretary of the United Nations Framework Convention on Climate Change (UNFCCC), emphasizes the critical role of women in addressing the climate crisis: "Women are not just victims of climate change; they are also powerful agents of change and essential partners in finding and implementing solutions. By empowering women and ensuring their full participation in climate decision-making processes, we can tap into their unique knowledge, experiences, and perspectives, which are crucial for developing effective and sustainable climate action strategies."

What if women-led initiatives were the norm in sustainable agriculture, water conservation, renewable energy projects, and disaster risk reduction efforts? It is essential to equip women with the skills, resources, and leadership opportunities they need to combat climate change and ensure their voices and experiences are heard and integrated into climate policies and strategies at all levels.

A study by the International Union for Conservation of Nature (IUCN) found that when women are involved in natural resource management and decision-making processes, there is a higher likelihood of sustainable outcomes and equitable distribution of benefits. However, the study also highlighted that women remain underrepresented in environmental decision-making, with only 28% of leadership positions in national climate change policymaking bodies held by women. Addressing this gender gap in climate leadership is crucial for developing effective and gender-responsive climate solutions.

The pursuit of gender equality in healthcare is another frontier that requires bold action. We must challenge the status quo where medical research, treatments, and healthcare policies are often male-centric or fail to consider the specific needs and experiences of women across their life course.

Dr. Paula A. Johnson, the founder of the Connors Center for Women's Health and Gender Biology at Brigham and Women's Hospital, emphasizes the need for a gender-specific approach to healthcare: "For too long, the medical field has taken a 'one-size-fits-all' approach, treating men as the default and failing to account for the unique biological and social factors that shape women's health experiences. By integrating sex and gender considerations into medical research, clinical practice, and healthcare policies, we can improve health outcomes for women and address long-standing disparities in diagnosis, treatment, and care."

What would it look like if women's health issues, from menstrual health and reproductive rights to gender-specific cancers and autoimmune disorders, were given equal priority and funding as those that predominantly affect men? Ensuring comprehensive, accessible, and gender-responsive healthcare is not a luxury—it is a fundamental human right and a prerequisite for women's empowerment and well-being.

According to a report by the World Health Organization (WHO), gender bias in medical research and healthcare systems has led to significant gaps in knowledge and treatment options for conditions that disproportionately affect women. For example, endometriosis, a debilitating disorder that affects an estimated 176 million women worldwide, has historically been underfunded and understudied, resulting in delayed diagnoses and inadequate treatment options for many women. By prioritizing research and investment in women's health issues, we can address these disparities and ensure that women have access to the care and support they need throughout their lives.

Let us not forget the power of representation. The media, entertainment, and advertising industries play a crucial role in shaping societal norms, perceptions, and aspirations. What if our screens, stages, and billboards were filled with diverse, complex, and empowering representations of women, challenging traditional gender stereotypes and inspiring a new generation of girls and young women to dream without constraints?

Geena Davis, the Academy Award-winning actor and founder of the Geena Davis Institute on Gender in Media, has been a leading voice in advocating for more positive and diverse representations of women in media. She emphasizes, "If she can see it, she can be it. By presenting diverse and empowering portrayals of women and girls in media, we can challenge harmful stereotypes, expand horizons, and inspire the next generation to pursue their dreams without limits imposed by gender norms or societal expectations."

By promoting diversity, inclusivity, and positive portrayals of women in media, we can challenge harmful narratives, dismantle damaging beauty standards, and foster a culture that celebrates and uplifts the strength, resilience, and multifaceted identities of women across all intersections of race, ethnicity, age, ability, and sexuality.

A study by the Geena Davis Institute on Gender in Media found that characters portrayed by women in family films are four times more likely to be depicted in revealing or sexualized clothing than their male counterparts. This type of representation not only objectifies women but also perpetuates harmful beauty standards and contributes to body image issues, particularly among young girls and adolescents. By promoting more diverse and empowering representations of women, we can challenge these harmful narratives and foster a culture of self-acceptance and respect for all body types and identities.

To galvanize these changes, we require robust legal frameworks, vigilant enforcement, and a commitment to upholding the principles of gender equality and non-discrimination enshrined in international human rights instruments and national laws. Legislation that penalizes discrimination, harassment, and gender-based violence must be strengthened, while proactive measures to promote women's equal rights and opportunities across all spheres of life must be implemented and adequately resourced.

According to the World Bank, despite progress in legal reforms aimed at promoting gender equality, many countries still have discriminatory laws and policies that limit women's economic opportunities, access to resources, and participation in decision-making processes. Strengthening legal frameworks and ensuring their effective implementation is crucial for creating an enabling environment for women's empowerment and addressing deeply rooted systemic barriers.

How do we create a judicial and legal system that is not only sympathetic to women's issues but proactive in safeguarding their rights and upholding principles of substantive equality? It is imperative that laws evolve to reflect the changing dynamics of society and that they are upheld and enforced to instill a culture of accountability, respect, and inclusive justice for all women, regardless of their backgrounds or intersecting identities.

Justice Ruth Bader Ginsburg, a pioneering advocate for gender equality and women's rights, emphasized the importance of a fair and impartial judiciary: "A prime part of the history of our Constitution is the story of the extension of constitutional rights and protections to people once ignored or excluded." By ensuring that judicial systems are free from bias and actively work to uphold the principles of substantive equality, we can create a more just and inclusive society that protects the rights and dignity of all women.

And what about men? Engaging men and boys as allies, partners, and stakeholders in the fight for gender equality is indispensable. Can we nurture a generation of men who are comfortable with women leading alongside them, who are vocal advocates for gender justice, and who actively challenge toxic masculinity, patriarchal norms, and the socialization that perpetuates violence and discrimination against women?

Michael Kaufman, co-founder of the White Ribbon Campaign, a global movement of men and boys working to end violence against women and girls, emphasizes the importance of engaging men as allies: "Men must recognize that gender inequality is not just a women's issue, but a human issue that affects us all. By challenging harmful gender norms, confronting toxic masculinity, and actively supporting women's rights and leadership, we can create a more equitable and just society for everyone."

Educational programs, campaigns, and community-based initiatives that promote positive masculinities, gender sensitivity, and allyship are vital components of this cultural shift. By transforming gender norms and fostering a culture of respect, empathy, and shared responsibility, we can create an enabling environment for women's empowerment and build a more equitable society for all.

Initiatives like the UNESCO Global Partnership for the Prevention of Son Preference and Gender-Biased Sex Selection have been working to engage communities, religious leaders, and educators in challenging harmful gender norms and promoting positive masculinities. By addressing the root causes of gender discrimination and violence, these programs aim to foster a culture of respect, equality, and shared responsibility between men and women.

As we chart the course for the future, it is essential that we adopt intersectional approaches and ensure the inclusion of diverse voices in shaping strategies for gender equality. Women are not a monolithic group, and their experiences, needs, and priorities vary based on factors such as race, class, sexuality, disability, age, and cultural context.

Kimberlé Crenshaw, the pioneering scholar who coined the term "intersectionality," emphasizes the importance of recognizing and addressing the multiple and intersecting forms of oppression faced by marginalized women: "It's not enough to simply acknowledge that women face discrimination; we must also recognize that women of color, LGBTQ+ women, disabled women, and other marginalized groups face compounded forms of discrimination and unique challenges that require targeted and intersectional approaches."

Recognizing and addressing these intersecting identities and forms of oppression is crucial in developing policies, programs, and initiatives that leave no woman behind. By centering the leadership, perspectives, and lived realities of marginalized women, we can build a more inclusive, representative, and responsive movement for gender equality that truly serves the diverse needs and aspirations of all women.

Tarana Burke, the founder of the 'Me Too' movement, has been a powerful voice in amplifying the experiences of marginalized women and advocating for intersectional approaches to addressing sexual violence and gender-based discrimination. She emphasizes, "The work to dismantle the systems that allow sexual violence to persist must include a commitment to addressing the intersections of race, class, gender identity, and other forms of oppression. We cannot achieve lasting change if we leave anyone behind."

International collaborations, global partnerships, and multilateral organizations have a vital role to play in setting standards, driving progress, and fostering accountability for gender equality efforts worldwide. The United Nations, through its various agencies, conventions, and initiatives like UN Women, the Commission on the Status of Women, and the Sustainable Development Goals, serves as a platform for nations to come together, share best practices, and hold each other accountable to their commitments to women's rights and gender equality.

Phumzile Mlambo-Ngcuka, the former Executive Director of UN Women, highlights the importance of global partnerships and collective action: "Gender equality is not just a women's issue; it's a human rights issue that affects us all. By working together across borders and sectors, we can build a global movement that amplifies the voices of women, challenges systemic barriers, and holds governments and institutions accountable for their commitments to women's rights and empowerment."

Strengthening these global partnerships, ensuring meaningful participation and representation of diverse women's voices and organizations, and translating international commitments into tangible actions on the ground are critical steps towards achieving universal gender equality.

The Beijing Declaration and Platform for Action, adopted at the Fourth World Conference on Women in 1995, remains a milestone in the global agenda for gender equality and women's empowerment.

However, progress towards implementing its commitments has been uneven, with many countries falling short of their pledges. Renewing and strengthening these international commitments, through initiatives like the Generation Equality Forum launched by UN Women, is crucial for driving concrete action and accelerating progress towards achieving gender equality by 2030.

Youth-led movements and the voices of the next generation are also powerful forces in driving progress and shaping the future of gender equality efforts. Young women and girls are not just the beneficiaries of the fight for gender equality; they are its leaders, change-makers, and agents of transformation.

Malala Yousafzai, the youngest Nobel Prize laureate and a global advocate for girls' education, has been a powerful voice for the youth-led movement for gender equality. She emphasizes, "With guns, you can kill terrorists; with education, you can kill terrorism. Let us pick up our books and our pens, and let us prove that we are powerful and that we are peace-loving people." By amplifying the voices and leadership of young women like Malala, we can ensure that the fight for gender equality is not only inclusive of the aspirations of future generations but also driven by their vision and determination.<

Empowering and amplifying their voices, creating spaces for intergenerational dialogue and knowledge-sharing, and fostering their leadership skills are investments in a more equitable and sustainable future. By engaging young people as equal partners and stakeholders in the development of strategies and initiatives, we can ensure that these efforts are responsive, relevant, and aligned with the aspirations and lived realities of future generations.

Initiatives like the UN Women Youth Leadership Programme and the UNICEF Gender Equality Youth Engagement Strategy have been working to create platforms for young people, particularly girls and young women, to engage in gender equality efforts, develop their leadership skills, and advocate for their rights and priorities. By investing in the next generation of leaders and change-makers, we can ensure that the fight for gender equality is sustained and remains relevant to the evolving needs and challenges of diverse communities worldwide.

Grassroots movements, community-led initiatives, and local-level activism also play a crucial role in driving change from the ground up and addressing context-specific challenges and needs. These efforts, often led by women who have experienced discrimination and marginalization firsthand, bring a deep understanding of the intersecting barriers and power dynamics that shape women's lived realities in their communities.

The Self-Employed Women's Association (SEWA) in India, a trade union of over 2 million informal women workers, is a powerful example of a grassroots movement that has been driving change and empowering women at the local level. Through collective action, advocacy, and community-based initiatives, SEWA has been instrumental in securing legal protections, access to healthcare, and economic opportunities for marginalized women workers, while also challenging deeply entrenched gender norms and power structures.

The success of SEWA highlights the importance of grassroots mobilization and empowering women to become agents of change within their own communities. By providing a platform for collective voice and action, SEWA has not only improved the economic and social well-being of its members but has also challenged the patriarchal structures and cultural norms that have historically marginalized women in India. This bottom-up approach to gender equality has proven to be a powerful force for sustainable and transformative change.

By supporting and amplifying the voices and efforts of these grassroots leaders and organizations, we can create more targeted, locally relevant, and sustainable strategies for achieving gender equality. Collaboration between local, national, and international actors, anchored in principles of mutual respect, shared learning, and a commitment to intersectional approaches, is essential for creating lasting and transformative change.

One such collaborative initiative is the Huairou Commission, a global network of grassroots women's organizations working to empower women, promote sustainable communities, and influence policies and decision-making processes at all levels. By fostering partnerships between grassroots leaders, local authorities, and international organizations, the Huairou Commission has been instrumental in amplifying the voices and experiences of women from marginalized communities and ensuring that their perspectives and priorities are integrated into global development agendas and policies.

In conclusion, the terrain ahead is vast and varied, but it is a landscape ripe for innovation, courage, and relentless determination. With every step we take, we must ask ourselves: Are we moving towards a future where every woman, across all intersections of identity and experience, can live without the confines of gender-based barriers? Are we forging a path towards a world where equality, justice, and the full realization of women's rights are not mere aspirations but lived realities?

As we navigate this terrain, it is essential to acknowledge the complex and multi-layered nature of the challenges we face. Gender inequality is not a standalone issue but is deeply intertwined with other forms of oppression and systemic barriers, such as racism, classism, ableism, and colonialism. Adopting an intersectional and holistic approach that recognizes and addresses these interconnected forms of oppression is crucial for achieving substantive and transformative change.

Every strategy we employ, every policy we advocate for, and every norm we challenge is a step closer to that future. It is a future where the contributions, leadership, and perspectives of women are not just valued but celebrated as essential components of a just, equitable, and thriving society.

In this pursuit, it is imperative that we challenge the very notion of what constitutes "leadership" and "success" in our societies. Too often, these concepts have been defined through a narrow, patriarchal lens that devalues and marginalizes the contributions and ways of being of women, particularly those from marginalized communities. By redefining these concepts through a feminist and intersectional lens, we can create a more inclusive and equitable society that celebrates and uplifts the diverse forms of leadership, knowledge, and power embodied by women across all intersections of identity and experience.

Remember, the pursuit of gender equality is not a solitary endeavor—it is a collective journey that requires the collaboration of governments, civil society, businesses, communities, and individuals across all sectors and spheres of influence. Together, we can build a world not just of broken barriers but of boundless opportunities for women and girls everywhere. This is our charge, our challenge, and our chance to make history. Let us seize it with both hands and hearts united in purpose, fueled by the resilience and determination that have characterized the women's rights movement throughout its storied history.

In this collective journey, it is crucial to recognize and value the diverse contributions and perspectives of all stakeholders, including those who may not traditionally be seen as part of the "women's rights movement." By creating inclusive spaces for dialogue, collaboration, and shared learning, we can harness the collective wisdom, experiences, and resources of diverse actors, from grassroots organizations and community leaders to policymakers, academics, and private sector entities, in the pursuit of gender equality.

The path forward is not without obstacles, but it is a path illuminated by the resilience, creativity, and unwavering spirit of women throughout history. From the suffragettes who fought for the right to vote to the activists who continue to challenge injustice in all its forms, we stand on the shoulders of giants. Their legacy is a reminder that change is possible, that no barrier is too high to overcome when we stand together in solidarity and intersectional allyship.

The history of the women's rights movement is one of resilience, perseverance, and collective action in the face of seemingly insurmountable challenges. From the abolitionist movement, which challenged the intersecting oppressions of slavery and patriarchy, to the labor rights movement, where women workers fought for fair wages and safe working conditions, the struggle for gender equality has been intrinsically linked to other social justice movements and the broader fight for human rights and dignity.

So let us go forth with courage, with compassion, and with an unyielding commitment to justice and equality for all. Let us create a world where every girl grows up knowing that her dreams are not just valid but achievable, where every woman can live free from fear, discrimination, and the insidious grip of oppression, and where gender equality is not an aspiration but a lived reality that shapes the very fabric of our societies.

In this pursuit, it is essential that we embrace a spirit of radical hope and unwavering determination. The challenges we face are significant, but they are not insurmountable. By drawing inspiration from the countless women and allies who have fought for gender equality throughout history, and by harnessing the power of collective action, we can overcome even the most formidable barriers and create a world where every person, regardless of their gender identity or expression, can thrive and realize their full potential.

This is the future we envision, the future we are building together, step by step, day by day. It is a future where women's voices are heard, their contributions celebrated, and their rights upheld in all their intersectional complexity. It is a future where the full potential of half of humanity is finally realized, unleashing a force for progress, prosperity, and transformative change that knows no bounds.

This vision of a more just and equitable future is not merely a utopian ideal but a tangible reality that we can collectively create through our actions, our choices, and our unwavering commitment to the principles of human rights, dignity, and justice for all. By challenging oppressive systems, dismantling harmful norms and stereotypes, and creating inclusive spaces for diverse voices and experiences, we can forge a path towards a world where every person, regardless of their gender identity or expression, can flourish and contribute to the betterment of our shared humanity.

Let this vision be our north star, guiding us through the challenges and uncertainties that lie ahead. Let it be the flame that ignites our passion, the spark that fuels our determination. For in the pursuit of gender equality, we are not just changing laws and policies—we are reshaping the very foundations of our human civilization, forging a new paradigm of justice, equity, and shared humanity.

As we navigate this journey, it is crucial to embrace a spirit of learning, humility, and openness to growth. The fight for gender equality is not a static endeavor but a dynamic process that requires us to continually reflect, adapt, and evolve in response to emerging challenges and evolving contexts. By fostering a culture of continuous learning, inclusive dialogue, and a willingness to question and challenge our own assumptions and biases, we can ensure that our efforts remain relevant, responsive, and truly inclusive of diverse perspectives and experiences.

The road may be long, but we walk it together, united in our belief that a better world is possible. With every barrier we break, every glass ceiling we shatter, we bring that world closer to reality. So let us press forward, with unwavering resolve and an unshakable faith in the power of our collective action, our intersectional solidarity, and our relentless pursuit of a more just and equitable future for all.

In this pursuit, it is essential that we also cultivate spaces for healing, self-care, and collective wellbeing. The work of dismantling oppressive systems and challenging deeply entrenched norms and structures can be emotionally and psychologically taxing. By creating supportive communities, fostering practices of self-compassion, and prioritizing the mental and emotional wellbeing of those on the frontlines of this struggle, we can sustain our collective resilience and ensure that our movement remains rooted in a spirit of love, hope, and radical care for one another.

For in the end, the fight for women's rights is not a fight for one gender alone—it is a fight for the very soul of our shared humanity. It is a fight for a world where every person, regardless of their gender identity or expression, can live with dignity, respect, and the freedom to pursue their dreams without the constraints of oppression or discrimination.

At its core, the pursuit of gender equality is a pursuit of human liberation – a liberation from the confines of rigid gender norms, oppressive power structures, and harmful stereotypes that limit the full expression of our shared humanity. It is a journey towards a world where every person, regardless of their gender identity or expression, can live authentically, free from the shackles of discrimination, violence, and systemic oppression.

That is the world we are building, brick by brick, story by story. And as we write the next chapter in this unfolding narrative, let us do so with the knowledge that we are part of something greater than ourselves—a movement that has the power to transform not just our own lives but the lives of generations to come, across all borders, cultures, and intersections of identity and experience.

As we embark on this transformative journey, let us be guided by the wisdom and resilience of those who have come before us – the countless women and allies who have fought, sacrificed, and persevered in the face of immense adversity to create a more just and equitable world. Their stories, their struggles, and their triumphs serve as a reminder that change is not only possible but inevitable when we stand united in our commitment to justice and human dignity.

So let us go forth, sisters, siblings, and allies, armed with the strength of our convictions and the power of our unity. Let us break barriers, shatter stereotypes, and rewrite the rules that have held us back for too long. Let us create a world where every woman, every person, can rise, where every voice can be heard, and where the very notion of inequality and injustice is a relic of a bygone era, remembered only as a testament to the human spirit's capacity to overcome and transcend even the most formidable obstacles.

In this pursuit, let us embrace the power of storytelling and narrative as a tool for transformation. By sharing our stories, our struggles, and our triumphs, we can inspire hope, foster empathy, and cultivate a deeper understanding of the intersectional and complex nature of gender-based oppression. Through these narratives, we can challenge dominant narratives that perpetuate harmful stereotypes and oppressive structures, and create new narratives that celebrate the diversity, resilience, and power of women across all intersections of identity and experience.

This is our moment, our mission, our movement. And together, there is nothing we cannot achieve in the pursuit of a more just, equitable, and inclusive world for all.

As we stand on the precipice of a new era, let us embrace the opportunity to reimagine and reshape our world, guided by the principles of justice, equity, and human dignity for all. Let us be bold, courageous, and unwavering in our pursuit of a future where every person can thrive, contribute, and realize their full potential, free from the constraints of gender-based oppression and systemic barriers.

Chapter 10
Conclusion

Section A: Summary of Key Advancements and Milestones in Women's Rights

The quest for gender equality has been a long and arduous journey, marked by countless struggles and triumphs. Have you ever paused to consider the immense courage it took for women to step out of the shadows of oppression and into the light of autonomy and recognition? This narrative unfolds the constellation of women's rights, woven with the threads of resilience, determination, and the indomitable spirit of those who dared to challenge the status quo.

Dr. Fatima Gailani, a prominent Afghan women's rights activist and former president of the Afghan Red Crescent Society, reflects on the challenges faced by women in the pursuit of equality: "The journey towards women's rights has been a long and arduous one, marked by countless sacrifices, setbacks, and hard-fought victories. It is a journey that has required immense courage, resilience, and an unwavering commitment to the principles of justice and human dignity. Yet, even in the face of overwhelming odds, women have persisted, their determination fueled by a deep belief in their inherent worth and the vision of a more equitable world for all."

One cannot speak of advancements in women's rights without tipping the hat to the historic suffrage movement that swept across nations in the late 19th and early 20th centuries. Owing to the tireless efforts of women like Susan B. Anthony in the United States, Emmeline Pankhurst and the militant suffragettes in Britain, and the countless unsung heroines who risked their lives for the cause, the 20th century heralded a new era of political empowerment for women.

The suffrage movement was not without its challenges and sacrifices. Suffragettes like Alice Paul and Lucy Burns, leaders of the National Woman's Party in the United States, endured harsh imprisonment, hunger strikes, and brutal force-feedings in their pursuit of the right to vote. In Britain, Emmeline Pankhurst and her fellow suffragettes faced violent opposition, heckling, and arrests for their militant tactics, including arson and window-smashing. Yet, their unwavering determination and willingness to endure hardships for the cause inspired generations of women to come.

With the passage of the 19th Amendment to the U.S. Constitution in 1920 and the Representation of the People Act in Britain in 1928, granting women the right to vote, societies took a monumental leap forward. How empowering it must have been for those first generations of women to cast their ballots, a symbolic act that declared their voices mattered and their civic participation was a fundamental right.

Ida B. Wells, an African American journalist and civil rights activist, played a pivotal role in advocating for the enfranchisement of Black women in the United States. She famously challenged the leadership of the national suffrage movement, calling out their racist attitudes and insisting that the fight for women's suffrage be intertwined with the struggle for racial equality. Her intersectional approach to advocacy highlighted the complex and interconnected nature of oppression faced by women of color and the need for an inclusive and intersectional feminist movement.

As the century progressed, so did the women's movement, blossoming into what would be known as the second wave of feminism in the 1960s and '70s. This wave crashed against the shores of institutional and cultural barriers, challenging deeply entrenched gender norms and fighting for reproductive rights, equal pay, and greater representation in education and the workforce.

The publication of Betty Friedan's groundbreaking book "The Feminine Mystique" in 1963 is often credited with igniting the second wave of feminism in the United States. Friedan's work exposed the dissatisfaction and unfulfilled potential of middle-class housewives, challenging the societal expectations and gender norms that confined women to domestic roles. Her book resonated with many women who felt trapped by the narrow definitions of womanhood and inspired them to demand greater freedom, autonomy, and equal opportunities in all spheres of life.

The introduction of the contraceptive pill in the 1960s was a game-changer, transforming the landscape of women's autonomy over their bodies and reproductive choices. Suddenly, women had the unprecedented ability to control their reproductive health, which in turn unlocked new avenues in education, career paths, and personal freedom.

The impact of the contraceptive pill on women's empowerment cannot be overstated. According to a study by the University of Michigan, the widespread availability of oral contraceptives was responsible for a significant portion of the increase in women's labor force participation and educational attainment in the United States during the latter half of the 20th century. By gaining control over their reproductive choices, women were able to pursue educational and career opportunities that were previously limited or denied to them.

The latter half of the 20th century saw a surge in women's representation in politics and the workforce, fueled by the hard-fought battles of the feminist movement. In 1981, Sandra Day O'Connor became the first woman appointed to the United States Supreme Court, a powerful statement on women's evolving role in governance and the shattering of another glass ceiling.

Justice Sandra Day O'Connor's appointment to the Supreme Court was a watershed moment in the fight for gender equality in the United States. As the first woman to serve on the nation's highest court, she brought a unique perspective and lived experience to the bench, shaping legal decisions and jurisprudence on issues ranging from gender discrimination to reproductive rights. Her tenure on the court paved the way for future generations of women to aspire to leadership roles in the legal profession and the judiciary, challenging long-held assumptions about the inherent capabilities of women in positions of power and authority.

Meanwhile, women like Indira Gandhi in India, Golda Meir in Israel, and Margaret Thatcher in the United Kingdom defied the odds to become the first female prime ministers of their respective countries. These towering figures shattered long-held stereotypes and paved the way for future generations of women to aspire to leadership positions in the highest echelons of power.

While the ascension of these trailblazing women to the highest offices of their nations was a significant milestone in the fight for gender equality, their tenures were not without controversy and criticism. Indira Gandhi, for instance, was accused of authoritarian tendencies and undermining democratic institutions during her time as Prime Minister of India. Similarly, Margaret Thatcher's conservative policies and confrontational leadership style drew criticism from various quarters, including from within the feminist movement itself. These complexities underscore the multifaceted nature of women's leadership and the ongoing debates around the intersection of gender, power, and political ideologies.

The fight for women's rights also extended to the legal realm, with landmark cases like Roe v. Wade in 1973, where the U.S. Supreme Court recognized a woman's constitutional right to abortion, affirming bodily autonomy and reproductive freedom as fundamental human rights. However, this hard-won victory would face ongoing challenges and threats, reflecting the contentious and ongoing nature of the battle for reproductive rights.

The Roe v. Wade decision was a watershed moment in the fight for women's reproductive rights, but it also sparked a fierce backlash from conservative and religious groups who viewed abortion as a moral and ethical transgression. In the decades that followed, numerous legislative attempts were made to chip away at or overturn the landmark ruling, reflecting the ongoing polarization and politicization of the abortion debate in the United States. This battle highlights the fragility of hard-won rights and the need for continued vigilance and activism to protect and expand women's bodily autonomy and reproductive freedom.

Landmark legislation such as the Violence Against Women Act of 1994 in the United States sought to protect women from domestic violence, sexual assault, and other forms of gender-based violence, recognizing these issues as societal ills that required comprehensive legal and institutional responses. Can you envision the relief and hope this law inspired in countless women who had long suffered in silence?

The Violence Against Women Act (VAWA) was a groundbreaking piece of legislation that not only provided funding for support services and legal protections for victims of domestic violence, but also recognized gender-based violence as a pervasive societal issue that required a coordinated response across multiple sectors. However, the implementation and reauthorization of VAWA have faced ongoing challenges, reflecting the persistent stigma, victim-blaming attitudes, and lack of resources that continue to hinder efforts to address gender-based violence in many communities.

As the 21st century dawned, the fight for equality continued to evolve, amplified by the power of digital connectivity and social media. The #MeToo movement, initiated by Tarana Burke and popularized in 2017, became a global phenomenon, exposing the deep-seated problem of sexual harassment and assault across industries and sectors. It sparked conversations, accountability, and a reckoning with the pervasive nature of gender-based violence and discrimination, underscoring a simple yet profound truth: women's experiences of injustice were universal, and so was their collective resolve to end it.

The #MeToo movement highlighted the power of social media and digital platforms in amplifying marginalized voices, fostering global solidarity, and holding powerful individuals and institutions accountable for their actions. However, it also exposed the challenges and backlash that often accompany such movements, with many survivors facing online harassment, victim-blaming, and retaliation for speaking out. This underscores the need for robust legal protections, support systems, and a cultural shift in attitudes towards survivors of sexual violence and harassment.

Education, once a privilege reserved for the elite, has become a more accessible right for girls worldwide, thanks to the tireless efforts of activists, organizations, and international initiatives. Malala Yousafzai, the young Pakistani activist who survived a Taliban assassination attempt for advocating for girls' education, and her Malala Fund have been at the forefront of this global movement. Who could have imagined a century ago that a girl from the Swat Valley would become a Nobel laureate, inspiring millions with her unwavering commitment to educational equality?

Malala Yousafzai's story is a powerful testament to the transformative power of education and the resilience of the human spirit. Despite facing immense adversity and violence, she has remained unwavering in her pursuit of educational rights for girls and women, inspiring a global movement that has mobilized resources, advocacy efforts, and policy changes to address the barriers that prevent millions of girls from accessing quality education. Her journey serves as a reminder that one person's courage and determination can spark a global movement for change.

On the international stage, groundbreaking treaties, conventions, and agreements have played a pivotal role in setting global norms and standards for women's rights. The Convention on the Elimination of All Forms of Discrimination Against Women (CEDAW), adopted by the United Nations General Assembly in 1979, is often described as an international bill of rights for women. It defines what constitutes discrimination against women and sets an agenda for national action to end such discrimination, serving as a powerful tool for advocacy and accountability.

CEDAW has been a transformative force in advancing women's rights globally, providing a comprehensive legal framework for promoting gender equality and addressing various forms of discrimination against women. However, its implementation has faced challenges, with some countries entering reservations that limit the scope of their commitments, and others failing to fully align their domestic laws and policies with the convention's provisions. Despite these challenges, CEDAW has been instrumental in shaping national legislation, informing policy debates, and empowering civil society organizations to hold governments accountable for their obligations to protect and promote women's rights.

The Beijing Declaration and Platform for Action, adopted at the Fourth World Conference on Women in 1995, marked another turning point in the global fight for gender equality. This visionary document set strategic objectives and actions for the advancement of women and the achievement of gender equality in 12 critical areas of concern, including poverty, education, health, violence against women, and human rights. It has served as a blueprint for governments, civil society, and other stakeholders in their efforts to promote women's rights worldwide.

The Beijing Platform for Action was a groundbreaking document that articulated a comprehensive and intersectional approach to achieving gender equality and women's empowerment. It recognized that gender inequality is rooted in multiple and intersecting forms of discrimination, and that addressing it requires a holistic approach that tackles various dimensions of women's lived experiences, including economic, social, cultural, and political factors. The Platform for Action's impact has been far-reaching, influencing national policies, mobilizing civil society action, and shaping the global development agenda, including the Sustainable Development Goals (SDGs).

Throughout history, women's rights advocates and activists from diverse cultural backgrounds have made significant contributions to global feminist movements, challenging oppressive systems, sparking important conversations, and inspiring generations of activists. From Simone de Beauvoir's seminal work "The Second Sex" in France to Wangari Maathai's pioneering efforts in environmental conservation and women's empowerment in Kenya, from Rigoberta Menchú Tum's advocacy for indigenous rights in Guatemala to Nawal El Saadawi's fearless critiques of patriarchy and religious fundamentalism in Egypt, these visionary women have left an indelible mark on the struggle for gender equality.

The contributions of these diverse women's rights advocates underscore the global and intersectional nature of the feminist movement. Their work challenged the notion of a monolithic feminism and highlighted the unique experiences, struggles, and perspectives of women from different cultural, racial, and socio-economic backgrounds. Figures like bell hooks, a prominent Black feminist scholar, and Gloria E. Anzaldúa, a Chicana queer theorist, have been instrumental in broadening the discourse and pushing for an intersectional understanding of gender oppression that acknowledges the interlocking systems of race, class, sexuality, and other factors.

The narrative of women's rights is punctuated by triumphs and setbacks, a testament to the complexity of the human spirit's quest for equality and the intersections of gender with other forms of oppression, such as race, class, sexuality, and disability. Every stride made is a beacon of hope for future generations, but it also serves as a reminder of the work that remains.

The ongoing struggle for LGBTQ+ rights, particularly for transgender and non-binary individuals, is an integral part of the broader fight for gender equality and women's rights. Transgender women and non-binary individuals face compounded forms of discrimination, violence, and marginalization due to their gender identity and expression. Figures like Marsha P. Johnson, a pioneering transgender activist who played a pivotal role in the Stonewall Uprising, and Sylvia Rivera, a Latinx transgender activist and co-founder of the Street Transvestite Action Revolutionaries (STAR), have been instrumental in advocating for the rights and visibility of transgender and gender non-conforming individuals within the broader feminist and LGBTQ+ movements.

For every barrier broken, new challenges arise, demanding our vigilance and sustained action. The ongoing battle for reproductive rights, the persistent scourge of gender-based violence, and the resurgence of conservative ideologies that seek to roll back hard-won gains are stark reminders that the fight for women's rights is far from over.

The ongoing battle for reproductive rights has been a particularly contentious and high-stakes issue, with conservative and religious groups seeking to restrict access to abortion and other reproductive health services. In the United States, the overturning of Roe v. Wade in 2022 dealt a significant blow to women's reproductive autonomy, sparking nationwide protests and reigniting debates around bodily autonomy, gender equality, and the role of the judicial system in protecting fundamental rights. This setback underscores the fragility of hard-won rights and the need for sustained activism and advocacy to protect and expand women's reproductive freedoms.

As we chronicle these milestones, we must not only celebrate the victories but also recognize the contributions of grassroots activism, community organizing, and local-level initiatives that have driven progress on women's rights issues. From the women's collectives in Latin America fighting against femicide and gender-based violence to the self-help groups empowering women economically in rural India, the power of collective action and grassroots movements has been a driving force for change.

The work of grassroots organizations and local initiatives has been instrumental in addressing context-specific challenges and amplifying the voices of women from diverse backgrounds and communities. For instance, organizations like the Association for Women's Rights in Development (AWID) have played a crucial role in fostering global solidarity, facilitating knowledge-sharing, and supporting grassroots women's rights movements around the world. By centering the experiences and perspectives of women from the Global South, these initiatives challenge the dominance of Western narratives and promote a more inclusive and intersectional approach to achieving gender equality.

The impact of technological advancements, such as the internet and social media, on raising awareness, facilitating global solidarity, and amplifying women's voices in the fight for gender equality cannot be overstated. Digital platforms have enabled the rapid dissemination of information, the mobilization of activists across borders, and the creation of transnational advocacy networks that have reshaped the landscape of the women's rights movement.

The rise of digital feminism and online activism has been a game-changer for the women's rights movement, enabling the rapid dissemination of information, mobilization of activists across borders, and amplification of marginalized voices. However, it has also brought new challenges, such as online harassment, cyber violence, and the spread of misinformation and hate speech targeting women and feminist activists. Organizations like the Association for Progressive Communications (APC) and the Web Foundation have been at the forefront of efforts to promote digital rights, online safety, and equitable access to technology for women and marginalized groups.

Yet, even as we celebrate these advancements, we must acknowledge the ongoing challenges and setbacks faced by women's rights movements in different regions of the world, often shaped by unique cultural, political, and socio-economic contexts. The diversity of experiences and struggles within the global women's rights movement is a testament to the resilience and adaptability of those fighting for gender equality, as well as the need for intersectional approaches that address the multifaceted nature of women's oppression.

In regions like the Middle East and North Africa, women's rights activists have faced significant challenges and backlash from conservative and religious groups, as well as authoritarian regimes that seek to suppress dissent and maintain patriarchal power structures. Despite these obstacles, women's rights movements in these regions have persisted, adapting their strategies and tactics to navigate complex cultural and political landscapes while advocating for fundamental rights and freedoms. Figures like Loujain al-Hathloul, a prominent Saudi women's rights activist who was imprisoned for her advocacy work, and Azza Soliman, an Egyptian feminist and human rights defender, have been at the forefront of these struggles, inspiring global solidarity and amplifying the voices of women from the region.

Let this summary serve as a reminder and a rallying cry. The path to gender equality is not linear, nor is it easy. Yet, with each step, we edge closer to a world where women's rights are not just recognized but ingrained in the very fabric of society. We must continue to stand on the shoulders of the giants who came before us and push the boundaries of what is possible, drawing inspiration from the trailblazers who have paved the way.

As we forge ahead on the path to gender equality, it is crucial to recognize and address the intersections of gender with other forms of oppression and marginalization. Intersectional approaches that acknowledge the unique experiences and challenges faced by women of color, LGBTQ+ individuals, women with disabilities, and those from low-income and marginalized communities are essential for building a truly inclusive and representative movement. By centering the voices and leadership of those who experience compounded forms of discrimination, we can work towards a more holistic and transformative vision of justice and equality that leaves no one behind.

The story of women's rights is still being written. It is a story of hope, of struggle, and, most importantly, of unstoppable progress. May we all be authors of this ongoing narrative, leaving our mark on history with the indelible ink of justice, equality, and the unwavering pursuit of a more equitable world for all.

As we continue to write this narrative, it is imperative that we foster intergenerational dialogue and knowledge-sharing, ensuring that the lessons and experiences of previous generations are passed on to the next. By bridging the gaps between generations and fostering a spirit of collaboration and shared learning, we can build a movement that is both grounded in history and responsive to emerging challenges and contexts. This intergenerational exchange not only preserves the rich legacy of the women's rights movement but also ensures its continued relevance and adaptability in the face of evolving societal dynamics.

The role of men and boys as allies and partners in the fight for gender equality cannot be overlooked. While women have been at the forefront of the struggle for their rights, true and lasting progress requires the active involvement and commitment of men and boys in challenging patriarchal norms, addressing harmful masculinity, and dismantling the systems and structures that perpetuate gender inequality. Initiatives like the HeForShe campaign, launched by UN Women, and the MenEngage Alliance have been working to engage men and boys as agents of change, promoting positive masculinities and fostering a culture of respect, accountability, and shared responsibility for achieving gender equality.

The COVID-19 pandemic has not only exposed and exacerbated existing gender inequalities but has also highlighted the resilience and leadership of women in times of crisis. Women have been at the forefront of the pandemic response, serving as frontline healthcare workers, caregivers, and essential workers, often while carrying the disproportionate burden of unpaid care work at home. This crisis has underscored the need for gender-responsive policies and resource allocation to address the unique challenges faced by women during emergencies, as well as the importance of recognizing and valuing the contributions of women in crisis management and recovery efforts.

Section B: Reflections on the Ongoing Journey Towards Gender Equality

As we navigate the complex terrain of the 21st century, it becomes increasingly clear that the journey towards gender equality remains a dynamic and multifaceted struggle. The path is not just marked by legal reforms and policy changes but also by a shift in the cultural zeitgeist, one that calls for a deep introspection of our inherited social norms and a commitment to intersectional approaches that address the diverse experiences and needs of women across all intersections of identity.

Kimberlé Crenshaw, a pioneering scholar and advocate of intersectional feminism, emphasizes the importance of acknowledging and addressing the multidimensional nature of oppression faced by women: "Intersectionality is a lens through which we can better understand and respond to the ways in which gender intersects with other identities and structures of power. It recognizes that the experiences of women are not monolithic, and that there are unique challenges and forms of discrimination that arise from the intersection of gender with race, class, sexuality, disability, and other identities."

The web of change is vast, and upon it, women continue to paint a picture of defiance against the status quo. The brushstrokes are broad and varied: from the ongoing fight for equal pay and workplace equity to the growing representation of women in science, technology, engineering, and mathematics (STEM) fields. We see a burgeoning recognition of the need for intersectionality, acknowledging that the fight for women's rights must encompass the diverse experiences of race, class, sexuality, ability, age, and other intersecting identities.

The push for gender equality in STEM fields has gained significant momentum in recent years, with organizations like the Association for Women in Science (AWIS) and initiatives like the European Union's Horizon 2020 program working to address the systemic barriers and biases that have historically discouraged women's participation and advancement in these fields. However, the challenges remain multifaceted, ranging from the perpetuation of gender stereotypes in early education to the lack of mentorship and support structures for women in STEM careers.

Yet, how do we ensure the inclusivity of this movement so that no woman, irrespective of her background or lived reality, is left behind? How do we amplify the voices and perspectives of marginalized women, such as women of color, indigenous women, LGBTQ+ women, women with disabilities, and those living in poverty or conflict-affected regions?

Tarana Burke, the founder of the 'Me Too' movement, has been a powerful voice in advocating for an intersectional approach to addressing gender-based violence and harassment. She emphasizes, "We cannot achieve lasting change if we leave anyone behind. The experiences of marginalized women, including women of color, LGBTQ+ women, and women with disabilities, must be centered in our efforts to dismantle systems of oppression and create a more just and equitable society for all."

Consider the persistent challenge of the corporate ladder, where many women still find themselves on the lower rungs, facing the proverbial glass ceiling and the maternal wall that hinders their advancement and leadership opportunities. Despite significant strides, the representation of women in leadership roles and decision-making positions remains disproportionately low, reflecting the deeply entrenched biases and systemic barriers that continue to impede gender equality in the workplace.

According to a report by McKinsey & Company, women remain significantly underrepresented in leadership positions across various industries, with only one in four senior leadership roles held by women in the United States. Furthermore, the report highlights that women of color face even greater barriers to advancement, with Black, Latina, and Asian women holding just one in 20 senior leadership roles. Addressing these disparities requires a multifaceted approach that tackles unconscious biases, promotes inclusive recruitment and promotion practices, and fosters a culture of diversity and inclusion at all levels of organizational leadership.

Mentorship programs, leadership training initiatives, and advocacy for equitable policies and practices are on the rise, aiming to nurture the next generation of female leaders and create more inclusive and supportive work environments. Can you imagine the transformative impact of a world where women hold equal power in the boardrooms, political arenas, and spheres of influence?

Organizations like Catalyst, a global nonprofit focused on accelerating progress for women through workplace inclusion, have been at the forefront of developing and implementing initiatives to support women's leadership and advancement. Their programs, such as the Catalyst Mentoring and Advisory Services, provide tailored guidance, skill-building, and networking opportunities to help women navigate the complex challenges they face in the workplace and unlock their full leadership potential.

The narrative of gender equality also unfolds in the subtleties of everyday life. It's in the shared responsibilities of parenting, the portrayal of women in media and popular culture, and the dismantling of archaic gender roles and stereotypes that confine both women and men to narrow, prescriptive identities.

The role of men and boys as allies and partners in the fight for gender equality is crucial. By challenging toxic masculinity, promoting positive masculinities, and sharing in domestic and caregiving responsibilities, men can play a pivotal role in dismantling the patriarchal structures and gender norms that have historically perpetuated inequality and oppression. Initiatives like the MenEngage

Alliance and the UN Women's HeForShe campaign have been working to engage men and boys as agents of change, fostering a culture of respect, accountability, and shared responsibility for achieving gender equality.

From the father who proudly takes paternity leave and shares childcare duties to the movies, television shows, and books that portray women as complex, capable protagonists – each act, each story, contributes to a larger cultural shift. But how do we amplify these individual acts of progress into a chorus of change that resonates throughout society, challenging deep-rooted beliefs and norms that perpetuate gender inequality?

The power of storytelling and representation in media cannot be overstated. When women and girls see themselves reflected in diverse, empowering, and nuanced portrayals, it can challenge limiting stereotypes and inspire them to reimagine their own possibilities. Initiatives like the Geena Davis Institute on Gender in Media have been working to promote gender balance, challenge stereotypes, and create a cultural shift through the power of media and entertainment.

The digital age has served as a catalyst for spreading awareness, fostering solidarity, and mobilizing action in the fight for gender equality. Social media platforms have become battlegrounds where activism can flourish and stories can be shared with a global audience. Campaigns like #MeToo, #NiUnaMenos, and #BringBackOurGirls have not only spotlighted specific issues like sexual harassment, gender-based violence, and the abduction of girls, but they have also amplified the collective voices of women, transcending borders and cultural divides.

The rise of digital feminism and online activism has been a game-changer, but it has also highlighted the need to address the digital divide and ensure that marginalized women have equitable access to technology and digital spaces. According to a report by the World Wide Web Foundation, women in low- and middle-income countries are 25% less likely than men to have access to the internet, limiting their ability to participate in online advocacy, access information and resources, and engage in digital entrepreneurship opportunities.

Yet, there is an undercurrent of resistance and backlash that reminds us the journey is far from over. We witness ongoing attacks on women's reproductive rights, a resurgence of conservative ideologies that threaten to roll back hard-won freedoms, and the persistent scourge of gender-based violence that pervades societies worldwide. The tug-of-war between progress and regression is palpable, and it begs the question: How do we fortify the advances made and guard against the erosion of women's rights?

The global gag rule, also known as the Mexico City Policy, implemented by the United States under the Trump administration, is a prime example of the ongoing threats to women's reproductive rights and bodily autonomy. This policy prohibited foreign non-governmental organizations from receiving U.S. global health assistance if they provided or promoted abortion services, even in cases where abortion was legal and performed with non-U.S. funds. The impact of such policies has been far-reaching, limiting access to comprehensive reproductive healthcare services and undermining the autonomy and decision-making power of women worldwide.

Education remains a cornerstone of empowerment, yet many girls still lack access to quality schooling, particularly in developing countries, conflict-affected regions, and marginalized communities. Initiatives that aim to close the gender gap in education, promote inclusive and gender-responsive curricula, and combat harmful practices like child marriage and gender-based violence are critical. For when a girl in a remote village holds a textbook for the first time, we inch closer to a world where knowledge is the birthright of every child, regardless of gender.

According to UNESCO, over 130 million girls worldwide are out of school, with poverty, cultural norms, and gender-based violence being significant barriers to their education. Organizations like the Malala Fund and the United Nations Girls' Education Initiative (UNGEI) have been working to address these challenges through advocacy, policy reforms, and community-based initiatives that prioritize girls' access to safe, quality education. By investing in girls' education, we not only empower individuals but also contribute to broader societal and economic development, as educated women are more likely to participate in the workforce, have healthier families, and break intergenerational cycles of poverty.

In this ongoing journey, we must also confront the specter of violence that looms over women globally. The fight against domestic abuse, human trafficking, femicide, and harmful cultural practices that violate women's bodily autonomy and human rights is far from over. Each story of survival and resilience serves as a poignant reminder of the courage that runs through the veins of women worldwide, but it also underscores the urgent need for comprehensive legal and institutional responses, societal shifts in attitudes and norms, and the dismantling of patriarchal structures that enable and perpetuate gender-based violence.

The pervasiveness of gender-based violence is staggering. According to the World Health Organization, nearly one in three women worldwide has experienced physical or sexual violence from an intimate partner, and even in the most developed nations, this figure is as high as one in four. Beyond the immediate physical and psychological harm, violence against women also carries severe economic costs, estimated to be as high as $1.5 trillion annually, according to the Copenhagen Consensus Center. Addressing this scourge requires a multifaceted approach that tackles root causes, such as gender inequality, harmful social norms, and the normalization of violence, while also providing comprehensive support services for survivors and ensuring accountability for perpetrators.

The COVID-19 pandemic has laid bare the deep-rooted inequalities that women face, exacerbating existing challenges and revealing new ones. Women have been disproportionately affected by job losses, shouldered the lion's share of unpaid care work, and faced an alarming rise in domestic violence during lockdowns. The pandemic has underscored the urgent need for gender-responsive policies, robust social protection systems, and a recognition of the vital role women play in sustaining communities and economies.

According to a report by UN Women, the COVID-19 pandemic has had a disproportionate impact on women's economic security, with women accounting for 54% of overall job losses globally. Furthermore, the report highlights the increased burden of unpaid care work shouldered by women during the pandemic, with many juggling paid employment, childcare responsibilities, and caring for sick or elderly family members. This added burden has taken a toll on women's mental health, economic well-being, and overall quality of life, underscoring the need for policies that address the unequal distribution of care work and support women's participation in the labor force.

As we navigate the path to recovery, we must ensure that the gains made in women's rights are not eroded and that the rebuilding process is inclusive, equitable, and prioritizes the well-being, economic security, and leadership of women across all sectors and spheres of influence.

The COVID-19 recovery efforts present an opportunity to rebuild more equitable and inclusive systems that address the structural barriers and gender inequalities that have been exacerbated by the pandemic. This includes investing in gender-responsive social protection programs, providing support for women-owned businesses and entrepreneurs, ensuring women's equal participation in decision-making processes, and prioritizing sectors and industries where women are overrepresented, such as healthcare, education, and service industries.

Art, literature, music, and popular culture have long been powerful tools in shaping perceptions of gender roles, challenging societal norms, and envisioning a more equitable world. From the subversive poetry of Audre Lorde and the unapologetic anthems of Beyoncé to the thought-provoking films of Ava DuVernay and the boundary-pushing comedy of Hannah Gadsby, women artists have used their creative voices to spark conversations, challenge stereotypes, and empower others to embrace their authenticity.

The impact of feminist art and cultural expressions extends beyond raising awareness and sparking conversations; it also plays a crucial role in fostering empowerment, solidarity, and resistance. Through their creative works, women artists have created safe spaces for marginalized voices, challenged dominant narratives, and provided a canvas for envisioning alternative futures. The poetry of Rupi Kaur, for instance, has resonated with millions of women worldwide, exploring themes of trauma, healing, and reclaiming one's power in a patriarchal world.

These artistic expressions have the power to shift cultural narratives, dismantle harmful representations, and inspire future generations of women and girls to dream beyond the confines of gender norms and societal expectations. As we reflect on the ongoing journey towards gender equality, we must recognize the transformative potential of art and culture in driving social change and empowering women to tell their own stories, on their own terms.

The power of storytelling and representation in media cannot be overstated. When women and girls see themselves reflected in diverse, empowering, and nuanced portrayals, it can challenge limiting stereotypes and inspire them to reimagine their own possibilities. Initiatives like the Geena Davis Institute on Gender in Media have been working to promote gender balance, challenge stereotypes, and create a cultural shift through the power of media and entertainment. However, more work remains to be done in diversifying the voices and perspectives represented in mainstream media, ensuring that the experiences of marginalized women are not overlooked or tokenized.

Moreover, the fight for women's rights does not exist in a vacuum; it is inextricably linked to other social justice movements and the intersections of gender with other forms of oppression based on race, class, sexuality, ability, and other identities. Women of color, for example, confront the compounded effects of racism and sexism, while LGBTQ+ women navigate discrimination and marginalization based on both their gender and sexual orientation.

The Women's March on Washington, held in January 2017, was a powerful demonstration of intersectional feminism in action. The march brought together millions of people from diverse backgrounds, including women of color, LGBTQ+ individuals, immigrants, and disability rights activists, to protest against the rollback of women's rights and advocate for a more inclusive and intersectional approach to gender equality. This collective action highlighted the importance of recognizing the diverse experiences and perspectives within the women's rights movement and the need to build coalitions that address the compounded forms of oppression faced by marginalized women.

Recognizing these intersections and working in solidarity with other movements – from racial justice and indigenous rights to disability rights and environmental justice – is crucial to achieving true equality for all women. The struggle for women's rights is, at its core, a struggle for human rights, social justice, and the dismantling of all systems of oppression that limit the full realization of human potential and dignity.

The environmental justice movement, which advocates for the fair treatment and meaningful involvement of all people in environmental decision-making, has been a powerful ally in the fight for women's rights. Indigenous women, in particular, have been at the forefront of the struggle to protect their lands, water sources, and traditional ways of life from the impacts of environmental degradation and resource extraction. Their resistance has not only defended their communities but has also challenged patriarchal power structures and amplified the voices of women in environmental governance and policymaking.

As we reflect on the ongoing journey towards gender equality, it is imperative that we recognize the power of collective action and the tireless efforts of grassroots organizations, global advocacy groups, and everyday citizens who are driving change at all levels. The achievements thus far are not solely the feats of remarkable individuals but the culmination of the efforts of many, each playing a role in this intricate dance towards progress.

The Association for Women's Rights in Development (AWID), a global feminist organization, has been at the forefront of fostering collective action and solidarity among diverse women's rights movements worldwide. Through its initiatives, such as the Feminist Futures program, AWID has provided a platform for grassroots organizations, activists, and advocates to come together, share knowledge, and develop collaborative strategies to address the intersecting challenges faced by women across different contexts and identities.

This reflection is a call to arms, a reminder that the fight for gender equality is not a relic of the past but an urgent, living cause that demands our sustained commitment and intersectional approach. It is a journey laden with challenges, yes, but also brimming with possibilities and the promise of a more just, equitable, and inclusive world for all.

As we heed this call to action, it is crucial to recognize that achieving gender equality is not only a moral imperative but also a driver of sustainable development and societal progress. According to a report by the McKinsey Global Institute, advancing women's equality could add $12 trillion to global GDP by 2025. Beyond the economic benefits, gender equality is intrinsically linked to the realization of other human rights and the achievement of the United Nations' Sustainable Development Goals, which aim to create a more prosperous, inclusive, and equitable world for all.

In the dynamic milieu of the 21st century, it is opportune to pay homage to the enduring legacies of trailblazers, before directing our attention towards the horizons awaiting our exploration. Let us continue to push boundaries, challenge norms, and forge new paths, drawing inspiration from the resilience and determination of those who have fought for gender equality throughout history.

As we forge ahead, it is essential to recognize the intergenerational nature of the struggle for gender equality and the importance of cultivating leadership and activism among younger generations. By empowering and amplifying the voices of young women and girls, we can ensure that the fight for gender equality remains relevant, responsive, and aligned with the evolving needs and aspirations of future generations. Organizations like Plan International and the Working Group on Girls (WGG) have been working to promote youth leadership, engage young people in advocacy efforts, and create platforms for intergenerational dialogue and knowledge-sharing.

For the story of women's rights is not a static tale but a living, breathing narrative that continues to unfold, shaped by the collective actions and voices of those who refuse to accept the status quo. As we turn the pages of this ongoing saga, may we each find our place within it, championing equality not as a distant dream but as an attainable reality for all, regardless of gender, race, class, or any other intersecting identity.

In this ongoing narrative, it is crucial to recognize the power of storytelling and the importance of amplifying diverse voices and experiences. By centering the stories and perspectives of marginalized women, we can challenge dominant narratives, foster empathy and understanding, and create a more inclusive and representative movement for gender equality. Initiatives like the Voices of Our Future program by the World Association of Girl Guides and Girl Scouts have provided platforms for young women and girls to share their stories, advocate for their rights, and become agents of change within their communities.

As we look towards the future, it is essential to embrace a spirit of innovation and creativity in our approach to achieving gender equality. The challenges we face are complex and multifaceted, requiring us to think beyond traditional solutions and embrace new paradigms and perspectives. This could involve leveraging the power of technology and digital platforms to reach and empower marginalized communities, exploring alternative economic models that prioritize care work and women's labor, or adopting more transformative approaches to addressing systemic barriers and deeply entrenched cultural norms.

The ongoing climate crisis has highlighted the disproportionate impact of environmental degradation and natural disasters on women, particularly in developing countries and marginalized communities. As we work towards a more sustainable and equitable future, it is crucial to ensure that climate action strategies are gender-responsive and inclusive of women's perspectives, knowledge, and leadership. By integrating gender considerations into climate policies and programs, we can address the unique vulnerabilities faced by women while also harnessing their invaluable contributions to environmental conservation, sustainable resource management, and resilience-building efforts.

Section C: Call to Action for Continued Advocacy and Activism in Support of Women's Rights and Empowerment

In the wake of the reflections on our collective journey towards gender parity, the question looms large before us: What more can be done to break the barriers still standing in the way of women's rights and empowerment? The constellation of progress is far from complete; it requires the persistent and passionate work of advocates and activists who are prepared to carry the torch of equality forward.

Alaa Murabit, a renowned international advocate for women's rights and gender equality, emphasizes the importance of sustained action and intersectional approaches: "The fight for gender equality is not a sprint but a marathon, one that requires our unwavering commitment and a recognition that women's experiences are diverse and shaped by multiple intersecting identities. We must be persistent, innovative, and inclusive in our advocacy efforts, challenging systemic barriers and oppressive structures while amplifying the voices and perspectives of marginalized women who have been historically overlooked or underrepresented."

Imagine a future where the term "empowerment" is not a buzzword but a tangible reality for every woman, regardless of her location, ethnicity, socio-economic status, or intersecting identities. This vision is within our grasp, but it calls for a relentless pursuit of justice and a steadfast dedication to intersectional advocacy and activism.

Chimimanda Ngozi Adichie, the renowned Nigerian author and feminist, reminds us of the importance of intersectional approaches in realizing true empowerment: "Empowerment is not a one-size-fits-all concept. It must acknowledge and address the unique challenges and barriers faced by women across different contexts and identities. Only when we embrace an intersectional understanding of empowerment can we create a world where all women, regardless of their race, class, sexuality, ability, or any other intersecting identity, can truly thrive and reach their full potential."

Consider the young girl with dreams as vast as the ocean but whose reality is confined to the walls of inequality, poverty, and marginalization. She is why our advocacy must persist. Think of the working mother juggling the demands of her job with the needs of her family, fighting a daily battle against a system that sets her up to fail. She is why our activism must intensify. Consider the indigenous woman whose land, culture, and autonomy are under constant threat from exploitative forces. She is why we must amplify our voices and demand change.

The experiences of marginalized women, such as those living in poverty, facing racial discrimination, or navigating the challenges of disability or displacement, serve as powerful reminders of the urgency and intersectional nature of the fight for gender equality. By centering these diverse experiences and amplifying the voices of those who face compounded forms of oppression, we can create more inclusive and effective strategies for advancing women's rights and empowerment across all intersections of identity and experience.

How do we then, as a collective, continue to push the envelope and demand transformative change? How do we ensure that our daughters, our sisters, our mothers inherit a world less burdened by the weight of gender bias, discrimination, and systemic oppression?

Transformative change requires a multi-pronged approach that addresses the root causes of gender inequality and challenges oppressive systems and structures at all levels. This includes investing in education and awareness-raising efforts to challenge harmful gender norms and stereotypes, advocating for policy and legislative reforms that promote women's rights and gender equality, and fostering a culture of accountability and zero tolerance for gender-based violence and discrimination.

We start by recognizing the power of our voices and using them to advocate for change at every level, from local communities to global platforms. Speak out against injustice whenever and wherever you witness it. Raise your voice, not just in the streets through marches and protests, but in every forum where decisions are made – in classrooms, boardrooms, and legislative chambers. Remember, silence often equates to complicity.

The Women's March on Washington, held in January 2017, was a powerful demonstration of the collective voice and advocacy power of women and their allies. The march brought together millions of people from diverse backgrounds, united in their demand for gender equality, racial justice, and the protection of human rights. This collective action not only raised awareness about the issues facing women but also demonstrated the potential of grassroots mobilization and intersectional solidarity in driving social and political change.

Engagement with policymakers, lawmakers, and those in positions of power is crucial. Legislation can be a formidable tool in securing rights, dismantling discriminatory practices, and holding institutions accountable. Are you in contact with your representatives? Are you voting for those who champion women's rights and gender equality? The political arena can seem daunting, but it is susceptible to the pressures of a vocal, informed, and engaged electorate.

Organizations like the National Organization for Women (NOW) in the United States and the International Alliance of Women (IAW) have been at the forefront of advocating for legislative reforms and engaging with policymakers to advance women's rights and gender equality. Through lobbying efforts, grassroots mobilization, and strategic partnerships, these organizations have played a vital role in shaping policies and laws that promote gender equity and address issues such as pay discrimination, reproductive rights, and violence against women.

Education is the cornerstone of empowerment, and it is our collective responsibility to support initiatives that aim to educate girls and young women, particularly in marginalized and under-resourced communities. When we invest in their education, we are not just teaching them to read and write; we are equipping them with the knowledge, skills, and confidence to challenge injustice, pursue their dreams, and become agents of change in their own right.

The impact of girls' education extends far beyond individual empowerment. According to a report by the United Nations Educational, Scientific and Cultural Organization (UNESCO), each additional year of schooling for girls can increase their future earnings by up to 20%. Moreover, educated women are more likely to participate in the workforce, have healthier families, and contribute to the economic and social development of their communities. By investing in girls' education, we not only empower individuals but also create a ripple effect that can break intergenerational cycles of poverty and gender inequality.

Mentorship, too, can be a powerful vehicle for change. By guiding and supporting one another, women can break through barriers that once seemed insurmountable. Can you lend your expertise to a burgeoning professional? Can you offer guidance to a young woman navigating her career path or facing challenges due to her gender or intersecting identities? The power of mentorship lies in its ability to foster intergenerational solidarity, knowledge-sharing, and the cultivation of future leaders.

Mentorship programs like the Women's Mentorship Network, founded by global advocacy organization Women for Women International, have been instrumental in providing support, guidance, and networking opportunities for women from diverse backgrounds and sectors. By connecting experienced professionals with aspiring leaders and entrepreneurs, these programs not only facilitate knowledge transfer but also create a supportive community that empowers women to overcome the unique challenges they face in their careers and personal lives.

The role of men and boys in this narrative cannot be overstated. Gender equality is not solely a women's issue; it is a human issue that requires the active engagement and allyship of all genders. Men must be partners, standing alongside women in the fight for equality, challenging the patriarchal structures that not only oppress women but also confine men to rigid stereotypes of masculinity.

The HeForShe campaign, launched by UN Women, has been a groundbreaking initiative in engaging men and boys as allies in the fight for gender equality. By providing a platform for men to take action and challenge harmful gender norms and stereotypes, the campaign has fostered a global movement of male advocates who are committed to dismantling patriarchal structures and promoting a more inclusive and equitable society for all genders.

By engaging men and boys as allies, we can create a more supportive and inclusive environment for women's empowerment, one that recognizes the shared benefits of gender equality and the need for collective action to dismantle systems of oppression that harm us all.

Michael Kaufman, co-founder of the White Ribbon Campaign, emphasizes the importance of men's role in promoting gender equality: "Gender inequality is not just a women's issue; it is a human issue that affects us all. By challenging toxic masculinity, embracing healthy masculinities, and actively supporting women's rights and leadership, men can play a crucial role in dismantling the patriarchal structures that oppress and limit the potential of both women and men."

Technology has given us a global platform, and it is our responsibility to amplify the voices of those who are often unheard, overlooked, or marginalized. Social media can be a double-edged sword, but wielded correctly, it can bring attention to issues that might otherwise remain in the shadows. Share stories, start conversations, and connect with like-minded individuals and organizations across the world, fostering solidarity and collective action.

The rise of digital feminism and online activism has been a game-changer in amplifying marginalized voices and mobilizing global solidarity around women's rights issues. Platforms like the Global Voices Feminist Resources, curated by the Rising Voices initiative, have provided a space for women activists, writers, and content creators from around the world to share their stories, perspectives, and experiences, fostering cross-cultural understanding and intersectional allyship.

Support for women-led businesses, organizations, and initiatives is another tangible way to foster empowerment and drive systemic change. By choosing where we spend our money, our time, and our resources, we can propel women entrepreneurs, leaders, and change-makers who are making a difference in their communities and beyond. Can we create networks that not only support but also celebrate the achievements of women, amplifying their voices and ensuring their contributions are recognized and valued?

Lastly, do not underestimate the power of local communities and grassroots movements. Grassroots activism has historically been the catalyst for monumental change, and it is at the local level where the seeds of transformation are often sown. Engage with local organizations, volunteer your time and skills, and contribute to building supportive environments for women and girls in your area, addressing the specific challenges and barriers they face.

In the midst of this call to action, it is essential that we also prioritize self-care and community care for those on the frontlines of advocacy and activism. The work of social change can be emotionally and physically taxing, and burnout is a real risk that threatens the sustainability and resilience of our movements. Create spaces for healing, reflection, and rejuvenation. Foster a culture of support, empathy, and collective well-being, recognizing that the fight for gender equality is a marathon, not a sprint, and we must nurture our collective energy and passion for the long haul.

Moreover, there is immense potential in collaborations between women's rights organizations, civil society groups, the private sector, academia, and other stakeholders. By pooling resources, expertise, and influence, we can amplify our impact and drive systemic change across multiple spheres of influence.

Imagine the transformative power of businesses prioritizing gender equality not just in their hiring practices but throughout their supply chains and corporate social responsibility initiatives. Picture the impact of cutting-edge academic research on gender issues informing policy decisions, social programs, and public discourse. These strategic partnerships can be catalysts for progress, leveraging the strengths and resources of diverse sectors to create a more just and equitable world for all.

Philanthropy and charitable giving also have a crucial role to play in supporting women's rights initiatives and empowering marginalized communities. By directing resources to organizations, projects, and grassroots efforts that promote gender equality, economic empowerment, education, and leadership development for women and girls, we can accelerate progress and amplify the impact of those working tirelessly on the ground.

Whether through individual donations, corporate giving programs, family foundations, or impact investing, philanthropic support can provide vital resources to sustain and scale initiatives that are driving transformative change.

In the pursuit of women's rights and empowerment, complacency is the enemy of progress. We must continue the fight with vigor, using every tool at our disposal to advocate for change in every sphere of society, from personal spheres of influence to global platforms. The barriers we face are formidable, but they are not insurmountable when we stand united in our commitment to intersectional feminism and the pursuit of justice for all.

Let us then move forward with a renewed sense of purpose and intersectional solidarity. Let us be the generation that stands up for the rights of women everywhere, across all intersections of identity and experience. Together, we can ensure that the future is not just bright but equitable and inclusive. The call to action is clear: continue to advocate, continue to fight, and continue to break down the barriers that stand in the way of women's empowerment. Will you answer the call?

Answering this call requires a commitment to lifelong learning and a willingness to confront and challenge our own biases and assumptions. The journey towards gender equality and intersectional justice is a continuous process of growth, self-reflection, and the courage to question and dismantle deeply entrenched systems of oppression. As bell hooks, the renowned feminist scholar, reminds us, "The consciousness of revolution must be cultivated continually, for only the commitment to struggle keeps alive the possibility of transformation."

As we close this chapter and reflect on the journey of women's rights, let us remember that every victory, every milestone, is a testament to the indomitable spirit of those who have fought and continue to fight for gender equality and social justice. From the suffragettes who braved imprisonment and force-feedings to the contemporary activists challenging discriminatory laws, harmful gender norms, and systemic oppression, these courageous individuals are the torchbearers of progress, lighting the way for generations to come.

The history of women's rights movements is also a testament to the power of intersectional solidarity and coalition-building. From the alliances forged between the women's suffrage movement and the abolitionist movement in the United States, to the collaborative efforts of feminist organizations and LGBTQ+ rights groups in the fight for marriage equality, the strength and resilience of social justice movements have often been amplified through strategic partnerships and the recognition of shared struggles against intersecting forms of oppression.

But the journey is far from over. As long as a single woman or girl faces discrimination, violence, or oppression based on her gender or intersecting identities, our work is not done. As long as girls are denied education, economic opportunities, and bodily autonomy, we cannot rest. As long as the halls of power remain dominated by those who uphold patriarchal systems and ideologies, we must keep pushing for transformative change.

The ongoing global refugee crisis, fueled by armed conflicts, political instability, and the impacts of climate change, has had a disproportionate impact on women and girls. In addition to facing heightened risks of gender-based violence, human trafficking, and exploitation, displaced women and girls often lack access to essential services, education, and economic opportunities. Addressing this issue requires a comprehensive and gender-responsive approach that prioritizes the protection, empowerment, and inclusion of women and girls in humanitarian aid efforts, conflict resolution processes, and long-term sustainable development initiatives.

The call to action is not just for women but for all of humanity, for gender equality is not solely a women's issue; it is a human rights issue that impacts us all. It is about creating a world where every individual, regardless of their gender identity or expression, can live with dignity, respect, and the freedom to reach their full potential, unencumbered by the shackles of oppression, discrimination, or violence.

The fight for gender equality is intrinsically linked to the broader struggle for social justice and the dismantling of all forms of oppression and discrimination. As Angela Davis, the renowned activist and scholar, reminds us, "We have to talk about liberating minds as well as liberating society." By challenging patriarchal systems, heteronormativity, and the intersections of gender with other forms of marginalization, we can create a world that celebrates diversity, embraces intersectionality, and upholds the fundamental human rights of all individuals, regardless of their gender identity, sexual orientation, race, ethnicity, ability, or any other intersecting identity.

So let us stand together, women and men, young and old, from all corners of the globe, united in our diversity and strengthened by our intersectional solidarity. Let us raise our voices in unison, demanding a world where women's rights are not just a goal but a reality, where equality is not an aspiration but a fundamental truth woven into the fabric of our societies.

The power of collective action and intersectional solidarity has been demonstrated time and again throughout history. From the civil rights movement in the United States, where women like Rosa Parks and Fannie Lou Hamer played pivotal roles in the struggle for racial equality, to the anti-apartheid movement in South Africa, where women like Winnie Madikizela-Mandela and Albertina Sisulu were at the forefront of the fight against oppression, the contributions of women to social justice movements have been immense and often underappreciated.

Let us be the change we wish to see, in our homes, our workplaces, our communities, and our nations, challenging oppressive systems and structures with unwavering courage and a commitment to justice for all.

Challenging oppressive systems and structures requires a multifaceted approach that addresses root causes and systemic barriers. This includes advocating for policy and legislative reforms, promoting inclusive and equitable practices in institutions and organizations, and fostering a culture of accountability and zero tolerance for discrimination, harassment, and gender-based violence. By working at multiple levels, from grassroots activism to institutional change, we can create a ripple effect that transforms societies and dismantles the foundations of oppression.

The path ahead may be long and arduous, but it is a path we must walk, together, in solidarity and with a shared vision of a better world. For in the end, the fight for women's rights is not just about breaking barriers; it is about building a more just, equitable, and inclusive future for all. A future where every girl can dream big and know that her dreams are within reach. A future where every woman can live free from fear, discrimination, and the insidious grip of systemic oppression. A future where gender equality and intersectional justice are not just ideals but fundamental truths that shape the very foundations of our societies.

As we embark on this path, it is essential to embrace a spirit of resilience, hope, and unwavering determination. The challenges we face are formidable, but they are not insurmountable. By drawing inspiration from the countless women and allies who have fought for justice throughout history, and by harnessing the power of collective action and intersectional solidarity, we can overcome even the most deeply entrenched barriers and oppressive systems. As Michelle Obama, the former First Lady of the United States, reminds us, "We cannot afford to be tired, or frustrated, or cynical. For the work ahead is overwhelming, and the future we want is not guaranteed. But if we keep showing up, if we keep fighting the good fight, if we lead with principle and with courage, I know that together, we can overcome anything."

This is the world we are striving for. This is the world we will create, together, through our collective advocacy, activism, and unwavering commitment to justice. So let us go forth with courage, conviction, and an unshakable belief in the power of our solidarity to bend the arc of history towards a more just and equitable reality.

As we forge ahead, it is crucial to embrace a spirit of hope and resilience, even in the face of setbacks and challenges. The path towards gender equality and social justice is rarely linear, and there will be moments of disappointment, frustration, and even despair. However, it is in these moments that we must draw strength from our collective vision, our shared commitment, and the knowledge that transformative change is not only possible but inevitable when we stand united in our pursuit of justice.

The call to action is ours to answer. The future is ours to shape. Let us seize this moment and make it count, for ourselves, for our daughters and sons, for generations to come. The time is now. The power is ours. Let us use it wisely and well, in the service of a world where every human being, regardless of gender, race, class, sexuality, ability, or any other intersecting identity, can rise, shine, and take their rightful place as an equal in the constellation of humanity.

The words of Malala Yousafzai, the renowned Pakistani activist and Nobel laureate, resonate deeply: "Let us pick up our books and our pens. They are our most powerful weapons." As we answer this call to action, let us wield the power of knowledge, education, and activism to challenge oppressive systems, amplify marginalized voices, and create a more just and equitable world for all. By harnessing the transformative potential of intersectional solidarity, we can shape a future where every human being can thrive and realize their full potential, unencumbered by the shackles of discrimination and oppression.

Onward, then, to a brighter, more just, and more equitable future for all. Together, we will break the barriers that stand in our way, and we will build a world that celebrates the beauty, strength, and resilience of our shared pursuit of justice and equality.

As we embark on this journey, let us embrace the power of storytelling and narrative as a tool for transformation. By sharing our stories, our struggles, and our triumphs, we can inspire hope, foster empathy, and cultivate a deeper understanding of the intersectional and complex nature of gender-based oppression. Through these narratives, we can challenge dominant narratives that perpetuate harmful stereotypes and oppressive structures, and create new narratives that celebrate the diversity, resilience, and power of women across all intersections of identity and experience.

The ongoing global climate crisis has highlighted the disproportionate impact of environmental degradation and natural disasters on women, particularly in developing countries and marginalized communities. As we work towards a more sustainable and equitable future, it is crucial to ensure that climate action strategies are gender-responsive and inclusive of women's perspectives, knowledge, and leadership. By integrating gender considerations into climate policies and programs, we can address the unique vulnerabilities faced by women while also harnessing their invaluable contributions to environmental conservation, sustainable resource management, and resilience-building efforts.

The COVID-19 pandemic has exposed and exacerbated the deep-rooted gender inequalities that persist in our societies. From the disproportionate burden of unpaid care work shouldered by women, to the increased risks of gender-based violence during lockdowns, and the economic hardships faced by women in informal and precarious employment, the pandemic has highlighted the urgent need for gender-responsive policies and interventions. As we navigate the path towards recovery, it is imperative that we prioritize the needs and rights of women and girls, ensuring that they are not left behind and that the gains made in gender equality are not eroded.

The fight for gender equality and women's rights is inherently linked to the broader struggle for human rights and social justice. By challenging oppressive systems and structures that perpetuate discrimination and marginalization based on gender, race, class, sexuality, ability, and other intersecting identities, we can create a more just and equitable world for all. As Ruth Bader Ginsburg, the late Supreme Court Justice and pioneer for gender equality, once said, "Fight for the things that you care about, but do it in a way that will lead others to join you."

As we continue to write this narrative of progress and transformation, it is essential to recognize the power of intersectional allyship and coalition-building. By fostering partnerships and solidarity across diverse social justice movements, we can amplify our collective voices, challenge intersecting forms of oppression, and create a more inclusive and representative movement for human rights and dignity. The words of Audre Lorde, the renowned poet and activist, remind us that "There is no hierarchy of oppressions. We cannot dismantle one system of oppression while leaving others intact."

The pursuit of gender equality is not only a moral imperative but also a driver of sustainable development, economic growth, and social progress. According to the World Economic Forum, closing the global gender gap could add up to $28 trillion to the global economy by 2025. By investing in women's empowerment, education, and leadership, we can unlock the full potential of half the world's population and create more prosperous, resilient, and equitable societies for all.